GOTTA RACE!

by Ken Schrader

with Joyce Standridge

COASTAL 181
PUBLISHER

CREDITS

Layout and Production *Jim Rigney*
Copyediting/proofing *Sandra Rigney, Cary Stratton*
Photo Archive *MaryRose Moskell*
Book Design *Sandra Rigney*
Cover Design *Joyce Wells*
Front Cover Photo *Dick Berggren, Speedway Illustrated*
Back Cover Photo *Ken Schrader Collection*

ISBN: 0-9709854-8-7

For additional information or copies of this book pleases contact:

Coastal 181
29 Water Street
Newburyport, Massachusetts 01950
www.coastal181.com

First printing March, 2006
Second printing May, 2006

Printed in the United States of America

Contents

Ernie Irvan
Sheldon Kinser
Steve Kinser
Terry Labonte
Sterling Marlin
Richard Petty
Kyle Petty
Larry Phillips
Tony Stewart
Dick Trickle
Rich Vogler
The Wallace Brothers
Darrell Waltrip
Michael Waltrip
Cale Yarborough
And I Could Go On and On

Part Three   *Even I Have to Come Out of the Race Car Once in a While*

Acknowledgements

WE'VE BEEN FRIENDS for nearly 35 years. As you read this book, you will realize how significant that was in Ken Schrader's decision to allow me to help him write his life story. There is little more important in his world than old loyalties—and, boy, am I glad.

Racing is as necessary to Kenny's life as breathing, and so it is with writing for me. When I'm a doddering old fool in the nursing home, I'll still be trying to figure out how to cop a pencil and paper. For a fair portion of my life, writing has been a way to keep the wolves from the door, but when I got the chance to do this book I was over the moon. And I stayed there because this ended up being even more fun than I had hoped. If you, too, don't laugh as you make your way through these pages, there's something seriously wrong with your sense of humor. The man is a genuine character, and thank God for that.

Joyce Standridge

I'm proud, too, that we've produced a book that is honest. No sweeping stuff under the carpet, no pretending that racing is populated with a bunch of choir boys. Because it is the real deal, you'll also find out that racers aren't the evil outlaws outsiders suspect either. Racing has never been more human than when it's seen through Ken Schrader's eyes.

There were many people who contributed to the completion of this book and a few thank-you's are in order. First and foremost is my husband Rick, who has ably filled the role of soul mate and best friend for nearly 35 years. I've loved racing all my life, but I would never have gained the background necessary to do this book without our years together. It certainly helps to understand what racing means to an obsessed diehard like Schrader when you've been married forever to another obsessed diehard.

My sister Kathy Stewart transcribed countless hours of tape, freeing me for the creative end. Kenny and I quickly learned to avoid restaurants with crying babies so Kathy didn't have to decipher words between squalls, but she gamely sorted voices, sometimes nonsensical comments and plenty of race-track noise throughout the process while also offering good suggestions about what she found interesting in it all. And she was reminded of why she loves racing, too.

Our good pal Bones Bourcier agreed to serve as unpaid, under-appreciated, unofficial editor and mistake-catcher. What a job that was! To have one of the very best writers in the business agree to help really gave our project some status, so thanks, Bones. We owe you.

Coastal 181, especially Lew Boyd, Jim Rigney, MaryRose Moskell and Cary Stratton, offered and provided assistance at any time we needed it. How wonderful to work with real racers who are also publishing pros. Mostly, we appreciated being able to write the book we thought we needed to do, and receiving encouragement every step of the way. Special thanks to Sandra Rigney for her book design, and Joyce Wells for her cover design. Finch Fenton, you were also a reminder to always find a way around obstacles—and to never take things too seriously.

Much love to Mom, Chris, Alicia, Richie, Dawn, Kyle, Bryan, Shelbi, Shawna and Cully the Wonder Dog for knowing when I needed a distraction, and then dragging my knuckles off the computer keyboard. And many thanks to my friends at the track and away who helped on that score, too.

Thanks to Kenny's family, friends and associates who gave of their time so unselfishly. Your enthusiasm for this project was so important to getting it right. Particular thanks to Ray and Sue for giving me total access at the race track, to Brian for being the ramrod we occasionally needed, to Donnie and Joey for letting me putter around the shop, and to Karen for helping copy records.

My gratitude also to Ken's many fans who, upon learning we were doing this book, came up to offer, "Be sure Kenny tells you about the time...." We weren't always able to use all those stories, but I hope it made everyone feel like they are a part of this story because in a very real way they are. Schrader fans really are terrific.

Ann Schrader, you're the best. After spending a bazillion hours getting your photos organized and in albums, you smiled gamely as I ripped through them taking what I wanted for this book, knowing full well you will have many more hours trying to get them back in place. You should know that when I went to the airport with the photos bulging out of a neon-yellow folder that had me bent toward the floor from the weight of it, the lady at the counter looked up and gasped, "*My God*, you need *wheels* for that puppy!"

Most of all, thanks to Kenny. It was pretty amazing that right from day one we were on the same page and of the same mind. We knew where we were going with this book and how we wanted it to be for the reader. The coolest thing of all about doing the book was this—I have liked and admired Kenny for lots of years, but after getting to know him so well as we plowed through many hours of conversation, I found at the end that I liked and admired him even more. That was a benefit I didn't see coming.

Now, get into it, reader. There are surprises, laughter, maybe a tear or two ahead as you read about the life of one of the most interesting people to ever go racing.

As for me, it's that time again—*Gotta Race!*

JOYCE STANDRIDGE

Foreword

by Rick Hendrick

WHY SHOULD YOU INVEST a few hours reading about the life of Kenny Schrader?

The odds are pretty good that if you've gotten this far you are already interested, but allow me to seal the deal for you. Even among people who know Kenny well, we've been waiting a long time for this book. The cliché, "they broke the mold," is inadequate to describe one of the most remarkable people to ever strap on a helmet, so we have always known there was a very interesting story whenever he got around to it.

Rick Hendrick

Here's the thing: If there's been some fun that's come out of the increasingly serious world of auto racing, it's likely it was begun by Kenny Schrader. I know this first-hand. I have always loved racing and I have always loved to laugh, but from the day I met Kenny there's been far more laughter in my life.

The most amazing thing is that he's backed that love of life with solid proof of his love for the sport. There are plenty of men and women who would like to race at the highest levels, but few are the genuine drivers whose zeal extends to every level of racing. Kenny Schrader leads that small parade, and it's deservedly earned him the love and appreciation of drivers and fans all across the country.

When he came to Hendrick Motorsports, we knew he wasn't going to leave the short-track world behind. I admit we were concerned about him getting hurt at that, but we never had to worry about him being distracted or failing to focus on the team. He did everything we asked him to do in the car and for the sponsor, so that was never an issue. And we also knew that he wasn't doing it for money—he was doing it because he loved it. You felt like you were depriving him of the joy in his life if you didn't let him go run. So, that's why we always worked around it. If there was a conflict, he knew what the priorities were and you didn't have to tell him. He's always been the consummate professional.

Even if you've never met Kenny, you probably have picked up certain things about him from commentators and in articles. Almost everyone in racing likes him and respects him as a driver. It's easy to do both. Kenny has that rare gift of making each person he meets feel like they are important to him because of the way he listens and responds. You'll undoubtedly read between the lines in this book and realize that yourself.

What may be less evident, because of his modesty, is his skill behind the wheel. I've always believed in his racing ability and if the trophy shelf isn't top-heavy, it's not for lack of effort or talent. The truth is that winning doesn't always equate with skill.

I saw Kenny as a NASCAR rookie, watched him drive and heard a lot about him before we hired him. Then when we met and got to know his personality, we found that in addition to making the whole thing a lot more fun for the people around him, we also knew that Kenny would make the best of his opportunities.

In our early days together, we could always run up front but we had a lot of mechanical failures and rough luck. I mean, Kenny would be leading the race and the back of the motor would crack—something that just isn't supposed to happen. Sometimes we didn't have the combinations right, but because Kenny had—and still has—so much talent we managed good finishes anyway. He wants to win as badly as anybody, but he also understands the nature of racing and how it isn't always going to happen even when it should. So, no matter how the day goes behind the wheel, when he gets out of the car, he puts it in the back of his mind and takes good care of the sponsors and the fans. If I had to sum it up, I'd say that it's hard to find someone who has the talent behind the wheel that he does, but still has so much personality and charm outside the race car, too.

Because of all that he can share with us from more than 30 years of racing, this is great timing for a book. Kenny remembers the era of short track racing when the cars were built from junkyard parts, but he's tremendously competitive today in the sophisticated short-track cars. He also can recall the days when NASCAR's top stars drove their pick-ups to the track, stayed in budget motels and could walk through the grocery store without being stopped. Kenny is part of the reason that's laughable today because he's one of the people who elevated racing. However, he has also kept the image of accessibility alive—because he really is accessible.

I think the young kids today could really take a page from his life story. Kenny has not changed from the time he started racing, the way he's kept his friends from the early days, and the way he has appreciated the fans. Success never went to his head. When he was The Man at Daytona—winning everything down there but the 500—he was still available to any fan who wanted his autograph or to talk.

Today, some of the kids get big heads. They work hard to get to the big time but then they develop a wise mouth and do things that create problems for the team and sponsors. They need to follow Kenny around. The Kenny Schrader I met the day we hired him is the same Kenny Schrader who worked for us and the same Kenny Schrader I know and love today.

I can't think of another driver who could become good friends with such different personalities as Dale Earnhardt, Sr. and Jeff Gordon. I also know what Kenny's presence on our team meant in terms of stability. He was a real ring leader, even though he wasn't all that old himself. If you had to have two guys who were accomplished veterans to be teammates with Jeff Gordon—

and not mind all the publicity that Jeff was getting—it had to be Terry Labonte and Kenny. They went about their work and did their job, and what went on around them didn't bother them.

Beyond that, Kenny was willing to share with Jeff when he was a young rookie coming in and trying to learn. There was no friction on our team, because Kenny wouldn't allow it. And what he meant to Jeff was one of the keys to the success we all enjoyed.

In particular, I remember a time at Talladega when Kenny went end-over-end about nine times. You'll see a couple of pictures from that experience later in this book.

I went to the infield hospital where they'd taken Kenny to be sure he was okay.

"What happened?" he asked, looking at me with a huge goose egg on his forehead and an eye that was already swollen shut.

"Buddy, it's hard to say."

"Well, who hit me? Somebody punted me."

And I admitted, "It was Gordon. He's all to pieces in the car. He's crying and saying he didn't mean to do it—asking us to please tell Kenny he didn't mean to do it."

Kenny—being soft-hearted as always—said, "Well, tell him don't worry about it."

Without thinking, I asked, "Well, Kenny, would you mind telling Jeff on the radio that everything's okay?"

He didn't hesitate. Kenny got on the radio and said, "Hey, Jeff, I'm all right. I know you didn't mean it, Buddy. Just go out and win the race."

Who else would do that? Who else would be laying on a hospital gurney, hurting like crazy, and then try to comfort the guy who put him there? I can tell you that Kenny razzed me pretty good about that later, but I know that if it had ever happened again, I could have taken the radio to the hospital, and he would have reassured the other driver.

Through all the years I've know him, I've also known this: You can always count on Schrader. You ask him to do anything, he won't turn you down. In fact, I think he's been good to a fault. I think throughout his career he's hung in with people he shouldn't have just to help them stay afloat. I also think he's given his own resources to other people, but that's because he's truly one of life's great people, on and off the track. He's just special.

He is family.

He's my brother.

That's what I want to close with. It's true that we gave him some professional opportunities to start with, but back then we couldn't have anticipated what we were going to get in return.

Racing is a huge family, complete with the crazy uncle and wild kids, but in general it's a great group. However, Kenny's place in it all is unique. In the darkest moments of my life, Kenny has been someone who has been there for me. Lots of people want to share the good times, but he is equally willing to share the difficult ones, too.

My mom and dad shared a very special relationship with Kenny and his family, as well. The race car Kenny drove for us was in my dad's name and it

was incredible to watch the feelings between them develop over time. Near the end of Dad's life, we had a birthday party for him and Kenny came, dressed in one of his old uniforms from the time he drove Dad's car. He was the life of the party, telling stories and making sure that Dad had a wonderful time. It's worth noting, too, that of the 80-some people who worked on the car during Kenny's time with us, all but a couple—and they were out of town—came. That tells you what it meant to all of them, and it's something I'll always remember.

Elsewhere in this book you will find a photo of Kenny and my dad in a rare, unguarded moment that requires no words to describe. But you can interpret that scene to include the entire Hendrick and Schrader families. Our emotional ties through many ups and downs, personally and professionally, have only strengthened through time.

The driver Kenny Schrader has had quite a career so far, but the man Kenny Schrader has had an even better life. That has led me—and many people who've known him—to conclude that the world needs more Kenny Schraders.

And there's your reason for taking time to read this book.

RICK HENDRICK
Concord, North Carolina

Foreword

by Bones Bourcier

Bones Bourcier

Aᶠᵗᵉʳ ᴍᴀʏʙᴇ 20 ʏᴇᴀʀs and Lord knows how many speedways—some big and fancy, some cramped and ramshackle—I have come to view Kenny Schrader as something of a pit-area psychologist.

Meaning that whenever something about this sport begins to bug me to the point where I'm ready to chuck the whole thing in favor of, I don't know, shuffleboard or something, what I do instead is check Schrader's short-track schedule, figure out when he's going to be someplace within driving distance on a Tuesday or Wednesday night, and then head there with an open mind and a willingness to grin.

After an evening at some little bullring with Dr. Schrader, everything is pretty much OK again.

You can get a terrific perspective on racing, and indeed on life itself, from my man Schrader, and I believe I've figured out why. It's because Kenny leads a good life doing what he wants to do, and he never forgets that. Lots of us who lead good lives doing what we want to do aren't nearly as diligent about remembering how lucky we are. So Schrader is my elbow to the ribs, my bookmark, my reminder that when it's all said and done, things can't be too bad if you're still able to get out to the racetrack, watch a good feature, and then maybe rerun the whole show with friends over a cold beer.

Schrader, I'm convinced, has no idea about his role in this process. I'm sure he figures I'm just showing up to catch a short-track show and bum a Bud Light or two.

I have been the recipient of his counsel at a wide range of tracks, from Charlotte and Daytona on one end of the glamour spectrum to homey joints like the Quincy Raceways in Illinois and his beloved I-55 Speedway in Missouri on the other end. I have watched him run Nextel Cup cars, Busch Series cars, Craftsman Trucks, midgets, and just about every conceivable configuration of late model and modified, on both dirt and pavement. I have watched him win plenty and, racing being what it is, I have watched him lose plenty. I have watched him as a journalist, pen in hand in plush press boxes, and I have watched him as an enthusiast, finding my seat on splintered boards in miniature pit bleachers as he ran his parade laps.

But you know something? It never matters much to me what type of car he's running, or how he finishes, or whether I'm there to see Schrader for an assignment or for leisure. I always know I can count on two things: First, that he's going to get the most out of whatever he's driving that day or night, whether it's for 35 laps or 500 miles; second, that win or lose he's going to be the same guy, that Everyman hero who never put himself above local racers and local fans, no matter what he accomplished or how well-known he became.

Two memories among the hundreds stand out to me as examples of the kind of fellow Ken Schrader is.

The first comes from 1993, when I tagged along with Schrader on a hectic weekend that included four events—an ASA show, a pavement late model gig, and two dirt late model races—in three states. His Saturday stop was at the Colorado National Speedway, owned at the time by millionaire racing enthusiast Marshall Chesrown, whose fortune was made through auto dealerships and land-development deals. Schrader was dismayed to discover that Chesrown, a classy guy who was simply being hospitable, had dispatched a white stretch limousine to pick us up at the airport. Clearly, it wasn't the fancy car itself that bothered Schrader; hell, it was actually a relaxing ride. No, I think what bugged him was the idea that such an ostentatious entrance might give track regulars the impression that he was a celebrity who needed—worse yet, demanded—a certain amount of pampering.

Later, Schrader was asked to tour the track in the long, white stretch, waving to the fans through the moon roof. He complied, because he is always an obliging guest, but he was clearly uncomfortable. "I don't like this," he said, fidgeting. "I mean, riding around the track in a limo."

He'd be happy, he muttered quietly, if any promoters interested in securing his services agreed to just meet him at the airport with a pickup truck, and drop him off at the pit gate.

Kenny Schrader, Everyman racer.

My second key memory dates back a bit further, to 1991, when I joined Schrader on a quick flight to the Seekonk Speedway in Massachusetts. Growing up in New England, I had spent a bunch of my teenaged Saturday nights there, so we talked about the track's history and its stars, including Bugs Stevens, a hell-raising NASCAR modified icon who by '91 had semi-retired but was still getting his weekly kicks running late models at Seekonk. Schrader had heard about Stevens, but the two had never met. He rectified that almost as soon as we'd gotten to the speedway, marching off toward to the Stevens pit, where the two chatted until it was time for the heat races.

This, I came to learn, was something of a habit for Schrader, wherever he went. Racing hard with the regional hotdogs was important, sure, but it was also important that he got to rub shoulders with them.

That night at Seekonk, he explained, "When you go to Springfield, Missouri, you listen to the Larry Phillips stories. If you go north of there, you listen to the Dick Trickle stories. If you go out to where they run modifieds around St. Louis, you listen to the Don Klein stories. Out here, you listen to the Bugsy stories.

"I didn't go over and talk to Bugsy to find out something about the track, or anything like that. I just wanted to *hear* him; I wanted to get to know him better."

Some years later, elaborating on this wonderful habit, Schrader told me, "I read a ton of racing publications, and I pretty much know who wins at these different places throughout the country. I'll read a guy's name a lot, and I may not know that man, but I'll feel like I know a little bit about him. Well, it's neat getting to meet people like that. I mean, these guys are heroes, and I get to go in and meet 'em."

Kenny Schrader, Everyman fan.

It has always troubled me that Schrader never became the Cup series champion I was once so sure he'd be. It's not that I feel bad for Kenny, because I know him well enough to believe that he's satisfied with the job he's done, if not always with the outcome. He is the sort of racer who can stomach finishing anywhere, whether second or 22nd, as long as he knows in his heart that he gave the job his all. I trust him when he says in this book that he doesn't much care how his career measures up against anyone else's. That brand of contentment comes only from a strong self-belief.

No, what troubles me is that Schrader would have been great for the role. There isn't a champion in modern racing as visible as the one who holds the Nextel Cup (or the Winston Cup before it), and all that attention would have been well-served by Schrader's quick wit and his wicked sense of humor. There are some drivers who try to be funny whenever they get near a camera or a microphone. Kenny Schrader could be funny just reading the phone book out loud. A Cup title, and the spotlight it would have brought, could have made Schrader one of the world's most popular motorsports figures.

Instead, he remains something of a cult hero. Some folks I know, the ones who believe "racing" consists only of what happens on their TV screens in those Sunday-afternoon 500-milers, have asked me why I think so highly of the guy. My answer is always the same: You either get Schrader, or you don't. And if you do, you recognize that he is an American motorsports treasure.

Ken Schrader has probably won in more types of oval-track cars than anybody; the only possible exception I can think of is his pal Tony Stewart. (As an aside, it is popular these days to describe Stewart, so full of fight, as this generation's A.J. Foyt. But I prefer to see Tony, especially in his lighter moments, as a latter-day Schrader, fueled by an enormous urge to just go racing.) I'm amused by the idea that Schrader has won at the biggest track of them all, the Talladega Superspeedway, and the smallest track I've ever seen, tiny Macon Speedway, out there amidst the Illinois cornfields.

In this book, my friend Joyce Standridge has done a marvelous job of drawing out Schrader's memories and philosophies. Joyce also captures Kenny's voice beautifully; that's not surprising, because the two have known each other since, as Schrader himself might put it, "nineteen-oh-shit." But knowing a person and acting as that person's ideal collaborator do not necessarily go hand-in-hand. On these pages, it's a perfect fit.

You'll come to know Schrader very well by the time you get to the final chapters. Along the way, you might even begin to see him as something of a psychologist yourself. That won't bother me a bit, so long as the Doctor can still fit me in the next time I come seeking some dusty, midweek therapy.

BONES BOURCIER

Part One

Racing Is All I've Ever Known

Ken Schrader Collection

Why Does That Angry Mob Want to Kill Me?

NOBODY EVER DROWNED at Lake Hill Speedway. Let me explain. When they paved the track, the owners didn't put any drains in the infield and there were a few times that we got caught in downpours. Rain hard enough and fast enough, there'd be spare tires floating.

Seriously.

It was never a real showplace on the order of an Eldora or Knoxville, nor was it famous even among the racing crowd. Head a couple hundred miles up I-70 and you'd be hard-pressed to find anybody who'd heard of Valley Park, Missouri, much less the race track there, but to those of us who called it our home track it was the best—floating tires and all. Anybody who's had their own home track knows what I mean.

A quarter-mile track that was paved in 1967 after many years as a dirt track, Lake Hill was surrounded by a wood-and-concrete wall that would suck you in if you were foolish enough to try to flirt with it or unlucky enough to have a tire go down. And if you had a rivalry going with another driver, he might just experience a brake fade as you got close to the wall. Or maybe it was a brain fade—either way the sparks looked pretty spectacular under the lights.

In its heyday, Lake Hill was a popular place to be on Sunday nights. The crowd was a blue-collar, beer-drinking bunch who really understood racing. Most of them recognized the difference between somebody who just mashed the gas and a real driver who could finesse a car around the track. The arguments about who belonged in which category was a big part of the fun of going there, and especially of hanging around afterward when we really ought to have been home in bed.

Of course, my Daddy, Bill Schrader, Sr., was the best driver who ever drove there. I might be a bit partial, but when I was little I had that very special feeling kids of a good racer have. It's hard to explain, but you kind of hitch up your shoulders a little bit when you walk through the gate. Reflected glory is really cool, even if you understand that you can't be a show-off. Daddy would have whipped us good if we'd ever strutted

around or acted like we were better than anybody else. He figured, rightly so, that you had to earn your place among the people to be admired.

Still, my younger sister Sherry and I were like hundreds of racer brats through the years. Even if your parent isn't a star, there's something special when you take your seat in the grandstand. The moon shines a little brighter, the lights on the track glow a little more, and the air just crackles with the feeling that this is your special place on earth.

In the years after I got out of diapers, and until they were forced to let me in the pit area, my routine was to accompany my mom, June, in the grandstand. She would gossip with the other wives and fans, but I was always ready to correct her if somebody asked about Daddy's repairs from last week and she didn't get it quite right. After all, I was the one down at his shop all week, every minute I could be.

I felt like those years until they finally let me get in a race car were both heaven and hell on earth.

Heaven because you were touched with glory without actually having to break a sweat, but hell because you knew that the respect you most wanted was withheld until you proved yourself. No way Daddy would see you as anything but a fuzz-faced kid until you *earned* his respect, and I'll bet that every adult reader of this book knows exactly how hard it is to get your folks to see you as a grown-up instead of the baby whose snotty nose they wiped. Other people will acknowledge your maturity long before your parents do.

I don't want to make it seem like I was hungering for Daddy's attention and approval. Our relationship was pretty uncomplicated, at least as much as a parent and child could have. We really understood each other because we knew what motivated us, and you can't get much more uncomplicated than living to race.

Even if he hadn't given his blessing, I would have had to race. I was smitten at an age so young I can't even remember it happening. Fortunately, however, not only did both Daddy and Mom turn me loose to chase my dreams, they supported me all the way.

Nothing like the kid taking up the family business, after all.

THE IMPALA

Lake Hill had a rule that you had to be 18 years old to drive a race car. Seemed like a pretty dumb rule to me. I was ready at about 12 or 13, but I was willing to be reasonable about it and wait until I was 16.

Let me amend that—the law wouldn't let me drive it until I was 16, although at that point I couldn't see what would be so magical from one day to another. It wasn't like I was going to wake up on my 16th birthday and overnight be ready, but the local judge ruling on the issue wouldn't budge to a day before that, even if he was a friend of my folks.

The day I turned 16 was May 29, 1971. A Saturday, if you're keeping score. Later on, I'll tell you something about my earlier years, but they all just led to this particular day, as far as I'm concerned, and I'm chomping at the bit to talk about it.

That Saturday we went down to the track and I ran about 20 laps, the first time I ever got behind the wheel on a race track. Nothing happened that afternoon to convince me that I wasn't ready.

Sunday night, I got behind the wheel and won the feature race.

A monumental day in my life—as my dad looks on, I sign in at the pit gate for the first time as a driver! Now that I was finally a race driver, I worked up the courage to speak to Danny Frye, Sr. (seated), one of the top open-cockpit owners in the area. Unfortunately, he wasn't ready to hire me as a driver. I don't think he was ready for me as a son-in-law several years later, either, but that's another story. (Rocky Rhodes photos; Ken Schrader Collection.)

And could that first night as a race car driver have a better ending? Daddy hands me the checkered flag for winning the feature! (Rocky Rhodes photo; Ken Schrader Collection.)

On Monday, my folks let me skip school and I went down to the DMV and got my driver's license so I could legally drive on the street.

Pretty cool, neat little story, huh? Except that it was more complicated than that. The problem was that *not everybody else thought I was ready.*

First of all, I had a car that had originally been Jerry Sifford's late model. It was a stock 1964 Chevrolet Impala and after a couple of seasons on the track it was pretty rough looking. However, I thought it was beautiful. It was a race car. Furthermore, it was *my* race car.

Daddy had bought the car back in December, 1970, when I was still 15 years old, because it was for sale at a good price and he was also anticipating my upcoming birthday. When the season began in early May, Daddy drove it a couple of weeks and Jerry drove it a couple of weeks in the sportsman division at the beginning of the Lake Hill season. And they won almost all those features.

The rest of the competition wasn't real happy, but they figured, *hey, the kid's getting in it and he can't find his head from a hole in the ground.*

And then I got in it and won the first three features I ran.

The other drivers were not thrilled. Some blamed my success on the car because basically the difference between the late model and sportsman divisions at that time was tire size, and the car had been good as a late model, too. But there were others who weren't willing to just leave it there. We were accused of cheating, even though the car got torn down and passed inspection more than once. I think the whispers in the pits went so far as to claim I'd been to race-driving school or practicing in secret locations.

I understand. It's really hard to just give young kids respect. The thinking—correctly, I believe—is that you need to earn a degree from the School of Hard Knocks, especially when you're talking about a short-track sportsman division. And if you are already a graduate, why should you be impressed with the 16-year-old kid who busted the track age rule with the help of a judge. I mean, that was a strike against me before we ever got on the track.

I figured out real fast that even if you do everything your folks tell you, try to be considerate toward others, do all the stuff you're told are the things a "good" person is supposed to do, there's probably somebody out there who is going to want to pull you down. Maybe it's jealousy, maybe it's a legitimate beef, maybe it makes no sense at all, but in the end you don't use it as an excuse to stray from what you've been taught. You just go out there and try to be the person you know you can be. Some people will appreciate it—and some won't. And eventually, time will pass, the respect will be earned, and if you're not exactly kissing and making up, at least things will calm down.

Heavier issues aside, my focus in the summer of 1971 was on racing even if I was the eye of an unwelcome storm. Winning those features made me feel really racy, and I was ready to speed up the pace. Six

Without Dean Roper's help, I probably wouldn't have gone to race at Rolla—at least not so quickly. We were really, really happy to have him in one of our race cars many years later for an ARCA show. It's 1995 at the Springfield Mile, a place he mastered during his career. (Kevin Horcher photo; Ken Schrader Collection.)

weeks or so into my "career," I got what was the ultimate compliment up to that point. It might have seemed even more momentous because there hadn't been all that many compliments in the early going, but there was a really good driver by the name of Dean Roper who ran Lake Hill at times. Dean became well-known as one of the best stock car racers in the history of the United States Auto Club and he ran a lot of different tracks so he was a big deal to us. Instead of just being a hometown hero, Dean was a real racer.

One night after the races at Lake Hill, he asked, "Kenny, why don't you go to Rolla?"

Rolla, Missouri, had a big ol' half-mile, paved track at that time. Like Lake Hill, it eventually fell victim to time passing it by, but in the early 1970s it was one intimidating, engine-eating, suck-'em-up track. You had to be a real racer to run there—and I wanted to be a real racer.

"Dean, my daddy won't let me go there," I told him.

He said, "Well, I don't have time right now, but remind me next week and I'll take care of that."

I re-ran that brief conversation in my head to the exclusion of almost everything else that eternally, infernally long week. School? Who had time for geometry or geography? Rolla was an oval—how's that for geometry? And it was 86 miles southwest of home—that's all the geography I needed that week.

Apparently, it was a more significant conversation to me than it was to Dean. After pay-off the following Sunday night, racers sat around rehashing the races like they always do, and the time started going by.

And going by.

And the next thing I knew, I saw Dean in his truck ready to leave.

"Mr. Roper!" I hollered, half out of breath after chasing his rig through the pits. "Mr. Roper, you told me you'd talk to Daddy."

He might have been tired, might have been more than ready to go home and get some sleep, but he'd made me a promise. And, Dean Roper was a man of his word.

"Oh, yeah, dammit," he sighed. "Hold on."

He put the truck back in *Park*, went over to the concession stand and got a six-pack. Tracked down Daddy and perched on a bench. I stayed out of it—clean away from them, but watching like a hawk. I didn't ask any questions when the conversation broke up and we all went home.

Next morning at breakfast, Daddy real casually tells me, "I think we're gonna go over to Rolla next week."

You'll not be surprised to learn that from that moment on, Dean Roper was My Man.

THE CHEVELLE

Running at Lake Hill in the sportsman division was a case of tunnel vision. I'm guessing most young racers know what I'm talking about. If you start out in a car owned by your folks you probably won't get fired, but it's twice as hard to get respect because everybody else knows you're not going to get fired, too. To be accepted as a driver, you have to figure out what you're doing, don't screw up anybody else and just hang on. You aren't charting out a career at that point. Yeah, everybody looks at the Big Time and fantasizes, but realistically your more immediate goal is to avoid bankrupting the folks or you won't be able to continue racing.

We did well that first season, so we got a little racey over the winter months and came back out the following spring running the same car but in the late model division.

We did not set the world on fire.

By the time we got through that season and headed toward the 1973 racing season, we were at a crossroads. It was time for some major, life-altering decisions, so Mom and Daddy sat me down and said, "Okay, we have three ways we can go here. The first is that you can go away to college somewhere."

Later, I'll be providing some background information about my academic career to that point which will clarify why, at this point, I was interested in hearing other alternatives. Let's just say Harvard wasn't calling with a scholarship offer even before this conversation.

"Secondly, you can go up the road to the junior college, and we'll continue to race the old Impala."

Better idea, but no goose bumps. Let's hear the final offer.

"Or we can build a new Chevelle."

Well, hell, let's build a Chevelle! Seemed simple enough to me.

Actually, I have great appreciation for the value of a good education, but at age 18 and with the prospect of a new race car dangling before me, there simply was nothing the educational community could have said to dazzle me into the halls of academia. Hell, I didn't even know what the halls of academia were.

So, Daddy and I, and our pals from his shop, built a 1973 Chevelle. It was a beautiful, beautiful car. One of the prettiest I have ever had in my entire career.

And it ran terrible.

Well, at the end of that '73 season, I was out of school and working full-time, because my folks weren't wealthy. Daddy took me aside then and said, "Okay, here's the deal. We're giving you the operation. The race car is yours, the spare engine is yours, and the trailer is yours."

I already had a nice pick-up truck. This was fantastic.

"So what's the catch?" I asked, knowing there had to be one.

"You have to pay the bills from here on out."

Heeeeyyyyy, no problem. Can life get any better than this? I mean, I got a decent job, my own race car and the stuff to go racing. I couldn't have been a happier camper if a bikini-clad Raquel Welch had called and asked to be on the pit crew.

Well, as you might imagine, my vision was a little short-sighted. Like every other Saturday-night racer in America, I had other bills and stretching my paycheck was a little harder than I had anticipated.

I worked at McCormick's Western Auto in Valley Park because the McCormicks were racing fans and I could get off to go racing. I had turned down a really good job at UPS, where I would have been making something like $7 or $8 an hour. In 1973, that was real money—like $17 or $18 an hour is today—but I would have had to work on Friday nights. Race night at another area track.

So that wasn't going to happen.

Over at the Western Auto store, I would sell tires—and then I'd mount them. I'd sell you a refrigerator—and then I'd deliver it. Easy

sales counter work? No chance. But, hey, come Friday night my carcass was outta there and off to the races.

Along about this time I also got an apartment. There's stuff 18-year-olds think they're old enough to do that their parents don't necessarily agree with. Besides, it's not cool to live with your folks. Kids do it more these days because it takes so much money to get out on your own, but it felt pretty expensive even then. I think the rent was $210 a month, and considering I was making about $5 an hour and trying to race, some basic economics began to eat into my brain. There's utilities, food, gas, the girl friend gets tired of the race track all the time and wants a movie now and then. Well, it adds up.

So I got stuff happening here. It would be good if I could drive someone else's race car sometimes, because I gotta race a lot. I mean, *a lot!*

However, it wasn't like car owners were lining up to hire me. There aren't a lot of independent car owners anymore, but in those days there were quite a few in all types of racing. These were guys who just loved to be involved and didn't have to get a fourth mortgage to own a race car.

Still, we hadn't been winning much.

Okay, in all honesty, we weren't winning *at all* at that point. So car owners who had their kid or their best buddy or just a good driver in their car weren't real inclined to throw them out and put me in just because my rent was due.

Not surprisingly, it was a friend who came to the rescue. Bob Mueller was one of my childhood heroes. When I was a kid, Bob was a real shoe and one of Daddy's pals, but by the mid-1970s he wasn't racing as often. As much as anything, he put me in his 1966 Ford Galaxy as a favor to Daddy. We ran the car at Tri-City Speedway, across the Mississippi River in Granite City, Illinois, and that was my first night on dirt.

The track is still among the best in the Midwest. Today, it's owned and run by one of my oldest friends and competitors, Kevin Gundaker, and his family. The track has always been a bitch to keep going as a solid business concern because it has a black-loam surface that provides a fantastic bite for tires. In the early days, it wasn't such a big deal because we couldn't get hooked up very well, but as time went by and the cars got more sophisticated, the power transferred from the bitey tires through the drive train meant that half-mile track ate engines like popcorn at the movies. That hurt racers financially, which in turn hurt the car counts. When promoters then tried to run the quarter-mile track inside the half, the fans didn't like it as well. It's been a challenge to keep the track going, but back in 1974, I couldn't have cared less how many owners were going to go broke in the future. At that time, Elvis and Florence Doolin were the owners and they had a terrific track, terrific crowds, and I was going to become a more versatile driver by adding dirt racing to my resume. Not even a legendary, car-chomping inside guard rail could intimidate me.

What a learning experience. And this is what I learned at the conclusion of that very first race on dirt: I was really, really glad that Wib Spalding was one of the most respected race drivers in the history of the track, because he was really, really helpful in keeping the other racers from killing me.

See, I didn't have respect for that guard rail. I hadn't eaten it before like most of the regulars, so I saw there was room between the other racers and the guard rail, and I just smoked 'er on down in there. Well, I wasn't used to how much that Ford was going to move around. We didn't have the kind of traction-loving suspensions we do today, so if you went down into the turn as hard as you could, you weren't going to stay next to that guard rail.

The regulars knew that.

I didn't.

And I have to say that the Ford of that era was a lot stouter than all those Chevys I was piling into.

I was a little confused that night because I had absolutely no car control. But I could see that if you got it figured out, it would be pretty neat. My learning curve ramped up pretty quickly after that, mostly because I came to love dirt racing in no time at all. I still love dirt. And I think at least a few of those guys from that first night may have forgiven me. A little Alzheimer's might not be a bad thing where that race was concerned.

Anyway, Bob didn't fire me. We took the car home, and changed the tires to go to Rolla the next night, because that was the technological difference between dirt and pavement in those days: You changed the tires. I recall also that we didn't have enough wheels, so we *really* changed the tires. Broke them down off the rims and mounted the tires on the few wheels we did have. Hard work, but, hey, we were going racing.

When he wasn't collecting checkered flags, Wib Spalding was keeping the angry mob from stringing up hard-charging kids from Valley Park. Man, am I ever glad. (Rocky Rhodes photo; Ken Schrader Collection.)

I broke it. There's a lesson here: It's not all checkered flags and cold beer. (Ken Schrader Collection.)

THE LEARNING CURVE

How do you like our tow rig? Made it all the way from Valley Park, Missouri, to New Smyrna, Florida, for Speed Weeks 1974. Later, you'll read a tale of Dale Earnhardt, Jr.'s coming-of-age, but that was a picnic compared to this trip, where Pat Walsh (right) and Bruce Hawkins (taking the photo) introduced me to worlds I had never known. By the end of the week, I had to literally hold my head on. (Ken Schrader Collection.)

I was still driving mostly for myself and that meant that I spent a lot of hours working on the car. Pat Walsh, who was a good late model driver in his own right, and Spence Bach, a friend I inherited from Daddy, helped me, but it was my baby. Nowadays, my crew won't let me do much more than run the grinder on the tires to get down to fresher rubber because as a mechanic, well, hell, I'm a pretty good grinder. But back then if I wanted it done, I had to do it.

And Daddy and the rest of the guys were doing what they'd always done, which is shoot the shit and drink some beer, only now they had the added sport of making fun of the kid. When you're young, ambitious and still on the short end of the learning curve, you don't have time in your busy evening to shovel the shit out of the way. I was getting tired of being an easy target.

I found a shop for rent at $60 a month and moved my race-car operation out of Daddy's shop. The new garage was about 12-foot wide and 40-foot long. Yeah, not ideal, even then, but it got me away from the harassment.

Took me all of about two weeks there before I realized a significant fact about having your own garage and needing help working on the race car. Due to this fact, I went out and bought a used refrigerator. And then I got somebody older to go get me some beer, because I found out no one would help work on the car if I didn't have beer.

With all that settled, my car-owner learning curve also got a lesson. Discounting a trip to Florida Speed Weeks in February, which was really just an excuse for underage drinking and watching other people race, I went back to Tri-City Speedway in April, ran well and I left there with about $400, which seemed like a lot of money. At that time, the purse was based on how many people came in through the gate and there was a great crowd, so we were immediately money ahead on this deal.

The next night we took the Chevelle down to Rolla.

Blew the engine.

Backed into the wall.

Got hit head on.

Second night as owner-driver, and I was done. Or so it seemed. Racers will tell you that circumstances often change in the light of a new day.

My old buddy Jerry Sifford came to the rescue and told me there was an old car down behind Tom Hannick's garage. Tom was another pal who had towed us before we had a trailer, and I think this was the car he'd run the year before.

Well, Pat Walsh and I went over and got it Sunday morning, put all my spare stuff on it and we were at Lake Hill that night. Nowadays you can do that, but it will cost you ten grand or more without breaking a sweat. You just buy it all, if you can. In 1974, there wasn't a lot of aftermarket stuff yet, so you took the stock car, put on some tires and a few other things, and you went racing.

Couldn't have been too hard to run an old car, because I set fast time

When we had our act together, we looked pretty good. Especially after I got a uniform to wear instead of driving in a tee-shirt. But then on my second official night as a car owner, I killed the car. (Left, Rocky Rhodes photo; Ken Schrader Collection; right, Ken Schrader Collection.)

that night. We ended up rained out, which was a bummer after sweating all day to get ready, but Pat and I left feeling pretty good about the whole thing anyway, and we ran good the following week back at Tri-City and Rolla.

Somehow, we got through that year, and then I learned something else useful that has stayed with me until today: Uncle Sam will be your friend, if you let him.

Let me explain. This was my first year working full-time, as well as being a race-car owner. So I went to a tax guy and he asked me, "Did you make any other money besides what you earned at Western Auto?"

"Well, I made $8,000 from my race car," I told him.

He blinked. "Does it cost you to run the race car?"

After I picked myself up off the floor from laughing, I assured him that it did indeed cost money to go racing.

"Do you have the receipts?" His words got prettier and prettier. "Your expenses may be deductible."

That's when Schrader Racing was formed.

There are some pretty specific rules and laws about this kind of thing, but after being slapped in the face all year with one expensive lesson after another, it was pretty neat to find out that Uncle Sam was the one guy who was going to take some pity on this poor racer.

And, I could afford to go racing next year.

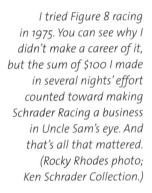

I tried Figure 8 racing in 1975. You can see why I didn't make a career of it, but the sum of $100 I made in several nights' effort counted toward making Schrader Racing a business in Uncle Sam's eye. And that's all that mattered. (Rocky Rhodes photo; Ken Schrader Collection.)

Don't Run Over the Rose Bushes in Turn One

2

ONE NIGHT I WATCHED A MIDGET RACE CAR zing down the backstretch with a stuck throttle. Slammed the wall good.

I was like, *I wouldn't drive one of them shitboxes for anything.*

But you can slam a wall with anything—and I have—so I changed my tune and decided that since they were occasionally running midgets on the same nights as late models at Lake Hill, why not double my chances of making some money by driving two classes? And, really, they looked like fun if you could keep them out of the wall.

During that time, midget car owner Bud Hoppe was working on a construction project near the high school I attended, and I would leave at lunch so I could track him down. I'd see him and beg, "Mr. Hoppe, Mr. Hoppe, let me hot-lap your car. Just let me practice some. That's all I'm askin'."

He knew better.

Now, some drivers have a hard time asking for a ride, and I'm telling you it's never easy at any level of racing, from the street stock division at your local track all the way to NASCAR Nextel Cup. You have to possess enough ego to believe your racing skills will get you hired, and, of course, if you don't believe in yourself why should anybody else? Like a lot of things in life, you'll hear "no," far more than "yes." If you are shy or lacking in self-confidence, your ego takes a battering from that kind of thing.

Not a problem for me.

It's not that I'm over-confident, but I just always subscribed to the nothing-ventured, nothing-gained philosophy, and not just in racing. I've never been quite satisfied to just hear about adventures of any kind. Why go secondhand when you can find out about something on your own?

So, I was pushing for rides about as often as I was shaving—not every day, but with increasing frequency. I was counting on car owners seeing hunger as a better deal than experience. In late models there were

more cars than in the midgets, but most car owners had their kid or a close buddy driving for them. It was a more laid-back atmosphere, too. Meanwhile, the midgets were a whole different circus.

If you are not already familiar with that era, in the early 1970s the St. Louis area was a real hotbed for midgets. The cars are a much smaller version of the Big Cars running Indianapolis before and just after World War II, and it seemed like almost every Midwestern track ran them as the premier division from the 1930s until the mid-1950s. Then, as has happened with almost every short-track division, over time they evolved, which translates into: they got a whole lot more expensive.

You'll always find people at every race track who are willing to spend whatever it takes to gain an advantage. You'd like to think that racing would appeal to a higher instinct, like we'll all run the same thing and the best man will win. I think that attitude lasted for 15 seconds all the way back in 1898 before the first driver figured out how to put on cheater goggles or something.

Promoters and sanctioning groups have tried ever since to figure out how to make a level playing field, but for every high-minded rule maker there's been ten-dozen mechanics, car owners and drivers trying to figure out how to make the rules work for them. Often, it boils down to writing a check and that was true in 1930, 1950, 1970 and today.

Although the midgets were no longer a weekly feature at most tracks by the 1970s, they were enjoying something of a popularity surge as traveling tours. There were little regional groups peppered all over the country, but a couple of really exciting sanctions were SLARA (St. Louis Auto Racing Association) and USAC (United States Auto Club). At that time, USAC still had the Indianapolis 500 sanction so it wasn't altogether unexpected for a guy to come into USAC at the entry level—midgets—and work his way up to sprints, dirt cars (also known as Silver Crown) and then to the Speedway. A lot of guys did it that way.

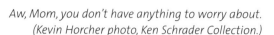

Aw, Mom, you don't have anything to worry about.
(Kevin Horcher photo, Ken Schrader Collection.)

Unlike the pre- and post-World War II years when deaths and serious injuries were common in open-wheel cars—mostly because they didn't have roll cages—it was pretty rare by the 70s. But it was still racing, still had an element of danger, and sometimes guys didn't come back to the pits when the race was over. That's why my folks, particularly my Mom, weren't really excited when I made the move into open-cockpit racing. The saving grace, at least where Daddy was concerned, was that I was going to drive for Bud Hoppe. I guess that I understand their hesitancy, but Daddy already realized I was going to race wherever I got a chance, and he felt a lot better that it was going to be in Bud's car.

MR. HOPPE GIVES ME A RIDE

Bud's cars weren't the fastest, hottest, latest stuff, which is why Daddy was comfortable with them. He figured that even if I drove "over my head," I wasn't going to be going fast enough to get a nosebleed, but I would be fast enough to learn a lot.

At that time, Bud had an older Kurtis-copy chassis with a Chevy II engine. The car had enough age that it had a bolt-on—instead of welded-on—roll cage. On dirt, we ran M & H tires, and sometimes also on pavement when we didn't have Firestones. If it had been 1963 instead of 1973, it would have been very racey. But we were into new technology and the real slick set-up was an Edmunds chassis with a Sesco engine (an aftermarket half-V-8 Chevy engine). You needed Goodyears and Racemasters for fast tires, and if you could mount them on chrome wheels you looked really slick. So, in the midget-racing world we were pretty good for our local racing but at a disadvantage in SLARA or USAC.

I could have cared less.

Bud Hoppe had been one of the really good post-war midget racers. He knew how to win races, and he knew how to do it without breaking

June Cox: Everything in Ken's life was racing. If he was going up the street, he would run and call it laps. He related everything in his life somehow to racing.

Let me tell you about his first midget race. There was a big wheel in the racing organization who didn't want Kenny to race. The rest of the officials told Kenny that he could, but it was suggested that if he got up to that guy on the track, don't pass him. Stay behind him.

So, Kenny was passing people like crazy. Well, when he got up to the guy he was warned about, Kenny just slowed down and did this real obvious turn so he stayed behind him. But everybody knew. They all knew Kenny could have beat him.

My Mom, June, with me and her second husband, Bill Cox. (Joyce Standridge photo.)

the bank. Even though I was still a kid, I was smart enough to know that his experience and his ability as a chassis man had to be worth thousands of dollars. You could buy technology, you could buy speed, but you couldn't buy the knowledge that came with those hundreds of nights when he'd made the right—or wrong—call in setting up his car.

By now you realize that my badgering at lunch time paid off. I was a midget racer, and I liked it. Never mind that the reason I got into it was because, unlike the late models where long-term relationships were the norm, in midgets long-term could charitably be called a season. The midget car owners were like, *hey, the kid didn't do any good tonight, so yer fired!* It was a whole different program, and I recognized there might be an opportunity in them. I just conveniently ignored the fact that I might be in and out of rides just as quickly as the rest of the kids.

Fortunately, in spite of our age difference, Bud and I hit it off immediately. I'd like to think it was because I've always been able to find common ground with people, and I'm sure that even though I was just a kid, I was eager to learn all I could from Bud and his peers.

And here's something I had already learned, but was confirmed by Bud: *Have a good time.*

Not everyone knows that Bud Hoppe was a damned good race driver when he was young. Notice that there's only a little roll bar on the car, proof also that guys of Bud's era were either brave or crazy—or both. (Ken Schrader Collection.)

I was sort of figuring that out on my own, but let's say that Bud accelerated the process. I remember one particular night when we started 18th in a feature at Belle-Clair Speedway, a little fifth-mile bull-ring in Belleville, Illinois, but a really good midget track. We won the feature, stopped on the front straightaway and got our picture taken. I'm 19 years old, I got a uniform that's still pretty clean for having run 20 laps on a dirt track, a checkered flag in one hand and my other arm around the trophy girl. Can life get any better?

"C'mere," says Bud. "You need to learn how to celebrate a win."

So, Bud and his helpers—who were all guys his age—took me to the girlie show over at the County Fair next door. Next thing I know, they've thrown me up on the stage.

"Dumb kid," Bud groused later. "You won the race, but you didn't care about those girls. What was wrong with you?"

Nothing. I didn't need to learn anything from middle-aged strippers with thick pancake make-up. There was a lot of shit I didn't know about, in fact, and I was eager to learn. In Bud I had a hell of a teacher about the whole after-race party shit. But at that point, I figured if I concentrated on the racing end, all the rest would come around, and I had plenty of time for girls later.

When we weren't studying Party-Time 101 or working on the race car, we raced at Lake Hill, Belle-Clair, St. Charles and other area tracks, but occasionally we got out on the road, even though it was pretty limited compared to the traveling we do today.

I also quickly learned at that time that if it's mid-August, 100 degrees with humidity to match, the pick-up truck has plastic seats and no air-conditioning, you'll separate the real racers from the wannabes. Especially if a thunderstorm rolls through and dumps an inch of rain on the track, the sun pops back out and no way will the promoter call it off since it's a Fair race and there's a big crowd guaranteed.

You're glad because you've already spent the money to get there, even though you know that if you have to change rear-end gears it will

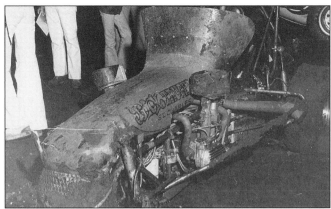

be in the middle of a mud puddle. And since it's Fair time, odds are pretty good that any breeze will blow through the livestock barn before it gets to your pit spot. But, you're racing and there's nothing to match it.

We ran a lot of little, flat horse tracks in those days. County fair boards could bring in midgets during the fair for a pretty modest purse and get a good field because there were so few options available for them. The tracks, even if they had started out as horse tracks and all looked pretty similar, tended to have some characteristic that made them memorable. For example, Fairfield, Illinois, had pea gravel on the back straightaway. You didn't want to start last in the field because you'd feel like you were under attack when the wheels of the cars in front of you kicked that gravel back. *Ping, ping, ping.* Like BB shot.

Over at Sparta, Illinois, turns one and two had a length of rose bushes. You get flipped into them and they'd tear up your uniform. Even just run into them and the garden club would run you out of town.

YOU NEVER KNOW WHAT'S GOING TO HAPPEN

Bud and I never got rich during the time we ran his cars, and sometimes we had to get creative to keep going. At times we borrowed other cars and Bud maintained them while I drove them. Made some really good friends doing that. One of the great guys we raced with that way was Hank Green.

We drove for Hank for a while in the '70s and then he moved to California. But within a few years he came back to the area. By that time, I was driving on the major midget circuits for Nick Gojmeric who had one of the best midget rides around. It was really first rate and sought after by a lot of drivers, so I felt privileged to drive for him.

When Hank came back from the West Coast he called us, and after a little noodling we figured out that the smart thing to do was for Nick and me to take Hank's car and run it. It would help Nick financially for a while, and it would get Hank back on the circuit.

Done deal. So, the first night of this collaboration Nick and I took the car over to Kokomo Speedway in Indiana, with Hank and Bud along. I won the heat and as I came around the track I spotted Hank and Bud—and gave them a big thumbs up.

Hank raised his fist in the air. Man, he was happy to be back.

They started back over to where we were pitted with the car, but Hank had gone only a few steps when he keeled over on his face. We were really shook up. You don't see a strong man like Hank go to his knees and then to the ground without it being bad.

While the ambulance was taking him to the hospital, Nick, Bud and I tried to figure out whether to continue racing or load the car. We knew Hank was pretty bad. Finally, we decided that he would want us to run, especially since the car was really hooked up and he'd been feeling so good about what we were doing.

I should have won that feature.

It was going to be the perfect storybook ending to a rotten night, but in the process of losing it, I cost the race for Rich Vogler, too. A lousy

Hank Green had just returned from living in California and was thrilled with how well we ran at Kokomo Speedway. But when he collapsed a few minutes after the heat win, I was determined to win the feature for him. Instead, I took out Rich Vogler (#74) and myself. Rich wasn't exactly a forgiving kind of competitor, but on this night he understood. (Jack Gladback photo, Ken Schrader Collection.)

night gone lousier. I just tried way too hard, wanting to win that race for Hank, and I ended up spinning and getting together with Rich and knocked us both out.

Afterward, we went up to the hospital, and I flat-out lied to Hank. We knew by then that he had suffered a massive stroke and wasn't likely to make it through the night. He was laying there, drifting in and out of consciousness, which was tearing us up, wanting so bad to hold on and bring him back to us.

I took his hand and squeezed it. Told him that we'd won the feature.

He managed to squeeze my hand back. He liked that. He was fighting for his life, but he really liked the idea that the first night back out with his race car, we were good enough to beat USAC's best.

Hank died later that night.

It was the worst night of my life to that point, but while Hank was an adult who'd lived a pretty good length of time, it was about that time that I got another lesson that we don't come into the world with a guarantee we'll live even as long as Hank did.

The first time I ever ran with the USAC midgets away from a home track was at the Indianapolis Speedrome, a really good, paved quarter-miler that operates on the other side of town from the big track. The quality of racing is so good they've stayed open forever, and part of the reason is because it's fast. That night, Johnny Gall's throttle stuck and the car got up on the wall on the cage side, clipped a light pole, and he was dead instantly. You didn't need an announcement to know. You were there, you were in the infield, you knew.

It was the first time I was ever at a track where I was so close to an

Cousin Mike watches the races from on top of the Schrader Racing hauler. (Joyce Standridge photo.)

Mike Edwards, cousin, driver, car owner, and father of NASCAR driver Carl Edwards: Kenny called me up and said, "There's this midget for sale and you need to own it."

So I bought it. It was a real nice car, the black #67 that Hank Green had owned. I raced it and didn't do too terribly good, but I didn't wad it up terribly either.

They had a 50-lapper at St. Charles. Kenny had been driving pretty regularly for Nick Gojmeric, but that car was broke. So they had me bring my car over. Nick brought some trick tires and wheels, different bars and springs, and they set it up. It was fast.

Kenny started in the top ten, got to third racing the wheels off it, and then caught the leaders. Everybody in the place was on their feet. Kenny really put on a lesson.

Well, in those days, Kenny remembers, if he won I gave him his pit pass money back. I don't remember it that way. But that night, he came over afterwards and told me, "You're paying me tonight."

He didn't have to ask twice. He earned it that night.

on-track death that I could have walked up and smacked the Grim Reaper. It was a wake-up call, a reminder that we're not playing tiddly-winks here. Made for a really long, really subdued drive home later.

That was the night that my thoughts about death behind the wheel began to take form. Racing was every bit as much fun after Gall's wreck as it had been before, but there was a whole new respect for what might be than I'd known in my short life to that point. I know everybody eventually encounters and deals with the topic, but I'm all for postponing that confrontation as long as possible. You're a kid before you deal with it. You can't be afterwards.

PUTTIN' ON THE RITZ

In spite of those heavy deals, the years I spent midget racing were mostly about fun. They had to be because they sure weren't about getting rich.

As I mentioned, money wasn't good in midgets, even though Bud's car kept the wolf away from my apartment door for several years. I can remember winning the heat, dash and feature at Lake Hill and taking home a whopping $167.

And I got only 40 percent of that.

But one night they had a $2,000-to-win USAC midget race at Belle-Clair. This was during the time I drove for Nick, and I'll admit we had a little swagger to us. Nothing obnoxious—at least not intentionally—but we had the best-running car and we knew it. So, we show up at Belle-Clair in our Hawaiian shirts, and our tow vehicle was Ralph Taylor's 1959 Cadillac convertible with a trailer hooked up behind it. We're styling and we're not afraid to tell people we're prepared to win.

Thank God we did.

We would have looked like real assholes if we hadn't.

Beyond questionable taste in tow vehicles, Nick was another great owner-driver. He had given up driving when he broke his neck driving

We showed up one night in 1983 at Belle-Clair Speedway towing with the pink pimpmobile and just a tad cocky. Damned good thing we won! That's Billy Taylor on the left, car owner Nick Gojmeric in the passenger seat, and I'm driving. Future wife Ann was wise enough to hide in the back seat. (Ken Schrader Collection.)

After winning the feature in Nick's car (that's him behind my right shoulder), I'm not sure if I was demonstrating how much I'd won by or clapping my hands because I was finally old enough to grow a mustache. (Ken Schrader Collection.)

the midget. Even though he came close to biting the bullet, he returned to racing as one of the most fun-loving car owners I ever drove for. He was always ready for a good prank—even at the expense of a mutual friend.

Remember the mention of Spence Bach helping with my stock car? Well, he was involved in my midget racing, too, although there was at least one night when he might have wished he'd taken up golf or something.

We were all supposed to be going to another show at Kokomo—up and back same day. It's about 300 miles one-way, but in those days of 50-cent-a-gallon gas we didn't worry about that kind of trip.

However, when Spence picked me up, I had a little suitcase that I threw in the car. "What's that for? We're coming back tonight, right?" he asked.

"Yeah, yeah," I said. "Just wanna change clothes after the race."

So then we picked up Nick and he came out of the house with a suitcase and put it in the van.

"Whatcha doin' with the suitcase?"

Spence was starting to get suspicious. He's not totally stupid. He knew that Nick wasn't going to drive, so why would he need to change clothes after the races?

"Ah, ya never know," Nick told him.

Then we went down the road and alongside an exit we picked up Billy Taylor, who was standing alongside the road—with a suitcase in his hand.

Well, hell, by now Spence knew he'd been duped but we were already a few miles toward Kokomo and you might as well go the other 290 miles.

We got to Kokomo at 5:30 P.M. At 6:00 it started raining and the promoter called off the races until the next night. So, we did what you're supposed to do when presented with a rain-out. We took up competitive drinking. Spence, meanwhile, was like, "What am I going to do?"

No problem.

There was an 8:30 P.M. flight out of Indianapolis to St. Louis. That meant Spence needed to stay sober, so he went over to the van and laid down to rest. He'd had a long, hard drive, after all.

At 9:00 P.M., he woke up.

We're still drinking beer and bench-racing.

You blankety-blankin' blankers! he hollered.

What about my flight?

"Well, hey, you missed it. Shouldn't have gone to sleep."

Yeah, I know, we sound like great friends. But if we woke him up and drove him down to the airport, we would have had to stop the bench-racing and there were still a lot of laps to go, y'know.

We're not totally irresponsible.

We won plenty of races in Gene Hamilton's midgets, including this one in his V-6 midget at Phoenix International Raceway. (Ken Schrader Collection.)

We took him into Indy, put him on the midnight bus to St. Louis, and arranged for him to be picked up at 7:00 A.M. so he could make it to work on time.

BUT I CAN SEE MY HOUSE!

As you might have guessed from the Kokomo story, these were the years that we were getting introduced to longer-distance racing—many hours away from our St. Louis base. The experience really helped us. Today we fly, or if we use the truck it's a semi with a sleeper. In those days, you drove a while, and then you stopped a while. At least, you stopped a while if you were with midget owner Gene Hamilton.

Gene had one of the best cars in the country. He wasn't afraid to pull a race a thousand miles away if the pay was good enough, but he had hard and fast rules about travel.

You got up and met in the lobby at 7:00 A.M. sharp.

Had breakfast.

Hit the road.

Pulled over at 12:30 P.M. for lunch.

Got back in the truck and drove until 6:00 P.M.

Pulled over, had a steak, a glass of wine and went to bed.

Repeat the following day. And so on.

One time, coming back from Phoenix, we got into Springfield, Missouri, at 6:00 P.M.—and he stopped.

"Uncle Gene, you're killing me! I can drive it easy!" I begged. "I can stand on the tire rack and *see my damned house!*"

"Nope. It's still three hours away. We're spending the night."

MIDGETS BECOME MEMORIES

Even if I had to stop mid-route, I went racing with Gene Hamilton as often as I could for years and years. Same with Nick and Bud. But it's been a while since I've run a midget. I went down to the Chili Bowl, a major mid-January race in Tulsa, a few years ago and had a great time, but generally it's hard to find a midget race that fits with my schedule. And another consideration is cost.

With a smaller group to work with, aftermarket parts for them are more expensive than parts for a sprint car or dirt late model—and the midgets also run for smaller purses. I'm no economic genius, but even I can figure out that it's not the best way to break even. And ultimately, that's what most racers hope for.

In the summer of 2005, Bud Hoppe (left) and I got together with my former sprint car owner Ray Marler (right) for lunch. (Joyce Standridge photo.)

Overall, the midgets were really good to me. The only time one of them sent me to the hospital was in Auburndale, Florida, during a Speed Weeks show. Injectors stuck wide open and I was off for the wall. Luckily, I ran over my future brother-in-law, Danny Frye, Jr. Slowed me down and I just got my bell rung. The car wasn't so lucky. Took from February to May to get it patched back together.

You may recall that Bud's operation was on a budget, so the first night back at the track afterwards, we were looking things over and I noted that the right front wheel was bent. Now, in that day you didn't just go to the tire rack and grab a whole bunch of tires. Bud's trailer did-n't even have the single tire rack my trailer back home did. He just had a single spoke with a spare—but it was a spare for the right *rear.*

I asked Bud, "Can't we put that one on?"

"I guess we could," he kind of scratched his head. "It's not really right, but, hell, it's holding air and the wheel's not bent."

So, we put the spare tire on. Everybody looked at us like we were crazy. But then they really looked us over like crazy when we won the feature.

Stuff like that bonds you—builds a base of total trust. That's why today Bud Hoppe is the only person I know that I can call at three o'clock in the afternoon, tell him to be at the airport at six, and we will be three drinks into the flight before he asks me where we're going.

This is a case of role reversal because 30 years ago, I was willing to go wherever he wanted, no questions asked, except maybe out of belat-ed curiosity. We go by plane a lot these days instead of a pick-up truck with no air conditioning, but there's never been a time throughout all these years that I wasn't absolutely tickled to spend time with Bud.

And the other guy I'll head down the road with any time at all is Ray Marler, who took my racing career in another, wholly unexpected direction.

So, That's *Why I Feel Sticky* 3

THE WHOLE OPEN WHEEL THING happened by accident. I know there are some fans out there who would like to believe I was dragged kicking and screaming from open-cockpit racing or was stolen away because Indy cars started hiring people from Sao Paulo, Brazil, instead of Brazil, Indiana. But I came from stock car people. My roots were firmly planted in roofs and doors.

Not that open wheel cars weren't good to me or that I didn't enjoy them. Considering that I got a couple of championships, my son's namesake, and a great business partner out of the deal, I would have to say the brief period I ran open wheel was a good time. And I mean that in every sense. If nothing else, they were pretty stable from a technology standpoint, and in the 1980s, late models barely even resembled cars. It was a wild time—and, for the most part, I didn't have to deal with it because for a few years I spent most of my racing time avoiding that craziness.

Not that open wheel isn't wild in its own right. As I noted earlier, midgets were a whole different circus from stock cars. And if midgets were a circus, then sprint and Silver Crown cars were *zoos*, complete with cages and animal instincts. I don't know if it's because there's an edgier feel to driving in an open cockpit car—I mean, sometimes you feel like you're riding out in the air with nothing but a helmet shield and luck between you and disaster—but there's a whole different atmosphere at those races, too.

Climbing into a 900-pound monster with 700 horsepower and knowing that hooking a rut can result in trashing $30,000 worth of equipment in the blink of an eye maybe has something to do with the different attitude. I suspect it requires *cojones* the size of a football because as you are turning one of those things over about a half-dozen times in airborne somersaults, you realize that if the boys aren't that big the centrifugal forces will try to shove them through your body and into your throat.

One of the good guys I drove for was Dean Adams. Here I was racing at Devil's Bowl in Texas with two of the better sprint drivers ever: Brad Doty #75 and Ron Shuman #21X. (Tracy Talley photo; Ken Schrader Collection.)

Still, I have to say that the people I encountered in open-cockpit racing added considerably to my understanding of how to have fun in a race car. And outside it. Seems like things were a little bigger than life: bigger wins, bigger wrecks, bigger lies to tell during the bench-racing later. Someday when I get arthritis in my shoulders from old injuries, I might wonder if it was worth it. But frankly, if a few of those open-cockpit crashes didn't scare some sense into me, I might not have been so well-prepared later for the world of Daytona and Talladega crashing.

GO AHEAD, STICK A FINGER IN MY FACE

I would never have raced open-cockpit at all if I hadn't wanted to go racing with Bud Hoppe so bad. Fueled, of course, by the need to pay the rent.

So, when Danny Frye, Sr., offered me a ride in a sprint car, I had to try. I'm not even sure the rent was due. Dan always had pretty good equipment, no matter what division. It was just always open cockpit, because that's what he'd driven and that's what he liked.

It was surprisingly comfortable. I think the clutch had something to do with that, even though that made the car pretty much unique. Most sprint cars have an in-out box and require a push to get started.

Not this one. Dan had gotten the car over in Indy and it was a day-glo red with a blue frame. One of the sharpest-looking cars I ever drove, although I don't remember setting the world on fire in it the few times I drove it. We did respectably, but I was surprised when Ray Marler approached me to drive the sprint car he co-owned with Dean Cook.

Considering how young I was at the time, it could have been easy to get a swollen head, but I didn't. Dean wanted to fire me about every other week, so I never got comfortable enough to let my ego take over.

Danny Frye, Sr., Kenny's former father-in-law and car owner: I had a lot of race cars, midgets and sprints, over the years. Like most guys of my generation, I started out as an owner-driver, but eventually I got too beat up so I put other people in the cars, including my son—and that wild kid, Schrader.

At one point when he was married to my daughter, they lived in the Big Bend area of St. Louis County and he kept the sprint car at their house. I stopped by one evening and before I got to the house, I heard this roar. There was Kenny, coming up the street in the sprint car. It was a King chassis that had been fitted out at George Bignotti's Indianapolis shop and it was nice. It also had a clutch.

Well, you let Kenny have a race car and it's not a race night but the car has a clutch—he's going to take it around the block.

Although he was terminally ill with cancer, Danny Frye, Sr. came out to a testing session at Gateway International Raceway in 2005. This is Rusty Wallace, who was also testing, Danny Frye, Jr., Danny Frye, Sr., and me. A few weeks later, Danny, Sr. was gone. (Joyce Standridge photo.)

It turned out to be a good lesson for every additional ride I got right up to today. Doesn't matter what the contract says, you're always no more than one phone call away from unemployment if you drive a race car for a living.

Not that I ever blamed Dean for being unsure about my skills. I had driven a sprint car maybe seven or eight times when they hired me. I imagine I was an unproven commodity in everybody's eyes—not just my car owners.

Add to that the fact that Ray and Dean had solid records as car owners separately, so when they teamed up, the expectations were pretty high. Ray's driver Tom Corbin retired after a long and successful career, but Ray wasn't ready to get out then. As a result, he pooled parts with Dean and they put together a race car. In those days, a homemade chassis wasn't at all unusual—in fact, it was pretty much the norm—and

In 1979, wings on sprint cars were just gaining popularity. At I-55 Raceway, I was running the Cook & Marler car, but notice that we didn't even have a nose wing yet. We were still on the learning curve. (Ken Schrader Collection.)

guys like Ray and Dean usually could be counted on putting together a real good car.

Except this time.

Now, I was a rookie and what I knew about sprint cars could be carved on an injector stack with room left over for a detailed instruction manual, but the car flat didn't feel right. Communicating that to Dean and Ray was made a lot harder by the fact that I got in the car at Granite City the first night out...and won the feature.

And then the second week—same thing—we won the feature.

The thing of it is, we shouldn't have done anything except maybe wreck. Nothing about the car's set-up was conventional to the thinking at that time. They had done some pretty funky things in the garage to get it to read right on the scales—meaning, getting the right balance of weight in ratio to where it should be on each tire.

It was fine on the scales, but it was a nightmare on the track. If the track was just so—slick and one-grooved—we could do what we did those first two nights, start at the front and stay there. But as soon as we went to Springfield Speedway, a totally fast quarter-mile dirt track in central Illinois where you *had* to be hooked up, we were in a fix. We still ran fourth or fifth in the feature, but I got out of the cockpit afterwards with my hands shaking like I had the DTs or something. Everything was shrunk up, and my eyes wouldn't blink for a while afterwards.

Man, there's something wrong here. But Dean was convinced it was the driver. So, one night when I was running a midget at Terre Haute, they put Herschel Jenkins in the car. Now, Herschel was one of the real veterans at the track. There wasn't a thing he didn't know about Little Springfield, and he had experience in a lot of different cars there beyond just sprints, so he was real capable of setting up a car to be as good as it could be.

He ran the car in hot laps. Pulled it in, got out, took his helmet off, looked Ray right in the eye and said, *You trying to kill that kid?*

But no car owner ever wants to believe his baby (meaning, the race car) is a brat. So we kept running it.

I never did get comfortable. In fact, I quit at least a dozen times during a single race night, almost every night. "I wouldn't drive that *blankety-blankin'* thing if you wrapped it up in a red bow and kissed my..."

Well, anyway, they pretty much ignored me, and I pretty much crawled in it and tried to herd it around a bunch of different tracks as best I could. But the tension was tough on all of us.

And here's the thing—eventually, those guys fired me.

Only time in my entire career that I was fired instead of walking away from a ride.

I stayed fired for about 10 hours. Then Ray called and told me to meet him at Steak 'n Shake in Fenton, which was our Sunday pre-race ritual. We met, rode to the track, raced all night and went home like nothing had ever happened.

Ray Marler, former car owner and current business partner: One night at Granite City, Kenny was leading the feature in the car that Dean Cook and I owned. The car running second was my old car that I'd sold to John Livingston, "The Garbologist." (He ran a garbage business.) Of course, no way did I want to see my old car beat my new car.

Kenny got the white flag—but he thought it was the checkered flag—and he pulled in, thinking the race was over.

Well, when he realized what he'd done, he avoided my partner because he knew that Dean would come unglued. So when Kenny got out of the car he came over to me.

And I came unglued.

Let me say he was fired only overnight.

Next day we met at Steak 'n Shake and went racing like nothing had happened, but he was out of the car overnight.

That's Dean Cook and Ray Marler behind the car in the middle. This was a rare night that Dean didn't want to fire me. (Ken Schrader Collection.)

But when the car is a mess and the driver is a rookie, things ain't staying calm. A bit later we went to Devil's Bowl in Texas and I was lining up for the feature. Goosed the throttle just a little bit—and hit the wall. Hadn't even gotten the green flag yet and we're busted. I may have still been wet behind the ears at the time, but I knew—I mean, *I knew*— that I hadn't done anything wrong. The problem is that I was the only one sitting in the seat—there were no co-pilots and no instant replays.

When I got back to the pits, Ray was mad. He started reading me the riot act, stuck his finger in my face and was shaking it.

So I reached out and tried to bite it.

Well, he had pinched it in the tool box earlier and that sucker was really hurting him.

I knew that. I didn't have to bite it. Just act like I might and it shut him up. He cradled that thing and watched me out of the corner of his eye for a long time, like he wasn't sure I wouldn't try it again.

And I would have if he'd started in on me again.

Most people who know Ray might be surprised by that story. Usually he's a quiet and very pleasant gentleman. He speaks softly and has more patience than almost anybody I've ever met. But when he loses it, he really loses it. I mean, ballistic.

Another time, another race trip, we were eating breakfast after the races at Sedalia, Missouri's fairgrounds track and he got to chewing me out pretty good. I don't remember what it was I did that made him so damned mad, but he just kept picking up steam.

So I took his glass of ice water and poured it in his lap.

I understand it was really cold, too, but it took several minutes for him to get his breath and tell me. Which was just fine with me.

We went through periods of time when our team separated by mutual consent. Ray and Dean put other people in the car and I drove for other car owners, but we stayed friends through all the ups and downs. I didn't have as close a relationship with Dean Cook, but I still like and respect him for what he did for racing as much as anything. We didn't see eye-to-eye on some things, but we shared a lot of laughs, too. And that's what I choose to remember.

Eventually, I drove for just Ray as solo car owner during one more period before he ended up with some health issues that caused him to get out of racing for a little while. But I kind of think it was meant to be. The time together as owner-and-driver gave us a chance to see each other up close, and we learned that we could really trust each other. It went way beyond simple friendship. By the time we got into the race track business together in the mid-1990s, we knew that in each other we had somebody we believed in. If the ship sank or if it was a huge success, we'd still come out on the other end probably a better person for what we'd done.

There's a lot of people I really like and trust, but there's very few I would trust with my cash. Ray Marler can get into my wallet anytime. He makes really good business decisions, and time has proven me correct about that. I'm glad we didn't have to test our friendship through a failure, but if the track had gone under I believe we would still be close.

Even if he never lets me forget that he's the only car owner who fired me.

And I still threaten to chew on his fingers.

Sue Marler, wife of former car owner and current business partner: Kenny is a self-made man. When he first started driving our sprint car he was in his 20s and broke. We would have to buy his pit pass and then he would hope to make enough to pay us back when the night was over.

He came to the house to work on the race car, but he was good at timing it so he could get in on dinner. Considering that he wasn't eating very well on his own, I didn't mind. And sometimes he would come in and head straight for the refrigerator.

He hasn't changed.

He can certainly afford dinner these days and Ann feeds him very well, but when he comes in my house now he still goes over to the pantry, gets the peanut butter jar and sticks his finger in it. Just for old time's sake.

I want to say, too, it's not just older people that he treats well. Our daughter became like a little sister and he was always very protective and considerate of her. That almost back-fired on him once. It was when he was driving our car and had been over to work on it. Shari had already gone to bed upstairs, so Kenny ran about halfway up and hollered "good-night" to her.

He started back down the stairs without paying attention to what he was doing. I was in the kitchen and all of a sudden I heard a "thud-thud-thud-thud-thud-thud..."

Well, he didn't break his neck. And the stairs were intact. But when I think back to how close a great racing career came to ending before it got a good start . . . let's just say I'm glad we have a one-story house now.

I drove the Marlers' sprint car in 1981 at the very last Knoxville Nationals that was run without wings. That's daughter Shari on the left, Sue, Ray and me. (Tracy Talley photo; Ken Schrader Collection.)

I've never had more fun in a race car than I did power sliding through the turn at the Terre Haute Action Track in Ray Marler's car. (Ken Schrader Collection.)

CHAMPION MATERIAL?

Never forgetting that I had to make a living, I picked up all types of rides wherever and whenever I could. If there was a race—stock car, midget, sprint car, whatever—within driving distance any night of the week, I wasn't shy about calling and asking if I could drive a car.

As a result, I had the pleasure of driving for more good people than I have room to mention here. I drove for a few assholes, too, but the overwhelming majority were salt-of-the-earth. It would be wrong, however, not to mention John and Glenda McDaniel, the first solid ride I landed in after Ray's and Dean's car. It was a handful but it hauled. We ended up winning races—and getting attention.

I have to say this about John and a lot of other people I drove for—nearly every time I got a chance to move into a little better ride, the car owners I drove for not only didn't stand in my way—they almost always encouraged me. It was like they knew they were nurturing a budding little career and they were happy to have done their part.

I guess I was exceptionally lucky in having driven for people who were realistic about their equipment. Nearly everyone had good stuff, but they didn't act like it was the dream ride of all rides. So, when the phone started ringing and better opportunities presented themselves, I usually got sent off with a pat on the back from the owner and a hug from the wife. That's why I hope that every time I moved up the ladder and had a little more success, it meant all those men and women took a bow and felt really good about it. Because without them, it wouldn't have happened.

One of those people who really got my name out among the racing movers-and-shakers was Damon "Blackie" Fortune. By the way, I think the reason he was called "Blackie" was because he was bald. In the perverse world of racing that made sense because at one time he had a full head of black hair, but during all the years I knew him, his head was like a cueball.

John McDaniel had good sprint cars but he was laid-back about it. Here, he kind of stands off to the side while Bud Hoppe, John's daughter, my dad (holding the checkered flag) and I get the glory. (John Poole/Apropo Studio photo; Ken Schrader Collection.)

I drove a variety of cars for Blackie, including Silver Crown. These are cars that time has pretty much frozen. Today they've got roll cages, sleeker bodies and faster engines, but they started out as Indy cars right after World War II. Back in those days you ran the same car at the 2.5-mile paved Indianapolis Motor Speedway that you took later in the year to the Illinois State Fairgrounds' one-mile dirt oval. In time, specialization meant the Indy cars evolved, but the dirt cars changed far more slowly and eventually became a division of their own. The Indy 500 was called the Gold Crown division of USAC, while the dirt cars were the Silver Crown. USAC lost their gold but the silver is still shining today.

We didn't start out to win a Silver Crown championship. Our original goals were pretty modest: run as well as we can, have some fun, take the car home in one piece, maybe balance the checkbook once in a while. We did those things—and then to our amazement we found ourselves in the hunt for the championship in 1982—just our first full year as a team.

Blackie Fortune and his crew gather around the car before the race. But I didn't always take good care of his stuff. If the race car is on one side of the photo and the right rear tire is on the other, it can't be good. This happened with two laps to go in the Hulman Classic, and it sucked because we were leading when the radiator hose came off. (Ken Schrader Collection.)

Running three and four wide at Eldora Speedway in Ohio—if you're a fan, it doesn't get any better than this! (Tracy Talley photo; Ken Schrader Collection.)

He had been retired as a driver for several years, but Daddy still knew how to sit in a race car. I think he would have liked to substitute for me if I'd asked. (Ken Schrader Collection.)

The only time in my career that I've gone hard after a championship was the first two years at Lake Hill in the Sportsman and Late Model divisions. And I got it the first year. But from the time I got into Bud's midget, I was racing for the purse. I ran so many different tracks, associations, sanctioning bodies, types of cars and so on that championships were a joke for me. So, when it got to be October of 1982's next-to-last race, and I was a close second to Ron Shuman in the Silver Crown standings, man, nobody was more surprised than I was.

I don't think that had anything to do with Shuman crashing me.

I broke a shoulder blade and a collarbone—on different sides. I was in a world of hurt, in more ways than one. But sometimes life is strange, and what happened next proves that.

The final race was scheduled for Nazareth, Pennsylvania. The schedule got bizarre with weather problems and some kind of business issues, so the next thing you knew—it was December 4th. A beautiful day, much nicer than we had a right to expect at that time of the year. I was healed up—sort of—at least well enough to get in a race car with a minimum of painkillers. They had about 30 cars—really nice turn-out—and decided to start 'em all with a random draw.

Guess who drew the pole? And I didn't even cheat at the draw, as has been alleged for a sprint car show or two.

So, we hot-lapped. And in no time at all, up into the clear, crisp blue sky of an exceptional December afternoon came the disgusting, burping eruption of an engine blowing up.

Mine.

Shit.

I had to finish like at least three spots ahead of Shuman to clinch the championship, but that's pretty hard to do on foot. So, I went down

to see my good friend Sheldon Kinser. I had kidded his car owner Benny Leyba for years about driving that car. Benny always said the only way I could drive for him would be if he called Sheldon and fired him long-distance.

"Well, let's fire the son-of-a-bitch," I always told him. "I'll dial."

It was all just a recurring joke for us—but, honestly, on this day I needed help. I asked Sheldon if I could drive his car, and great friend that he was, he agreed.

I brought my tires to his pit.

"What's that?" he asked.

"Stuff I'm gonna change."

Sheldon sighed, not too patiently. "You just need your helmet. Just drive the damned thing, okay? Don't think. Just drive it."

He was inferring that the car was a real honey, and turned out it was. In fact, I came from dead last up to fourth. I knew Ronnie Shuman was about 10th because I'd passed him, and I had gone through the field to a position behind Rich Vogler. Great driver, but he was known for running fellow competitors pretty hard. It was a risk-versus-reward situation, and it didn't look like a safe pass, so I just tucked in behind Rich.

Lap 56 or so, somebody turned over, and because it was getting dark they called it a race.

I was a champion. An aching, sore champion because the shoulders weren't totally healed up yet, but you don't really care about that when they hand you the trophy. You can soak in the tub later.

It was a USAC championship, so that meant bringing our team to the banquet that winter to celebrate. We were going to share the stage with their other champions, including the Indy 500 winner, Gordon Johncock—as well as our old pal Dean Roper, who'd won the Stock Car championship.

As it worked out, I had been out West racing and had to fly to Indianapolis. Lots of friends and family drove up there from St. Louis, and somehow all the people made it—but my dress suit didn't.

I didn't much care. I would have felt more comfortable in jeans, but

Left: We banged wheels and really went hard at it on the track, but when the engines shut down, Ron Shuman and I liked to talk because we had nothing but respect for each other. (Hugh Baird photo; Ken Schrader Collection.)

Right: I wouldn't have won the 1982 USAC Silver Crown championship if Sheldon Kinser and Ben Leyba hadn't loaned me their car. A great car, great guys and a great moment in my life. (Hugh Baird photo; Ken Schrader Collection.)

There aren't very many ladies like Sylvia Bach, who patched my clothes for a banquet, among many kindnesses over the years. That's Spence next to her. (Joyce Standridge photo.)

USAC was pretty serious about dressing up and looking professional. So, the ladies in our group went shopping and Sylvia Bach tailored the store-bought stuff to fit me in a matter of a few minutes. Her husband had handed me my helmet for my very first race back in 1971 at Lake Hill, and here she was years later making sure I didn't embarrass myself at my first national championship.

See the value of old friends?

DON'T GET TOO COMFORTABLE, BOY

Through Blackie I got an invitation to try out at Indianapolis. It was a pretty typical deal for a rookie who hasn't blown into town on a load of hype and mega-resources. The car looked real racey to me, though, and I got it up to 193 mph, but we were having engine trouble—blown a couple of them, in fact—so I parked the car on a Monday afternoon running comfortably.

The following day, I crashed big time.

They say that I cut a tire when I was trying to finish my rookie test, but all I remember is getting into the car and then later walking out of the care center after the ambulance dropped me off, which was a significant gap in time.

And if that wasn't painful enough, consider that you had to reach only 186 mph that year to get in the race, and we'd been doing that with ease. I figured that they would just pull the engine and put it in the other car.

Not so fast, Schrader.

It cost $1,000 entry fee in those days, and the rather low-buck team I was running for hadn't officially entered the second car. I don't know why it was sitting in the garage—maybe to taunt me or to scavenge parts? Sell a ride to somebody else?

Anyway, I was out of luck.

The famous mechanic Grant King was working on the car that year, and he missed the excitement. In fact, as I was leaving the infield care unit, he pulled up in his car and hollered at me to help him carry the lunch meat, soda and ice into the garage.

"We got problems," I told him.

"Hey, we'll fix it," he said.

Yeah, right. Easy to be optimistic from the parking lot.

Once he saw the extent of the damage, he conceded that it was more than his 25 years of experience could correct.

As I headed for the exit with my tail between my legs, guys from other teams came by and wanted to know if we wanted to run their cars. They asked, "What do you have?"

"I've got this brand new helmet that Bell gave me," I smiled, perking right up.

"No, no. What kind of sponsors do you have?"

Ummm. This nice, new helmet and a nice, new uniform. That's about it.

The days of bringing a helmet and a shitload of desire had passed at Indy. Unfortunately, that was all I had to bring to the garage.

Well, that's when I made up my mind that it was time to start planning seriously to go South. Like I said, I'm a stock car guy, and I guessed my pit stop in Indy pretty much sealed the deal for me. There are countless race drivers who would love to race the Indy 500, and it certainly is an impressive place with great history, but I have to say that I enjoyed my later visits there in a stock car a whole lot more.

PATCH ME UP AND PUT ME IN THE SEAT

I didn't go straight to Charlotte. The commitment to run for Blackie took me through a pretty great racing season in 1983. We won the USAC Sprint Car Championship, finished second in the Silver Crown, and got a third in the midget division while running only about half the shows. Again, we hadn't gone all out to win a championship, but we were tooling along very well.

That was also the year of The Lost Eyeball Wreck.

I was racing out West and took a major dump I'll always remember in those terms. They put the neck brace on, probably because I was incoherent, but I had bigger worries. I reached for my left eye.

Oww. Something hurts there.

I reached for my right eye and, oww, something hurts there.

I thought I was playing it cool and taking care of the equipment at the Indianapolis Motor Speedway in May, 1983. I knew the car owners didn't have a lot of spare parts—but I still wrecked it. Sure liked the place better when we came back with the NASCAR Winston Cup/Nextel Cup Series. (John Mahoney photo; Ken Schrader Collection.)

Any idiot can flip over a guardrail. It takes a special kind of idiot to drive through one. Wasn't much left of the car after they pulled it back out. (Left: Kevin Horcher photo; Ken Schrader Collection, Right: Tracy Talley photo; Ken Schrader Collection.)

I got some issues here.

Both shoulders hurt and I'm getting a little concerned, but legendary driver Leland McSpadden came over and told me to just calm down.

"Leland, are my eyes open?"

"Yeah. Wide open."

"Shit. I can't see anything."

I mean it was pitch black, so they put me in the ambulance and Leland got in with me. But as we start to leave, I ask the attendant, "Do you have a mustache?"

"Yeah," he says.

It was like a miracle—I was starting to see again. Turned out I just got my bell rung pretty hard and once the Tweety-birds stopped circling my head, my vision slowly came back.

"Stop the ambulance!" yells Leland, and they do. "Hell, if you aren't blind, I'm gonna stay and watch the feature."

I'd been real concerned because Leland had been real concerned. He'd taken some flips and crashes I never wanted to happen to me, so I figured he knew what he was talking about. I can recall one time at Erie, Colorado, when he did an end-o flip on the front straight. It was really, really bad, and a few minutes later the rescue helicopter came in to land at the track.

We were watching the helicopter land and all of a sudden, Leland is standing behind us. He tapped me and wanted to know who the LifeStar was for.

Uh. You, I told him.

Doesn't matter what type of car I get in, my stomach doesn't want to get in at the same time. I pretty much don't eat on race day, at least until later. (Larry Kave photo; Ken Schrader Collection.)

And he stayed to watch that feature, too, although later he asked Ron Shuman to take him to the hospital because, "I don't feel so good."

WE'RE SUCH A CLASS ACT

On another long-haul trip, I was conserving my energy between races. In those days, we caught sleep when and where we could because there was always a race the next night, but it might be 300 miles down the road. Even if we could have scraped together the money for a Motel 6, we didn't have the time.

Now, some of the guys with me were bored and tired. Bored and tired equated to thirsty and there was a cooler full of beer in the truck.

This cannot be good. Especially because I cannot join in.

Car owner wasn't going to stop every 20 minutes so they could pee, either, so it meant getting resourceful. Took a little while to get the engineering figured out but they found a spare exhaust pipe.

I think what they did next would be frowned upon by every environmental group in North America, every Sunday school teacher and a few cars and trucks that happened to be on the road that night.

"That better not be why I feel sticky!" I hollered at them when I woke up.

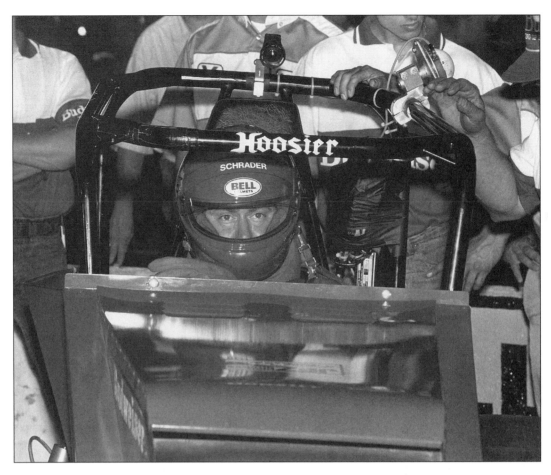

Ann sometimes teases me that I've grown into my nose, but the truth is that I've raced literally thousands of times and the helmets have squeezed my face into my nose. And here's the proof. (Al Steinberg photo; Ken Schrader Collection.)

The Check's Not Bad Until Monday

4

MONEY WAS ON MY MIND in the late 1970s and early 1980s. When you don't have any, that tends to happen. And while I think a lot of people from my generation spent a little starving-artist-type time, my time seemed to be extending itself.

So, I took stock of my situation.

I'd already figured out that it was smarter to drive other people's cars than try to find the time—and money—to run my stuff all the time. More years than not, I had a race car or two, but it wasn't unusual for the cars in my garage to belong to somebody else.

To run other people's stuff, I had to get there, and sometimes getting to the races was a challenge. For example, at one time I had a 1967 Plymouth station wagon with a Mac bulldog hood ornament. Real babe magnet. Just ask my wife, who was my girl friend at the time. She wouldn't even ride in it. She made me meet her places.

Reliability was a factor with the station wagon, too. So, when there was a race I really needed to run and the distance exceeded the expected range of the wagon, I had to find somebody to con into taking me.

Once I conned my sister and her husband, counting on their lack of knowledge about geography.

"Need to get to Winchester," I told them.

"Where's that?"

"Not far at all."

"What time should we pick you up?"

"Five."

"Five? *In the morning?* What time are the races?"

"Oh, they're starting them early."

I couldn't tell them it was a five-and-a-half hour drive.

They'd have said "no."

After that experience, though, they checked the map. You could usually get away with this only once before you had to find another geographically challenged chauffeur.

Talk about getting out of town—I went north of the border to Sanair Speedway in Canada during the summer of 1989. By then, I wasn't counting pennies anymore, thank goodness, because they're not worth a penny up there. Winning over the likes of Brett Hearn (left) and Jack Johnson (right) felt like a great accomplishment. (Ken Schrader Collection.)

I found out that if you put on a barrel and a hard hat and go into a bar near Slinger Speedway, everybody else will get stupid, too! God, I love the people in Wisconsin! (Dave Drew photo; Ken Schrader Collection.)

A few times in those days we chartered planes to make far-flung races. Mostly, you got on, took a nap while the pilot got you where you needed to go, ran the races and flew home. But a couple of times, we had memorable flights.

I woke up on a return trip from Kokomo, Indiana, and realized that it was very, very quiet in the plane. Now, even a rookie passenger knows that it's supposed to make noise. You hear that on television and in the movies, and it was making noise when we took off. But one fuel tank was dry and the pilot couldn't get the switch to the other tank to work.

Well, obviously he got it to work eventually because I'm here to tell the story.

Another time, the pilot hit piled-up snow at the end of the runway and knocked off the right-side landing gear. Needless to say, the plane tipped over to that side. No one was injured—but my fingerprints are still imbedded in that dashboard and it's 25 years later.

We actually chartered from the same firm again, but we requested a different pilot and got a new one. She was good. She was real beautiful, too, so we didn't much care whether she could fly or not.

Of course, most of the time, we were on the highway towing. For a long time, with or without the race car in tow, we got to the track in what had been a Purolator courier van in a former life.

It didn't have rear seating. Had blue carpet and tan bucket seats, so then we added a red velvet couch in the back. An insensitive person might have described it as a pimpmobile, but we drove it 100,000 miles and then took it to an auction because it was still running and we were ready to step up.

That's about as nervous as I'd ever been to that point in my life. I mean, I had my life savings wrapped up in that thing. It sold for $4,500. Then I sold an old race car for $3,000. And I did something with the money that I'd never done before: I bought a house.

I've always believed that real estate is a good investment. As I've told my banker more than once, "They're not making any more land."

I financed $27,000 on that house in Fenton, and the house payments were $990.

Sounds like a lot, doesn't it, for just $27,000? Well, here's the deal. It would have been easier to make a house payment every month, I guess, but I waited until I got that registered letter every three months. The real bad one that said send them $990 or I was going to have to find somewhere else to live.

It wasn't a totally bad thing, though. With that incentive you knew you were gonna win some races that week.

JUMP(ER) RACING

Like I had with the open-wheel cars, I drove for a lot of different late model car owners through the years, and that was real instrumental in keeping the wolf from the door. The mid-week, local late model shows didn't get me a lot of attention, but when I was writing the check for the mortgage, those races were critical to the check being good.

By the late 1970s, I'd worn out a lot of the early car owners from Lake Hill, but I found a real good friend and car owner in Ernie Jumper, not least of all because he was so trusting.

Ernie would go down to the lake to do a little fishing and his kids—who were maybe 13 or 14 years old—would call me.

"Daddy left the keys in the truck," young Donnie would say.

"Well, let's go racing," I'd answer.

With luck, Ernie might have left $50 in the cab for gas and pit passes. If not, the kids and I would go to the gas station and fill up. In those days you could write a check for cash in addition to the gas, and I would. No ATMs, which was just as well because there usually wasn't anything in the account on Friday night anyway. And I would be back on Monday morning with cash to replace the check, because, really, the check wasn't bad until Monday morning. It didn't hurt that we went to Hank Sieveking's station, because Hank knew us—and he'd hold that check on Monday morning for a little while if we were a little slow rolling out of bed.

More often than not, Ernie didn't leave the car for the kids and me to run. He usually went to the track, too. People used to think that Ernie was tardy getting the car to the race track an awful lot, but the truth is that he had learned his lesson early on.

If the track was real wet during hot laps, I had a tendency to wreck it. Not on purpose, but I did more than my share of eating the wall. We also seemed to blow engines in hot laps, too. Voodoo or something, but eventually Ernie figured out that if he arrived just in time for the final heat race, we'd probably win it and get a good run in the feature, too.

Ernie Jumper's late model in the late 1970s really was a "stock" car, but for the times it was a fast little Camaro. (Ken Schrader Collection.)

Paid a whole lot more to win the feature than to win hot laps, plus he'd save the cost of having to replace a wheel, a tire or some suspension parts.

One night, however, the usual good fortune deserted us. During the feature I ran out of gas.

Man, that pisses you off. Ask any race driver. It's a dumb, dumb reason to fall out of a race.

So, I changed my clothes and got up on the trailer to watch the rest of the race. Well, the guys on the track wrecked, and then they restarted.

And they wrecked, and they restarted.

Many minutes later they still hadn't gotten in another lap that counted, so Ernie looks at me and says, "You think we ought to get back out there? We could gain a lot of spots on the pay-off list."

"Nah." I was still pissed. "I ain't going out there. You go."

So, he got in the car and went out there for the rest of the race. Clearly, he was unimpressed with my attitude.

I helped on Ernie's race car quite a bit, too, not because I particularly liked to work on race cars. And we've established that I'm not the best mechanic in the pit area, either. But if I got to Ernie's house at 5:30 P.M., his wife Jenny would have supper ready. And she always insisted that I pull up a chair and eat with them. Considering I was a bachelor for much of that time and eating off the wrong end of the food pyramid, I saw the opportunity. I had gained 20 pounds at Ray Marler's because we worked a little on the race car, and then we ordered pizza. At Jenny's table, I ate really well, too.

I don't want to say that food determined who I drove for, but it sure didn't hurt.

Mike Edwards: I was racing the Volkswagen class at Lake Hill and they kept saying to bring it over to Belleville. But I didn't know how to drive on dirt. I figured I could drive on pavement because I drove back and forth to work on pavement.

Well, I finally went over there and while I was waiting to get in, they had the biggest pile-up in turn one. They were on the wall, on top of each other, and I was thinking, I'm not taking my car out there. Before, I didn't think I wanted to go dirt racing, but then I *knew* I didn't want to go dirt racing.

Kenny was there, racing another class that night and he said, "I'll drive it. Don't worry, it'll be fine."

Well, they started them three wide, but they were four, sometimes five wide going into the turn. Kenny started 18th, but he led it coming off turn two. He went around the top side. Worry about wrecking it? Not if it's your cousin's car. He'll fix it!

Our biggest night was winning the mid-season championship. It paid $66 and two cases of beer.

Nice trophy, though.

Still got the trophy.

That's my uncle Jim on the left; the goofy one in the middle is me; and on the right is cousin Mike Edwards. I drove his doodlebug at Belle-Clair Speedway and I can only guess that the fumes got to us all. (Ken Schrader Collection.)

MAKING AN IMPRESSION (IN THE PIT WALL) IN DAYTONA

Much of my short-track late model career is associated with Hank and Don Sieveking. People in the St. Louis area recognize their delivery trucks because the family runs a real good operation supplying gasoline, propane and heating oil in the area. Jerry Sifford drove for them, but when he got hit by a car in the pit area at Lake Hill and was hurt, Hank and Don needed a driver. That's how I got the chance to drive for them.

Just one thing.

They ran Fords. Now, there's nothing wrong with a Ford. I've had some pretty good races in Fords, from Bob Mueller's Galaxy that I ran in my first dirt race, all the way to today. The problem back then was that not too many other dirt-trackers ran Fords, so if you had a problem that you were trying to diagnose it was hard to find somebody to bounce ideas off. The bow-tie guys could always put their heads together and talk it out, but we were on our own. And for a while, we really struggled. We were calling Jack Roush, who was Ford's development chief in Michigan at the time, and he tried his darnedest to help us.

One day during this period the phone rings and it's Jack telling us to change the intake manifold. *It'll be better,* he assures us. So, we look at the clock and sure enough we have just enough time to make the change and still get to the track. We put a taller box intake on the engine, but then the hood didn't fit back on.

Well, my patience gave out.

"If these *blankety-blankin'* intakes were any good, every *blankety-blankin'* Chevrolet in the country would be running one!"

Don Sieveking just chewed down on his cigar, looked me in the eye and said, "Well, if you want to drive one of them Chevrolets, you just go right ahead and drive one. But if you want to drive this son-of-a-bitch, finish putting the hood on it."

In that moment I understood just how fully committed the Sievekings were to running a Ford. We made that hood fit and we made it in time to race in Eldon, Iowa. But Don didn't go along.

He was famous for going to bed early, too, and we knew that. So, we got done racing, visited with all the fans who came by the car, loaded up, went back to the motel and had a nice little late meal.

Then, about one o'clock in the morning or so, we called Don.

"Run fourth," we told him. "Would have been even better but I had to run the 5/8-mile line while everybody else was running the 3/8-mile part of the track. I couldn't go down on the bottom because if I let off the gas, it wouldn't run."

"Okay," I could hear him shrug. "We had to try it."

He hung up on me and went back to sleep. And I didn't even have the satisfaction of getting a rise out of him.

Don and Hank enjoyed getting out on the road and trying to mix it up with everybody we thought we could race with. It certainly helped my career, and I think the Sievekings had a great time. We were competitive in USAC and ARCA (Automobile Racing Contest Association), and even though the car was heavy, we were competitive at a lot of short track events, too. We even tried NDRA (National Dirt Racing Association), which was the raciest, fastest, coolest thing happening in short-track racing at the time.

It was also with Hank and Don that I went to Daytona for the first time. We started 33rd in the 200-mile ARCA race and got all the way up

to fourth when the fuel pressure needle started bouncing going down the backstretch.

Time to pit.

I swear I thought I had my speed down to 60 mph when I reached pit road.

Estimates are that it was actually about 120.

The car started to slide. First it hit the pit wall forward, then it spun and hit it backward. Finally, it spun 180 degrees, but now it's straight, so I dropped it into second gear, popped the clutch and ran 'er on up to our pit.

I got stopped and tried to act like nothing much was going on, but everybody is just staring at me.

Don hollers over, "You done?"

"Uh, yeah."

Assured I wasn't going to try to pin them or run over them, then the pit crew came over the wall to service the car. The Granada's body by now looked like it would fit on a compact car, but I was hoping nobody was looking. I mean, the chances that superstar car owner Junior Johnson was going to run down pit road and thrust a contract inside the car for me to sign was pretty unlikely even *before* I crunched the car's body, but after that I was hoping he—and the rest of the NASCAR car owners—were having a cook-out in the infield or something.

We left Speed Weeks just a little worse for wear even though we managed an 8th-place finish in the ARCA race, and it was back to reality. At that time, not only did I depend on Hank and Don for race cars, but also to keep me from starving. Racing paid a lot of the bills, but when the weather got too cold and crappy to race, I drove a propane truck for the Sievekings.

Hank would call me every morning and wake me up. He'd figured out that I needed a keeper, and if Mom wasn't around to roll me out of the sheets, he made sure I got up and on the road.

In the summer, Hank still called and got me up, just not so early. And instead of jumping in the truck to make deliveries, I met him for breakfast. Then I worked on the race car. Considering that I bought my

Remember the photo of me drilling the DuQuoin guardrail with a Silver Crown car? Well, I tried the same thing with Sievekings' USAC stock car. Apparently I wasn't going as fast because I destroyed only the car instead of getting the guardrail, too. (Kevin Horcher photos; Ken Schrader Collection.)

There is a mistaken impression that you can race on asphalt and stay clean. Well, maybe if you're not in the car because Robert Hanke and Tommy Mottle look fine, but I look like I've been mud-wrestling. (Don Bok photo; Ken Schrader Collection.)

house in Fenton from Hank, it wasn't a big surprise that eventually they let me take the car over there to keep and work on it. In fact, long after I quit driving for them and moved to North Carolina, we kept the house and Joey Walsh worked on race cars in the garage there. But if we needed an additional place to work on the cars we knew we could count on the Sievekings' garage, too.

We didn't just waltz into NASCAR and leave the past behind. You don't even want to think about that when you've got great friends back home like the Sievekings.

DAMMIT, THE CAR WILL FIT

I inherited from my Daddy a real appreciation for clean and neat garages and towing equipment. I figure if everything is in order, it's a whole lot easier to find tools and parts when you need them.

Now, in spite of having really sharp-looking cars, the Sievekings' hauler was a disaster area. It was a crew cab with a 30-foot box on it and we liked that. But the crew simply tossed tires in the box and it just killed me. So, I announced that I was going to put tire racks in it.

"It's fine like it is," I was told.

"No. We're *gonna* put racks in it."

So, one night I started measuring to get it ready, and Don got mad. "I told you not to mess with them things."

"It'll be fine."

"I don't think the *blankety-blankin'* car will fit if you put tire racks in it!"

The disagreement escalated from there.

It's now 10:30 at night, and I called Donna, Hank's wife, who had a brand new Ford Granada. "Can you come down here, please?"

She must have heard something in my voice because she came without any argument, in spite of the hour. I winched her car into the truck just to make sure everything would fit.

It did.

I built my tire racks, and Don never said another word about them. But he sure hated that I was right, so he ignored them the rest of the time we had the hauler, even though the tires went on the racks every night.

And you wondered how life-long, close friendships get started.

One of the deals we did later on with Hank and Don involved an Allied modified. It's actually in the museum at Talladega now, but this was back in the mid-1980s. The cars still looked pretty stock then and they had put a really sharp new Thunderbird body on the car. Additionally, even though the body was one piece, according to the Allied association rules, the doors had to be welded or chained shut.

Well, I hadn't done anything to aggravate Hank and Don for a

while, so I put ugly, completely unnecessary plastic chain around the door posts just to piss them off. Did a good job of it. But that was part of my job, too. Just wasn't in writing. Keep 'em on their toes.

When they decided to stop owning race cars, I bought the car off them. These days Hank sponsors Dandy Don Klein. Don Sieveking passed away in the mid-1980s, but Hank still goes to tracks and watches racing with us. We wouldn't want him to get too comfortable with retirement. That's still part of my job, too.

Don Klein, veteran St. Louis racer: When Kenny first started driving, I don't think anybody in our area realized where his career was headed. He was just another kid getting started. But it became clear real quick that he had a whole different attitude about racing. I don't believe I've ever seen anybody more committed to it. He had a job at Western Auto to pay the bills, but it was obvious that his mind was on racing rather than becoming a big shot at Western Auto.

When we realized how determined Kenny was, and how he was willing to drive just about anything to advance his career, we began to think about him getting well beyond being a St. Louis shoe. And considering what a great kid he was, I don't think there was much of anybody who didn't wish him well.

What's happened since then has been great, but if he'd had just a little bit more good luck, I believe he would have been a legend on the order of Earnhardt. As it is, Kenny's got nothing to apologize for. He's done a fine job with everything he ever drove, from the beginning to today.

A few years ago, I got together at Belle-Clair Speedway for a photo with my long-time pal and childhood hero, Don Klein. He was in his late 50s then, but he is still a competitive racer as he nears 70. (Ken Schrader Collection.)

I had my dirt late model on the track at I-55 Raceway in Pevely, Missouri—our track—during the summer of 2005. A little while later, the whole right side was missing and my nephew/crew chief Joey Walsh was welding on the bent door bars. (Joyce Standridge photos.)

THE BEST LAID PLANS. . .

After the 1983 season, with that championship in USAC sprints, really strong finishes in other divisions and some late model wins, we figured we were ready to move up. Because of the Sievekings we'd made a connection with Roush, and we started bugging him to do a little more racing. Through Jack, Ford decided they were going to get us engines and a sponsor to go racing with ASA (American Speed Association), which at that time was the best way to move up and eventually into NASCAR.

I had Sievekings' nice truck and trailer, so, I took all my point fund money, called Ray Dillon, who was building the hottest pavement-racing short-track cars in the country, and I ordered two new cars. I hired Boyd Breiton to turn the wrenches, and we ordered our engine.

And then we waited.

And waited.

And waited.

And, eventually, come spring, they called to say the engine was ready to pick up. But we had a bill and still no sponsorship.

I had already known that a promise is as good as the paper it's written on, and even then it's subject to change. But if all you've got are verbal promises, things can be real slim come racing season.

There are two ways you can deal with this kind of situation: you can whine and cry and get really bitter about it, or you can go racing. Just take a step back, and go racing.

I didn't let Ford totally get away with it. I continued to bug Lee Morse until I'm sure he was tired of taking my calls. Thank goodness there wasn't Caller ID back then. I'm sure I would have gone to voice mail, do not pass GO, do not collect two cents.

Eventually that persistence paid off. But first, we had the 1984 racing season to deal with.

It turned out far better than anything so unplanned should have. I had quit all my good rides from 1983, but I found out that I got a $250 appearance fee for being the defending champion if I just showed up at the USAC races.

I showed up a lot.

And I drove a lot of different cars everywhere they had a race. By the end of the season, we had paid the mortgage pretty close to being on time, and we'd had a lot of laughs. From a disastrous start, we'd pieced together a successful year.

We had also run five NASCAR races.

Fly Down and Talk To Me, Bubba

5

WHEN THE ASA DEAL FELL THROUGH I was real disappointed. But it wasn't like they poked my eyes out or something. I got over it. And the 1984 season pretty much confirmed my feeling that I could make a living in a race car—a pretty good one, at that—even if I continued to patch together rides on the short tracks.

But while I was coming up with new and interesting ways to have an excuse to call Lee Morse at Ford, he was working behind the scenes on my behalf. Toward the end of the 1984 racing season, I got a call I'd hoped to get—but hadn't expected without some seasoning in ASA.

I was going NASCAR.

BRING MONEY

Elmo Langley was a former NASCAR driver from the days when it meant running 60 times a year on both dirt and pavement. The "wear-and-tear" finally convinced Elmo to hang up his helmet, but he hadn't completely cured himself of the racing bug. As a driver, he'd been what is usually called a "journeyman." That means he never had the equipment to challenge Petty, Jarrett, Lorenzen and Johnson, but he had earned a lot of respect for driving clean and as fast as he could. That's a very honorable thing. There have always been drivers who were real fast but they don't earn any respect because they're selfish or stupid—or both. Elmo was never in that category. I don't think there was a driver in the 1950s through 1970s who didn't enjoy racing with Elmo.

When he became a car owner, he still didn't have top-of-the-line equipment, but his cars were a really good place to get experience. Elmo wasn't opposed to a driver bringing some cash, too. In fact, it was sort of a requirement.

Lee Morse had told him something like, *hey, let's put that Schrader kid in your car.* I never knew the details, but I would guess that they threw in some parts or something to get Elmo's attention.

More than one car owner thought this cartoon was funny—and accurate. (Ken Schrader Collection.)

Then I talked to Elmo. He told me, "Give me $3,000 and a set of tires for each race."

At this point, I'm making about $300 a night at Granite City and thinking it's pretty good money. So, Elmo's request is a blow, but I'm lucky. I've got people who believe in me, believe that I can make it in racing's big leagues if I can just get attention. A couple of guys from home, Larry Hill and Timmy Delrose, bought me four races in Elmo's car.

Then it came to the fourth race and I can't go beat on these guys for more money. It would have just been asking too much of them. But we'd done pretty decent in Elmo's car, so he dropped the rental, and, hell, I could afford a set of tires. It meant that I got five races in Elmo's car, the maximum a driver could run back then without actually affecting his status in the run for Rookie of the Year, which was an award that could help a career.

Our first race with Elmo was at Nashville. At that time, NASCAR ran the show at the old state fairgrounds track near downtown. It's still a good little oval track, and for a guy with limited big-track experience, it was probably a good choice for our first race.

At the introductions before the race, I really caught it from some of the drivers. Because I had tried to break into Indy racing the year before, I had a fantastic driver's uniform—but it was triple-layer, and I had the fire-resistant underwear, too.

"You're gonna regret that, son," I was told.

Boy, was that an understatement. I found out that not only are summer afternoons in Nashville damned hot, but they're long, too. Really, really long when you're drowning in your own sweat. You got air flow in an Indy car. You got the sauna experience in those old stock cars.

I had qualified on the back row, but we finished a very respectable 18th that day. My childhood pal Rusty Wallace, who already had his

NASCAR career going, finished one spot ahead of me. We were nine laps down at the finish, but Elmo's other driver was like 22 or 23 laps down, so the team was pretty thrilled with me.

So was I. Even though they had to literally drag me out of the race car.

I told the guys at the sprint race the following day that they didn't have a clue how hard those S.O.B.s in NASCAR run. The longest race I'd gone through to that point was a Silver Crown 100-miler at DuQuoin, which was about an hour long. In Nashville, we raced for three-and-a-half hours. And only one idiot was wearing triple-layer!

Next NASCAR race, I had a lot thinner uniform on. In those days, there were no vents, no air ducts other than maybe poking your left hand out beside the window netting and trying to redirect some air inside, but at a lot of the tracks in those days, you were working too hard and didn't have time for that. We hadn't even dreamed of air-conditioned helmets yet.

Elmo and I got comfortable together real fast, and I enjoyed the time I spent with him even though it was limited. I learned a lot from him about the cars, the competitors, and how to drive at that level. He really helped me a bunch and we stayed close friends for the rest of his life. After Elmo gave up owning cars he became NASCAR's official pace car driver. Unfortunately, Elmo passed away from a heart attack while driving the pace car when NASCAR raced in Japan a few years ago. But throughout my career I could count on Elmo giving me good advice and I always followed it.

Except once.

Another driver wrecked me at the Darlington Labor Day race. Now, he'd wrecked me before, so it wasn't like it was the first time. We spent about 80 laps fixing the car. I got back in, headed to the track, and what

Left: Even after we got into Winston Cup racing, we went racing everywhere. Here we ran—and won—at Phoenix in the Seymour family's Silver Crown cars. With Ann and me in Victory Lane was the great J.W. Hunt, who was renowned for adding money to the purse—especially if he liked the way you drove the race. (Nate Mecha photo; Ken Schrader Collection.)

Right: I'm not sitting in the passenger seat. In 1990 I went Down Under and raced in Australia. Having the steering wheel on the right side was disorienting, but we had a lot of fun once we got used to it. (Ken Schrader Collection.)

do I see immediately ahead of me? The guy who'd made a long, hot day even longer and hotter—because there's nothing like trying to make repairs to a race car in Darlington's infield on Labor Day weekend.

So I wrecked him.

Then I limped back to the pits, got out of the car and found that my crew didn't mind much at all. Sometimes you just need to hand out a good whack, and even though we didn't finish the race, the guys didn't care that they were going to have more work back at the shop.

NASCAR, however, wasn't quite so thrilled.

I was told that they wanted to see me at the trailer. If you're not already familiar with NASCAR procedure, the sanctioning body has a mobile office set up at every track where they run. At least a few top honchos from Daytona are there and ready to deal with whatever issues come up, so when you were told you needed to report to the Big Red Trailer (as it was called then), it meant it was pretty serious. They weren't just sending word down to the pits through one of the trackside guys of some little deal on their minds. It meant the big guys wanted a word—*Now!*

So, I left the track.

I got in the truck and went home. I figured I was in big trouble, so I probably wasn't compounding it a whole lot. And frankly, I needed a little time to compose myself, too.

Elmo called me that night and said, "You're in a little bit of trouble."

"Yeah, I know."

"Well, you're gonna have to go see them next week before you get on the track, and no matter what, you need to tell them that you only made it a half-lap when your steering broke."

I don't feel like he was encouraging me to lie so much as trying to save my butt. Dick Beatty and Les Richter ran the show in those days and they were the tough dudes. They had to be to keep the circus under control. They were reasonable and fair, but if you wanted to piss them off big time, ignore a summons to the trailer. Elmo knew that.

But I didn't do as Elmo suggested, and here's why.

A few years before, I had come back to the home track near St. Louis after having a really racey midget series in Houston. About the eighth lap of the sprint feature, Lee James passed me. Well, I was still wizzed up from running real fast all weekend with the midget. Nobody had passed us in Houston. So, I went down the backstretch—pulled the belts a little tighter—and went down in the turn hard to pass Lee back.

POW—Got the right front up over the cushion and took the front end off John McDaniel's nice little sprint car.

Three or four people came down to our pit area with different stories about what they figured had happened. One of them said he saw a piece come off the front end of the car as it was going into the turn. Another said he saw something coming off the back of the car going into the corner. And yet another said he saw the wing drop down.

We listened to all these theories, and then everybody left. I said, "John Mac, you know what happened, don't you?"

He said, "I think I do. Why don't you tell me?"

"I run down in there and ran it over the cushion."

"I thought that's what you did."

There was no sense trying to pretend otherwise. I knew that's what I'd done. And John Mac knew that's what I'd done. We hadn't made a habit out of trashing his car, so he wasn't going to fire me because I'd made one mistake.

And that's what guided me when I went to talk to Les and Dick at NASCAR's Big Red Trailer. When I got there—and I'm not sure it was a bad thing that we'd all had a week to think about things—I was asked, "What happened?"

They probably weren't real surprised by how my explanation started. "We spent 80 laps fixing the car, and I went down there in the turn on new tires because I was coming out of the pits. I was going to pass him underneath and I started to turn left. Car started to go left, and all of a sudden I decided—piss on it."

I admitted, "That's the second time this year that driver wrecked me, so I wrecked the son-of-a-bitch."

They looked at each other and then one of them said, "Okay. That's what it looked like."

We all nodded our heads in agreement and then they continued, "Well, we're going to have to fine you $10,000 for wrecking him intentionally. But since you 'fessed up, here's what we'll do. If you don't try to wreck him for the next three weeks, we'll give you $3,000 a week off the fine."

One of the reasons I got to run Ben Bowen's car more than once, along with a lot of other car owners, was that I didn't wreck a lot. But if I did, and if it was my fault, I owned up to it. (John Mahoney photo; Ken Schrader Collection.)

No matter where I've raced or for how many years, the same cast of characters is usually hanging out. In this instance, it's my former midget car owner Nick Gojmeric and my forever pal Pat Walsh. Either we were relaxing between races or we were plotting some mischief. Could have gone either way. (Troy Hogan Racing Photos; Ken Schrader Collection.)

They also brought the other driver into the trailer and we had a kiss-and-make-up session. Can't say we became best friends, but I could afford to be big about the whole thing because, after all, I'd had the satisfaction of paying him back at least partially for those two times he'd wrecked me. I still owe him another shot.

About a month after our session in the Big Red Trailer, I got a bill for $1,000. I tossed it. I know NASCAR got their money somehow—probably withheld it from my winnings—but I didn't care. It's just like it was with John Mac. I didn't make a habit of this kind of thing, so I probably got cut a little slack because of that.

And I never told Elmo that I hadn't followed his advice. I always wanted him to understand how much I valued his advice and help. Didn't seem like there was any point in telling him that I'd dealt with the situation on my own and it probably worked out better.

THE JUNIE YEARS

During the period I was driving Elmo's car, I wasn't just hanging around the NASCAR garages like a hungry puppy. I may have been one, but they didn't need to see me to know that. So, I was still running every short track race I could.

In November of 1984, Ann and I got married (more on that later) and went out to California to spend some time racing with Hank and Rosemary Green. Had a great time, but the whole time I'm thinking ahead. If I can come up with $125,000 I can drive Elmo's car all year. Even a down payment of $20,000 would get us going.

I got home from California and there was a message on the answering machine: *You need to fly down here and talk to me, Bubba.*

It was Junie Donlavey, one of NASCAR's real long-time car owners.

Man, what a rush. I scraped together the $700 for a plane ticket—probably on Ann's credit card—and high-tailed it down to North Carolina. There was simply no place in the sport where it was better for a rookie to get hooked up. I didn't know until much later, but Elmo was real important in this deal—he'd been talking to Junie and helped me get the ride.

Now, beggars can't be choosers, right? I was thrilled, and I talked to one of my friends, Tim Delrose. Smart businessman that he is, he wanted to know about the contract.

What contract?

No, Tim, it's not going to work like that. I drive the car. Junie gives me 40 percent. He gets me a motel room everywhere we go—I pay for it, but he gets me one. I get that 40 percent and that's easy enough to remember so we don't have to write it down. That way, if a better opportunity comes along, I can go do what I want.

Ann Schrader, Kenny's wife: When Ken got the call from Junie, I was excited for him. I thought he was truly worthy of the opportunity because he has done everything the right way from the beginning.

He never burned a bridge and he has always been congenial with everyone he's worked with.

I feel for some of the wives who think they've got to run into their husband when he stops walking, or they need to be walking around with a clipboard. I don't need to be on the pit box. I couldn't keep track of what goes on. My mind wanders to other things. I couldn't even keep the lap count at DuQuoin. I was like, Oh—did he come by?

I'm too busy talking. I'd rather go to a suite and have a nice meal and a drink. They don't need me in the pits. I have no interest in working on a car or learning how to do tires. That's not putting down anyone who feels they must. God bless them, some feel like they have to have those radios by their ears, but I think it's important to be your own person. I've seen how easily you can get chewed up and spit out by the sport, and how often marriages don't last. I just needed to be me, going and doing what I like—with Kenny's blessing—so I could be comfortable with who I am.

Even when you go to the race track now, you are hanging out with people you like. It's not drudgery to be at the track. You're talking, everybody's kids are there and having fun. At least, I am. That makes it a lot easier.

Ken will say, "I'm going to qualify with or without you being there. Life will go on."

For me, too. I tell the young girls in the sport, this is not a dress rehearsal. If you don't have fun, life is passing you by.

A lot of our dating and marriage years have been spent like this—figuring out where the next race track is down the road. (Harry Dunn photo; Ken Schrader Collection.)

"What if a better opportunity comes along for Junie?" my friend asked.

"Well, I think he's got the same options," I responded with exaggerated patience.

But I could live with that. And I did, for three fantastic seasons, and we pulled off that 1985 Rookie of the Year Award that did nothing but help my budding career.

Here's the deal: I couldn't put a price tag on what I learned driving for Junie. There's a good reason that nearly everybody who's ever driven or worked for the man absolutely loves him. He was as kind and patient as anyone I've ever driven for, and that's why he was considered the best place for a youngster to start out racing.

Things have changed a lot. Today, young guys who come into Nextel Cup have really good equipment and they are expected to produce immediately. If they don't, they're gone, and that's a shame. Some people need a little more time to develop, and I can't help thinking it means that some really good drivers are not getting the opportunity to prove they belong in the top tier. When I began, however, financially marginal operations like Junie's could still operate. The costs were high, even then, but it was relative. Everybody in racing seems to spend everything they make and as much more as they can hustle, but at that time the differences between the haves and have-nots were in terms of hundreds-of-thousands instead of millions.

Because of his situation, Junie needed to finish races and not have his driver tear up the car. I understood that, and I was okay with it. We might be the 26th best car on a given day, but we'd wind up 15th because we put the premium on finishing. He put a car under me that wasn't going to drop out due to attrition, and I wasn't going to put it in the wall.

I also read the entry form pretty close. Figured out that it was good to finish first, second, third, fourth—or tenth. You didn't back up from sixth to tenth on purpose, but it was real easy to drop back one spot to tenth because it meant more contingency money.

In those days, we had two-day qualifying, too. We probably could have gone out and gotten maybe 12th or 13th quickest on the first day. But if we were the fastest car on the second day, we'd pick up $2,500 or $3,000.

"Let's get that $2,500, Bubba."

"Yessir, Mr. Donlavey."

And we did pretty regularly.

I think Junie might have had the opportunity to pick up more sponsorships and move himself up to a higher level as a car owner. He certainly had the knowledge to do it, and because everybody liked him, I'm sure some doors opened to him at times. But, you know what? He was doing it to have fun. Especially as he aged, he saw the value in avoiding ulcers and headaches. When he went to the track, nobody there had a better time, and if you were lucky enough to go with him, you were sure you were going to have fun, too. He was also extremely loyal to the sponsors and friends who'd been helping him to that point. He recognized how racing was changing and he knew that in time it was going to pass him by—and he didn't care. He raced his way, and, man, you just gotta respect that.

I didn't know it until several years afterward, but Junie was

Of course, it wasn't all checkered flags and sitting on the pole. Sometimes, we tested out that safety equipment. (Ken Schrader Collection.)

instrumental in getting me my ride with Hendrick Motorsports. But, I loved Junie long before I knew that. He had recognized that I was going to move up the ladder from his operation, and he wanted to make sure I went someplace where I got a chance to run more consistently at the front than I could in his car. What an unselfish person, because he did that for other drivers, too.

STRADDLING TWO WORLDS

When I got into Junie's race car I realized that I was going to be spending about 30 weekends a year racing for him. It also occurred to me that I was going to have another 22 weekends that I wouldn't be, not to mention all those mid-week days. I was already used to racing at least 100 times a year, so what was I going to do with my time?

Hell, I was going racing!

So, during those three years with Junie, I continued to run as many short-track events as I could possibly jam into the schedule. Mostly, I ran around home in the Midwest because I still had my operation there. But early on in my NASCAR career, I found out that a lot of tracks will pay you a nice little fee (and I still worried about things like mortgages and truck payments at this time) to just come in and sign autographs for a while. They'd like it if you raced, but the majority of NASCAR drivers didn't want to do that, or their car owners and sponsors didn't want them to, in case they wrecked and got hurt.

My car owner was a real racer, and he recognized the need in me to race as much as I could. By this time, I think we were all realizing that for me, racing was more than a way to avoid getting a real job. You can be a junkie on drugs or you can be a junkie on racing. Play your cards right, and the racing might not cost as much as the drugs.

Ann and I waited a year before moving to North Carolina. During 1985, we drove back to St. Louis after every race—planes were still a luxury—because she was a nurse and had to get to work on Monday morning. This turned out to be a good thing when we moved South, because bankers like to loan money to stable people with a good work record.

In our case, that would be Ann.

We found about five acres of land west of Concord that looked just perfect. We could have a stocked pond and a good-sized garage to house most of the various race cars I had started accumulating. It was shaping up to be a promising situation, and thanks to Ann's stability, we got the loan to do it. I mean, boards of directors are real funny about guys who run around from race track to race track with no guarantees regarding income. They like R.N.s, like Ann, a whole lot better, and we had found a bank that would take a chance on a nurse, if not a race-car driver.

But my situation was improving steadily, so I couldn't resist rubbing it in when our race team hit a real landmark in February, 1987. From Daytona I called Tim Crist, one of the bankers who had become a friend. "Hey, Buddy, now what do you think about that property loan?"

"What do you mean?"

"We just won the Twin 125!"

Silence. Long silence.

"What's a Twin 125?"

Well, at that point, I knew that it was time we expanded Tim's horizons. So we started taking him to the races with us sometimes and introducing him to other drivers. It wasn't too long before Rusty Wallace started doing business with Tim, too.

And then one day the phone rang at Tim's bank.

"This is Dale Earnhardt."

Yeah, right, thought Tim. *And this is the President of Tanzania. It's a Schrader prank, for sure.*

Fortunately, Tim didn't say what he was thinking, because it turned out that it really *was* Dale Earnhardt, and he joined a long list of drivers—starting with me—who have done business with Tim.

When Ann and I moved to North Carolina, Dale Earnhardt helped us find acreage a few miles from his farm, and then our sponsor Oakwood Homes brought us a nice little mobile home to live in. A little while later, Oakwood replaced the singlewide with a doublewide, which is still there. My dirt crew chief, Joey Walsh, lives there now. (Ken Schrader Collection.)

We got our Oakwood deal—including a home to live in—in part because our P.R. person Darlene Patterson put it all together for us. So, when we made it to Victory Lane, we made sure that she and her husband Wayne got their pictures taken, too. (David Chobat photo; Ken Schrader Collection.)

Tim Crist, banking executive and close friend: I met the Schraders when Kenny was Rookie of the Year in NASCAR. I was just starting a bank at the time, and some friends recommended that I get involved in racing a little bit. I didn't think I wanted to, even though people thought the business side of racing was about to take off. Just a couple of weeks later they came in, wanting to buy some land. Earnhardt had been driving Kenny around and they found some acreage not too far from Dale's land. I remember listening to an interview with Kenny on Ned Jarrett's old *Wrangler World of Racing* show where he talked about buying the land and putting up the garage. It was just the greatest thing in the world to him, more than he'd ever had in his life, and he owed it to racing.

I liked him from the start, but it was a while before he convinced me to go racing with him. It took only once. You know you're going to be the last people to leave. I've seen Security give him the keys and tell him to lock up when we leave.

He treats everyone the same. Doesn't matter if you are a street cleaner or a senior vice-president. Friends don't get left behind either. He just keeps accumulating more and they all have to learn to mix. Which is a real easy thing to do when your ringleader is Schrader.

Beyond actually beginning to have a little money to think about investing—and therefore needing a banker—I had a real racing career. And it was about to get even more exciting.

It's a driver's meeting and already the kid is paying more attention than I am. (Ken Schrader Collection.)

The Ultimate Trust—
I'm Not Buckled In and
There's a Wall Coming At Me

6

I SPENT A FABULOUS DECADE in Rick Hendrick's cars, but it came as-close-as-this to not happening. I told you that Junie Donlavey had been quietly lobbying with Rick to hire me, but I hadn't heard anything from the Hendrick garage because they all thought I was under contract to go to Bud Moore's team in 1988.

I thought I might be going there, too. Except you may recall that I had this sort of loose relationship with legal documents to that point. That turned out to be a really important issue in advancing my career.

This is what happened: In the summer of my last season with Junie—when we all knew that it was time for me to move along and for Junie to nurture another young, ambitious racer—my nephew Kenny Williams came to North Carolina for a visit. He was a huge Darrell Waltrip fan, so I took him over to Darrell's shop one day. While Kenny was having the time of his life, I got into a conversation with Waddell Wilson, who was one of the guys in charge over there.

"Boy, you gotta be excited about next year," he said, referring to the move over to Bud Moore's stable.

"Oh, yeah," I responded. "Pretty big jump."

"Congratulations. You earned it and you ought to feel good."

"Yeah, as soon as we get everything signed, I'm gonna feel wonderful."

Lengthy pause.

"You're not under contract yet?"

"Well, uh, no."

An hour later the phone rang back at my shop and it was Jimmy Johnson, general manager for Hendrick Motorsports (not the race driver).

"Come on over and have a little meeting with Rick," he said.

He didn't have to repeat himself.

That was on a Tuesday. When I got to Darlington that weekend, Jimmy had a contract ready and I signed it.

That's Jimmy Johnson, the general manager rather than the race driver (who spells his name Jimmie), between Rick Hendrick and me. Jimmy was instrumental in bringing me to the team. (Ken Schrader Collection.)

The legendary Bud Moore. I nearly drove for him, but circumstances brought me to Hendrick Racing instead. Still, Bud and I have been friends for many years. (Mike Adaskaveg photo.)

Let me say Bud Moore is one of the true gentlemen of the sport and he took the news well. Maybe he hadn't been all that wild to get me—I don't know. But it was important that Bud understand why I went with Hendrick. Everybody has enormous respect for Bud, and there was a time when his car was a much-sought-after destination for any driver. But from the day Hendrick Motorsports arrived on the scene, they boosted the competition level considerably. Anybody who has ever been offered a ride with them tries to make it happen.

If we'd had a contract with Moore, we would have honored it. As it was, we didn't even have a handshake; just a loose sort of understanding. More importantly to me, Bud and I remained friends, and that was also the case with Michael Kranefuss and Lee Morse of Ford, who had been working behind the scenes to engineer the Moore ride.

That's been the pattern throughout my career—and my life. It's been important that friends stay friends. I've seen people who came through racing, as well as a lot of other high-profile careers, who think nothing of using and then discarding the people who help them along the way.

The winner in life is not the guy who dies with the most toys. You can't take them with you anyway. And, although I'm not opposed to having a lot of toys, I do believe you can have them as long as you didn't earn them off the backs of other good people.

I've seen too many examples of people who made it to the top and then realized that wrapping yourself in fame and fortune can be pretty lonely, especially when you know that the hangers-on are just there to pick up the crumbs. I'd a lot rather just have crumbs and know that there's a never-ending circle of friends to share them.

There are many people I've come to appreciate, including Bud Moore, whose fantastic career didn't end up including contributions from me, even though I'm happy that NASCAR's history will always include Bud's accomplishments. But there are just a few who hold a very

special place in my heart. One whose name immediately comes to mind is Rick Hendrick. And it's not just because of the great professional opportunity he gave me.

MEETING MY "BROTHER"

I'm really glad I got those years in the Hendrick race car, and there's no doubt that many people consider that the pinnacle of my driving career. That's where I got my Winston Cup wins, a lot of pole positions, almost a guarantee each year that I would finish in the top ten in points, and I made a lot of money as well. All of those are good things. But the best thing about being in that ride was that it gave me a chance to spend some quality time with Rick.

Rick Hendrick, the irrepressible racing ambassador Linda Vaughn, me and Ann enjoy another great moment in Victory Lane. (David Chobat photo; Ken Schrader Collection.)

There's a myth that oval track racers don't like road courses. But it's like I told Northeast ace Dave Dion when he was about to go out on one, "Forget everything you know. Right now your name is Nigel." He got the idea, and I've had as much fun on a track like Watkins Glen, here, as anywhere. (David Chobat photo; Ken Schrader Collection.)

He's like an older brother to me and we've had an incredible amount of fun together. In my mind, I have set him on a pedestal and he deserves to be there, not just for what he's accomplished as a self-made professional, but even more for the way he treats people. I don't say this about very many people, but Rick is truly a class act. You simply couldn't have a better friend. Let me tell you how much I trust him.

We went to the road course at Topeka one time to test for an ARCA race. Now, Rick's a good little race-car driver and he's there testing cars, too. I had an older car, but Rick was running one of the regular Cup cars during the test. I'm running around there a little bit quicker than he is, so he says, "Climb on in here and show me what you're doing down here in turn one."

I climbed in. And we smoked on down into turn one. He wheel-hops and off into the weeds we go. Now, I'm riding shotgun. I got a fire suit and a Bell helmet—and as hard a grip as I can get.

No safety harnesses.

We're sliding through the grass and we're looking at that wall coming up. So, we looked at each other. Then back to the wall. And then back to each other.

It's a matter of seconds, but it's incredible how much time you have for all this stuff to go through your mind. And you kinda know what's going through the other guy's mind, too. Rick knew I was thinking, *Hey, buddy, I'm committed to you. Not everybody would do this shit.*

Well, we stopped short of the wall, thank goodness. And I'd get into a race car and ride shotgun with Rick Hendrick again any day of the week. I'd kind of hope he'd take it a little easier in Topeka's turn one next time, but I know that if we didn't make it through there, it was just meant to be.

THE REST OF THE FAMILY

Because of the way the NASCAR rules were, a car owner could have only two cars and get all the perks like provisional starts in races. So, technically my car was owned by Papa Joe, Rick's dad. That was just fine with me because it meant spending a lot of time with him. I can recall winning at Charlotte and seeing Papa Joe and his wife Mary pictured with me in the newspapers, with them identified as my parents. I was cool with that. Even though we didn't share the genes, families don't come any closer than how I felt about them. And the Hendricks are a package deal anyway.

When Papa Joe died in July of 2004, I hadn't driven for the Hendricks in several years. I was in another part of the country when his formal funeral ceremony was held, and while I felt bad for missing it, I knew that there would be 2,000 people there. I also knew that the family had always understood how I felt about Papa Joe.

Well, I got a call that Saturday night from Rick and he said, "You're going to be at the funeral tomorrow, aren't you?"

I was stunned for a moment. "Rick, I thought the funeral was the other day."

"That was the ceremony. This is the actual burial in Virginia. Just family mostly, but we'd like you to be there."

He didn't have to say any more. The brother thing kicked in once again, and you couldn't have kept me away. Later, Rick told me things about Papa Joe and how he had felt about me that I hadn't known, too.

See, I was brought up in the *yes-sir, no-sir* school of thinking. You always, always treat your elders with respect. In Papa Joe's case, that sort of thing was pretty important to him. I hadn't realized at the time what it meant to him, but I guess I can understand. Rick and his brother John have been successful men who'd come from pretty humble beginnings. They didn't leave Papa Joe behind, but there were fringe people who treated him like they were just tolerating an old guy.

I didn't.

And I'll tell you why—Rick and John wouldn't have been so successful if Joe and Mary hadn't raised them they way they did, taught them great values and encouraged them. They were every bit as wonderful and accomplished people as their sons. They just didn't have as much money. I think Joe and Mary Hendrick are the proof that money isn't the most important element in figuring out how "successful" people have become.

THE OTHER BROTHER

I mentioned John Hendrick. I didn't know him well in the beginning of my time with the team, but before too long we ended up down at Daytona for a testing session. When it was done, John, the crew and I went to Hooters. About three hours later, I called Rick.

Left: In an unguarded moment when we didn't know there was a camera around, Papa Joe Hendrick and I shared our feelings for each other. I really loved the man and I still miss him today. (Ken Schrader Collection.) Right: Sharing a memorable time with Papa Joe and Rick. (Ken Schrader Collection.)

He asked, "What are you doing?"

"I'm at Hooters with your brother."

There was a funny little gurgling noise at the other end of the phone. Maybe a tight laugh, maybe a groan.

"Why didn't you let me meet him earlier?" I continued.

"Uh, there's a reason I've kept you two apart."

"Uh-huh. Well, I wanna drive for *him*."

Rick didn't let it happen, but think what we could have done for Hooters' stock!

Tim Crist: Kenny was in Topeka to qualify on a Saturday afternoon. He was also taking the Brain Trust (a group of friends from North Carolina) to Erie, Colorado, for a short-track race. We knew we were going to be hard-pressed on time, so Kenny asked Rick Hendrick if we could use his plane, since it was faster.

"What are you going to do in Erie?"

"I'm signing autographs."

That was okay with Rick, and we left for the airport.

So, we got to Erie too late for qualifying, in spite of the quicker plane, and Kenny started dead last in the field. It was one of the most incredible races I've ever seen. I watched him maneuver from dead last to win the race.

And then he signed autographs.

It was the usual deal when you go with him. Again, you don't leave until everybody else is gone. Then you jump on the airplane and get back to Topeka when the sun is coming up.

The Brain Trust went to bed. Kenny went to the track to get ready for the Sunday afternoon race.

"How was last night?" Rick asked when Kenny got to the track.

"We won."

That got Rick's attention.

"What do you mean, you won? I thought you were going to sign autographs!"

"Well, yeah. I did. I signed a bunch of autographs. But I raced, too."

Rick shouldn't have been surprised. They had race cars, they had an organized event, and Kenny was there.

I'd have figured that one out before I gave him the keys to the plane.

The core of the Brain Trust: The Banker Tim Crist, The General Manager Brian Buchauer, The Tile Man Walter Hannah, and The Lawyer Tom Grady. Why a Tile Man? Well, you just never know when the time is going to be right for that terrazzo patio. (Joyce Standridge photo.)

IN THE #25 CAR

I didn't replace Tim Richmond. I can't tell you how many times I've heard references to having taken his place, but I didn't. And it bit me that first year.

It's correct that Harry Hyde was Tim's crew chief before he was mine. And that Folgers Coffee came to us after sponsoring Tim. But Hendrick had two Folgers cars before I came on board, one driven by Tim and the other by Benny Parsons. Tim was the #25 and Benny the #35. I got the equipment from both cars but I got the points from the #25, which hadn't run all the races the previous year.

If you don't recall the 1987 season, Tim Richmond raced only periodically. For a long time, the Hendrick team tried to hold a place for Tim's return, but by Speed Weeks in 1988, it was clear that Tim was too sick to race. Within another year, unfortunately, Tim was dead.

At about the same time, Benny was retiring from driving to go on to his highly successful television career. That was planned, which is why I got Benny's equipment. But come the 1988 racing season, my car has the #25 on the door. That brought Folgers on board with us, too, and we were happy with the situation. First race of the year at Daytona, we sat on the pole.

Wow.

Next week at Richmond, we didn't even qualify for the race.

Damn.

Turns out that the car didn't have any provisional starts because that car number ran only four or five races the previous year. At Richmond, the stupid clutch was slipping, so we had to load up and I ended up in Buddy Arrington's car. I really appreciated that, and it kept us in the running for points, but it was a frustrating experience going from the pole one week to a pick-up ride the next.

I'm not the first.

I won't be the last.

But it ain't my favorite memory.

Pacing the field for the 1988 Daytona 500. That's Davey Allison on the outside front row and eventual winner Bobby Allison starting right behind me. (Ken Schrader Collection.)

Racing with Rusty—we've been doing this literally since we were kids, but the stakes at Charlotte are a little higher than they were at Lake Hill. But only a little. (Mike Adaskaveg photo.)

Left: This is a rare moment when Harry Hyde and I were happy with each other. We'd just won our first Winston Cup race together and he deserved the kiss. Rick is on the left, with Dennis Connor and Papa Joe to Harry's immediate right. (Dorsey Patrick photo; Ken Schrader Collection.)

Right: In 1992, I had a horrible time at Bristol. After the front end was destroyed and the back end was destroyed, I climbed up on the roof and made sure that no part of this damned car was going to survive. The fans loved my Bristol Stomp. I don't recall the race team being as pleased. (Joyce Standridge photo.)

In fact, that time with Harry Hyde wasn't my favorite time in a race car either, even though Harry is deservedly a legend in auto racing. What he accomplished through many years as a crew chief for some of the best drivers in history just defies description. It was a coup for Rick to hire him to run a team. Certainly, Harry and Tim clicked.

But Harry and I didn't click.

It's not that we didn't have success. We won at Talladega together. We had a lot of strong finishes. And it's really bizarre that we didn't communicate real well because throughout my life I have *always* gotten along exceptionally well with men who are older than I am. On a purely personal basis, Harry and I got along just fine. But when it came to the race car set-up, we differed. Even winning, I was telling Harry that I couldn't get the cars to feel comfortable.

So, I'm getting aggravated.

And Harry is getting aggravated.

And we went to a meeting with Rick, who said, "Do what you've got to do, change whatever you want to change."

We walk out of the meeting and Harry stops me. He says, "See what I mean? Rick won't do nothing."

I stopped in my tracks. "Harry, what are you talking about? He just told us to do whatever you wanted—whatever you need to go faster."

"Yeah, but he don't mean it."

Well, I got Harry by the arm and took him back to Rick's office.

"Rick, I'm a little bit confused here. I was just in this meeting and you told us to change whatever Harry wanted to change. But he says you don't mean it."

Well, the meeting continued with just Harry and Rick. And it came out that Harry was real concerned that if they made changes and we didn't go faster it would be blamed on him. From that meeting they decided it would be better if they weren't together anymore, and they parted ways. No friendships lost—it was just time to do something different.

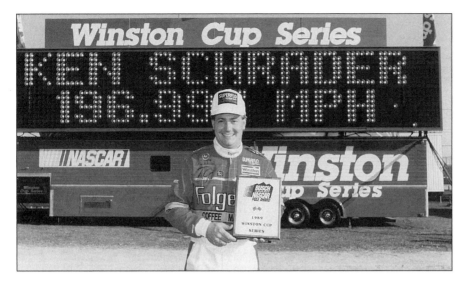

I had several other crew chiefs during my time at Hendrick, and I liked them. We all learned to be a team, too, and the credit for that goes right back to Rick. It was a natural thing that if you found a little something that worked, you'd want to keep that information to yourself. I mean, it's really, really tough to be competitive at the top of the NASCAR food chain, and even if you have a lot of confidence in yourself, you still like to have an ace in the hole if you can.

But Rick wouldn't have that business of hoarding information. These days, it's not unusual for teams to share information, but back in the late 1980s it was hard enough to get teammates to admit they had a teammate, much less help them out.

Still, no matter what we did, outsiders regarded us as the third team. Jeff Gordon was winning races and championships with Hendrick, Terry

Labonte snuck in there and won a championship in 1996, but no matter how well we ran—and sometimes we ran extremely well—we seemed to get bit on the butt. We didn't wreck a lot, but we broke, usually when we were running best.

There are people who think that we were the step-child, or that we got lesser equipment, or that we were a research-and-development car. None of that was true. Not ever. Rick always believed in our team and made sure we had the opportunities. But here's what would happen: they would have three engines come out of the shop, race-ready. We could choose first, but I guarantee you that whatever engine we chose would drop a cylinder. Or a valve. Or the engine would run fantastically but we'd blow out a tire. Or something incredibly stupid would fall out of the sky and end our day or just cripple us. We still ran very well, got a lot of great finishes and found our way to the stage for the NASCAR banquet. But when you have the potential, and you know you have the potential, and you still can't make it happen, eventually it wears on you—and the whole team.

I might still be in the Hendrick car if not for the final crew chief. Now, I want to say here that I've been happy with my later rides with other teams, and I'm never one to look backwards and say, *What if?*

Even though my relationship with Rick was one-of-a-kind—and it still is—when the final crew chief started working the guys in the shop to the bone, that guy and I were sure gonna butt heads. There was no valid reason. It was just that he didn't have a life, so no one else should. If you've been reading from the beginning of this book, you know that I don't share that philosophy at all. I know it takes hard, hard work to be successful, especially in NASCAR racing, but there's a fine line. And I felt we'd gone over it.

Although it can be helpful to know what your teammate is running and what his set-up is, it doesn't mean that it will work as well for you.

Drivers have different styles. But, because Jeff Gordon was winning a lot, we were expected to do the same with his information and set-ups.

Well, I'm not Jeff, any more than Jeff is me. Whenever I got comfortable with a car, it seemed like a crew chief wanted to change something on the car, because *that's what Jeff is running.*

And then at Watkins Glen in 1996, I was really happy with the way the car was running. Pulled it in from practice, parked it and told the crew I was happy. But the crew chief directed a change because *this is what Jeff is running.*

And my days with Hendrick Motorsports became numbered, not least because I had a new opportunity that made staying with a team where my input was limited look a lot less appealing.

I would also like to point out that not much has happened with the #25 car from the days I was there. It's still considered by a lot of observers outside the organization as the third car in the stable—maybe the fourth. And I know for a fact that Rick continues to give it as much support as the other cars but at a lot of events it still seems snakebitten.

Sometimes, no matter how hard you try, it's just not meant to be.

Sweet. But look at Ann's right hand. It's refreshment and the tab has been opened. And you wonder why I go home with the girl after the race? (David Chobat photo; Ken Schrader Collection.)

I'M NOT GIVEN TO TEARS, BUT . . .

I got that "Guy Thing" going. You know, avoid situations when your heart gets ripped out and handed to you on a platter. But if you love the Hendrick family, you have to wonder why The Big Guy has been so hard on them. And you have to go looking for your heart occasionally.

When Rick was diagnosed with life-threatening leukemia, my wife Ann and I were just devastated. To see one of the most dynamic men I've ever known being attacked by disease took the stuffing out of all of us who care about him. It figures that Rick would take a disaster and figure out how to make something positive for a lot of others. He motivated a lot of people, including me, to help work for bone marrow registration. And, ultimately, he appears to have beaten the disease, although it has taken a toll. That made me happier than all my race wins put together.

But, just when it looked like Rick and his wonderful wife Linda were back into a normal life, they had to face the worst challenge imaginable—losing a child. And if that wasn't enough, they lost Rick's brother and two nieces at the same time.

Just months after Papa Joe died, one of Rick's planes was trying to land in the fog near the Martinsville Speedway. All ten people on board were killed when the plane flew into the mountainside, including Rick's and Linda's son Ricky, brother John and John's twin daughters. It was unthinkable.

When I walked in the door at home that night after getting back from the race at Martinsville, I was literally in shock. I couldn't think, I

After Ann and I had Dorothy, I understood that special bond between parent and child. That went some way toward understanding how Rick and Linda felt when they lost Ricky—but only some way. I don't want to ever know what it's really like. (Mike Adaskaveg photo.)

couldn't feel. I just wanted to hide, because like so many people in NASCAR racing, I'd just lost some people I cared for very deeply.

But Ann was thinking straight, thank goodness.

"C'mon. Let's go," she said.

"Where are we going?"

"We are going to Rick and Linda's house."

I shook my head. "I'm not going to bother them. There will be so many people there."

"I don't care," she said. "I don't care if we do nothing but walk up and give them a hug. We're going to go down there and let them know that we hurt for them."

And we did.

And you know what? There were only about 30 or so there. I guess most people thought like I had: that everybody would show up and it would be too much for them.

Ann has talked me into a few things in life that I didn't really want to do, but turned out okay anyway. This turned out to be something I'm really glad we did. We couldn't take the edge off their hurt, but it helped us to be there for them.

I've often said that if I was in a bind, I would not hesitate to call Rick. Not even if it was three o'clock in the morning. And even when he was sickest with the leukemia, he would have come to help me. That's the kind of friend he is.

So, I'm very happy that a tiny ray of sunshine came out of that terrible tragedy. It turned out that Linda was holding an engagement ring for son Ricky. When he got back from Martinsville, he was going down on one knee for his Emily. And if the wedding never happened because of the accident, the baby they were expecting did happen.

Little Ricki was born a few months after her daddy died, and no child could be more loved. I think she must be the salvation for Linda and Rick, and I'm glad.

I'm really, really glad.

The Princess and the Pe(tree) **7**

I F YOU'VE BEEN A NASCAR FAN for any length of time, you'll recall a first-rate race driver by the name of Harry Gant. He was famous, as much as anything, for an unreal number of second-place finishes, but then one year he put together a string of wins in a single month that earned him the nickname of Mr. September.

I mention Harry by way of bringing up what a good team he was driving for at the time. So, when Harry and his car owner Leo Jackson started talking about retirement, it was a natural that there would be other people interested in buying what they'd built up. One of the most interested was Andy Petree.

Brian Buchauer, General Manager for Schrader Racing: I started out in racing as a track announcer in upstate New York, but worked my way through a series of jobs before I went to work for Kenny full-time. I spent about 10 years working for U.S. Tobacco as Harry Gant's P.R. man, as nice a man as has ever raced. I used to call him "Sara Lee," *because nobody doesn't like Harry Gant*. So I've worked for two really good guys.

Back in the late 1980s, I went with Kenny and Harry to a benefit race in Florida. When we get to the track, they've got two semi-tractors for them to race.

Well, Harry climbs up, struggles a bit but finally climbs in through the window. Schrader watches him, cocks his head and then climbs up to the window. "Hey, Harry, let me show you something neat about these things."

And he opened the door.

Schrader Racing's general manager, Brian Buchauer. (Joyce Standridge photo.)

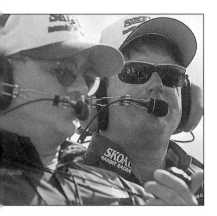

Andy Petree on your side is a definite advantage. (Mike Adaskaveg photo.)

It's rarely a happy thing to be on pit road, under green, alone. (Mike Adaskaveg photo.)

It's hard to imagine there might a race fan who hasn't heard of Andy, but for the few who might be thinking about a Google search, I'll save you the time: Andy was crew chief for Dale Earnhardt, Sr. through Cup championships six and seven. Need I say any more about his racing instincts and smarts?

You may wonder why somebody who put together back-to-back killer seasons would pass on the chance to make it three in a row and be a part of Earnhardt getting that record-breaking eighth championship. You wouldn't wonder, however, if you'd ever been in the pressure-cooker world of a championship hunt. They really were hard on everybody, not least of all Earnhardt and Petree.

Plus, Andy's stock was very, very high. There wasn't anybody on the NASCAR circuit who didn't want Andy to be on their team.

That included me.

So I was paying attention the day he came roaring up to my shop in a beat-up old S-10 pickup. (Andy's not into status symbols. Besides, working 80-100 hours a week like he had been, he didn't have time to go truck shopping. But you gotta love it when the currently most-successful crew chief in racing is running around in a vehicle that even a hitchhiker would hesitate to get in.)

Andy doesn't waste a lot of time on small talk. "Hey, I'm buying Leo's team, and I want you to drive for me."

I was stunned.

"Well, I'm driving for Rick, but I'd really love it if you'd come be crew chief for me. I don't think there's a problem with that happening, if you did," I managed to understate with a straight face.

Now, if I were given to looking backward, I might stop at this point and speculate that if Andy had agreed with me, we could possibly all be happy campers today. Me, Rick and Andy. Sounds like a winner to me.

But then, maybe we wouldn't have been able to get out of our own way. Maybe we would have blown up or wrecked so many cars that we would have broken Rick. Maybe.

That's why I don't look backwards. Life, as you know, isn't about the maybes. I understand why Andy wanted his own team. He's one of the smartest guys in racing and he saw that if you came into racing middle class but you wanted to be rich, you had to be smart and you either had to become a successful driver or car owner.

Did you catch the most important word in that last sentence? It's "successful." There are plenty of people who have come into NASCAR through the years and left poorer than when they started. Maybe most of them. But a few guys have hit the Mother Lode thanks to racing.

Andy is a good race car driver. He might have made it as a driver, but he had just seen Kirk Shelmerdine, his predecessor at the Childress-Earnhardt garage, leave to go racing—and struggle. With his good business sense, Andy could take an already-good organization like Leo Jackson had assembled and potentially make it a powerhouse. And then

The Skoal Bandit car was a great-looking, great-running car. (Mike Adaskaveg photo.)

he and his family would never again have to worry about a wolf at the door. Makes sense.

"Well, here's the deal," Andy continued our conversation, "I'm going to own the team, but I'm going to be the crew chief, too."

Wow.

Here I was with a less-than-perfect situation at the time, and Andy tells me that if I go drive for him, I can have him as my crew chief.

But Andy is nothing if not honest, too. "Only thing is, I'm not sure about sponsorship yet."

Deflate the balloon.

"Just think about it," he said, and I did.

A lot.

A lot more than a guy who's happy with his ride is going to be doing. So, when that deal at Watkins Glen happened—when I was expected to change a really good-running race car to a set-up I knew wouldn't work as well for me *because Jeff's running it*—well, I walked over to Andy and told him he had a deal.

I think agreeing to drive for Andy probably helped him keep the lock on the sponsorship he needed, but regardless, we started off the following season in the #33 Skoal Bandit car.

AS IT TURNED OUT...

. . . Andy wasn't my crew chief.

Hell, I knew that with the demands on his time from the front office, sponsorship deals, and a hundred employees, Andy wasn't going

When you're sitting around, might as well do a little helmet maintenance. (Mike Adaskaveg photo.)

At the front. Doesn't get any better than that. (Mike Adaskaveg photo).

to be able to sit on the box on race day and direct what happened with me. I think I probably knew that even before I took the ride. But, by the time it was official that he wasn't going to be crew chief, we were in too deep to back out.

Our relationship didn't turn out to be a bad thing for either of us. Andy probably got me more focused, and I think I was able to help him lighten up a little bit.

Boy, is he tense. I mean, it's all about the finish, and if commitment to the cause was the determining factor, Andy would be the guy every other car owner was gunning at today.

At the time, Andy and his wife Patty didn't have baby Johnnie yet, so it became a kind of mission for me to introduce them to having a little more fun in their lives. Patty was real open to the idea. Andy took a little more work, but I think we got the job done.

You'd think he would have been an easy convert. I mean, he's married to one of the most beautiful women in a pit area full of beautiful women. Patty is a former Miss Winston.

In the days when Winston was the series sponsor, they had several lovely young women who were goodwill ambassadors for the brand and appeared in the Victory Lane photos, so you would look at shining hair and gorgeous smiles instead of the dirty, sweaty race driver in the middle. Nice distraction, good idea. And to keep things on the up-and-up, the ladies were not allowed to date the racing crowd.

Isn't there a cliché that rules are made to be broken?

My former teammate Jeff Gordon is the most famous instance of breaking that rule, and considering the way it turned out long-term, maybe Winston knew what they were doing. But while we've lost like four of these lovely ladies to people in the series, the Petree marriage seems to be taking very well. And Patty is a smart lady—far more than window dressing or a trophy wife. From day one she was involved with the team in a major way. I always think it's nice if the boss is good to look at, but she is also one of the sweetest, most caring people I've ever met.

And since she had been a Miss Winston, we called her Princess. Also because she had been a Miss Winston, she had manners, so she didn't call us what we deserved.

DOING AS I'M TOLD

Of course, on the way to being a Super Team, we encountered the gremlins that haunt every team that doesn't quite make it to that level of superstardom. We had the right elements, but we also had rotten luck at times.

We got wrecked at Daytona in our very first race together, which is a common statement during the Age of the Big One. It sure wasn't the

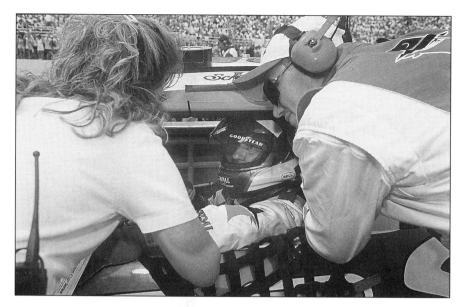

Getting last-minute instructions. Or maybe just shooting the shit with Heidi Stoddard and Wally Rogers. There's always a lot of time to kill before the race starts. (Mike Adaskaveg photo.)

way we wanted to start off. But we had some good times, too. When we went to Charlotte in May that year, we qualified very well, and then about 30 laps into the race we passed Jeff Gordon for the lead. Mr. Hendrick told me that his whole suite went wild. They were happy for us. And that made me happy because as far as I was concerned, those people were still very special to me.

Of course, just as we were truckin' along and doing well, fate had to bite us. We broke a cylinder head that day, but we had that moment in the sun. A really good moment—the kind that sparks hope and keeps you going.

Also, I found that when Andy would tell me to do something different on the car, I was willing to give it a try. I respected him that much. Sometimes what he suggested didn't work for me, but often it did. In fact, the whole crew did exactly what Andy told us to do because there was never any question about who was in control.

For example, we were at Watkins Glen and I walked in the garage on a Sunday morning and the crew said that Andy's not here.

What happened?

"Patty went into labor so he flew home."

Before leaving, Andy had left instructions for us. Among our marching orders was that in the 90-lap race, we were to pit on lap 30 and lap 60. That's what you did then.

Well, about lap 52 I smoked on down into turn one and had to get all over the brakes. I was about to get into another driver and didn't want to take him out, so I just locked up the brakes, spun off course and flat-spotted all the tires. I didn't get stuck, but when I got back on the track that thing was vibrating like a hundred sledgehammers were hitting it.

The Princess and the Pe(tree)   **81**

"W-w-w-hat l-l-l-lap is it?" I hiccupped over the radio to the pits.

"You're on lap 53," came the word back. "Get in here and get some tires."

"Uh-uh," I keyed. "A-A-A-ndy said t-t-t-thirty and s-s-s-sixty."

So I just ran around there with that thing jarring my fillings for another seven laps. I wasn't going to pit when Andy hadn't told me to pit.

DAY-*OUCH*-TONA

During the time I drove for Andy, we seemed to be kind of snake-bitten at Daytona, which is odd because it has always been a really good track for me. Slap a restrictor plate on those suckers, even up the horsepower, and I'll make a race out of it. Like a Saturday night shootout at a short track, but at 175 mph, so when you wreck it hurts a lot more.

Obviously, it makes a lot of sense to get up front because most of the wrecks happen back in the pack. Proof of this theory came during the 1998 Twin 125. We had qualified well so we were locked in to running the 500 on Sunday. During the race we pitted late and we were running at the back of the pack but decided that since we weren't running real well, we needed to take care of the car and think about Sunday. A starting spot in a 500-mile race isn't always critical, so we thought we'd go conservative in our approach this time.

Of course, we wrecked.

Big time.

Broke my sternum.

Some of the best racing anywhere, anytime, is at Daytona. Here, we were going at it with one of the great racers, Mark Martin. (Mike Adaskaveg photo.)

I'm over at the Halifax Hospital with Andy, Patty, Ann and Heidi Stoddard (wife of another crew chief, Frank), who was our P.R. person the three years I was with Andy's team. I was laying there and I asked Heidi and Ann where we'd qualified.

Qualifying had been several days earlier. They looked at each other, but answered me anyway.

So, how did we wreck so far back in the 125? I asked.

Again, they were patient and explained the late pit, and so on.

Thirty seconds later, I asked, *Where did we qualify?*

Rung my bell pretty good, I guess. They're all used to me being goofy, but I think they really were worried about how bad I was hurt when I started asking the same questions over and over.

And, man, I was hurt. I've been injured in race cars before. Broken shoulder blade, collarbones and such, but the difference when you break your sternum is that you can raise your arms.

You just don't want to.

And you don't want to breathe.

The Twin 125s traditionally are run on Thursday. On Friday, I didn't even get in the race car because I hurt too much. Morgan Shepherd shook down the back-up car for us that day, and then on Saturday I got in it for the final test session. The shocks we were running on the car at that time had so much rebound in them that they pulled the cars down aerodynamically and it was almost like they didn't have a suspension. I mean, you could run over seagull shit on the back straightaway and feel it.

We ran decently but when I got back to the pits I told Andy, "Hey, this thing doesn't feel like it did. What did you do to it?"

"Well, I changed the rear shocks. The other ones would beat you apart."

"Yeah, but's it a lot faster with them on."

"But, I don't know if you can do it with them on."

"Well, I ain't gonna feel good regardless, so let's put them back on."

We did. I took a couple more practice laps and decided it was the right thing to do.

Now, because of the 125 wreck, I had to start in the back of the 500 on Sunday. For some reason, maybe the Big Guy felt sorry for us, I was able to find holes all day and run in them about two-thirds of the way back in the pack. I felt safe and didn't need the relief driver who was standing by. I definitely didn't want to be in The Big One—the huge wreck involving a lot of cars that seems to happen at least once every time we run the restrictor-plate tracks. Shoot, I didn't even want to *see* The Big One.

About fifty laps to go, I realized that everything was cool.

Okay, we need to go to work.

And so we headed to the front.

More than once I've been glad for—and needed—a pre-race prayer. When you share it with your family— note my daughter, Dorothy's hand—it's even more special. (Mike Adaskaveg photo.)

HE WASN'T GOING TO WIN

Dale Earnhardt, Sr. was not going to win that race.

The record books all say he did, and that 1998 was his one and only Daytona 500 win. Nobody was happier than Andy and me when he did.

Just as I still had a lot of emotional ties to the Hendrick team, Andy felt the same way about car owner Richard Childress and Dale. Beside that, Dale was one of the first friends I made among the NASCAR drivers. He actually drove me around to find the property for my shop just a few miles from his farm. We shared a lot of laughs and some pretty important moments in our lives, so Andy and I could live with the idea of Dale winning the 500. Several times would have been okay, in fact.

But just not that day.

And the thing is, I don't know who was going to win. Coming down toward the end there was a pack that included Dale, Bobby Labonte, Jeremy Mayfield, Rusty Wallace and me. Mike Skinner was a lap down, but he was a factor for a little while just by being there. Even though he and Dale were teammates, they weren't exactly president of each other's fan club. Still, I think Mike wanted to keep his ride and he knew that he better help rather than hinder Dale, or he wasn't going to want to see Mr. Childress when he got back to the pits.

After a few laps we booted Mike back into the pack and got down to serious business. Dale was in the lead, but there was no way he was going to be able to block all of us. Maybe two of us, but we were all fast enough—and hungry enough—that we didn't care about a storybook ending for Dale. We all had our own stories to write.

So much for strategy.

On the 199th lap of 200, coming for the white flag, we also saw the yellow flag. John Andretti, Jimmy Spencer and Lake Speed had tangled and brought out the caution.

The field froze as soon as we crossed the line with that yellow flag.

We all know what that meant. The only major feat that had eluded Earnhardt was the 500, and he wanted it more than Al Gore wanted a Florida recount back in 2000. When we knew that Dale had achieved the prize he wanted so badly, we all quit thinking about our own situation and got really happy for him.

Andy Petree was one of the first people among the hundreds lined up on pit road to high-five Dale. I would have been one of the first drivers to congratulate him, but, damn, I couldn't get out of the car! I had that broken sternum (which Dale knew all about, having broken his at Talladega some years before). We did get a chance to talk later, though, when I could stop gritting my teeth with pain.

And, as this is written, the rest of us in that lead pack have yet to win the Daytona 500, so maybe you have some sense of just how hard we were all willing to race. You get only so many opportunities. But when one passes you by, you can't help being happy to see a friend have his moment in the sun.

And on that February day in 1998, we got fourth place: That meant Mr. Petree was a happy camper.

I had to have help getting out of the race car: That meant I wanted to cry. But I couldn't catch my breath to sob.

I BEAT THE BOSS

Several times in my career I've driven for people who knew how to race. There's advantages and disadvantages to that, even though it wasn't a reason I ever chose a ride. The advantage is that you can cut the bull. When you come in from a test session or a race, you can talk in the kind of shorthand that exists between people who understand first-hand what it is you do out there. The disadvantage is that you have to beat their on-track performance.

I told you about testing with Rick Hendrick. Well, I also tested with Andy Petree, a fine driver in his own right. Especially at Hickory Motor Speedway, a paved short track a little west of where most of us live in North Carolina. It's not at all unusual to go out there on an "off" weekend from Cup racing and find guys having some fun. Several NASCAR drivers got their start at Hickory, too, so it's a real racey place.

It's also a place that Andy runs well. And one day when he was testing a car over there, I arrived about an hour after he'd started.

"Take it out there and see what you think," he told me.

Well, he's run Hickory a lot—this is *his* car—and I can't just get in it and take it out there. I mean, I have to go faster than he goes. Otherwise, why does he need a hired gun in the Cup car? If he can race as fast as I can, then he can save himself a bunch of money by just hiring himself.

I strapped in and took the car out there. I ran like six laps—and the sixth lap was finally faster than Andy's laps had been. I mean, I was side-

I kept one of the Skoal cars for the collection I have at our new shop. Race fans can stop by and see the car—as well as others— and you might even run into Andy Petree when he stops by for visitation rights. (Joyce Standridge photo.)

My man, Andy Petree.
(Mike Adaskaveg photo.)

Andy Petree, close friend and former car owner: Oh, yeah, he will tell you that he out-qualified me at Hickory, but he doesn't tell you that it took four tries!

Later, he talked me into racing on the dirt at DuQuoin, and it was my first time on dirt, but I out-qualified him for the race. However, I'll be honest and admit that coming off turn two, I heard over my radio that Kenny was coming up on the outside. I couldn't believe he'd passed that many people on the first lap, so I looked over and sure enough—there he was.

I looked too long. I had the steering wheel cranked for the turn and didn't let off soon enough so I ended up spun out.

That was his fault 'cause he made me look.

The second time I spun out later on was just my fault.

ways, like I was on dirt. It wasn't pretty. In fact, Andy had some grave concerns about his car and whether it was going to come back in to the pits in one piece.

But I was one-hundredth of a second faster. That's .01 of a second—less than an eye blink.

"You ran the same speed I did," Andy said.

"No, I did not run the same speed," I pointed out patiently. "I ran one-hundredth of a second faster."

"Yeah, right, a whole one-hundredth of a second," he jeered.

"Andy, let me explain this to you," I responded. "In this little deal we just had, the whole field qualified, and I would be in the Bud Shoot-out in Daytona for all the pole winners next February—and you would not be."

End of argument.

A NEW OPPORTUNITY

I still feel really close to Andy and Patty, even though I spent only three years in their car, 1997-1999. Some people are just such good human beings that you feel better for having spent time with them. I wish things had turned out for them as car owners as it should have. I mean, if being successful in racing was based on quality of character, the Petrees would be superstars.

But racing rarely works that way.

I hope I helped them. I want to believe that I made my time in their cars a good time for them as much as it was for me. But we just couldn't seem to get the Good Luck Fairy to drop by.

A race at Talladega kind of sums up how things went for us. We were leading with just a lap-and-a-half to go. But I had the Labonte brothers behind me.

Now, Terry, who'd been my teammate at Hendrick, is one of the

Racing with Bobby Hamilton when he was driving one of the most famous cars in the history of racing, the Richard Petty-owned #43. (Mike Adaskaveg photo.)

good people who is like a teammate for life. And I think the world of Bobby. We're all really good friends.

Except when there's a lap-and-a-half to go at Talladega.

You need a "dance" partner at Talladega to create a usable draft that will allow you to go to the front. If I'd been followed by a couple of selfish assholes, no problem. I'd have won the race. But you knew that, friends or not, when it came time to dance, the brothers were going to be together.

And that's how it went even when we ran well at other times. We couldn't buy a break. But my stock hadn't fallen off the chart, so when my pal Ernie Irvan got hurt for the final time in his star-crossed career, the seat in the MB2 Motorsports car opened up.

And I'd always loved M&M Candies.

It hadn't been easy to leave Rick Hendrick, but he's a huge businessman who'd always had lots of employees and understood people moving on. It never affected our personal relationship.

With the Petrees, it was a lot harder.

They were struggling to some degree. They were always having to worry about sponsorships because they didn't have the largest Honda dealership in the western hemisphere to fall back on like Rick Hendrick did. Then, Skoal, our sponsor at the #33, was forced by the Feds to choose between NASCAR and drag racing. For whatever business reasons that made sense to them, they chose the drags.

But I had been putting together a deal with Oakwood Homes. They sponsored me when I first came to North Carolina, as well as helping Andy's Busch car during this period. We had a nice package put together that was going to move them up to the Cup. So at least I wasn't leaving the team high and dry.

But it was at Richmond in the fall that I told Andy I was moving on.

It wasn't good.

It wasn't good with Andy or Patty. For about a week, things kind of simmered, and I certainly understand why. You don't ever mean it to be

My "little brother" and teammate while I was at Petree, Kenny Wallace. Here's he's signing autographs, but it looks like hard work. That's K...E...N...N...Y... (Ken Schrader Collection.)

a rejection, but whether you are leaving of your own accord or you've been fired, it can't help but have somebody feeling like the divorce papers are being served. Even if it's civil, it hurts.

At Loudon, we sat down in their motorhome and talked for quite a while. It was an emotional deal for all of us.

When people say that a team split was just a business deal, they're either lying or they don't have much depth to them. Business enters into it—I had a terrific financial offer from MB2 or I wouldn't even have considered it. But the will to win, the need to stir the pot to try to make the wins happen, are a big part of it, too. Sometimes you feel that a change will help everybody concerned.

Nothing personal? Bull. It's real, spitting personal. We've all got our feelings invested in this deal as much as our finances. So, when you have come to care for people like I did with Andy and Patty, the last thing you want to do is hurt them. And in the process of unintentionally hurting them, it hurt me, too.

In a fairly short time, we all got over it. And it did help, at least in the short term. We had become a two-car team during my time there, with my old St. Louis pal Kenny Wallace driving the other car. A little later, Andy had Joe Nemechek and Bobby Hamilton in his cars and they got wins with them.

But sometimes it seems like big time racing is a cold, cruel, heartless world. The cost of racing these days is a killer. And eventually, Andy found maintaining a shop across the state from the hub of racing was too much. He sold off a lot of his stuff, dropped back to lower classes.

But when it comes to the human being inside his skin, Andy Petree is still one of the classiest guys the racing world has ever seen.

I just wish we'd had more moments like this on for Andy and Patty. (Dorsey Patrick photo; Ken Schrader Collection.)

Asleep at the Wheel — and Rudder

8

IF YOU WANT TO BECOME A RACING HERO to your own kids, get M&Ms as your sponsor. There are plenty of other things you can do, but having an unlimited supply of candy in the house is a short-cut, trust me.

That wasn't the reason we went to the MB2 Motorsports ride in 2000, much as I let my kids think so. And it wasn't the preferred way to gain a ride, either, because it came as a direct result of a good friend's injury. Ernie Irvan had made a storybook recovery from near-fatal injuries to once again win races—and then back to yet another serious wreck that ultimately ended his NASCAR driving career.

One afternoon during the period shortly after Ernie's accident, I was standing on pit road when Jay Frye, the team's general manager, walked by. Just as a common courtesy I asked the same question everybody was asking of their team members: "What are you going to do?"

"Dunno," he said. "You can come drive it."

We both laughed and went on our way. But then I got to thinking. Teaming up with Andy hadn't worked out as either of us planned, and it looked to improve odds for both of us to try something different.

In the case of the MB2 car, it was owned by three guys, Tom Beard, Read Morton and Nelson Bowers, all of whom were new to the Cup world but came in with pretty good sponsorship support and looked to be around for a while even though they'd lost their driver. Jay Frye and I had a good history that went back many years to when he worked for Budweiser and then later with Valvoline. Plus, I had a relationship with M&Ms' parent company, which also owned Pedigree dog food, through an associate sponsorship in our Hendrick days.

MB2 was getting engines from Hendrick, as well, so in some respects racing with MB2 would be sort of going home. There were other familiar faces there, too, but what sealed the deal for me was when Rick Hendrick said the team owners were good guys. That's all I needed to know.

Added to all the turmoil the team had been through, they were still operating out of a tiny shop in Mooresville. Might have been 10,000 square feet, which would be very comfortable if you wanted to run a Saturday night dirt-track operation, but it was really difficult for Cup racing, even if you're not building engines in-house.

The second season I was with them, they built a new, 40,000-square-foot shop on a nice bit of property near Concord that was partially owned by Ann and me. And even though I haven't driven for them for a while, in 2005, they moved from that shop into a new 144,000-square-foot shop for their growing team, and it just happens to also be on property that Ann and I are partners in. I have to say that I've pissed a lot of money away on race cars, but real estate has been very, very good to me.

While I was with MB2, they brought in a second team by convincing Valvoline to invest. Just about everything in racing is related to knowing somebody, and I'm sure Jay helped make that happen, but I was really pleased. Even if you don't love your teammate, having somebody to share notes with sometimes makes a lot of difference in how well you're going to do over time. For starters, NASCAR now limits the amount of testing you can do, so obviously if there's more than one team, there are more notes to share. And even if you and your teammate have different styles, if you pay attention to what they're doing, you can figure out how to adjust what they've learned to what you need to do.

In this case, the teammate was Johnny Benson, a good pal of mine. Johnny and I had worked together for several years on a television show, so we were well beyond the "hi-how-are-ya" stage. There's no question that working together was a plus, even if the results don't support that claim as much as we both would have liked. Once again, we spent too much time flirting with Lady Bad Luck. Just one of too many examples of what I mean was when we were running in the front pack at Daytona in 2001. We did nothing wrong, but still ended up being involved in Earnhardt's crash, the most famous fatal wreck in NASCAR history.

By 2002, we recognized that changes were coming. The M&M peo-

It's Daytona and everybody's excited. Well, not everbody. My son Sheldon's nap seems to indicate that he wasn't overly impressed. (Mike Adaskaveg photo.)

ple were shopping around, and here's what happened with that deal: They wanted to win.

Hell, every sponsor that comes into racing wants to win. It would be stupid to want anything else. But you can't get on the top two or three teams because their sponsors are very happy and unlikely to move on. So, you come into Cup racing on a single-car team or as a new addition to a multi-car team, and you either wait for an opening at one of the top teams or you hope that the team you're with develops winning ways.

When M&Ms moved the following year, they also upped their involvement by about 50 percent. That's a real common deal, so I took no offense from that. All the sponsors do that all the time—it's just part of way things are.

But here's the economics. A single-car team struggling along might be spending about $12 million a year. Sound like a lot of money? Seems like it to a former pit rat from Lake Hill, too, but the top multi-car teams won't add another car for less than about $15 million, and that car would be able to share expenses with other teams. The very best teams, in terms of money available, are on a "budget" of about $20 million.

You better like close quarters when you hit the big tracks. (Mike Adaskaveg photo.)

The only thing that's really changed over the years is the number of zeroes behind the first number or two. Back in the days of Petty, Allison and Yarborough, top teams ran on a budget of a million dollars or so, as outrageous a figure in 1975 as $20 million seems today. Who knows what it will take in another 25 or 30 years?

A lot of people think the difference between winning teams and the also-rans is a matter of money. It sure doesn't hurt. But think about it: If every driver had *exactly* what he needed, you'd have 43 cars that were *supposed* to win, and you'd have 42 who would have to explain to the car owner and the sponsors afterward why they didn't. And the car owners and the sponsors would be asking, "Why not? Why didn't you win when you had everything you needed?"

It's maybe just as well that some teams spend time playing catch-up.

It's great when you are accompanied at the track by the loveliest lady there, my daughter Dorothy. (Mike Adaskaveg photo.)

JUMPING THE GUN

One of the most difficult things about racing is knowing when to move on. Sometimes, a car owner will make that decision for you, ready or not, but most racers like the illusion of control. And that, folks, is how Silly Season has continually gotten earlier and longer each year.

If you're not familiar with it, "Silly Season" is the period that the rumors of team changes begin and sometimes go completely out of control, but usually have some basis in fact. You can make a phone call to put out some feelers, thinking it's just between you and the person you've called. But in the media-hungry world of NASCAR, the phone lines apparently are tapped, because rare is the call that doesn't result in Internet postings or newspaper articles.

So, if you are giving any thought to changing your circumstances, you better be ready and willing to move quickly, because when the word gets back to your current car owner—*and it will*—you might find yourself with a not-so-gentle shove toward the garage door. I'd rather not experience that, so I've tended to not go looking unless it's really time.

As I said, M&Ms was looking to change, and even though we continue to have a great relationship and they sponsor the biggest night of the year at our short track, we knew that they probably weren't coming back to MB2 for the 2003 season.

I was looking at driving the #43 for the King.

For about 15 minutes.

The problem is that I quit the #36 during that time. I thought we had a deal at Petty Enterprises, but we didn't. It's too bad, because I'm a huge fan of Richard Petty and all he did to make racing what it became. I'm also a close friend of Kyle Petty's. Kyle runs the Petty operations these days in addition to driving one of the cars, and I can't help feeling we would have had a great time together, but sometimes things just don't work out the way you plan. However, keep in mind that Kyle felt really bad when our plans fell through. This will end up being important to me.

It got to be Christmas 2002, and we were having a party at Schrader Racing shops. Everyone was having a really good time—but that's when it hit me that everybody in the room had a job except for one person.

And that person was me.

Then it wasn't so funny.

I've said before that the difference for me between racing the Cup series and racing short tracks is just a matter of adding or subtracting zeroes in the budget. I don't try any harder at one race than another. I mean, there are races that mean something special and you'd really like to add that win on your resume, but frankly, they all matter to me. If there's a race, I want to run it, and I want to win it. So, running something other than Cup is fine with me.

But I want to do it on my terms.

One of our M&Ms cars is on display at the North Carolina shop. (Joyce Standridge photo.)

And I wasn't ready yet to give up on Cup racing. So it was time to do something about it if I wanted to race in the Cup during 2003. It was time to return the telephone call from BAM.

EMERIL'S NOT THE ONLY "BAM" AROUND

Some girls are thrilled to get diamonds for Christmas. Beth Ann Morganthau got a race team, which pleased her no end. I mean, Beth Ann is one of the original gear-heads, and I say that with complete affection. When she was a kid, she would get on her bicycle and ride down to the paved track at Hialeah, Florida, to watch the races. Now, how many gals can you say that about?

On that Christmas a few years ago, she opened a package that had a little racing scene. "That's cute," she said. "But what's it about?"

"Those are the toys," husband Tony told her. "The real ones are in Charlotte."

Pretty cool angle for a photo that shows how intense it is when you're inside the race car. (Autostock Images.)

Unfortunately, this happened to us too often when we were in the BAM car—wrecks that were no one's fault. When a right front tire goes, your ability to be competitive gets beat right through the fender. (Mike Adaskaveg photo.)

When I needed a friend at Daytona so I could make the race, Kyle Petty stepped up and made a difference by keeping a whole pack of cars behind me. (Mike Adaskaveg photo.)

They started out with a couple of cars, a rented shop and a shot at running ARCA. They did it for a year or so, and then moved up to Cup racing. Consider that even as sponsorship has grown for the team, they are still paying a lot of bills—like a few million—out of their own pockets. Welcome to Nextel Cup racing.

They had established themselves as a race team by the time I came on board, but only just. And they had AT&T as sponsors for about ten-to-twelve races that year. I really liked the shop they had, though, and it appeared we had the tools we needed to get rolling.

Except provisional starts.

You may recall this issue being raised when I started out driving for Andy. Doesn't matter how much experience you have as a driver or how well you ran the season before. Those provisional starts are all based off the car owner's performance the previous year.

So, we went to Daytona needing a really good finish in the Twin 125 if we were going to run the 500 at all. That meant at least 15th place.

Well, before the 125, Kyle Petty told me that he would help me any way he could. And, boy, he did, or we would have had to load up and go home on Thursday afternoon, instead of following the 500 on Sunday.

Toward the end of the 125, I was running all by myself in 15th. Now, if you know anything at all about Daytona and the whole restrictor plate racing deal, you know that running alone on the track at speed has about the same sense of security as a rabbit headed across the desert floor. He's going as fast as he can, but the turkey vultures are circling on wind drafts, and that means it's just a matter of time.

Kyle was 16th and leading a pack that was closing on me about two seconds a lap. Didn't take a math genius to figure out that before the end, Kyle was going to start another row forward, and I was going on the trailer for home.

But when the checkered flag fell, that pack still hadn't caught me, even though there were cars in the group that needed the finish, too.

Because the same parent company owns Schwan's and Red Baron Pizza, we got to run the special paint job a few times, and it was a bit of nostalgia for long-time fans as well as our team because Red Baron was one of our first major sponsors in NASCAR. (Autostock Images.)

Kyle got us in that race. I'm not really sure how he did it—maybe got really wide, because you can do that at Daytona as long as you don't have to do it for too long or hold back too many—but he did it.

How's that for friendship?

We needed friends while we were in the BAM #49 as we faced the on-going struggles of a single-car team. Still, we usually had a good time, and it's good to know that they've been able to stay in the sport even as I moved away to another opportunity.

I'LL FLY AWAY

It's been interesting to watch racing at every level change so much over the years, but to see how we've become a real road show as opposed to just a regional series is pretty amazing. It's altered how we approach racing in so many ways that we could make a huge laundry list of changes.

However, nothing has changed more than how we get around the country for the many responsibilities we have. When I first came to Cup racing in the mid-1980s, only a handful of drivers had their own airplanes, and those were slow and small. Over time that got better as surely as the race cars themselves.

I decided I wanted to learn to fly.

Bobby Allison could fly his own planes, Rusty was flying, and there were others deciding that they wanted to, so I figured it wasn't rocket science even if it involved getting off the ground.

I started out by getting a plane. I needed to get somewhere in a hurry after a race at Richmond, so when a guy offered to sell me a plane, spur of the moment, I bought it.

Of course, I couldn't just jump in it and go. Wasn't like going from a motorcycle to a car had been when I was a kid. Car had more gauges and dials than the motorcycle but the principle was the same—keep it between the lines.

There ain't no lines in the sky.

I'm looking down the flightline in front of the Concord Airport hangar that we co-own with Rusty Wallace. (Joyce Standridge photo.)

Harry Gant put me in touch with Earl the Pilot. Started out that Earl Blanton was going to give me lessons so I could pilot my own plane. But after a while, it became real clear that it wasn't going to happen. Earl starts bugging me that he's got a good job offer so he needs to finish up this business of teaching me. We might have made it but I had this habit of falling asleep at the wheel.

See, the thing is my life is a little bit hectic. So, when I get a few minutes where I don't have to do something, or I get bored, I have a tendency to catch a quick nap. Mostly, it's not a problem, but at 10,000 feet in the air—well, let's just say that Earl had to grab the controls a time or two.

Eventually, we reached a point where we had to make a decision about this whole deal. Either I had to put everything else on a back burner, knuckle down and get my license, or just hire a pilot to get us around.

For those who wonder how in the world I could fall asleep at the wheel of an airplane, this may show how I trained. This quick nap in the Seymour Silver Crown car was real refreshing and I went on to win the race. There were no trophies for napping in the plane, tho'. (Steve Koletar photo; Ken Schrader Collection.)

Earl Blanton, Schrader Racing pilot: Kenny would be sitting in the left seat—that's where the student pilot sits—and I'd be in the right seat. He'd be flying along and the next thing I knew, he's sound asleep.

Well, I'd just reach up and grab the controls and fly along. He'd sleep 15-20 minutes and then he would wake up and say, "I got it."

I thought, you know, this isn't going to work. It's not because he didn't have the ability. He had plenty of ability. He would have made a fine pilot but he didn't have the time to put in the effort it required. The worst of it was that he would have to sit down and study to take a written test as part of getting the license.

Did he mention that he isn't really into school work?

Earl Blanton, a.k.a. Earl the Pilot. We adopted him years ago so nobody else could have the fun—and thrills— we've had. (Joyce Standridge photo.)

Well, I looked over in the other seat and there was this perfectly qualified commercial pilot. Better yet, he was equipped with a wicked sense of humor that suited my family, friends and me. *What the heck?*

This is the guy who has taken us through more than one occluded front—whatever that is. I can recall a really bumpy flight when one of my friends asked Earl, "Do you think we're gonna get down?"

And without missing a beat, he replied, "Yup."

His confidence started to spread to the rest of us. Then he added, "Never known one of these things to not come back down—one way or another."

When we thought about it, we couldn't argue with the logic.

Another time, bad weather sent us in the direction of a different airport than the one we headed for originally. But when we got close to that one, the weather had beaten us there, so we were diverted yet again. When the third airport sent us on to yet another one, I asked Earl, "Do you think we'll land at the next one?"

"Yup."

I'd sort of learned about his one-word answers by now. "What makes you so sure?"

"Because by then we'll be out of fuel."

Some of the race tracks we go to are not exactly big city. If you've never heard of Rossburg, Ohio, don't look for it on most maps, even though it's home to Eldora Speedway, about as famous as short tracks in America get. Same with places like Winchester, Indiana; Knoxville, Iowa, and Fonda, New York.

So when one of these trips resulted in coming down onto a landing strip literally in the middle of a cornfield, we weren't all that surprised. We got off the plane and looked around.

Tim Crist: Our little group consists of Tom The Lawyer, Walter The Tile Man and me, but it always expands to include anybody else brave enough to come along. Only requirement is that you have to revert to irresponsible childhood until you come home. Schrader considers this one of his charitable deals: he takes otherwise responsible adults and lets us misbehave for a few days. Who knows what we would do if we didn't go racing with him? I mean, we had all this repressed stuff inside before we met him.

We fly, we race, we party, repeat, repeat, repeat.

On the way home after the first time we did a road trip, Tom said, "Schrader, when you told us we were gonna race all these races, do all that other stuff, and live to tell it, I figured no way. But it's just amazing what you can do when you give up eating and sleeping."

On one of our jaunts, we bought a mini-stock ride for Tom the Lawyer. He was 60 years old and had never raced before. On the cell phone he promised his wife he would just toodle around the back, but when the green flag fell, he drove right through over half the field. She never knew—until now. But we like a raciness in a lawyer. (Joyce Standridge photo.)

Corn on all four sides.

A light pole.

A dirt road that led to a paved road.

Well, that last one was promising. We trooped over to the paved road figuring civilization might be in that direction. No hangars, no reception area, in fact no nothing but rows and rows and rows of corn. Guess we wouldn't starve.

We're standing alongside the road when a farmer in a pick-up truck came along. We flagged him down and asked if he knew where the race track was.

"Yup."

Where have we heard that before?

"Could you give us a ride over there?"

"Yup."

He got beyond one-word answers as he told us that he'd seen us coming in for the landing, and thought he better drive over to see what was going on because they didn't get many airplanes coming in here.

Gee. That didn't sound promising.

Well, when we got to the track, I gave him $50. I didn't know until later when we compared notes that so had my friend Tim.

As had Tom.

And Walter.

And just about everybody else in our group. I'm guessing the farmer went back home with about $500 more than he started out with.

And I'll bet he's still sitting in the front yard watching for us to come back again.

The point of that little story, in addition to the gullibility factor, was that Earl Blanton sometimes takes us into places that not just any pilot would be thrilled to go into. And, so far at least, he's gotten us there safely every time. We like reliability in race cars, but we really appreciate it in a pilot. Earl's been with us for about 18 years now, working on that 20-year pin we keep promising.

Don't tell him it doesn't exist.

This poster is signed by all the drivers on it, including the late Alan Kulwicki. At an auction, Rusty and I were bidding against another guy for it and figured out that if we teamed up we could outbid him. But then we had to have someplace to hang it that both of us could enjoy. So we bought a hangar. And it's the first thing you see when you walk into the lounge. (Joyce Standridge photo.)

In the conference room at our hangar, there are large framed photos of Rusty and me. In between, in a large window that looks out onto the hangar floor, you can see one of my planes. (Joyce Standridge photo.)

Above: The lounge inside our hangar is very comfortable whenever we're forced to wait for take-off. Right: I can also go in my office. Sometimes I drive out here just to get away from all the craziness and spend a little quiet time getting things done. (Joyce Standridge photos.)

Part Two

People Who Don't Wear Helmets— And a Few Who Do

Jim Compton photo; Ken Schrader Collection

The Motorcycle's Stuck in the Creek

9

I WAS NOT HATCHED under a helmet as has been rumored. I think my interest in racing might have begun around potty-training days, but I'm not sure because it was earlier than I can actually recall.

But there is more to my life than just racing. My family is extremely important, my friends are *like* family, and my hometown is very much a part of who I am. None of what happened on the track would have happened without the earlier—and continuing—influences of other people.

VALLEY PARK

There are people foolish enough to call Missouri "fly-over country." Of course, part of the reason it's a great place is because those uppitty snobs stay away and we don't have to put up with them. But if you have a choice of where to be born and raised, you could do a lot worse than spend time on the streets where I grew up. It was a little too blue-collar to be a Norman Rockwell painting, but in our own way it was just exactly right for me. I don't know that Mom ever locked the doors, although I suspect she was tempted when Dad came home from the shop after the beer flowed a little too freely. But she didn't, so there were no huge fights between them. I think she just sighed a lot.

We lived in Valley Park, a suburb of St. Louis, Missouri. I know the race track announcers say I'm from Fenton, another southside 'burb, but that's the last place I lived before heading to NASCAR country. Most of the kid years were spent in Valley Park on a street that could have been indistinguishable from all the rest—except for the race track.

That's right, I grew up on the coolest street possible. The same road you had to take to get to Lake Hill Speedway.

One time Mom and Daddy decided that we were going to move away. They had picked out the house and it was definitely nicer than the one we lived in. You could go to school and kind of brag about it,

The St. Louis Arch is recognizable the world over. The other photo shows downtown St. Louis as it appears from the windows in the Arch. (Joyce Standridge photos.)

Kenny on being from St. Louis: In my childhood, St. Louis was a brewery town. Still is, come to think of it. They make a lot of dog food there, too, and other useful things because we're nothing if not down-to-earth. Sometimes the city fathers apologize for it being a working-class town, but they really ought to be bragging it up, in my opinion. People work hard there, come home tired with honest sweat, and pop the top on a cold one. I don't see any reason to say you're sorry for that.

You can't live in "The Lou," as some locals call it, and be a wimp. Besides being a hard-working town, it has the worst weather in the country. And we're darn proud of that.

It's as cold and windy as North Dakota in the winter, hot and humid as Alabama in the summer. In fact, all the old sections—and many of the new—were built with Mississippi River-mud brick, which turns a city rimmed by hills and bluffs into a virtual oven in July and August. Before air conditioning was widespread, a lot of people slept out in the open at the huge central-city park. Of course, if you tried to do that now the cops would hope some identification was left with your body, but I guess that would be the case in any city.

I tell you this by way of explaining how St. Louis hasn't really changed a lot. There are some very classy suburbs, but most of the 'burbs look a lot like the city because people just moved out away from the summer heat. The houses don't sit on top of each other like in the city, and there are a lot of shade trees, but without roadside signs you'd have a lot of trouble telling when you ran out of St. Louis and into the 'burbs. That's cool with most residents because for an urban area, St. Louis has a small-town feel to it. And we'll hold on to that, thank you very much.

My sister Sherry and me. We had to borrow a dog from our neighbors, the Kettlers, for this photo since we didn't have one. But as far as Bud and Dorothy were concerned, we were their kids, too. (Ken Schrader Collection.)

Daddy is the proud papa. Trouble is, we can't remember whether the baby he's holding is Sherry or me, but he was so happy when each of us was born that it didn't really matter. In the other photo, however, we are sure that it's me, just over three months old. I'm the cuddly looking one. (Ken Schrader Collection.)

in fact. But my folks told us kids that we'd have to tighten the financial belt a bit. Bigger, nicer house meant bigger, not-so-nice mortgage.

We wouldn't have so many "toys."

No more new motorcycles and stuff.

What do you mean, no more new toys??? we screeched.

Bigger, not-so-nice mortgage, they reminded us.

Well, heck with that! Let's stay where we are, we told them, and we did. And the toys kept coming, you'll be relieved to know. We sure were.

Daddy had his shop on the street there, too, and it was my favorite place in the whole world. Even better than the race track, and that's saying something. Didn't even need a tow trailer because you'd just fire up the race car, look both ways and goose it the eighth-of-a-mile to the pit gate. And nobody ever called the cops on us either!

This is the only photo I have of my favorite childhood hang-out—my daddy's garage in Valley Park, Missouri. But I can close my eyes and see it just as clear as if it was yesterday. Because we lived on the same road as our race track, we didn't have to buy a trailer to tow the race car. I just climbed in my Sportsman car while Daddy or one of our friends pushed me down to Lake Hill Speedway. (Ken Schrader Collection.]

THE PEOPLE WHO WHUMPED MY BUTT WHEN I NEEDED IT

My daddy might have been the greatest of my early influences. Certainly, he was a man who made impressions wherever he went and we all adored him. My mother continues to this day to be a gentle power in my life, and I feel blessed to have a sister, as well as a half-brother from Daddy's first marriage, both of whom make my life better.

Kenny on his father: Bill Schrader, Sr., was close to 40 years old when I was born, so he had lived a whole other life before we came along.

I know it's natural for people who've got a good relationship with their parents to kind of play them up, ignore their flaws and sort of clean up the details. Well, my dad was a good man who doesn't need any apologies offered for him. He was a product of the Midwestern work ethic and culture, which pretty much consists of working until you could drop and then either finding a second job or taking up a hobby that makes you sweat some more. His generation sure didn't sit around the swimming pool contemplating their navels.

I'm not sure how much education Daddy had, but in The Lou if you could learn to read instructions and do enough math to be sure you didn't get cheated on your pay stub, you made up for education deficiencies with a strong back and a stubborn determination to make life better for your kids. He sure did that for us.

As a young man, Daddy married and had a son, my half-brother Bill, Jr., and I'll tell you more about him in a minute. Daddy's wife died of tuberculosis while she was still a young woman, and I can't imagine how hard it was for him and Billy.

Daddy wasn't a real reflective person, so I don't suppose he spent a lot of time sitting around feeling sorry for himself. I expect he just went back to work even harder than before. In fact, he started racing to pay the hospital bills. You can figure out pretty fast what kind of race car driver he was by the fact that he paid off all those bills. Probably it says something about the changing cost of medical care, too. I can't imagine somebody doing that today.

It didn't take long for Daddy to be as big a star at the race track as he was anywhere he went in his life.

My father, Bill Schrader. Doesn't he look like Clark Gable in the movie "To Please A Lady"? He continued to go to the races all his life. In 1990, we captured him relaxing during practice at Charlotte. Within another four years, he was gone. (Top: Ken Schrader Collection; bottom: Mark B. Sluder, Charlotte Observer photo; Ken Schrader Collection.)

A happy time in my mother's life, sharing some fun with Daddy, Ann and me. (Ken Schrader Collection.)

Kenny on his mother: My mom is still one of the most attractive women in the world, but I figure that when she was young she was a dazzler. In spite of that, June didn't marry young. She was a career girl before very many women did that, but I think part of it was because she was the oldest of ten children and she ended up helping raise the younger ones. As well as all the brothers and sisters, she had lots of cousins—including one who was married to Bill Schrader.

Mom started out doing filing for a real estate company. Within a few years, though, she went to work for the telephone company, staying there even after she married. When you hear her voice you can understand why she was so successful as a chief operator in the days when you could dial "o" and talk to a live person who was neither surly nor insulted that you needed help with your call.

The hours were long and irregular, and there was no such thing as a day care center. So after about 20 years with the phone company, she left to take care of my sister and me, having married Daddy and started their own family. Besides, she wanted to be more hands-on, and—okay, I'll say it—Sherry and I needed it. I'm thinking she probably wanted to keep an eye on us because we occasionally pushed the envelope, as they say.

Mom was no soft touch, but the limits she placed on us were always reasonable. For example, after we got a little older, if she left the house for a little while, Mom expected us to stay right there in the house or at least in the yard.

Did I mention we pushed the envelope?

One time I decided to go motorcycle riding with a friend who was older, and I figured Mom would be okay with it. I just didn't bother to wait for her to come home, yet I suppose it reveals something that I left her a note so she wouldn't worry—too much.

We went down to a creek not far from the house. There was a pretty good bank on it and it was a blast to fire up the bike, tear down the bank and across the creek. You'd get a huge spray that looked cool. This time, however, I didn't make it across the creek. In fact, I hit one hell of a mud bog and came to an immediate stop right in the middle. I was so stuck that I could literally get off the bike, walk around it and try to figure out how we were going to get out.

The photo has darkened with age, but then so has the tale about how I stuck the motorcycle in the creek. (Ken Schrader Collection.)

I'll add that I didn't go home and ask Mom for help. She had always told me to stick around home, and on my first venture of testing the limit I found myself up the creek without a paddle—literally—and water running through the spokes. We finally got it out and didn't try that trick again—for a while.

I guess it tells you a lot about my Mom that I could 'fess up to the whole episode and she didn't ground me or yell at me. My folks were pals as much as parents. I mean, it was neat to go to school and thump your chest because your dad was a race car driver—not that very many people were impressed in those days. All the same, in a world full of working stiffs, my dad was special and I knew it. My mom, too.

They were both people who were warm and friendly to others, maybe in part because they had jobs where they worked with people and had to be easy-going to some extent, but the friendly exteriors were covers for very strong personalities. I don't think they were going to let life get them down or keep them from doing what they wanted, and that's been the real legacy to their kids.

But my family doesn't stop there. Living next door was my second family.

With both of my folks working when Sherry and I were little, Mom didn't have to look far to find help through the neighbors. Mrs. Crocetti was an elderly woman who had lost a leg to diabetes, but in spite of limited mobility she was really good at looking after us. She and her husband lived with their daughter and son-in-law, Bud and Dorothy Kettler in a household with no children. They treated Sherry and me like the kids they didn't have, and we ate it up! From about age six, I began spending one or two nights a week over there until I was 16 and need-

My second mom, Dorothy Kettler, in May 2005 during one of her regular visits to us in North Carolina. Unfortunately, I don't have any pictures of her husband Bud, except in my mind. He took me to Cub Scouts and sat me behind a steering wheel for the first time. I can't describe how important they've been in my life. (Ken Schrader Collection.)

ed a keeper instead of a babysitter. Sherry was over there as much as I was, and it took a long time for us to realize that not everybody has two sets of parents.

Mom and Daddy worked as hard any two people I've ever known and I have the utmost respect for them, but it was a fact that there were only so many hours in a day and time was sometimes precious. With all the demands in their lives, my folks appreciated that the Kettlers and Mrs. Crocetti were willing to spend so much time with us kids. All those normal kid activities we might otherwise have missed out on, the Kettlers were there for us. It was Bud who took me to Cub Scouts and the Pinewood Derby. My very earliest memory of driving a passenger car, I was sitting on Bud's lap turning the steering wheel while he ran the pedals.

Kenny on his sister: My sister Sherry is less than two years younger than I am and she has always been one of my favorite people. She's hell on husbands, but fantastic with brothers.

I'm just kidding. At least I'd better be because I think she could still beat the tar out of me if she took a mind to. But when she married Pat Walsh a few years ago, the family sat her down and told her, "Look, we've known Pat as long as we've known you and we're all on Pat's side."

She had to be pretty tough to put up with all the abuse I gave her. Just sibling rivalry stuff, but that happens when you're the older one and you've got somebody trying to tag along. Whatever I did as a kid, Sherry wanted to do it, too. She played with the motorcycles and went to the races, which is how she met Pat, who was a really good late model driver in his day. Pat's boy Joey works for me these days in my dirt-track shop, keeping several race cars ready to go whenever my schedule allows me to run them.

We're all really close and we look out for each other. But I'm really proud of Sherry because of the way she looks after Mom. When we were kids, Daddy wasn't around a lot because of work and racing. That's how it's been for me, too, although I'm always looking for time I can carve out for family and old friends and really happy when it happens. But Sherry's there in the St. Louis area and she spends a lot of time with Mom.

After Daddy died in 1994, it was really hard on Mom but in time she met and married Bill Cox. He pampers Mom and makes her life as good as he possibly can. I respect the fact that he puts Mom's interests ahead of his own—or mine. He doesn't hesitate to remind me of my duties as off-spring. He putters around our shop, takes Mom to see me race and makes sure she's happy.

Mom's been sick for a while now—an age-related thing. She's still fun to be around, and I admire the way Bill's been so good to her and how well Sherry's handled it. She's calm and patient. She tells Mom we'll get through this, and you end up believing her. Makes me really glad Mom and Daddy had her so she could be the glue that holds us together, even if I can't remember feeling quite that charitable toward her when we were kids.

You can see that even when we were kids I got to be the (pretend) race driver and Sherry was the (pretend) fan. Years later, when she got married, Daddy, Mom and I posed with her. (Ken Schrader Collection.)

I want to emphasize that Sherry and I never felt ignored or unloved where our folks were concerned. As I said, we thought having two families was a normal thing, and as we grew older we realized that in fact we were incredibly lucky. And Mom and Daddy never "dumped" us on the neighbors. On the contrary, they were really close friends, too. They were only sharing us with Bud and Dorothy.

Think I'm kidding? Well, you remember how Sherry and I wouldn't let Mom and Daddy move us to a nicer house? A few years later Daddy bought a house that was five or six miles away. This time, voting was suspended. He came home and said, "Oh yeah, hey, I bought a house and we're moving."

Mom ran out of the house crying. She went straight to Dorothy and told her what had happened. A little later Bud came home from work and found them clutching each other, still in tears. "What's wrong?" he wanted to know.

Between sobs they explained.

So Bud went out and bought the house next door to the house where we were moving. Problem solved.

Too many years ago, Bud passed away and there's a hole in my heart these days—pretty large one—where my two daddies used to live. Most kids would be happy to have one good father. I had two.

Dorothy is still an important part of our lives. Even in advancing years, she comes to North Carolina and spends a few weeks a year with us. When my kids were young, we'd send the plane for her and she babysat to the delight of the kids, too. Most people would be happy to have one good mother. I had three, if you counted sweet, old Mrs. Crocetti.

Kenny on his brother: There was a time when my half-brother and I didn't see eye-to-eye. It wasn't anybody's fault, and maybe Daddy could have helped the situation some, but I just don't think he knew how to mend things. Time took care of that eventually, thank goodness.

I understand—and understood at the time—why Bill, Jr., and I didn't have a good relationship, but I sure didn't know how to change that. You only have to look at how Billy's life went for a while. I guess I wouldn't have felt much differently if the roles had been reversed.

Billy is 18 years older than I am. His mother died when he was still pretty young. Today, single fathers seem to just pick up and go on to raise their kids, but in the late 1940s and early 1950s, it was a different world. Daddy did what any widowed father did at the time. He took Billy to his grandmother's while Daddy worked long, hard days. Then went racing, at least in part to pay his late wife's medical bills. It didn't leave much time for a kid.

I don't want to put Daddy in any kind of an unfavorable light because I thought he was the greatest, but I guess maybe he let Billy down a few times, too. In later years, Billy told me about a time when he was just a kid and Daddy was going to come pick him up. Billy sat on the porch until nine o'clock or so, when he finally realized that Daddy either forgot or something came up. I don't think that was the only time. Since Daddy was such a strong person and so popular with the racing crowd, you can understand why it was important to Billy to have some of Daddy's attention—and how it must have hurt when he didn't.

We have a really good friend, Warren Gallaher, who got drunk one night back in the '60s and joined the Marines. He sobered up the next day and realized what he'd done, so he got Billy drunk and talked him into joining the Marines too.

Great friend, huh? Well, actually he was, and still is. But as a result of that, I never met my brother until I was five years old and he came back home. Then Billy got married, had three kids and lived in California for a long time.

When I was 16, his family moved back to Valley Park, but imagine how he felt then. When he was 16, he was an orphan living with Grandma and Grandpa, grasping for straws where Daddy was concerned and looking at a future that was up to him to build. He comes back from California years later, saddled with the responsibility of his own family, and he sees this teenager who's got it all, at least all that Billy had ever wanted and didn't get. He resented the hell out of me, and I still don't blame him. I only wish we could have gotten back those years somehow. The eventual improvement in our relationship was thanks to a battery thief.

I was coming home from the races and saw some guy stealing a battery out of a car at the shop, which—by that time—Billy had bought from Daddy. I chased that thief for miles, but a truck and race-car trailer aren't the ideal tools for a car chase. I finally gave up and called Billy.

"Hey, some S.O.B. was stealing a battery at the shop," I told him.

This is the middle of the night and he mumbled something like, "Oh, okay."

Well, I figured, *if you don't care, bro', I don't care*. But ten minutes later, he showed up at the shop, and between us we were plenty pissed about that battery. Ours wasn't the kind of neighborhood where people stole from each other.

It's funny, but that shared anger focused on somebody else opened a gate for us that all the efforts of our folks and everybody else had never been able to do. Billy took me to a bar in town and we ended up talking all night long. Didn't matter I was under-aged. At that point, we weren't splitting hairs. We'd

When I married Ann, my half-brother Billy came to the ceremony. We hadn't always been close but by the time this was taken in 1984 there was nobody in the world I'd rather spend time with. (Ken Schrader Collection.)

finally found some common ground and there's nothing like some heart-felt, long-term heartaches shared over a cold beer to fix a relationship. You'd think the politicians of this world would figure that out.

It's been a solid relationship ever since. Billy's son Eddie bought the shop in later years. They've done Daddy and all of us proud with the way they've kept it an honest business that cares about the customer and the neighborhood. My nephew is almost as old as I am, so it was a natural for him to go racing with me a lot when I was starting out around St. Louis. We still go as much as we can.

My brother Bill served in the Marines so it wasn't a huge surprise when his son Eddie (pictured) went military, too. Eddie now runs the shop he bought from his dad, who had bought it from our dad. All in the family. (Ken Schrader Collection.)

On my wedding day, my sister Sherry and brother Billy came to lend support— and warn Ann. (Ken Schrader Collection)

The Bird Bath Never Had a Chance 10

S HERRY AND I DIDN'T GET TO GO to the races when we were really little. Mom said it was because they stayed out too late and it wasn't fair to us to lose that sleep. I think it was because they stayed out too late and didn't want to have to take sleepy babies home instead of enjoying good times with their friends.

Well, I don't blame them. I grew up to enjoy the after-race socializing as much as anybody. Another legacy from Mom and Daddy.

But the racing influence was always there anyway. When I was still not much more than a toddler, my folks fixed up a little go-kart for me and tethered it to a pole in the yard. The steering wheel wasn't workable, but the kart had an accelerator. I'd race around in circles for hours, making my own racing noises until it ran out of gas. And then they'd put more gas in it, and we repeated the deal enough times to wear *them* out.

One day, my mom was sunbathing while I was driving my little kart. All of a sudden, she heard a change in my noise and she knew something was up.

Something was up, all right.

The tether had broken and I was headed across the yard. Remember, it didn't have any real steering. The wheel was just there for something to hold on to. And what did I know about brakes?

I stayed on the gas, with my mom running behind me, all the way across the lawn, until I crashed into the concrete birdbath.

I was having a riot.

My folks looked pretty concerned.

But the bird bath survived, the kart was fixed, and Mom sunbathed with one eye on me after that.

Even people who aren't fans have heard the story about my folks tethering a go-kart in the backyard when I was three and I would race until the gas ran out. This is it. You can just see the tether in the lower left, but the soon-to-be-clobbered bird bath isn't in this shot. (Ken Schrader Collection.)

GETTING READY TO GO RACING

We weren't supposed to go to the race track with Mom and Daddy until we got into first grade, but I weaseled my way in by the time I was in kindergarten. Anybody who's gone short-track racing and watched the racers afterwards has seen a kid just like I was. The other racers' children and I would run around the track on foot like we were racing. We'd play in the dirt while our folks bench-raced and had a few beers. They could totally ignore us because they knew we were safe. Nobody was going to snatch us even if they'd wanted to, and it was just the kind of unique family atmosphere that's become increasingly rare over the years.

For a long time people coming in the back door at our house had to step over the circular braided rug where I had all my little toy race cars lined up. Mom never made me pick them up, so you had to watch your step. I don't think I ever expected to one day have my own race track, but it was a whole lot easier manipulating those little cars. Plus, my favorites always won those races. And that leads me to telling you about some more favoritism.

The starter's wife made me a complete set of flags when I was in grade school. Since we lived on the road to the race track, I would wait outside and flag the racers as they came by. I knew them all and recog-

It doesn't take long to get through the downtown area of St. Louis and into the neighborhoods. My family has been in the area for nearly 100 years now. (Joyce Standridge photo.)

June Cox: Kenny never forgot his roots. I think that's why he's remained so popular. His dad used to tell him, "Ken, you'll do fine. I know you're going to do fine, but there's two things that I want you to remember: be kind to old women and little babies, and don't forget where you came from."

Well, Kenny was really impressed and later he asked Bill, "Who told you that?"

And Bill said, "My dad told me that."

It was a great story. Turns out, according to Kenny's grandmother, that Bill's dad hadn't said it. But it was really good of Bill to give the credit to his father instead of taking it himself. I thought Bill was a great man, and I think Kenny has turned out to be a lot like him.

Bill's family has been in the St. Louis area for a long time. They came from Germany and the family name was "von Schroeder." But it was around World War I, and it wasn't popular to have that name or "von"-anything, for that matter. So, the family dropped the first part and changed the spelling to the phonetic Schrader.

My background is English and Irish, going back a long way, too. There were a lot of us, and almost all of them thought it was great when Kenny got into racing. They'd seen what he could do on a motorcycle and a go-kart. A lot of them watched him grow as a driver and they're proud of his accomplishments.

I think most of the people who knew Kenny when he was little right on up to now would say he's a really great guy, but just wish he would have had a little more luck. I've never heard anybody say anything negative, which is probably a good thing, because I would have blown their heads off if they did.

nized their tow trucks. I'd give the green or checkered flag for the ones I liked, and the red flag for the ones I didn't.

My earliest hero, besides my Dad, was Bob Mueller. This was in the days of coupes and real stock cars. He was a big star at Lake Hill Speedway, our home track. He raced with Daddy there and at other area tracks like Belle-Clair Speedway and St. Charles Speedway, and eventually I got to drive for him. Wib Spaulding was another of the stars then, and throughout the years, I've also been a huge, huge fan of Don Klein.

Don's almost 70 years old now, and still racing. Won something over 500 races. He's great with the fans and his fellow competitors, and he's always known how to have a good time. When I got old enough to race, Don was one of the people who taught me how to have fun.

I wouldn't call it corrupting a young kid. I think I pretty much knew the drill anyway, but it was nice to have him take me under his wing, so to speak, and make sure I understood that you'd better be looking for the fun in it. It's why we all got started. Anybody who gets into it to get rich and famous is probably going to end up bitter and heart-

Don Klein: Most people who know him today would be surprised to know that he was a bit of a stick in the mud when he was a kid. He was so focused on racing that he didn't know how to relax and kick back.

But we taught him. Right outside the race track gate in the parking lot. And he was a good student. Didn't take long at all. Might have been in the genes—his dad Bill was a great partier. But Kenny figured out real fast that no matter how good a driver you are or how far you take your racing career, there are going to be some rough nights. And if you go to the races with the idea of having a good time, you probably will. You can turn a bad night into an "okay" one if you just have the right attitude.

And, boy, did that lesson ever take!

My dad (left) and I (right) both drove—and won—at some point for Dandy Don Klein. The thing of it was that the guy hardest to beat on the track was Don! He's still racing at nearly 70 years of age. Wanna guess whose tire tracks I want to follow in? (Left: Ken Schrader Collection; right: Ronald M. Poehl photo, Ken Schrader Collection.)

broken. But, if you look for the fun, you'll end up like Don and Blanche Klein, still running down the road and enjoying it as much as anybody in the game.

Don's still competitive, but you know what? It doesn't matter. If you have to make a living from it, then you have to be competitive and be able to win or finish well every night. But if you're racing just because you love it, then it doesn't matter. Race until they can't load you in the car anymore.

I always wanted to *grow up* to be like Don. Now I want to *grow old* and be like Don. But, that's getting ahead of the story.

THE KID GOES RACING

Not surprisingly, our folks got Sherry and me into racing early. I don't remember how old I was, but it was grade school and we got a quarter-midget that we took over to a little pavement track in St. Charles, Missouri. It was strictly a play deal. Mom and Daddy weren't looking to gain reflected glory through what Sherry and I did. We had a good time and I remember it with fondness—except for one thing.

To this day, I cannot blow a bubble with bubble gum. I've never been able to do that. But we'd be at the quarter-midget track and this girl named Linda King would roar by with her ponytail flapping in the wind, blowing a bubble.

Man, it was a traumatic experience. I didn't much care that she had a faster car, but I'm pretty sure she knew I couldn't blow a bubble and was just rubbing it in.

We motorcycle raced, too, and I still love bikes, including the one that embarrassed me so bad in the creek that time when I snuck out of the house. But the focus was always—*always*—on cars. I knew I was

My very, very first competition checkered flag. I was 7 years old (take that, Jeff Gordon) and drove for George Egans. I drove for him again in the big-boy toys. (Red Meyer photo; Ken Schrader Collection.)

going to follow in Daddy's tire tracks, hoped I would be half as good and half as successful, but whatever happened I was going to race as much as I could afford, or as much as other people who owned cars would let me.

First I had to finish growing up, and patience was not my virtue.

THE REAL INFLUENCE

My best friends weren't from school. They were at Daddy's shop and there weren't kids there. It was Daddy's friends, who then became my friends. That's why a lot of my pals even today are so much older than I am. They're still the same bunch who hung out at the shop.

Among many others, the gang included Pat Walsh, who's now my brother-in-law; Warren Gallaher, the former Marine; and my cousin Mike Edwards, who is NASCAR driver Carl Edward's daddy. Spence Bach handed me my helmet the first night I ever drove a race car. Spence works around the Missouri race shop—he did all the interior and finish work there—and at the race track I'm a partner in. I can't imagine life without these guys, and I guess they must have been hard up for friends because they're still hanging out with me.

That was the deal: I came with the shop.

If they wanted Daddy to do all this shit for them, it meant they had to jack with me, and I'm still not sorry that was the shop rule.

Daddy's shop was a masterpiece to me. There was always neat stuff in there because he had a lot of parts around. It was full, but he knew where everything was, and we washed that floor every night. Kept it real neat. That's why I like my shops and haulers cleaned up. Daddy gave me that appreciation.

He educated me on how to be a real mechanic, instead of just a parts-changer, too. I remember when a lady came in with her car's engine knocking really bad and somebody else had told her it was a rod

This was Daddy's tow truck. I managed to track it down and then restored it in our shop. It is on display at our North Carolina facility these days. (Left: Ken Schrader Collection; right: Joyce Standridge photo.)

bearing. She didn't have the money for an overhaul. Well, Daddy listened to it, took the air cleaner off, revved it and kept pouring a glass of water down the carburetor. Finally it quit knocking. It only had a piece of carbon on a piston, and he figured that out.

He also taught me how to read people so you know somebody who's maybe just a little down on his luck as opposed to somebody who's trying to use you. Example: There was a family headed to California. They'd saved forever to make a trip to Disneyland, but their car broke down on a highway near the shop. Got towed in. Daddy worked on the car and before he could finish up, they were spending the night at the house with us. They were going to have to spend their vacation money on the repairs, but he told them to go on and send him the money later. On the way back from California, they stayed with us again and brought little gifts for Sherry and me. When they got back East, they wired the money to Daddy, proving him right.

He always did read people well. He helped out folks who didn't have the cash at hand, and I don't think even one of them ever disproved his trust. I remember one guy who came by and left three dozen eggs in our refrigerator every week. His car ran perfectly, and we never wanted for eggs.

You did things like that in the fifties and sixties.

HARVARD MATERIAL, I WAS NOT

Mom insists I was a good student in school (although not as good as Sherry, she reminds me). If I got good grades it wasn't from effort. Now, I wouldn't encourage any kid to approach school the way I did. Most people who become successful in some measure, including those in racing, put a lot of effort into getting a good education. It can sure help, especially now that racing is such a business. You get a good education and you'll have the confidence to deal with all kinds of people. You'll also probably be able to make sure nobody's taking advantage of you or your money.

But that's not how I got here. My path took me through school with minimal effort and attention. Even if I wasn't enthused about school I did get along with most of my teachers. In fact, my driver's ed teacher used to come watch me race when I was just 16; I don't think it helped my grade, but my ego enjoyed it. And another teacher, who's now retired, has a motor home and used to periodically show up at my races. Makes me glad I didn't burn too many bridges back then.

By the time I got to high school it got to be a real test of patience—for them and for me. Since I wasn't taking any classes I didn't have to, I didn't need study hall, so I worked in the office and got to be friends with the principal and office staff, too. This became really important, as you will see.

Senior year, I got kicked out of math class. I had been getting A's on homework and D's on tests.

I think the teacher figured it out.

I won't tip my hand on who was actually doing the homework, but the final straw was the day I got caught reading a racing magazine in class.

"You're just taking up space," he told me. "You don't want to be here."

So, I just worked in the office some more. Came time to graduate and the principal said, "C'mere. We got a problem. You're a quarter-credit short to graduate."

"Dang. What are we gonna do?" I said, with the emphasis on *we*. Notice I didn't offer to take a summer class or come back the next year. Ain't no way I was coming back after May, and I think he knew it.

"I'll give it some thought," he told me.

Anyway, they finagled and I ended up with a quarter-credit for working in the office. I don't think the fact that the principal moved that year and I loaned him my neat little '67 Chevrolet pick-up that week had anything to do with it.

Well, anyway, I escaped more than graduated, and it probably wasn't a minute too soon.

In addition to being total terrors of the neighborhood, a bunch of us participated in organized motorcycle racing by the time I was in my early teens. Although he's not pictured here, Rusty Wallace was one of the crowd. And when we weren't under organized control, we were tearing up the back roads and tracks. It's a wonder my Mom didn't have an ulcer. (Ken Schrader Collection.)

TWO-SPORT MAN?

While I was chomping at the bit to turn 16 and get on the track, I decided that my life needed rounding out. My life's always been about racing, but I'm not totally ignorant. I know there's a lot of other things going on in the world, and people seem to find a lot of pleasure and satisfaction doing stuff that doesn't have anything to do with racing.

So, I decided to play football.

Well, right off the bat I was late for practice the first day because I couldn't find my pads. I get out to the field and Coach tells me I have to run four laps for being late.

Shoot.

That's a mile, and I got madder and madder with every foot.

Now I'm really pissed, sweat running in my eyes for no good reason that I could figure. Then they turned us loose on the tackle dummies. I hit it like it was the Coach, but proving that football coaches are maybe not the most intuitive people in the world, he announces to the team, *Number Seven really wants to play football!*

Number Seven was me. (Daddy's contemporary and my favorite at the time, Don Workman, had that number at the race track.)

Thing of it was, I woke up the next morning and my neck hurt like heck from hitting the dummy so hard. I got to thinking about what a football injury could do to my racing career and I was just a few months from driving age. So, that morning my football career was over. I turned in the pads and never even went to a game after that.

The only other time our family's attention was focused on something other than racing was during a period that my dad had some heart trouble and had to stop racing for a while. He came home with a small, 48-passenger Dodge school bus and started making a camper out of it. Mom wouldn't even look at the thing. When they were about three-quarters of the way done with it, though, she start getting enthused. Finally, she asked, "Don't they make longer school buses?"

So, we went out and got us one and built a trick bus. It had all the motor home stuff in it and ended up really nice. During that time we went camping every week, and had as good a time as you can without a race track.

Even then I knew you needed a race track to have a really good time.

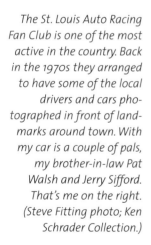

The St. Louis Auto Racing Fan Club is one of the most active in the country. Back in the 1970s they arranged to have some of the local drivers and cars photographed in front of landmarks around town. With my car is a couple of pals, my brother-in-law Pat Walsh and Jerry Sifford. That's me on the right. (Steve Fitting photo; Ken Schrader Collection.)

Are Those the Right Earrings, Honey?

11

RACE CARS WERE NOT THE ONLY THING I came to appreciate as I got older. I guess I had my share of girl friends, but really, with my schedule it was hard to get a serious relationship going. So while I did some dating, I did a lot more racing.

However, I was not destined to be a monk. And there have been two attempts to make a permanent relationship. The first time was a huge wreck, but on the second go-around, I've been able to convince her—so far—that I'm almost worth the trouble.

If you want matrimonial advice, here it is: Don't ask me. That I'm married is due solely to Ann's effort and wisdom.

And I didn't have her effort and wisdom to guide me the first time around.

THE SPIN CYCLE

Back in the mid-1970s there was a cute little blonde bouncing through the midget pits. Man, you'd have to be blind to miss her. The fact that she was tied to some really good racing people was just a bonus.

Debbie Frye's father, Danny, Sr., owned some of the best midget equipment in the Midwest. Her brother Danny, Jr., racked up some pretty good statistics as a midget driver for his dad. In those days, women weren't yet allowed in the pit area until after the races, but then I could usually find an excuse to stop by the Frye cars, and it wasn't just to jaw with Danny, Sr. and Danny, Jr..

It didn't take long before Deb and I were spending a lot of time together—without the guys—and then it got really serious. Let's face it, she wasn't going to be hollering when I headed out the door to go racing. She had grown up around it, loved it, was loved by a lot of people who were involved in it, and it just felt like a good fit. Marriage centered around a shared love of racing just had to work.

I was wrong.

Deb, Mom and me at the races. (Ken Schrader Collection.)

Left: The house in Fenton, Missouri, was a gathering place for our friends. In front of the garage, you can see my former midget car owner Nick Gojmeric and Danny "The Dude" Lasoski. The Dude and his wife went with Ann and me on our honeymoon. (Ken Schrader Collection.)

Right: At one of our parties, the Birthday Fairy showed up, and even though it wasn't my day, he convinced me to get up and dance with him. Can you believe that this photo never made the NASCAR media guide, even though I was a Winston Cup driver by then? (Ken Schrader Collection.)

Having fun after the races is easy. Trying to make the mortgage payment when you're just kids making little more than minimum wage is a whole lot harder. Maybe if we'd been older we could have figured out how to make it work, but it seemed like the little nagging problems before we married ended up growing bigger and bigger.

To prove that we still weren't really adults when we split four years later, I'll tell you just how petty we got. Deb was moving out. It was my house; I'd bought it from Hank Sieveking, and she couldn't have made the mortgage on her own anyway. So, I left the night of the break-up to go over to Ray and Sue Marler's house and work on the race car. I told Deb to back up the truck to the door and take whatever she wanted.

Boy, did she take me literally. I came home later that night to find the house was stripped. I mean, the curtains were off all the windows, and even the shrubs had been dug up out of the front yard.

Somehow, though, her family couldn't fit the washer and dryer in the truck. They were coming back the next day for them.

I threw a fit. I said, "Nope, you had your one trip to take what you wanted, so I get to keep the washer and dryer."

Bear in mind that I have never done a load of laundry in my life. I'm sure I could figure it out, but I just never have. It didn't matter. I wasn't budging, not even for a return of the curtains on the windows.

Fortunately, we both matured a bit along the way. As a couple we were a disaster, but as people we were—and still are—really good friends. I remember camping trips to the DuQuoin, Illinois, fairgrounds that were part of our racing, and her whole family was there. The laughs we had are still with me, and I'm glad the Fryes were a part of my life. They are still today, in fact.

Deb has not remarried, but she has made a success of her life, post-Schrader, I'm very happy to say. She has a great job as head accountant at a swank St. Louis hotel, and she's been able to buy a real nice little place for herself. We still talk fairly regularly and I would do about anything for her. As I said, we were lousy as husband and wife. But as friends, I couldn't ask for a better one.

THE BILL CAME DUE

I was a little gun-shy about serious relationships for a while after Debbie. When it came to women I was skating along the surface in the early 1980s. I was really busy with the racing, too.

At the time, I was driving for the Sievekings and they had several guys who were pitmen for them. One of the guys who came around occasionally and went to the tracks with us also brought along his wife. She had the most striking blue eyes imaginable, although it was her smile and her ability to make everybody around her laugh that really captured attention.

But she was married.

Well, I was at the shop one day when the husband came in and said he might be getting a divorce. That's guy-talk for "she's kicking my ass out."

I knew that Ann had a really great job. She was a nurse, but at the time she was working for a pharmaceutical company. If you aren't aware, pharmaceutical companies tend to pay well and have lots of good benefits. Her husband, on the other hand, wasn't real crazy about working.

Now, I have noted numerous times in the past that I race so hard because I don't want to have to get a real job. It's not that I'm opposed to working. In fact, I put a lot of effort into everything I do, but I just didn't want to punch a time clock. I would have done it right if the circumstances had required it, and maybe I worked even harder at racing than I would have if I'd stayed at Western Auto or gotten on at UPS.

Still, I have nothing but respect for all the people out there who work in the real world. They deserve more credit than I do because when I have a bad day at work, I still get to drive a race car and pop a cold beer afterwards. When they have a bad day, they have to keep from popping the boss in the nose.

Well, about six months after the conversation at Sievekings' garage, I was cleaning out my desk when I came across Ann's business card. I'm holding this card and remembering that this is a really fun girl. And since she's just coming off a divorce, I'm guessing she's probably not wanting anything more than a few laughs, too.

So, I called her. We went out to dinner, and same as was the case in the past, we talked, laughed, and thoroughly enjoyed ourselves.

But nothing clicked. It was no love-at-first-sight. It wasn't even first sight, of course, but the only click was in renewing the friendship. It wasn't like seeing somebody across the room and thinking, "I gotta find out who that is."

For her, too. In fact, she even tried to set me up with her friend Marcy. It seemed that Marcy needed a date for the wedding of a mutual friend, and Ann went so far as to send Marcy with me to buy a suit.

We were getting our picture taken at the Chili Bowl in Tulsa when Ann decided that she really needed to save the world from that ugly ol' trophy girl! (Ken Schrader Collection.)

Marcy didn't take. Not even for a short-term thing. But when I needed a date for a racing banquet that winter, I called Ann, and again we had a good time. A couple of weeks later we met for dinner, and then again another week later. Mostly these were deals where we did stuff with other people along and it was always a riot. But it wasn't fast-forward at all. In fact, all this played out over about eight months or so.

But then—and I can't really put my finger on why—the frequency picked up. We didn't go into a deal thinking that this was going to be a relationship person. We started out as friends helping each other through that bad time following a divorce, when you're wondering what's wrong with you and whether you'll ever even want to get serious again.

I had a house in Fenton with no shrubs—I wasn't quite ready for that commitment either—and she lived in a duplex her parents owned about seven or eight miles up the road toward St. Louis. And that's the way it stayed. There was going to be no living together, because her folks did not subscribe to that kind of stuff at all.

I got questioned occasionally by Ann's mom and I had to tell her that I was coming by at ungodly early hours to pick up Ann for breakfast, and that's why my car was parked out front at 6:30 A.M. I don't think she bought it all the time, but I don't guess I think fast on my feet at 6:30 A.M..

We drifted along like this for quite a while. Couple of years, actually, and then we got into a little discussion about where we were going.

I was going racing.

Ann had different ideas.

Not about the racing. She's always been cool about that, but she had gotten beyond the divorce pain and was starting to think long-term.

I'm hedging about the whole thing—when she presents me with a bill.

Sue Marler: When Kenny and Ann started going out regularly, one of their first dates was to a race in Indiana and we all went in our van, which was brand new.

We stopped at a truck stop on the way back and they got milk shakes. Next thing we knew Kenny and Ann were spitting ice cream from the shakes through straws at each other!

It took me a week to get all the ice cream stains out of the van, but I couldn't get mad about it. They had Ray and me in stitches when it happened, and then there was the matter of seeing Kenny so happy and carefree again.

Ann is as smart as anybody I know and has great business sense, but when it's time to get silly she's as much fun as anybody you'll ever meet. I never saw it, but there is a legend that one time when Kenny fell asleep on a road trip she painted his toenails red —and he didn't notice it until the next day in the shower!

No kidding.

Over the time we'd been dating, she'd sometimes picked up the tab for dinner, or paid for a tank of gas, or paid the phone bill so it didn't get shut off. I hadn't thought much about it at the time. I mean, I'd paid for stuff for both of us, too. But as many, many people have noted over the years, there's nobody smarter than Ann. And she's nobody's fool to be taken advantage of, either, as the $2,500 itemized bill proved. Heck, I've ignored bills from NASCAR, for pete's sake, but I took this one seriously.

It's time for a decision.

I can pay back the bill, but it's worked as far as making me think: What does Ann mean to me? I mean, I know that I love her. We have a lot of fun together, and she's nothing but an asset. I can walk away from this but do I really want to cuddle up to a tail pipe every night? And what is out there in the dating pool these days anyway? There's barracuda out there, for sure.

Some guys need a wake-up call to see things straight. Count me in that group.

Ann and I have joked for years about that bill, but you know what? If I married the girl, I could get the $2500 debt forgiven, and I could get health insurance. She had a great job with benefits, remember. And if you're already in love…

Well, on November 13, 1984—a Tuesday at noon, if you're keeping score—we went to a little church near where she worked, and we got married. I wore the suit Marcy made me buy for that other wedding. Ann actually bought something new to wear—and she looked great, even if we didn't do it up big and fancy.

Ann was president of the Women's Auxiliary of Motorsports (WAM) for several years and she included our short track in fund-raising activities. At the M&M Night of Stars, she organized a duck race. Yup, little rubber duckies.
Next to Ann is Brian Bell, Industry Relations Manager for WAM.
(Joyce Standridge photo.)

Afterwards, we went by her office and my grandparents' home, and then just rode around to see friends and family. That night we went back to my house, and her mom finally didn't ask any questions about what we were up to.

The next day I pulled out of the driveway, taking a midget to California for the Turkey Night Grand Prix at Ascot. Ann flew out later, and we spent our honeymoon sharing expenses with driver Danny Lasoski and his wife. Just the four us. It was wonderful.

When we got back, the phone message from Mr. Donlavey was on the machine, solving our problem of how we were going to scrape together the $125,000 I needed to continue in Elmo Langley's race car.

I think it's worth noting that while a lot of new wives would have been planning on how to get me working more regularly, Ann was totally supportive from the start. And frankly, if I had decided to go on driving a propane truck for the Sievekings instead of racing full-time, she would have been fine with that, too. She let me make the decisions about what was right for me, and she has fitted her life into mine extremely well. That's a big part of why we're still together more than 20 years later.

That, and the fact she's licensed to kill in four states.

Ann and me on our wedding day. (Ken Schrader Collection.)

DID THE CLAMPETTS MOVE LIKE THIS?

As I noted earlier, during the first couple of years that I was in NASCAR, Ann and I went to the races on the weekend and then drove home to St. Louis on Sunday nights. She went to work, which was still real important to keeping our heads above water and the foreclosure notice off the front door, and I messed around with short-track racing to supplement the NASCAR deal. Eventually, though, it became clear that I needed to make the commitment of living in stock-car country if I was going to stick in NASCAR.

We spent a week looking around in the Charlotte-Concord area, and that was when Dale Earnhardt, Sr. helped us find the property we bought. It was great land.

This is our original race shop on Windy Road near Concord, North Carolina. Now there are four large buildings on the acreage. (Joyce Standridge photo)

It was questionable, however, regarding living arrangements.

Bless her heart, Ann agreed to the move, and you gotta give the girl credit. We didn't have anything fancy back in Fenton, but we had four solid walls, curtains again and even some new shrubbery. But this North Carolina property had only an old mobile home on it.

Ann tried. She went to Wal-Mart with a couple of the ladies whose husbands worked for Mr. Donlavey and they spent about $100 on cleaning supplies. After two days, though, Ann came back to the shop and told me the situation was terminal. There wasn't enough Mr. Clean in all of North Carolina to make that dump livable.

That's when Darlene Patterson, our P.R. person at the time, put the foundation in place for our Oakwood Homes relationship. We weren't asking for anything big or fancy, just something clean and free of bug poop.

When we finally left Fenton, it was with a couple of pick-up trucks piled high with our belongings, thanks to our neighbors' help. We went to Bristol to race first, then on to North Carolina. I hoped every time we went around a corner that we still had everything and didn't tip the truck over. All we lacked was Mr. Drysdale and Miss Jane waiting for us in Concord.

Came around the corner, and there was the new, single-wide trailer. Didn't have any electricity or steps, but there it sat.

Actually, when you think about it, we were sort of the Clampetts in reverse. We hadn't hit any oil wells in our part of the Ozarks, and there sure didn't seem to be any likely in North Carolina either, but I gotta say that Ann was an enormous help in putting a happy face on the gamble. She had given up a great job, but it wasn't all that bleak. Norrell Health Care, the home-health service she had been working for the past couple of years after leaving the pharmaceutical company, thought so much of her that they opened a hospice in North Carolina. I should have been so valued by an employer, huh?

Ann is a huge fan of the nursing profession for what it did for her and for us, what it does for people in need, and how well she carved out

In one of our storage buildings we hung race car bodies from the rafters. The light coming through the skylights make them look pretty cool. Also, at the shop on Windy Road the walls were covered with trophies and momentoes. (Joyce Standridge photos.)

her own identity as a nurse. She also worked at Schrader Racing, paying the bills and tending to payroll for quite a while. Even now she is very active, and stays involved in all my business matters, while she has also become a community activist. But mostly she's a fantastic, full-time mother. Considering the amount of time I'm on the road and away from home, our kids are damned lucky to have a mom who's spent so much time raising them and being available for them.

And that brings us to parenting.

WE'RE HAVING A BABY, MY BABY AND ME

We were, by far, the oldest couple in Lamaze class. We weren't successful getting pregnant right away, so by the time Ann was expecting our first baby, we were both over 30. But Ann's a nurse, so we're not going to panic, right?

I was at the shop one night when she called. "I think my water broke."

Oh, hell. I couldn't even think. By this time we were living in a real house in Concord, a few miles away, so I was Ricky Ricardo tearing down a dark back road for home. I think I turned on the headlights at some point.

When I got there, I showered, dressed and was ready to go in like two minutes. In the meantime, Ann is trying on earrings.

What are you doing?

I tried to be calm. I might have screeched, I don't know. It was late and I had no idea of how much time we had between water breaking and delivery. All I knew was that I was not prepared to do the delivery, no matter how easy it looks in the movies. For all I knew, it would be like it was for Will Smith in *Men In Black*, with aliens beating me against the car multiple times.

"If I put little earrings in, they won't make me take them off."

Pause.

Flashes of breathing exercises wasted because we didn't make it in

Ann Schrader: I worked in infectious diseases at St. Louis Children's Hospital, and later I worked in the neo-natal ICU in North Carolina for a while. I worked in pediatrics because I like kids and always wanted them. I have lots of nieces and nephews, so there have always been kids around.

If we weren't in this sport, I would have had five kids, but because we are in racing I figured out that you have two hands and two kids so you can get through an airport.

We had some challenges getting pregnant but once I was expecting Dorothy, I didn't want to tell anybody until we were sure everything was going to be okay. Well, Ken tells mouth of the south, Dale Earnhardt, who then told just about everybody. So we had a lot of interest and support through our pregnancies.

time. *What the hell goes through women's minds at times like these?*

Well, Ann had plenty of time to examine her jewelry collection before heading to the hospital because nothing happened all that night or the next morning. We're well into the following day and I'm trying to help her with the Lamaze stuff.

At no time in all the classes we took did they ever tell you a woman 20 hours into labor is going to become a shrew who will criticize your best efforts to help, and then proceed to tell you exactly what you can do with the equipment that helped create this hell-on-earth creature tearing up her insides and refusing to come out.

So I did what I could do to help her through the contraction.

And when it was done, I leaned over and ever-so-gently whispered, *Did you have the right god-damned earrings for that?*

For some reason, it didn't go over well.

"THERE'S LOTS OF STUFF I CAN TEACH THIS KID"

Some of Ann's testiness might be due to the fact that our daughter weighed 10 pounds, 13 ounces at birth. She was "Catch of the Day," according to the staff.

The kids have enjoyed going racing with Daddy at the short tracks, too. Here, they got to pose in Victory Lane and it's as much fun as it is at the NASCAR tracks. (Al Fortner photo; Ken Schrader Collection.)

We named her Dorothy, not a real common name these days, but she meant an awful lot to Ann and me so it seemed important to name her for people who were already special in our lives. You may recall that my next-door mom was named Dorothy Kettler. Ann also had an aunt Dorothy who was very special to her. And we have a good friend back in the Midwest, Dorothy Allgaier. With her husband, they had built a Hoosier tire dealership from a rented, two-car garage into one of the biggest distributorships in the country, and she has remained until this day one of the sweetest people in racing. If our daughter grows up to be anything like her three namesakes, we are going to be very proud.

After Dorothy's birth, I ran back to the house and put a message on the answering machine announcing her birth—then to the shop and did the same—and finally back to the hospital.

At 7:00 P.M., Ann yawned.

A few minutes later she dozed off.

So much for our New Year's Eve.

So I called and got a driver. Went to every party I knew about. I had my baby's first photo in my pocket and I was ready to celebrate. Of course, I had some catching up to do with everybody who was already hard at it.

Next morning, I laid in the hospital bed with Ann—and the worried nurse took my pulse first.

I was a lot less nervous when our second child came along. Because of Dorothy's size, the doctor set up a C-section for Ann, and let me tell you that it's pretty simple when you schedule that stuff.

Dorothy was six years old by then, and we were at Sears Point, California, when we called and told her that we were getting her something special. When I got home, she was more than ready. "What did you bring me, Daddy?"

"Well, we gotta go by the hospital first."

Wise as six-year-olds are, she was nervous to be in the hospital, but she was sitting on my lap when they ran the ultra-sound over Ann's stomach. The doctor says, "There's the heartbeat."

Daughter looks up at me with big eyes and says, "Am I gonna be a big sister?"

"Yes, you are. That's your surprise. Do you like it?"

"Oh, yes."

"Are you sure?"

"Oh, yeah," she says with total conviction. *"There's a lot of stuff I can teach this kid."*

Sheldon was our "little" guy. He weighed only eight pounds, eight ounces, which had Ann muttering about why they couldn't have switched on sizes.

Like Dorothy, our son was named for a very special person, and I'll tell you more about the namesake a little later.

Sheldon and I look at a photo taken of us earlier the same year. It now hangs on the wall of my office at the shop. (Ken Schrader Collection.)

This is the crew—Dorothy, Sheldon and our cat Goblin. Ann and I rescued him from a dumpster in Phoenix, and he lived 19 long, happy years before going to cat-nip heaven. (Ken Schrader Collection.)

THEY GROW UP TOO FAST

As this is written, Dorothy is 16 and in her sophomore year of high school. She finished the freshman year with a 4.5 g.p.a..

You're thinking—can't get a 4.5—but it turns out that if you take advanced classes you can. Obviously, she has her mother's brain, but she's like me in that she is outgoing and really enjoys having a lot of friends. Last summer, she went to New York City and did a program with the Radio City Rockettes, which for a dedicated dancer like her was just great. She also reached 5'7" tall, which is the minimum for a Rockette, so Dorothy is thrilled and has her sights set on a future on stage.

And then there is Sheldon.

So far his interest in school rivals his old man's, so when he got straight B's once, we were real proud of him. He's not dumb at all—he's just having trouble getting motivated. Right now, at age 10, he plans to grow up and design video games while also being a cook in a Japanese steak house.

Actually, Ann thinks Sheldon may end up in advertising or marketing because he's always coming up with clever stuff. A reporter once asked him about driving race cars, and he very solemnly responded, "No, I don't believe so."

"Are you sure you're not?"

"Oh, yeah, I'm sure."

"And why not?"

"Looks a little bit dangerous to me."

Yeah, like twirling knives in the Japanese steak house isn't. But, he's not into bikes or anything that "looks like I could get hurt." Smart kid. At least I'm not going bald tearing my hair out over crazy things my kids are doing.

And how does my kids' lack of interest in racing careers feel to me? I couldn't be happier.

Ann Schrader: We try to do things together, like vacations at Christmas and New Year's. We have created some holiday traditions, too, for our kids, but they're going to remember the fun stuff. They're not going to remember how many times we took them to Toys R' Us. So, I have game nights at home and we go places, travel beyond just going to the races. I try to make sure they are well-rounded and have an appreciation for things beyond racing.

It's hard for Ken because his family's life centered around his dad. His mom would get up at three in the morning to fix bacon and eggs if that's when he got home and what he wanted.

I don't do that. Ken doesn't expect me to do that. I have interests and activities of my own, the kids have theirs, and we all respect each other for being strong individuals.

In 1997, we had a family portrait taken—where else—at a race track. Dorothy was seven and Sheldon wasn't quite two. (Dorsey Patrick photo; Ken Schrader Collection.)

I mean, it was the right thing for me, no question. If I had it to do all over again, I would in a heartbeat. But I also have seen the down side to being a second- or third-generation racer. Hell, even a first-generation racer.

I don't know that Dorothy or Sheldon wouldn't do better than I have, but I really like the idea that they've both found things they enjoy, that they are good at, and they can make their own names doing.

I just hope they don't mind growing up before I do.

Ann with Sheldon—one of my favorite photos—and ol' Dad with Dorothy in 2005. Now that you've seen how lovely Dorothy is these days, you'll understand why I have a shotgun ready for the dating deal. (Ken Schrader Collection.)

I think this was for a charity event, but generally while I leave car-pooling the kids to Ann, she leaves the race cars to me. However, she's a great sport when it comes to doing things that help other people, and, no, she didn't wreck it.(Ken Schrader Collection.)

Big Shoes 12

U NLIKE COLLEGE FRATERNITIES, the racing crowd doesn't have a hazing where they try to humiliate new guys. Our people know you can do that on your own, and it's called figuring out the gears and clutch.

I don't know how the college guys feel about their group, but once you've been accepted as a race car driver by your peers it's a special feeling that isn't the result of being allowed into the group based on social standing or a matter of buying a pin. You don't even have to get exceptionally good at it to understand that it's a tremendous accomplishment.

Part of having made it as far (and for as long) as I have, is that I've been fortunate to race with some of the best drivers of the past quarter-century. I can confirm the theory that some of the better racers have never made it to NASCAR's top division for a wide variety of reasons, but I think it's probably a matter of not being in the right place at the right time. I mean, the car owners in NASCAR aren't stupid. These days they need guys who can sell the sponsor's product, for sure, but they also get tired real fast of writing checks for wrecked cars, so they want the right drivers, too. It's impossible to see every driver around, but it seems that, for the most part, they've done a darn good job of finding quality drivers.

But that's a whole other chapter we'll get to shortly. Right now, I'm going to share some thoughts I have about a few people whose names are pretty well known and are guys that I've had the privilege to race with. They are in alphabetical order because I don't think I could rank them by favorite or any other measurement. And bear in mind, this is just a drop in the bucket. I've raced literally thousands of drivers around the country and could level a forest for the paper to talk about all who made an impression. These are just some of the guys that you might be curious about.

BOBBY ALLISON

1983 Winston Cup champion, 84 WC wins, but he was Schrader before Schrader was, because he would race just about anywhere, anytime, and he never looked at it as going backwards to run with the Saturday night racers.

At the end of Bobby's career I wasn't really racing with him. I was just out on the race track at the same time, you know. I was learning and he was one of the guys who was contending for the win every week. But he was approachable to rookies like me, and if you wanted to learn how to race hard-nosed, but smart, he was a guy to follow on the track.

Then he had the bad wreck at Pocono that almost killed him. It was touch-and-go for so long, but after a lot of years healing up, he's a welcome sight in the pits these days.

We like having him around so he's always welcome in our hauler. I can remember a particular day when Dale Inman was there, too. Dale is Richard Petty's cousin and was his crew chief through most of Richard's career. In their time, Bobby and Richard were tremendous rivals, so on this later day there were a lot of "war" stories going back and forth. It was pretty funny to watch Dale going out of his way to piss Bobby off and then calm him back down—and then doing it all over again. It was really something.

I can't imagine what it was like for Bobby and his wife Judy, losing their sons Clifford and Davey. It was so intense that it broke them apart for a while. But when Adam Petty was killed, Bobby and Judy decided that they should go to the Pettys together. I know that Adam's parents Kyle and Pattie have said that it really helped them, but it had the unexpected bonus of making Bobby and Judy realize they needed to be back together. I think they're as happy and content now as they've ever been.

I made the decision on my own many years ago to continue racing on the short-tracks as much as I possibly can, so it wasn't Bobby's influence that kept me out there. But I sure did respect him for what he did and I am still a huge fan of his today.

In 1992, Bobby Allison was still recuperating from his near-fatal wreck four years before, but it was a thrill for me to have my picture taken with him. I still thoroughly enjoy having him stop by our hauler when he's visiting the tracks. (Ken Schrader Collection.)

BUDDY BAKER

1980 Daytona 500 winner, first NASCAR driver to top 200 mph at Talladega.

It's telling that Buddy's wins came on the biggest, baddest, hardest tracks, like Talladega, Daytona, Darlington and Charlotte. He just wore out the gas pedal on a race car, and while maybe he would have won more if he'd been a little friendlier with the brake or at least a little easier on the gas, then he wouldn't have been Buddy Baker.

In 1987 I drove the Red Baron car, but the following year he became the Red Baron driver. I've continued my relationship with them through the years (the parent company is Schwan's), so I spent some time at events with Buddy and shared a lot of laughs with him.

I knew when I made him mad on the race track because we'd be following him, maybe kind of reminding him we were there, and all of a sudden that big, ol' right arm would come up and he'd make a fist.

But then I found out that he did that to everybody all the time. Like, if you were on the race track with him—you shouldn't be.

Buddy really is a gentle giant. As fierce as he looked, especially if he came out of a race car mad, you might not believe that, but it was good that he had all that time as a television announcer because then people got to know him as the really funny, good guy that he is.

All you need is a helmet and a fist in the air, and you, too, would know how it felt to follow Buddy Baker around the race track. Hard to believe from this photo but he's one of the nicest guys who ever raced. (R. N. Masser photo.)

JOHNNY BENSON

Former Busch Series champion, 1995 Winston Cup Rookie of the Year, currently on the Craftsman Truck Series.

This is a pretty deep friendship that goes back to ten years of sharing hosting duties on a television show as well as running on the track. We were teammates for a couple of years at MB2, and in addition to enjoying his company I found it really helpful because he's so smart when it comes to race cars.

Johnny has built race cars literally from the ground up. Not even a frame to start with. He just jumped in and built late model stock cars that won races. He's part owner of Berlin Speedway, back home in Michigan, so he's got his hands in that, too. Like I think I'll wind up back in St. Louis one day, I think Johnny will be back in Michigan eventually.

I was glad to see him end up being in a good Truck Series deal in the meantime, though. I don't think it bothered him too much to do what some people think is taking a step backwards. If you love to race as much as Johnny and I do, you are just happy that somebody wants to put you in something competitive and you don't have to worry about the tire bill.

I have as much respect for Johnny Benson—on and off the track—as almost anybody I've met in racing. (Mark Gross photo.)

DALE EARNHARDT, SR.

So damned famous I don't have to tell you his accomplishments.

He became Elvis in the sense that his fame was just incredible, but he wasn't Elvis in that the fame and wealth never changed him a bit. I mean, in the end, even with imported Italian marble inside his race shop, he was still the same guy who struggled to run out of his daddy's two-car garage thirty years earlier. Dale learned to talk to the media and do the stuff he had to, but he never liked it, and that was actually part of his appeal. I don't think anybody else could have gotten away with stuff like he did, but he knew that no matter what he said or did, it was all going to be the same anyway, so he stayed true to who he was inside.

This isn't a great-quality print but it was the last one taken of me with one of my first friends in NASCAR, Dale Earnhardt, Sr., and his wife Teresa. It was 2001, and a few hours later Dale was gone. (Ken Schrader Collection.)

As far as being the Intimidator on-track, it didn't win him any popularity contests with the rest of the drivers. He called it "bump-and-run," but I always just thought it was knocking people the hell out of the way.

But then you'd get out of the car and you couldn't stay mad at him. I mean, you *could not* stay mad. He'd jack with you until you got over it. Tell you how it was really your fault, and just when you thought you couldn't get any madder, you'd end up laughing— and have no idea of how you got there.

When I was driving for Mr. Donlavey, the team was kept up in Richmond, Virginia, so when I first moved to North Carolina I had a lot of time on my hands. Dale took care of that. This was when he bought the first part of his farm and I'd go over there every day. I'd help him do stuff around there and I learned a lot. Sure was different for a city boy like me and I enjoyed it. In return, Dale helped me considerably with business stuff. With his direction, I knew who to call for this, who to call for that, and how to make the most of what was coming my way.

I know, also, that no matter what I've done in racing so far or ever do in the future, my career will always have an asterisk that is tied to Dale's final wreck. It was my rotten luck to be the first person to walk up to the car afterwards. And, I'll say, just like everybody associated with it has, that it was nobody's direct fault the wreck happened. It's the last lap of Daytona and unless you've sat in the seat and felt the intensity, known what it's like to be *sooooo* close to winning the biggest prize in our sport, you can't know how fast and furious things happen. It wasn't the first or last wreck that's going to happen at the end of that race. It's just one that's especially notorious.

While it was happening, I was pretty pissed to be caught up in the wreck. I mean, I had a solid finish going to happen, too, and it was going up in tire smoke and a crunched front end. I also figured, as I got out of my car and walked over to Dale's, that he was going to be really mad, but at least he wasn't going to be mad at me.

I walked up, took down the window net and knelt down to jaw with him about our shared bad luck. But the first word never got past my lips.

People who were watching on television tell me that my body language said it all, but, in fact, he wasn't gone then. I mean, I wasn't a fool—I knew he was hurt bad and it didn't look good. It was bad enough to scare the hell out of me, and that's why you saw some pretty frantic waving for help.

The hardest part was talking to his car owner Richard Childress in the Infield Care Center a few minutes later. If you are not already aware of it, NASCAR sensibly requires everybody involved in a wreck to go get checked out, even if you're positive you're fine. It can be aggravating— as much to the health-care workers having to deal with racers who may be mad as hell at the guy on the next gurney—but more than one driver has been a little bit in shock or too mad to realize he's hurt, so it's a good idea.

But in this case, I knew Richard would be coming to the Center and I didn't want to see him. They'd already taken Dale directly to the hospital, but Richard knew that I'd had a view nobody else had. And I knew that Richard was closer than a brother to Dale so I wanted to just shrivel up in the corner when I heard him come in.

"What's the deal?" he asked.

"He's hurt, Richard."

"Like, he's going to be out for awhile?"

I said, "No, Richard. I mean *hurt*. Like, maybe no good at all."

You could see Richard's face just crumple. I mean, he was still holding on to hope just like we all were until we were told otherwise by the medical personnel, but I guess we probably knew even then.

I've been asked countless times since then about what I saw when I let down the net. I don't think most people have a ghoulish insensitivity about the wreck. I suspect they just want to know that it was peaceful for Dale, that he wasn't in any pain. But I've never talked about those few minutes with anybody in any detail, and I never will. I figure this is one thing that needs to be between Dale and me. And nobody else.

It's enough for everybody to know that he was The Man.

DALE EARNHARDT, JR.

1998-99 Busch Series champion, hugely popular Nextel Cup competitor and son of The Man.

When the kid was 16 years old, he went on one of our weekend racing trips. From earlier stories, you might have gotten the idea that there is a little bit of partying going on during these trips.

You would be wrong.

There is a *lot* of partying going on.

We use our heads and stay out of trouble. Mostly, we laugh, make other people laugh, and regress to pranks, practical jokes and tricks on each other. It's the kind of thing that many people do as they are growing up but forget how to do by the time they've got mortgages and kids. But when you're young and curious, it's a good idea to test the limits in the company of people who will take care of you.

At least that's what I told myself Dale, Sr., must have thought when he allowed the kid to go with us. Dale's older son Kerry was already grown, and daughter Kelly was always sharp about the big, bad world out there. But Dale, Jr., had led a pretty sheltered life—which is a good thing—and Senior figured that if he was going to experiment and try out things, it was a whole lot better to let him go with me and my crowd than with a bunch of other 16-year-olds and wind up in jail or worse. It also couldn't look to Senior's wife Teresa like it was his idea. She might have been the kid's stepmother but she'd done a good job in her part of bringing him up. And, at that point, Teresa was just way too trusting, but we fixed that.

The Lost Weekend began when we went to Granite City, where we won; then on to Topeka; Moberly, Missouri; back to Topeka where we won again; and then back to St. Charles, Missouri. During that weekend, Junior got acquainted with his future sponsor, so when we got back to Topeka the second time—where we knew we were going to meet up with Dale, Sr., once more, we said, "Now, don't look at your daddy, don't tell him nothing about what we did, and whatever you do, don't breathe on him."

He must have breathed because later on I got cussed and yelled at, and I took it quietly because I had it coming. But after the rant went on long enough, I asked Senior, "I guess this means we can't take Kelly next year?"

I got a pretty strong suspicion about a couple of those "bump-and-runs" I received later that year.

But Senior knew I would keep the kid safe. You have to remember that a pretty similar thing had happened to me when Bud Hoppe got hold of me, and I turned out...

Maybe I better think of another comparison.

Dale Junior is well past legal age now and we still get together pret-

During the infamous lost weekend with Dale Earnhardt, Jr. in 1991, we stopped partying long enough to win a feature at Granite City, Illinois. (Allen Horcher photo; Ken Schrader Collection.)

ty regularly. I have had a long association with Budweiser, his current car sponsor and mine for much of the time I was in the Hendrick car. We do personal appearances together, and we usually sample a little of the sponsor's product, too. He's not at all bothered about that trip years ago—in fact, it's taken on the status of a legend. But things have changed a lot for him. In those days, even with his name and his father's fame, he could hit the road with a bunch of over-the-hill kids like us and let his hair down. Most people had no clue who he was.

I will tell you who he is today—that same kid. He just doesn't have the life he had. The way people react to him—and I suspect it would be this way even if his daddy was still alive—is incredible. It's like a cult following. I mean, it's like Palm Sunday at the race track.

The thing of it is, he doesn't give a shit about it. Don't get me wrong, he appreciates his fans, but he didn't ask for it to get so crazy. He just wants to drive the damned race car, and he proved that quite a while ago because his father didn't make it easy for him. Senior figured—rightly—that if the kids had to struggle at least a little they would better appreciate whatever they achieved, and they all do. Rich and famous is incidental. First and foremost, Dale Junior is a lot more than just a name—he's a real race car driver.

Usually you get blinded by the Carl Edwards smile, so I figured let's run one where he's actually serious for a change. (Autostock Images.)

CARL EDWARDS

Winning driver all the way from hometown short tracks to Nextel Cup, and, as mentioned earlier, my cousin.

The neatest thing about Carl is that he made it to Nextel Cup racing and he did it with just desire and ability. No check or sugar daddy.

When he was still pretty young, he came down to our shop in North Carolina, and we put him to work pushing a broom. He thought we were going to put him in one of the race cars. You know, play the relative card and by-pass or speed up the learning curve.

I told him, "Go home and race."

"But I don't have any money."

"Doesn't matter. Drive any piece of shit you can drive. Anything. Just get laps."

And he did. Man, he excelled in a lot of different stuff. There's this mistaken belief that he didn't win and had never shown promise until he got in the Roush ride, but that's wrong. Carl won races, but he accelerated his career so quickly that it wasn't a matter of winning over a period of decades. And then, he advertised for a ride. It was a pretty gutsy thing to do, but it worked, and then he backed it up with ability.

Carl's going to have a good career in Nextel Cup. He's aggressive, but he's learning how to make that work for him. And it doesn't hurt that he's a sponsor's dream. Got those damned dimples.

His dad Mike, who's won about 200 races, lived with us the summer he was 18 and I was 13. He's got the dimples, too, and he told me that summer that he got them when he was spiked playing football.

And I believed him.

Well, little Carl got spiked, too.

What a coincidence.

RED FARMER

Legendary Alabama short track driver still racing past 70 years of age. Probably the greatest driver to never become a major NASCAR Cup star.

A real hero.

I raced against Red very, very few times, but I was always in awe of being on the same track with him. He's won in just about everything he ever got in.

As you get older, and if you've raced forever as Red has, you know that hitting anything with a race car hard enough to leave a mark is going to hurt. You don't see many older short track drivers wreck a lot, in part because of experience, but also because they'll back off rather than get bruised up and sore for a week.

Well, I can't say that I ever saw Red back off. He's been mashing the gas for decades and he's still a force to be reckoned with.

I wish more of the kids coming up these days could watch Red because then they could see how you can make fast, smart and good last as long as you want it to.

Red Farmer, founder of the famed Alabama Gang, may not have achieved the same level of fame as some of the rest, but there's no one, anywhere, who's raced longer, better, or with more enthusiasm. (Bruce Bennett photo.)

JEFF GORDON

Four-time NASCAR Winston Cup champion, Jeff began racing at the age of five and won at every level on the way up.

Anytime people don't like you and the only reason they can come up with is that you win too damned much—well, I'm sorry but you better come up with a better reason than that. I remember when I was a kid and people responded to Dandy Don Klein that way, and there's been others, too, but probably nobody has been as much a lightning rod as Jeff has been.

Jeff is a good person. Period.

He's done so many good things for so many people, a lot of it quietly and without credit, so he owes no one an apology for anything except possibly for raising the bar for everybody in racing.

The first I ran with Jeff was in Silver Crown cars all those years ago.

I was an adult already and Jeff wasn't even shaving. I can remember thinking, "Damn, that kid's gonna be a pain in another year or two."

He's the reason car owners now want young kids instead of veterans—or maybe I should blame Jeff's step-dad because he recognized the extraordinary talent at a very young age and helped him realize the potential. Everybody wants the next Jeff Gordon without realizing that he is one-of-a-kind. That kind of phenomenal talent is probably unique to that one individual, but it doesn't stop parents across the country pushing their kids whether they've got talent or not. They might not find the lure of money and fame so attractive if they realized what it's done to Jeff.

I mean, he's got financial security for the rest of his life in spite of that messy divorce, and more power to him. He's earned it. But, in a way that's different from Dale Junior, Jeff can't have anything remotely like a normal life. There are people who adore him like Junior's fans feel about the younger Earnhardt, but if you use the word "cult" in connection with Gordon it's probably with the group of people who hate him with such venom it defies explanation. It doesn't seem a fair trade-off for all he's done to elevate racing.

There have been a few drivers who've advanced racing, including Richard Petty, Cale Yarborough, Darrell Waltrip and the Earnhardts among others. You have to include Jeff in that group, because he brought attention and sponsorships to racing that wouldn't otherwise have happened. He won so many races at a young age, while leading the way with that baby face and an inability to be arrogant about his accomplishments. But it's brought him as much grief as satisfaction.

I'm a huge Jeff Gordon fan, never mind that during those years he was my teammate I was often expected to use the same equipment and set-ups even though we have different styles. That wasn't Jeff's doing, and he was never anything but supportive then—and now.

Even though Jeff hasn't won 13 races a year recently—and nobody has because the level of competition has caught up to Jeff rather than his team sliding back to the rest of us—the reactions to him have not really changed. So I think in time—even though he's never known anything but racing in his life—Jeff will probably walk away from racing and try to find something resembling a normal life. Unfortunately, he'll never have it as long as he stays in racing, and I figure he's earned some peace and quiet.

ERNIE IRVAN

In a relatively short NASCAR career, Ernie won over $10 million and had 15 victories, including the Daytona 500.

Ernie moved from California in the early 1980s and he was a local hero at the short tracks pretty quickly. He raced with Mark Reno, another Westerner who'd moved to Charlotte to advance his career. Mark built a lot of fast race cars, but it was as Ernie's car owner that both hung their stars.

Not long after I moved to Concord, I was out running around with Earnhardt one day. We stopped by Mark's shop. I kept my short-track car there for a while until I had my own place. On this day, the conversation led to good things because it resulted in those guys getting sponsorship from Dale for a car Ernie was going to drive in the World 600. This was a real shoestring operation at the time—Ernie and Mark had written a lot of checks to go racing that weren't real good until after the race. Talk about inspiration to race well, and Ernie did. I kind of helped con Dale into giving those guys a break and buying some tires for the race, too, so Dale and I felt like we had a hand in Ernie's launch.

Ernie Irvan (right) shares a laugh with other partiers at our shop a few years back. (Ken Schrader Collection.)

Occasionally, we wondered what we'd unleashed. Ernie's style was aggressive. It won him some races and fans, but it also challenged his on-track friendships, too. He stood up at a Talladega drivers' meeting and apologized and that kind of helped him, but there wasn't anything he could do about those two big hits on the head. Darn near killed him the first time, but he came back Hollywood-style and won again when he healed up. The second time, though, was just too much.

He's had some rough times off the track, too. A fire gutted his home and destroyed all the racing memorabilia, but Ernie's a real survivor. He continues to do charity work to help people less fortunate than he is, and that's a pretty neat thing.

Sheldon Kinser's life and brilliant racing career were cut short by cancer. There should have been a lot more Victory Lane photos with his family, but since there weren't, we cherish the ones like this. (Ken Coles photo; Ken Schrader Collection.)

SHELDON KINSER

1988 USAC sprint champion, Indianapolis 500 racer, cool dude.

The whole Kinser clan has tough guys. They're big, strong, and they take their racing real seriously. From the perspective of today, Steve is by far the most famous, but Mark, Karl, Randy and Bob all have a lot to be proud of. What you may not realize is that back in the 1970s and 1980s, the most famous and accomplished Kinser at that time was Sheldon, another of Steve's cousins. I think many observers felt that Sheldon was the one who was going to be a huge star before it was all said and done.

Sheldon always got attention whenever he walked into the pits. Where Steve, and most of the Kinsers, are blonde and bulky, Sheldon was dark and big as Buddy Baker. You kind of wondered how he got all that size into a sprint car, but he did. He drove really good cars, too, which explains in part why he won 37 USAC sprint features (sixth all-time) in his career. But he earned those rides with his skill, and when you beat him you felt like you'd really accomplished something.

When he was driving for legendary car owner Ben Leyba, we had a lot of fun after the races. Benny, Sheldon and Sheldon's wife Susie, who is the daughter of another short-track legend Bobby Grim, all knew how to turn the after-race time into something as memorable as the racing was. It was also Sheldon and Benny who loaned me their car at Nazareth, Pennsylvania, so I could win the Silver Crown championship.

You always knew where you stood with Sheldon. You sure didn't want to piss him off because he could be relentless on the track and next thing you knew, you could screw up because of that pressure. He didn't do anything wrong or dirty, but he could make his presence known.

I've known too many drivers who died on the track, but there's something especially horrible about a big, tough guy brought to his knees by cancer. Most on-track deaths are swift, mean little events that shock you and leave you shaking your head. But the nastiness of cancer, the wasting-away of a vibrant force like Sheldon was almost unthinkable.

He died the day after we won our first Winston Cup race.

When my little guy was born a few years later, it seemed like a challenge, giving him the name of one of the best men who ever walked through a pit gate. It's a lot for my Sheldon to live up to, but the original Sheldon would have been cool that his namesake is going his own way in the world. He'd be the first to tell my boy that you just need to be able to look yourself in the mirror in the morning, and he would be speaking from experience.

STEVE KINSER

Umpty-zillion wins in sprint cars, King of the Outlaws.

We've been friends and occasional teammates for about 25 years now. Steve's got one of the most interesting careers of anybody I've known, too. In sprint cars he has a winning legacy that I doubt anybody will ever match in the future. But his sprint car career might not have been so long if he'd had a better situation during the year he tried NASCAR.

Nobody I've known has better demonstrated how important it is to have the entire package come together to have success at the Cup level. I mean, Steve proved his ability in the International Race of Champions series where they put drivers from all types of racing into cars that are as close to the same as they can make them. That kind of pavement, late-model style of race car isn't like what he's used to, but he won anyway, and against unbelievable competition. Back on the NASCAR circuit, however, things didn't go well at all—and I know it wasn't the driver.

He got a couple of raw breaks right off the bat. Steve was dumped a couple of times—just plain old dumped—when it wasn't his fault. So, it was easy to go back to sprint cars and excel at what he did so well and had so much more control over. He was already a legend, but the years since have just been phenomenal. As this is written, he is still completely dominating the premiere sprint car circuit, with no signs of slowing down.

I might have mentioned that the Kinsers are a tough bunch. Steve might be the toughest. He certainly has no patience for *Here's your sign* silliness.

For example, I can remember a time at the Chili Bowl race in Tulsa when a midget got dumped over the Jersey barrier around the track. Steve and I were standing together when this young kid walks past us and says, "Went over the wall, huh?"

Steve took a puff on his cigarette, gave the kid one of those looks that makes 200-pound men shiver in their shoes and said, "I don't see no holes in it."

I just chuckled. I mean, I know the kid just wanted to say something to the greatest sprint driver ever, and Steve wasn't trying to be a dickhead. It was nothing personal and it wasn't meant to be intimidating either. It was just that southern-Indiana, plain-spoken way that has contributed to the legend that will live on long after Steve is bench racing on the porch of the old-folks home.

Have you ever seen such intensity in a driver? Well, Steve Kinser gets into it every time he gets in a race car. (Terry Bourcy photo.)

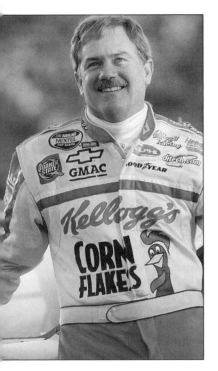

Terry Labonte is one of those rare people who becomes a teammate and friend for life. They don't make them any better. (Autostock Images.)

TERRY LABONTE

NASCAR Winston Cup champion 1984 and 1996, IROC champion 1989.

Terry was my teammate at Hendrick and I was involved in helping getting him hired. You treat him right, and he becomes a teammate for life.

He's a lot different from most of the drivers. I mean, you need a butt-load of self-confidence to get to NASCAR's top division. You have to convince car owners to take a chance on you and then you have to go out on the track and prove that you belong there. You can't do that if you don't believe in yourself. That also makes the testosterone level pretty high during drivers' meetings.

Terry, on the other hand, is about as quiet as anybody around. He's really good, really focused, and I'm sure that's how he got championships so far apart. He just never let what got him into NASCAR ever get away from him.

He and wife Kim have a big charity event down in their hometown of Corpus Christi every year, and Ann and I enjoy going. It's great to see how the fans react to the Labonte brothers, too. Being the strong, silent type is not a liability in Texas.

Terry does know how to let down his hair, though. You don't want to get him mad, but it's a lot of fun to get him around a campfire and put a beer in his hand.

One night in Michigan, there was a small group of us sitting around, and I will note that alcohol was involved. I happened to mention a crew chief that I'd always wanted to work with.

You don't want to work with that blankety-blankin' blanker, Terry said.

Man. I'd never heard him talking this much. I'd never seen him this animated.

So we gave him more Budweiser and encouraged him some more. I mean, *Terry, tell us how you really feel.*

But when he fell off the chair the second time, we didn't care what he thought. We were putting him to bed.

Damn chairs can be tricky.

STERLING MARLIN

Long-time NASCAR driver, winner of back-to-back Daytona 500s.

I always thought Nashville, Sterling's hometown, was a lot like St. Louis—a nice working-class river town. Good, hard-working people there, but just as I wasn't gonna make dog food for a living in my hometown, Sterling knew he wasn't going to pick cotton.

His daddy, Coo-Coo, was a terrific race car driver, too, and I know that had a lot of influence on Sterling. He won a lot of championships and short-track stuff before he moved into NASCAR, but he's still exactly the same guy. Totally got his feet on the ground. Even when he was running for the Cup championship a few years ago and broke his neck, he never varied in his approach to the racing, the fans or the media, staying cool and calm as he had been in the short-track days. But, I sure hated to see that happen because you always want to win or lose on the track and not be sidelined, watching it unfold.

We really like Sterling. Ann and I took him and his wife, Paula, on a New Year's Eve trip to the Bahamas. Now, we like to pull the occasional harmless prank, so we told him that the place we were going was real dressy and that he needed to wear the tuxedo we'd told him to bring. But when we all gathered together in the hotel lobby, everybody else was in flowered shirts and shorts—just what you'd really expect in the tropics. We all got our laugh at Sterling's expense and then told him to go change.

"Nope," he said. "I dragged this dang thing all the way down here, and I'm gonna wear it."

And he did.

After we pulled a fast one on Sterling Marlin by insisting he bring a tux to a New Year's Eve party, he insisted on wearing it. We didn't complain because it meant his wife, Paula, looked pretty spectacular, too. (Ken Schrader Collection.)

RICHARD PETTY

Seven-time NASCAR champion, unmatchable 200 wins.

There's nothing more you can say but that he's the King. Even his son Kyle calls him, "King."

Nobody influenced our sport more than Richard has. He just has always hit every note right. He had that mega-watt smile that could charm a corpse, the wrap-around sunglasses that added some mystery, and the cowboy hat that he's never traded in for something else, which was one of many ways he's proven that he's unwavering in what he does.

It was all the autographs, staying until the last fan was satisfied that did more than anything to propel our sport. People argue that drivers can't do that anymore, but I've still never seen the King walk away from requests.

Richard used to have a greater spotlight, but I'm glad he's not one of the original stars who faded away and doesn't come around anymore. Just seeing him in the pits is a reminder of how much we have to be

grateful for, and how the guys like Richard made it all possible. We still joke around with him in the pits, but we're always glad to see him.

Thank you, Richard, for all you've done. We don't tell you that nearly often enough.

KYLE PETTY

NASCAR driver, Petty Enterprises CEO, and one of the most charitable people on earth.

We came to NASCAR racing about the same time, but from opposite directions. I mean, there was never a need for Kyle to hop in any sportsman or midget ride that happened to be open. The name opened doors, and it should have. The dues just got paid on a bigger stage. Kyle's such an important part of NASCAR that I hate to think what it would have been like if he hadn't taken an interest in racing.

The thing is that Kyle has always had so much going for him. He was a really good high-school athlete who ended up with multi-sport scholarship offers. He toyed with a Nashville singing career at one point, but happily he stayed in the driver's seat.

You know, most racing fans have no idea of how much Kyle loves to drive a race car. I don't think anybody can ever match the King's 200 wins, if for no other reason than that we don't run enough races anymore to make it feasible. But can you imagine the standard it set for Kyle?

Fortunately for his own well-being Kyle realizes there is a lot more to life than just driving a race car. He's so darn smart and capable with sponsors that he was a natural to take over Petty Enterprises and keep it an important part of NASCAR. Other drivers, car owners and sponsors from the building days have faded away, but the Petty cars are still on track and that's very much because of Kyle's ability.

When his son Adam was killed in an accident at New Hampshire, it changed Kyle. He'd been a great dad, but he became obsessed, I guess is the word, with realizing Adam's dream. You see, Adam was like his granddad—soft-spoken, a little introverted, and less interested in the business aspect of racing. In fact, the Victory Junction Gang camp for sick children was originally Adam's idea. It's just that Kyle and Pattie have thrown so much effort, energy and enthusiasm into it, I suspect it's all happened a lot faster and a lot bigger than it would have with only Adam behind it. I know that Ann and I are such strong believers in what they've done that we have put a lot of our charity emphasis into it, too.

I'm sure all the effort for Victory Junction has impacted Kyle's driving career. I'm equally sure he doesn't care.

He's got his priorities right.

Kyle Petty is a guy blessed with a heart as big as all get-out. And it's meant wonderful things for a lot of people, but especially for sick kids. (Mike Adaskaveg photo.)

LARRY PHILLIPS

Midwestern short-track star, winner of five NASCAR Weekly Series championships.

Larry first came over from Springfield, Missouri, to Lake Hill in the early 1970s. He came in and set a track record, started last in the feature and was in the lead on the first lap, but then dropped a driveshaft.

He had our attention.

When he came back the next week, he was told that his car's body was too rough-looking for our nice track, so he returned the following week with a new body and set another track record before he won the feature.

When he came back again, they told him the car was too light. Never mind that we didn't have any scales. So, they made him bolt on some old cylinder heads as ballast—sort of like adding an anchor—but

Larry Phillips (right) was one of the great stars of short track racing. Here he talks with Ray Callahan who built some of the fastest chassis of the 1980s and 1990s, but really Larry could have taught everybody how to make a living at racing. (Joyce Standridge photo.)

it didn't matter. He was the best. Everybody started buying stuff from him because they couldn't beat him.

I was only 13 when Jerry Sifford (one of my earliest influences, you may recall) took me to Springfield to run a four-hour motorcycle race. I ran the mandatory, non-stop first hour with a hole in my knee after I fell. I ended up needing six stitches later.

After the race, Larry and his girlfriend gave me a screwdriver—the drink, not the tool—and suddenly I didn't feel so bad. But even though it didn't hurt anymore, the knee got really stiff and swollen on me, so I had to go to the emergency room. Pretty big deal to have Larry Phillips carry you into the hospital.

Larry was racing for a living when almost nobody else was doing that on the short tracks. He'd build you a new car and then he would beat you. If you didn't like that, hell, he would sell you the car he just beat you with—and then he would beat you again. I mean, you were gonna get beat.

He wasn't a warm, fuzzy kind of guy. He went to the race track to win—not to get fans and friends, but he did okay on that, too. For a while there, a group of mostly senior citizens would follow him to tracks and they were called the Cowbell Brigade. It was a neat deal.

I wish he was still here. Like Sheldon, Larry got his career taken away by off-track illness. When Larry passed away it created another big hole in racing that will never be filled. He wasn't an easy guy to get to know or to like, but he was a big influence because his career proved that you could go racing full-time. Larry taught me that you could leave the race track with the money.

TONY STEWART

USAC Triple Crown winner, IRL and NASCAR champion.

It kind of surprises me that more Dale Earnhardt, Sr. fans haven't migrated to Tony, because he's got the same kind of personality in that he's got a heart of gold but he's not comfortable with people knowing that.

Tony has changed quite a bit over the last couple of years, at least as far as his temperament is concerned. I don't think he's changed inside, but it looks like he decided that being 100 percent honest about things wasn't worth the hassle it brought him.

I believe it helped him a lot to go back to living in Indiana. Certainly, it causes more problems in scheduling and moving around the country than if he was down in North Carolina where the main NASCAR deal is located, but we always like it when people don't turn

If you had as much talent as Tony Stewart, you'd smile, too. (Autostock Images.)

their backs on their roots. I believe it's been very good for Tony to be around the people who loved him when there was nothing he could do for them.

I've been a big fan for a long time, and I was really impressed when he won the USAC Midget, Sprint and Silver Crown championships in one year. When I got a first, second and third in a single year, I think it was the first that anybody had come that close, or even given it much thought. But no matter how hard you go after a goal like this (instead of backing into it like we did), there's so much that's out of your control, so Tony's championships were huge.

What I especially like about Tony is how much he just loves to race. He'll have an off week and drop in unannounced at a dirt track. I think Indiana driver Steve Barnett keeps a late model dirt car for him, along with all the open-cockpit cars Tony owns, and it makes it possible for Tony, aka Smoke Johnson, to just go play. Definitely, it's a matter of loving racing more than viewing it as a job, and it doesn't seem to be lessening in Tony's case, at all.

DICK TRICKLE

Retired NASCAR veteran who won around 1,000 short-track races in the upper Midwest.

Dick Trickle could teach a lot of people how to race on the track and how to have fun off it. (Mike Adaskaveg photo.)

I didn't mature as a driver like Rusty Wallace and Mark Martin, racing pavement full-time. The home track was paved, but otherwise I was pretty much learning on dirt, so I didn't race with Dick very much. That doesn't mean I didn't hear about him. In the 1970s and 1980s, you had to have your head in a locked, iron helmet to not hear about his growing legend.

One of the paved short tracks we've run occasionally is Slinger Speedway, up in Trickle Country. There's a bunch of tough paved tracks in Wisconsin, but Slinger was one that you didn't stop by the first time and master. So, I'm there for a multi-race show, and I'm running just terrible. In the bar after the first night, I asked Dick if he would take my car out and shake it down the following day.

Sure, he tells me, but the next afternoon he says, "You probably don't need a driver. You're not wet behind the ears, so you probably just need a crew chief."

He had me go out on the track for five or six laps at a time and then come back to the pits, telling him what the car was doing and he would make changes. He got me running a whole lot better in a short time.

I never figured out why Dick didn't have the same success when he went NASCAR Cup racing, but it didn't happen for him. Still, he owes no apologies. He was as fine a race car driver as I ever saw run.

And the whole thing about him racing and then drinking all night and then going on to win a race the following night is kind of exaggerated.

Not a whole lot.

Just a little bit, because it's based on some fact.

RICH VOGLER

Winner of the first Chili Bowl race, holder of seven USAC open-cockpit titles.

Rich was one of the most controversial short-track champions ever. You either loved him or hated him, although sometimes it could be a little of both.

I got always got along with Rich, even though there were a couple of times I wanted to kill him. He was driving Louie Seymour's car out in Colorado one night when he started running out of fuel. I was coming up on him down the front straightaway when he hooked a right to block me. I thought there was going to be a big crash, and there would have been if I hadn't hit the brakes.

Rich was fueled more by desire than anything. He heard me coming and he was prepared to do whatever it took to hold on to the win. He didn't care if he made you mad, as long as he ended up in Victory Lane. And you might recall that I wrecked him one night when I was trying to win a race for the dying Hank Green. Whatever my reason, whatever Rich's ever were, sometimes desire trumps the situation.

The 1983 USAC champions, Gary Bettenhausen (Silver Crown); Tom Sneva (Indy cars); Rich Vogler (Midgets); me (Sprints) and my old friend Dean Roper (Stock Cars). (John Mahoney photo; Ken Schrader Collection.)

That's why I settled for fourth at Nazareth the day I borrowed Sheldon Kinser's ride. Rich couldn't have cared less about my situation in trying to win the Silver Crown championship that day. I knew I had enough distance on Ron Shuman. It was getting dark and they were going to call the finish early, so it didn't seem worth taking any chances trying to get around Rich, who was only going to be thinking about protecting third place.

I fell asleep in front of the television the Saturday night they televised that sprint race from Salem, Indiana, in 1990. Ann woke me up to tell me that Rich had just flipped and hung his car on a pole. They didn't show any replays, and I knew from the way they were talking that it wasn't good. The following day, they announced that Rich died in the wreck. What few people remember is that he was qualified for the Sunday Winston Cup race at Pocono.

I don't know what kind of Cup career Rich would have had. He couldn't have continued exactly the way he'd run on the short tracks, because the Cup guys wouldn't have stood for it. Hell, neither would Bill France. But, if he could have harnessed that incredible desire he had, Rich might have conquered NASCAR, too.

THE WALLACE BROTHERS

Rusty was the 1989 NASCAR Winston Cup champion and is one of the all-time race winners in NASCAR. Middle brother Mike came east later than the rest but has turned out to be a solid racer. Youngest brother Kenny is a hoot.

I've known the Wallaces all my life. There was a time in the St. Louis racing scene when Schrader and Wallace meant Bill and Russ, our fathers, so we all grew up around the race track.

Rusty is just a year younger than I am and we were close during those early years. We were a couple of gear-heads, too, so it was a natural and we didn't live all that far apart. We spent a lot of Sunday afternoons racing motorcycles and then Sunday nights racing cars.

For just a little while, Rusty dated my sister. I knew that nothing good could come from that, but fortunately it was a very short deal. And that had nothing to do with me—unintentionally—almost killing Rusty.

We were out riding our motorcycles one day when we were in our mid-teens, I guess, and we were screwing around jumping creeks and climbing hills. We came to this one hill we decided to fly over, like the jumps they do in motocross. So, I told Rusty I would ride up and check it out first. I hollered back that it was fine, and he proceeds to roar up

Three life-long friends, Rusty, Mike and Kenny Wallace. (Left and middle: Autostock Images; right: Dick Berggren photo.)

the hill and sail over the crest—only, there was no hill to come down on the other side. Just a cliff.

I thought I'd killed him, but fortunately, he was a lot tougher than he looked.

Not too long after that, Rusty started building and selling chassis. I don't think it had anything to do with that little episode on the bikes. He was always just a whole lot more into the technical end of racing. I wanted to race but I didn't want to spend 60 hours a week working in the garage, even though there have been periods of time when I've done just that. Rusty's career took off on short, paved tracks while I was running primarily dirt. We met up again in NASCAR, but our commitments have kept us from doing a lot together (*he's Miller, I'm Budweiser, for example*), although we co-own an airport hangar in Concord, North Carolina. Rusty was quick to expand his business interests and since many of them are in East Tennessee, I doubt Rusty will ever return to St. Louis.

Mike and Kenny are another story. Mike was the last of the brothers to come down. He married, had a family and tore up the local tracks back home. Between an accident that killed his little boy and the fact that the rest of his family was out in North Carolina, Mike eventually decided to try his hand in NASCAR, too. For a year-and-a-half he drove my Craftsman truck for me, and Mike's driven for a lot of different car owners in trucks, Busch and Cup cars, as well. It's hard to predict what Mike will do in the long run because his career has been less in his control, but I feel he will do fine, whatever he decides to do.

I've become closer over the years to Kenny, whom we all call "Herman." We just continue to be better and better friends, and part of that is our ties to home. He and his wife have a real nice place back there and he's become a huge St. Louis Cardinals baseball fan, too.

Kenny used to come home from high school and spend literally hours practicing pit stops. Before he went to North Carolina, he was already an outstanding pit man. But sometime along the way he decided he wanted to drive, too, and his success didn't turn out to match his skill. There's been a few major setbacks, but he always manages to come back from adversity. Part of it is his personality—I mean, it's almost impossible to dislike the guy. He does well in public appearances and on television, too, which keeps him in the public eye. As this is written, he's got a real good Busch deal going and he tells me he could care less about a Cup ride at the moment. It's neat to see him happy.

The three brothers are as different as can be. They've got different personalities, interests, results and situations. I like them all, but Kenny tells people that I'm his other older brother, and I'm real cool with that. I suspect we'll be friends for the rest of our lives.

DARRELL WALTRIP

Three-time NASCAR Winston Cup champion and a winner in all types of racing, he's now the color announcer for Fox television's racing broadcasts.

I drove for Darrell Waltrip. He was sitting in his Busch Grand National car at Dover in 1991 and I walked up. Told him, "You need to let me drive that car." So he did, and I finished 5th. (Ken Schrader Collection.)

When I got to NASCAR, Darrell was the main man. In the early 1960s it was Fireball Roberts and Joe Weatherly; the 1970s belonged to Richard Petty, David Pearson and Cale Yarborough, but in the 1980s they had to make room for Darrell and he was a whole different breed. Darrell wanted to talk, he was *gonna* talk, and you couldn't shut him up. That got him the nickname "Jaws," but eventually it also got him a great gig as a television announcer.

He was controversial for a while. Sort of like Jeff Gordon but not as bad because there weren't as many fans then, and Darrell was a Southerner instead of a Californian. He also knew when to back off, although his duels with Dale Earnhardt, Sr. were the stuff of legends. There was Darrell, the first clean-cut, handsome dude who never saw a microphone he didn't love, and there was Dale, a kind of scruffy mill-town boy who never saw a microphone he couldn't turn his back on. It was ironic that at the tail end of Darrell's driving career he ended up driving for—and having his final success with—Dale as car owner. Talk about the Odd Couple making peace!

Darrell has two sides to him. One is the public person, and he really likes the limelight. There's probably nobody better at it, either, and he can put on a real show. The other side is a really normal, down-to-earth guy who is as good a friend as anybody could want. In my early NASCAR days, I could go to him with questions and always get a thoughtful, good answer. He was so good that he was never threatened by helping other people step up their program.

Part of the appeal also is his wife Stevie. They have been very, very good friends to us and it's great to see them still at the track and an important part of the whole scene. He's got plenty to offer the racing fan on television and young guys getting into racing, and she's a warm and wonderful person of faith.

Even though Darrell was a huge winner, one memory that stands out for me is the time he wrecked real bad at Daytona and broke his leg. I went to the emergency room with his brother Michael, and Darrell still wouldn't shut up, but it was a mess. He kept asking us what happened, and we're having trouble looking at him with the bones sticking out and stuff.

About a year later, we were at Ditka's restaurant in Chicago and I asked the waiter for a bottle of wine. Darrell was something of an expert, so we turned to him to ask what to order, but he says, "I quit drinking."

Huh?

"After the wreck, I quit drinking."

I started laughing. "Well, hell, Darrell, you quit, but after seeing you in the emergency room after that wreck, I *stepped up* my drinking!"

MICHAEL WALTRIP

NASCAR veteran, television veteran and all-around good-time veteran.

We've done a television show together for over 10 years now, and apparently a lot of viewers like the way we play off each other. Mikey and I have been in the same boat in our racing careers because both of us are just literally amazed that we haven't had to get real-world jobs yet.

I imagine his last name opened some doors initially for Mikey because Darrell was the big dog when his little brother came up, but in general those doors haven't been very wide or as productive as he planned. When he finally got where he needed to be to win, and Mikey headed for Victory Lane for the first time, his car owner died and didn't even see it.

Dale Earnhardt, Inc. couldn't easily fire a guy who's won the Daytona 500 and has the kind of personality that sponsors just love. But the reality is that Mikey's connection at DEI was Dale. It's not that they haven't been good to him, or that he failed them in any way—it was just that things changed.

With the support of NAPA—a company smart enough to realize that Mikey's sold a lot of filters and spark plugs for them—he has moved on

to Bill Davis Racing. Mikey acknowledged how much times have changed in NASCAR, with some of the big teams now grooming drivers through development programs, when he said on our show, "I want to thank Bill Davis for *not* taking a chance on a younger driver who *doesn't* have a sponsor."

Once upon a time on the show, Mikey showed a folded-up picture of just a set of eyes and asked the viewers if they didn't think it looked like Schrader. Even I thought it did. Well, then he unfolded the paper and showed them that it was actually a photo of Larry Fine of the Three Stooges.

So, how do you fight back with a guy like that?

Well, it's true that he has two more Daytona 500 wins than I do, but in terms of overall wins in NASCAR, we're tied! And we're not done trying to beat each other.

We were just puppies, Michael Waltrip and me, not knowing that we would share a television show, a ton of memories, and more laughs than I can count, in this instance with former NASCAR driver Rick Wilson. (Ken Schrader Collection.)

CALE YARBOROUGH

Three-time Winston Cup champion and Daytona 500 winner.

What I learned real quick about racing is that everybody hates to lose. But I'm thinkin' not very many hate it as much as Cale did.

He's a little fireplug of a guy that you couldn't knock over. And he is just as tough mentally, so you not only had to beat him with better equipment, you had to out-smart him, and not very many people ever did that.

Cale's one of the guys who made racing better. I didn't get to race with him very much because by the time I got competitive he had cut back his schedule to part-time. It's hard to continue that way very long because it's difficult for your team to retain its sharpness if they're not

running every week, and sponsors want you on the track all the time.

When he stopped driving, Cale tried owning a team, but when there wasn't enough sponsorship money to go around he real wisely got out of that business. We've always been told that he was especially smart with his money. Guys in his era didn't make near what even the back-markers of today make so a lot of them didn't end up on Easy Street. Still, last I checked nobody was putting a gun to our heads to make us race, so we all make of the racing and the money what we can. It just seems that Cale, who came from a real poor background, did well and he set a standard that the rest of us have tried to follow.

Few people did more than Cale Yarborough to make racing a major deal. I have so much respect for him and the example he set for all of us to follow. (Mike Adaskaveg photo.)

AND I COULD GO ON AND ON

As I said at the beginning of this chapter, I can't begin to comment on all the people who've made an impression. This is barely a good start, actually, but I need to save some room for other topics.

Let the observations end with this: There have been very, very few people I've met in racing that I didn't like. It's been my experience that guys without talent or desire don't last long, while the ones who last a long time seem to have an unquenchable passion. So, if there's a driver you wish I'd mentioned but didn't, let me say this: He's probably good, I probably raced with him, and I probably like him.

Part Three

Even I Have to Come Out of the Race Car Once in a While

Jim Compton photo

You Have to Hustle Up a Couple Million a Year

13

IBECAME A BUSINESSMAN at age 18. Not in the sense that I had to go out and buy a tie and hold meetings with staff. But in the eyes of the IRS—*and this is extremely important*—I qualified as a businessman.

Quite unintentionally I've seen my business grow to the point where I own a couple of ties—don't necessarily wear them, but I've got them when needed—and I attend way more meetings than I'd like. But it's not like I drew up a Business Plan or a Five-Year Plan or even a Five-Minute Plan. Stuff just happened over time and I was smart enough to realize that if I didn't get organized and take advantage of opportunities that came my way, when the Day Job (driving a Nextel Cup car) went away, I might actually have to punch a time clock.

We weren't having that.

So, thanks to good advice from business associates, hiring the right people, listening to Ann, and following what have turned out to be pretty good instincts, I've managed to accumulate more than I've spent. And considering how much I've spent on race cars, I can make that statement with some pride—and surprise.

Welcome to Schrader Racing in Concord, North Carolina. (Joyce Standridge photo.)

SCHRADER RACING

Daddy gave me the race car when I graduated from high school, you may recall. But for a long time, Schrader Racing was a pretty small operation. There was usually a race car in the garage at the Fenton home, but it was strictly a fall-back position. As much as possible, I hounded car owners for rides because early in Schrader Racing's formative years I figured out that it was a much better deal if somebody else was paying the tire bill and springing for the repairs. It also meant that I got to run around the country with some great ladies and gentlemen, so I liked that set-up and we did it as long as we could. Still do, occasionally.

When we moved to North Carolina, though, it got a lot tougher to continue with what we'd been doing all along. I continued to fly back and run Midwestern shows, but coordinating the schedule got tougher. And some of those car owners went on to other deals. I mean, if you have a race car and you've invested more and more into it—which is the case over the years as short-track racing has gotten a lot more expensive—you want to see it on the track. If you can hire somebody good enough to win, he or she is gonna want to know that they can race it all the time, not just when Schrader is off doing something else. Some car owners kept a spare car for me over the years, but mostly we kept the friendships and changed the business end.

Shortly after relocating, I bought a Busch car. Running around with Earnhardt kept me mostly busy and mostly out of trouble but that wasn't real profitable. And while I was used to working on race cars, I recognized that keeping a Busch car going would take too much time as I tried to gain security on the senior circuit.

The first employee was hired.

Tim Kohuth was crew chief, although it was only part of his duties. I worked on the car, too, but anything that wasn't hired out—like painting the car—was his job, so really Timmy was also the janitor and took care of anything else that needed doing. When we went to the races my Cup team would run the pit stops for us.

Tim also started a real Schrader Racing tradition—he stayed with us for years. We can't compete with the big Cup teams in terms of pay and perks, but we must do something right because people come to us as

The original Schrader Racing shop was on Windy Road, several miles west of Concord. We built the well-stocked, spring-fed pond because Dorothy and I had so much fun fishing over at Earnhardt's farm. Time passes and things change. Dorothy doesn't want to go fishing so much anymore, and we recently sold the Windy Road facility. (Joyce Standridge photos.)

their first or second full-time racing job, and then they stay. We play it straight with them when they are interviewing. We don't paint it to be a glamorous job and we don't make promises we know we can't keep. So, when you come to work for me, you know where you stand today and where you'll stand tomorrow, too.

We also won't work you to death. As we've said, we firmly believe there is more to life than working.

We have occasionally hired the relative—Carl Edwards is an example, although he never actually went on the payroll, and Joey Walsh, who is my sister's stepson and currently my dirt-car crew chief—but this happens only when there's an opening for somebody who's otherwise qualified. There's an area Mission for charity. There's also a lot on the line for all of us so we can't carry dead weight on the payroll. Everybody who comes to work here, no matter the route, has to be prepared to do whatever is required. I mean, our general manager Brian Buchauer's duties include ordering toilet paper, and then he may be the one to go put it on the hanger. Nobody around here is too good to do whatever needs to be done, and that includes Ann and me.

Schrader Racing's uncontrolled and unplanned growth came out of desire to go racing rather than sound business planning, but we've avoided over-reaching what we can do, too. Our growth started with a second Busch car, because having only one car wouldn't get it done on the NASCAR short tracks and at Daytona, too. Then we got what's called a Southwest Tour car, which is a short-track pavement car that conforms

Tim Kohuth was our original crew chief when we first went to North Carolina and he stayed with us for a very long time. Loyalty among our staff members is pretty well known. (Ken Schrader Collection.)

Brian Buchauer: Most people think Kenny is an open book. Or they believe that he's only what he seems to be most of the time, which is a happy-go-lucky guy. But there's some real depth to him, which isn't so apparent.

First of all, people who know him well are aware that he's very smart and a good businessman. He's invested much of the money he's made, and not just in race cars.

He is also deeply caring. My wife died of cancer recently and during the difficult period of her illness, there couldn't have been anybody better to be working for than Kenny and Ann. Their understanding and support made all the difference.

And he never wants to hurt anyone he cares for. When he made the decision to leave Hendrick and move over to the Petree car, he thought about it a lot more and a lot longer than it seemed to most people. As important to him as his career is, it was equally important that he not hurt Rick Hendrick.

Kenny doesn't show it, but some things really disturb him, and leaving Rick was one of those things. I don't think I've ever seen him more upset than trying to figure out how he was going to tell Rick he was leaving the team.

But Rick's an extraordinary businessman and he understood. And then Kenny learned even more from Rick about how to conduct yourself as a businessman.

Brian Buchauer, Schrader Racing's General Manager. And one of these days, he'll tell me what a general manager does. (Joyce Standridge photo.)

Joey Walsh, nephew and dirt late model crew chief: Because my dad and Kenny grew up together and were real good friends, I started going to the local dirt tracks around St. Louis and I'd hang out, work on his dirt cars. Eventually, he asked me to help him take care of the cars he had there. We ran out of a shop I had in Missouri, but after about three years I moved to North Carolina and started taking care of all the dirt cars. I've been here for seven years now, and I like the resources we have in our shop.

It's kind of far to drive because most of his dirt races are in the Midwest, but it's fun here. With our new program, the new shop and everything, everybody works on everything—the dirt cars, the ARCA cars and the trucks. You learn a lot that way.

Joey Walsh, nephew by marriage, dirt car crew chief by choice. (Joyce Standridge photo.)

Left: At the back of the shop we have a covered area for loading and unloading the trailers. My bus is also parked there before and after trips. I spend about 110 nights a year in it, so it's home almost as much as home is. Right: Craftsman Truck Series racers in various stages of building or repair. (Joyce Standridge photos.)

to the rules out West, because if you want to race in the winter months that's one of the few places you can go and do it.

When the Craftsman Trucks Series began in 1995 we kind of thought we needed to get involved, especially when AC Delco wanted to help us do that. Of course, we had to have a dirt car, and then we felt like an ARCA car was a good investment. We found that with a little planning we could find markets for our sponsors, who in turn helped us get on the race tracks in those areas.

We're running a very limited schedule—maybe 20-25 races with ARCA and NASCAR Craftsman Trucks—except the dirt cars, which we run as many as 50 races a year. With good sponsorship you can also win enough prize money to about break even, which is always our back-up goal whenever the original one of coming out ahead fails. The hardest division to make that happen in is the dirt car, because we have to go into tracks where the local heroes run every week and know exactly what kind of set-up they need. We're always playing catch-up with these deals.

Even when cars are outdated, we don't get rid of them. Fans who come by the shop for a visit enjoy looking over the variety. But they're not available to take for a spin. (Joyce Standridge photo.)

It's less expensive to go into a track and drive somebody else's car, but you also have a lot less control, and sometimes it can be really hard to jump in a strange car and be as competitive as you want to be. We've kind of learned over the years where we can go and do that, so we gear at least part of the season to that.

With the Nextel Cup car added in, we are racing in excess of 100 times a year.

About once a week, Brian gets with me on how we're doing. He oversees everything but the dirt operation, which Joey and I control, and I think the dirt car kind of irks Brian's business senses. He'll tell us we did okay this week—we lost only an arm and a leg on the dirt deal. But we've got a really good, open relationship and he undoubtedly keeps me from wasting too much money on losing deals. He can't stop me altogether, but it's good to have another set of eyes on the books.

This Maynard Troyer-built modified is actually licensed and street legal. I love to take it out for a spin with Sheldon riding shotgun. (Joyce Standridge photo.)

We also still love motorcycles so there's an assortment on hand to play with. (Joyce Standridge photo)

My first general manager was Roger Hamilton, a nephew of one of my former midget car owners, Gene Hamilton. That was really a case of knowing somebody a long time and having faith that he would keep our best interests at heart. Roger came on board in 1990 and stayed until he had the opportunity to go back to Indiana and buy into a General Motors store. We not only wished him well, we recently bought into the store, too.

We hired Brian to replace Roger because Brian had done a lengthy stint with U.S. Tobacco and was very well-respected in the NASCAR community. He was the first person who ever quit a job to come to work for us. There's been a couple more since then, even though I always said we wouldn't hire anybody that stupid. But getting back to Brian, we sort of backed him into a corner where he had to come work for us because we told everybody at the track that we'd hired him before we told him. He didn't have much choice.

In addition to our receptionist-secretary, Karen Burnett, who's also a long-term employee, we have truck and motorhome drivers, plus our pilot. At the shop, as well as the track, we have the talented veteran Donnie Richeson as crew chief on the various NASCAR and ARCA vehi-

Donnie Richeson, pavement racing crew chief: I was actually sitting on a beach in Aruba when I got the call from Kenny to come work for him. I needed a job, he needed somebody, and we found each other out of necessity, but it was a good mix.

This racing is a pretty small industry and everybody knows everybody. I always tell people, "Don't rob a bank with anybody in NASCAR there, because by that afternoon everybody's gonna know what happened."

There were never any horror stories about working for Ken Schrader. Everyone knows him and Ann, and you realize people have been here 10, 11, 12 years, so it's pretty obvious that they take care of employees and treat you like you're part of their family.

Made it an easy decision.

Donnie Richeson is our crew chief for the ARCA cars and the Craftsman Truck Series. (Joyce Standridge photo.)

cles. There are also full-time mechanics, who may have to stock toilet paper if Brian doesn't have time, because like I said, everybody has to do what needs to be done. We've never had to worry about anybody saying, "That's not my job," but if they did, we'd be pointing to the door. At that point, they would become former employees of Schrader Racing.

OTHER THINGS SCHRADER RACING HAS TO CONSIDER

These days, we have 16-18 paid employees, a drop in the bucket compared to the 200-300 at the major Nextel Cup shops, but just the right size to keep our organization humming along. We're close and committed to what we do. But the financial end of the business goes well beyond the importance of having good workers.

Our original shop—the one that Earnhardt helped us locate—was really neat. It's about 30 acres out in the woods, with a stocked pond. We liked the peace and quiet, and we liked the idea that when the stress got too much we could always get a fishing pole and clear our minds for a couple of hours before going back to work.

But times change. In order to grow Schrader Racing we needed an upgraded facility. And we had race cars scattered all over the place from our home, to Missouri, to other race teams' shops. We needed more room to work, too.

So in 2004, we bought some property and a 35,000-square-foot shop where we could keep all the cars and employees under one roof. It's also closer to Concord so we're closer to home for most employees, including me.

The shop is just part of the physical stuff we have. As this is written, we have three tractor-trailer units, three motor homes and two airplanes. There's also a cube van and a 24-foot trailer. We also have an old-style ramp truck that we're pretty proud of because it's our own design,

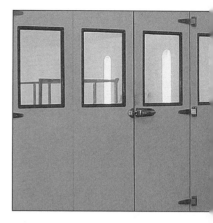

Having a paint booth is a real help. We also have a booth for the bondo body work. This keeps the fumes out of the rest of the shop. (Joyce Standridge photos.)

Being behind the desk is a place I spend more and more time, and that phone is about glued to my ear these days. As long as I can still get to the race track, I guess we'll just have to tolerate it. (Joyce Standridge photo.)

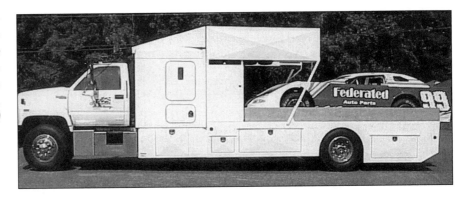

The design for this truck started out on a napkin one night. We're happy that it ended up being practical and pretty darn sharp-looking, too. (Ken Schrader Collection.)

with the help of a couple of bottles of wine and a napkin. We're especially proud of the fact that the end product is remarkably close to what we originally sketched, so maybe the wine didn't go as far as we thought.

Because we can be racing anywhere from three to seven times a week in a variety of classes at several tracks, just the logistics of getting things done is pretty incredible. I can remember being out at Phoenix once upon a time with three cars, three tow rigs, an airplane and a bus, and thinking, "Why are we doing this shit? This ain't makin' sense at all."

But we keep on doing it, and occasionally we literally meet ourselves coming and going. With the hundreds of thousands of miles we've done on the roads, we also have a remarkable safety record. The only accident I can recall was a few years ago with the dirt car operation, going from St. Louis up to Quincy, Illinois, for a special there.

Joey was laying there on the ground after the wreck with his wrist bent over at a really unnatural angle and Tim the Banker was laying next to him with the mother of all hangovers from the previous night's partying. The EMTs took both their pulses—and wanted to transport the Banker first.

Even though we won't be slowing down, I don't see us growing past a full-time Truck or Busch Grand National team. We don't anticipate

Joey Walsh: I broke my wrist in that accident and ended up going to the hospital in an ambulance. The nurses kept telling me that my friends hadn't gotten there yet, but I knew where they were. They'd gone on to the race track.

But I got the last laugh. They couldn't figure out how to get the door open on the trailer, so they ended up not racing that night!

Two of the dirt cars and an ARCA car on the right take up only a little space in the shop. (Joyce Standridge photo.)

hiring on-track drivers in the future, but you never know. We didn't always anticipate hiring the ones we've had in the past. You just figure out whether it makes sense to keep all the cars (and trucks) on the track, and much as I would like to, I can't drive them all every week.

At its most basic level, nothing has changed. It's just that things have grown, which means more headaches at times. But all I've ever done is jack with race cars, whether it was one car in the shop out behind the house in St. Louis or in the shop now with a dozen and a half of them.

You just gotta keep a couple million dollars a year hustled up so you can keep everybody working.

NATURAL EXTENSIONS

We didn't intentionally get into other areas of the racing business either, but in 1995 I found myself leasing a track back home, in partnership with my former car owner Ray Marler. This has turned out to be such an important part of my professional life that I'm going to devote the next chapter of the book to it, but for now, we'll note that I-55 Raceway got me thinking beyond just running race cars all over the place.

In 2005, having grown the I-55 Raceway business into a solid producer, I decided that in the right circumstances another track would be a good investment. Not just any hole in the ground either. It needed to be something that wasn't going to have to overcome a truly horrible reputation or that had been run into the ground and chased off all the fans. But we were looking for a place that still had room to grow and develop more potential, because if it's already at its maximum, it's also expensive.

This investigation took on a somewhat accelerated pace when I was joined by two new partners. I've never been opposed to having partners—in fact, I think it's a really good idea because you've got an on-going infusion of ideas and enthusiasm from other smart people, while it makes the rewards more enjoyable and the risks more tolerable.

When I've partnered, I've gone with people who aren't afraid to tell me when I'm wrong or my ideas won't work. That has saved my butt

I've kept all my helmets over the years and there are about 50 of them in storage at the shop. All my old uniforms are there, too. These are the Winston Cup/Nextel Cup uniforms, but I have dozens of others in another room. I have no idea of how many there are, but I can guarantee it's a hell of a lot more than the number of business suits I'll ever own! (Joyce Standridge photos.)

The sign above the door leading to the employee-only area says it all, as far as I'm concerned. (Joyce Standridge photo.)

more than once through the years. I also look for people who are smart, full of ideas and not afraid to work. That's why Ray Marler—and in fact, his whole family, because it was a package deal—was a natural.

But Ray and the gang have their hands full at I-55 Raceway and I really like the idea of their focus remaining on that track. We've not realized all our goals there and I wanted the family to stay focused on making it the premier race track we envisioned when we started. We're getting a lot closer—but we're not quite there yet.

So, for the next track, I'm looking for other people I trust. And along comes Bob Sargent, a really good young promoter out of central Illinois, who's looking to expand his horizons.

And from a completely different direction, interest in short-track ownership comes from Dale Earnhardt, Jr.

Seriously.

For a kid with unlimited opportunities, it says a lot about his total devotion to racing that he wants to invest in a dirt track. He'd told me that if I saw something good come along to let him know. So, when Paducah International Speedway quietly went on the market, we were interested.

It's a pretty grand name for a 3/8-mile dirt track in Kentucky, but if you don't believe in yourself, why should anybody else? They've got a pretty solid core of race cars supporting the track, and even though there's not a huge population in the area, there's also very few other entertainment draws we have to compete with.

It's too early yet to know how well our vision for the track is going to work. Unlike I-55, where I got a working partner with a whole family willing to invest time and energy, at Paducah we had to hire a manager and the rest of the employees. It's a different can of worms, for sure, but Bob and Dale wouldn't have invested in it if they didn't think it has a promising future.

. . . AND MORE RACING VENTURES

One of the most important sanctioning bodies in the history of short-track racing is the United Midwestern Promoters (UMP). The brain-child of the late Bob Memmer, UMP in its infant years didn't overly impress a lot of people. Bob was so down-to-earth that some people were convinced it would never succeed because he couldn't waltz into corporate boardrooms and dazzle the Suits.

Well, UMP had its struggles and for many years functioned without major sponsorship, but what it had was credibility. It was obvious that Bob wasn't in to get rich and then walk away. For him and his dog Trouble, it was their lives, right up to the end. And you didn't need a lawyer going over a contract with a fine-toothed comb because Bob's word was good as gold.

When he knew that his health was failing he went looking for somebody to take over his baby and try to keep it where he'd built it or make it even bigger. Bob Sargent had promoted a bunch of UMP shows and impressed Mr. Memmer, so it was a natural to start talking with him.

But Sargent didn't have the time to assume ownership of UMP on his own, so that started our first partnership along with Howie Commander and Robert Lawton, two other veteran promoters.

For a couple of years, we kept Mr. Memmer's dream going on, but it became clear that it was too hard to keep up with the many issues a sanctioning group has to face, from rules to rules infractions by race teams, adding tracks while keeping the currents ones satisfied, and growing purses in the face of tough economic times for a lot of the people who came to the tracks. These were issues that needed full-time attention instead of the couple of phone teleconferences a day we tried to carve out. Sam Driggers did—and still does—a fine job of day-to-day operations management, but too much was beyond our control.

We believe in preserving racing history when we can. We have rescued a few historical cars and restored them and will continue to do so in the future. (Joyce Standridge photos.)

Along one wall of the shop are several "classic" Winston Cup cars I've driven. We have visiting hours for fans who'd like to come by and take a look for themselves. (Joyce Standridge photo.)

And then Boundless Motorsports—which is now DIRT Motorsports as this is written, but could well be called something else by the time you read it—came along with the promise to keep it the best weekly racing sanctioning group around. With some trepidation, we sold our interests.

We genuinely hope that UMP is a force forever, for Mr. Memmer's sake if nothing else. He deserves that. But while Bob Memmer, and our group for that matter, were always accessible and talked the racer talk, it's been different for the DIRT group. There are layers of bureaucracy and the talk is business-speak. That's not necessarily a bad thing, even if it appears they're awfully leveraged, but it makes racers nervous. Most drivers don't want to see a monopoly running racing—not even NASCAR—because if they fail or they stop being receptive to the average racer, the whole sport could suffer. Maybe even die, though I don't think you can kill racing, even with government interference. Somebody is gonna get together with somebody else in a cow pasture and pass the hat—and I'll probably be there. I don't think you can ever totally kill racing.

But the uncertainty about UMP is why Bob and I retained ownership of the North American Late Model Series, which we own along with managing partner Bill Nelson. We've got a nice little group there, solid racers supporting it, all of it functioning well but without demanding a huge chunk of our time. And it's there, just in case everything with UMP goes bad.

BUT THAT'S NOT ALL . . .

Never put all your eggs in one basket, especially when you no longer have the NASCAR Nextel Cup money pipeline available to replenish your nest-egg. So, I have been fortunate enough—and it's mostly because I met people racing—to have bought into a couple of auto dealerships. I am 50 percent owner of Kirby-Schrader Chevrolet in Whitmire, South Carolina, and 60 percent owner of Ken Schrader's Linton Motors, a GM dealership in Linton, Indiana. Come on by and we'll do you a nice deal.

These are not huge mega-lot dealerships, but the advantage of having a place midway between Spartanburg and Columbia, South Carolina, and another place just southwest of Bloomington, Indiana, is that you can run them like family-owned businesses. Doesn't mean you give away the vehicles, but that you get to be friendly with your customers and develop long-term relationships. You might have noticed, if you've been reading from the beginning, that I'm sort of into that kind of thing.

The problem with taking a truck to the track, especially one as tight as Martinsville, is that you'll probably have repair work when you bring it back. (Joyce Standridge photo.)

Through my business partner Bob Sargent I was able to track down and buy the original hand-painted sign that hung outside Springfield Speedway. The track has been closed for 20 years now, but it was the scene of my earliest midget fun and a place where I ran—and won—sprint and late model races. In time I will have the sign restored and hung at the shop. (Joyce Standridge photo.)

For quite a while, Rick Hendrick and I have talked about co-owning an auto dealership somewhere and sometime, too. I think we'll do it one of these days, and for sure, with Rick's background and knowledge, we'll end up with something bigger than what I have now. But, frankly, I don't care about the size. I just really like the idea of sharing with him on a professional basis once more.

Beyond that, we're dabbling in other things like real estate. Like I told my banker, they're not making any more of that, so if you buy some dirt, even something you have to sit on for a while, eventually you can turn a profit.

And that matters, because it's all that stands between us and the time clock.

I tracked down the car we ran the year we got the USAC Silver Crown championship and had it restored right down to the motor. I believe it's the only Silver Crown car on display in the Charlotte-Concord area. (Joyce Standridge photo.)

A Track Owner Is a Promoter With a Mortgage **14**

PROMOTING RACES is like driving race cars. If you do it really well, you make it look easy. As a result, an awful lot of racers and fans who have been to a well-run race track think the sum total of promoting races is that you open the gate, take in the money, count the money, figure out a way to screw everybody else, and go home.

Okay, that's not really fair. At bad tracks, it feels that way, and I imagine almost everyone with a long-term racing career has thought so at times. Most folks will give a promoter the benefit of the doubt. They know it takes effort to prepare the track, get food and drink in the cooler and do a little advertising. But there are very, very few people who have a real grip on what an incredible amount of work is involved. I admit that while I had a pretty good idea, actually getting into the promotion business has been an eye-opener.

I am going to share with you just a little of the background. If I told you everything, you'd be convinced that Ray Marler and I need straight-

This is an aerial view of our 3/8-mile dirt track at Pevely, Missouri, the I-55 Raceway. (Ken Schrader Collection.)

My partners at I-55 Raceway, Ray Marler in a rare moment of rest as he watches a feature event, and, at right, his lovely wife of 40 years, Sue. (Joyce Standridge photos.)

jackets for doing this. And I want you to bear in mind something else—even if you are not a NASCAR fan, you need to appreciate what it takes to put on a single race at the Cup level. Because they're doing all the things we do at I-55, *times a hundred*, because they're also dealing with crowds in excess of 100,000, television and radio, and about a zillion people who think they deserve special perks even though they don't. Yeah, it means huge sums of money, too, but a lot of that is going out as well as coming in.

Even on our level of racing, with a 3/8-mile dirt oval on about 161 acres just south of St. Louis, we wrestle with the bank balance as much as the Federated Auto Parts store clerk sitting in our grandstand on Saturday night does after paying bills on Friday night. As I've said about the difference between running a NASCAR Cup team and the guys at our track, it's all a matter of how many zeroes you add to the starting figure.

CROSSING THE LINE

From the first time they passed a hat to pay for a race, promoters and racers have been on different sides of the same fence. It's Catch-22. You can't promote races without the cars and drivers, and you can't race without the prize money generated by a well-promoted race. Sometimes all concerned get to be such adversaries that they forget about the fans, who have no stake at all in racing except for the enjoyment they get. That's why more and more short tracks are back-gate-driven financially, which is a whole other can of worms.

I never planned to be a promoter. I mean, I'm like every race driver who ever walked past the pit gate. I've looked around and said, "If I was a promoter, I'd…" and then proceeded to say what I'd do. This is always done without knowing why things are done the way they are or what restrictions—financially, environmentally, governmentally or what-

A huge crowd of several thousand waited hours in 100-degree heat to get autographs. I can't think of another group of fans of any other sport who would have done that. (Joyce Standridge photo.)

ever—the track owners and promoters face. Communicating with the racers is an important part of the promotional deal, and track owners need to work on that. You don't need to tell the racers everything about your business, but there's nothing wrong with letting them in on some of the headaches.

Being both promoter and race driver can be a conflicted feeling at times. The more I understand about both sides, the more I'm convinced we don't understand one another at all.

I could have avoided this drain on my brain.

The long road to being a track owner started back in the early 1990s when a lot of talk was centering on I-55 Raceway in Pevely, Missouri. The track has been around for quite a while and known success in the past, but at that time it was struggling somewhat. Carol Smotherman was the owner/promoter following her husband's death, and while the Allied Auto Racing Association (AARA) was running the races for her and they had a good car count, the track was showing its age. A lot of the guys I talked to at the time were concerned about the future.

Carol was no dummy. This was not only her main source of income, it was also a tribute to her husband in her eyes and she wanted to do

Late Model heat race action in turn four at I-55 Raceway. On good nights cars run two and three wide. (Joyce Standridge photo.)

A Track Owner Is a Promoter With a Mortgage **179**

When you're a co-promoter, you get to do neat things like chauffeur The King around when he visits. But then you get to do not-so-neat things like clean up behind everybody else. (Ken Schrader Collection.)

well. I don't think it really needs saying that promoters don't go into business to fail, but a lot of people get into it thinking they have all the answers and they won't listen to a dispassionate suggestion or two.

Carol wasn't in that group.

She started calling Ray Marler for advice. Ray had been the managing partner at St. Francois Speedway in Farmington, Missouri, for several years and had built that county fairgrounds track into a showplace. They had great car counts, plenty of fans in the grandstand, and good shows during that period, so Ray was a logical person to turn to. And he would help anybody, even other promoters where he stood to gain nothing at all.

The thing of it was, when you saw Ray, sometimes you saw me. And I did a couple of "drop-in's" to race at Pevely when Ray was also on hand. In no time, the Internet message boards got to buzzing.

Finally, one day we were flying to Charlotte with Ray and his wife, Sue. Russ Wallace—father of Rusty, Mike and Kenny—was on-board, too. He turned to Ray and said, "Hell, Rayburn, everybody says you're going to take over I-55. So when are ya gonna do it?"

We blame Russ.

We really hadn't considered doing it, but the conversation went from "you're nuts," to "well, what would it take?"

From that conversation, over an extended period of time Ray negotiated a lease for the facility, starting with the 1995 season. For the next six years we were just the promoters—people who don't own the track but operate a race-track promotional business at the facility—and then we purchased the track from Carol. She was a very reasonable landlord, but you hate to continue to pour money and effort into something that isn't yours, especially when you are located in an area where it's only slightly more difficult to get permits to build a world-renowned, 600-foot Gateway Arch on the riverfront than it is to build six new stalls in the rest rooms at the track.

Leasing would be simple if everything was in place, and I think of Ralph Capitani's situation at Knoxville, Iowa, where the county board recognized what a wonderful thing racing could be for the local economy, and have supported Ralph 100 percent. That doesn't usually happen. So, when you want to install better lights, new concession stands, a VIP tower and such, you're really doing it for somebody else unless you own the track.

A race track, as you will see, is a lot more than just a hole in the ground that needs watering.

BEFORE YOU OPEN THE GATE

You could write an entire book about what it takes to run a race track, but we'll go with the Reader's Digest version.

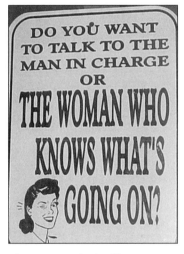

This sign is in Sue's office. We know better than to argue with it—or her. (Joyce Standridge photo.)

In our corner we have Sue Marler, who has a completely appropriate sign just outside her office that sums up her value to our team. It says, "Do you want to talk to the man in charge, or the woman who knows what's going on?"

Sue has seen maybe a half-dozen races in the ten-plus years we've run the track. We've held several thousand races if you count all the heat, dash and semis along with the features. She comes out to watch the Nickel Toss we occasionally have for the children because she enjoys it so much. But most of her days, nights, weeks, months and life are spent in a 10-by-12-foot cell...er...office that has no view whatsoever, unless you count the heads bobbing past as people walk up to the back door. We keep saying we're going to build an office adjacent to the VIP tower so she can see the races, but I'm not sure she would have the time, because come the green flag she shoos everybody else out to go watch and she handles the telephone, walk-ins, complaints, headaches, demands and, once in a while, a smiling visitor.

Long before race night, however, she's put in long hours making sure that we have all the permits we need to operate our business. She works with the accountant and the banker to see that we've got enough money set aside to pay the light bill, mortgage note, payroll, beer and hot dog bills, and all the other invoices in the overflowing stack.

Sue has also made sure the insurance bill is paid so we are protected, the racers and the fans are covered, and we can stay in business. She has checked that somebody was around for all the deliveries done from

Ray and his daughter Shari Stanfill set up pay-off for the races. Most racers will tell you this is important, but they'll also tell you that being treated with respect and appreciated for being on hand to help put on a show is just as important. (Joyce Standridge photo.)

Monday through Friday. And, once in a blue moon, she takes off to go get her hair done or spend a little time with the grandchildren who are the apple of her eye.

Sue doesn't do all the office work alone. Although daughter Shari Stanfill doesn't clock in every day, she knows as much about running the joint as Sue, because Shari fills in at times, supplements Sue's efforts all the time, and is frequently the go-to person when employees, security staff, racers and fans need answers.

The guys aren't just sitting around waiting for Saturday night, either. Sue's son, Chip Marler, is in charge of the concessions, which is a whole lot more than just tossing hot dogs and beer to fans on Saturday night.

Ray and son-in-law Mark Stanfill often start working on the race track surface immediately after the last checkered flag on Saturday night. They will get the equipment out and knock down the cushion of dirt around the racing surface, working five or six hours toward breakfast on Sunday.

On Monday, the grandstand and surrounding areas get hosed down to get any dirt that flew out from race-car tires churning up the surface, as well as getting the interior walls of the track cleared. This coincidentally puts several thousand gallons of water onto the track. Then Ray and Mark will work most days of the week tilling, disking and working in the track. If it's a hot summer week—*and what summer week in St. Louis isn't?*—they'll put thousands and thousands of gallons of water on the track. (And those of you who've visited I-55 wondered why we have such a pretty pond at the back of the facility!)

Ray often gets called away from working the track because, believe it or not, there are people who want to talk to the man in charge instead of the woman who knows what's going on. That was said tongue-in-cheek. The truth is that most decisions are a joint effort. Day-to-day is ably handled by the extended Marler family, but it's not at all unusual for them to call me.

Which brings us to my part of the deal.

Until I move back to the area, I'm pretty limited as to what I can do in terms of hands-on help. Still, I care passionately about this track and its success, not only for my family's well-being, but also for the 150 or so drivers, their car owners, mechanics, families and fans. This is a huge commitment for all of us, and I have come to realize that the complaints and zingers I hear or see about what we do is only because people care. If they didn't, they would ignore us. But the track and what happens there matters maybe more than almost anything in their lives, too, even if they don't have to worry about the light bill. I wish sometimes that they would try to put themselves in our shoes and face all the stuff we are juggling, but I remember wearing only the racer's boots, and it does look different when you cross the fence.

Besides calling the track a half dozen times on race night to check on how things are going, I have been able to bring some billboard sponsorships to the track. This has been very helpful, especially in providing the income to make facility improvements. But while you will see M&Ms and Budweiser on billboards, you will also see more and more Pevely- and Missouri-based companies as they've come to realize what a good, captured audience we have for them.

With my contacts, I have been able to bring in some pretty big names for specials. We have an annual charity event that we tag onto NASCAR shows in Michigan or Indianapolis so it's not real inconvenient for people to come. The first M&Ms Night of Stars featured Dale Earnhardt, Jr., and our 5,000-seat facility strained to hold 9,000 folks.

That was interesting.

This is what it looks like from inside a truck cab as you pack in the dirt track to get it ready for racing, complete with a couple of mud clods on the windshield. Sometimes, it looks a whole lot different because if you lose momentum you slide sideways to the wall on the inside. (Joyce Standridge photo.)

Dave Blaney (left) and Casey Mears sign autographs for the fans. Dave has raced in the area as a sprint-car driver so he already had a fan base, but Casey is a smart young guy. He introduced himself around and earned a bunch of new fans, too, that night. (Joyce Standridge photo.)

Over the years, we've had most of the Cup, Busch and Truck Series drivers come in for the special. For example, in 2005 we had Kenny Wallace and Carl Edwards (who also raced in the regular show with our usual gang of drivers, in addition to the NASCAR-only race), Jimmy Spencer, Bobby Hamilton, Martin Truex, Jr., Casey Mears and Dave Blaney. We have given as much as $100,000 at a time to charities such as the Petty family's Victory Junction Gang Camp, but we've also made sure that the guys have fun, too. They love getting close to the fans, racing in dirt-track cars that are totally unlike what they are used to, and we usually share a few laughs at an impromptu party later.

Mark Martin told me last year that he wanted to come out to one of our shows. I started to check the calendar for the Night of Stars date, but he stopped me. "No, I want to come out on a night when *you* can make some money."

Mark appreciates that we don't have more money than God, and I sure appreciate what he did for us. So did his fans, who didn't have to fight for space alongside the fans of all the other guys at a Night of Stars event.

When Carl Edwards won a modified race, of course he was expected to do one of his patented back flips. Well, Kenny Wallace couldn't stand to be shown up, so he introduced his new signature move— a slow-roll somersault. Hey, we all do what we are capable of doing! (Joyce Standridge photos.)

AND THEN THEY DROP THE GREEN FLAG

Even if you do things well, when it comes time to race, you're lucky to see any of it if you're the promoter. A lot of people think that Ray spends his time running around in his golf cart and that's it.

Well, let me tell you that the smartest thing we could have done was to keep the race operations and the track operations separately managed. Allied Auto Racing Association continues to run the show for us, which frees us up for the 5,000 things that have to be done to keep the fans happy. It's not unusual for Ray to have garbage stuffed in bags in his cart because he's stopped and picked up junk as he drives around. He doesn't want fans coming in to think we don't care how the place looks. As I've said before, I like my things to be neat and clean, and so does Ray. So, even if the fans are the ones dropping crap all over the place, ain't nobody too big to stop and pick it up.

In the course of the evening, Ray may be called up to fix leaking pipes, knock down a too-tall cushion on the track, check areas where kids are trying to sneak in without paying, back up Allied officials when there are disagreements with racers, and keep notes about what they've done with the track preparation for this event. And, while it may look like he's puttering around socializing with fans and racers, that's actually a very important part of his job, too.

Because no matter what the racers tell you, they don't care about the money. They want to be treated with respect and appreciated for what they do. That's the most important thing we have to do as promoters. And Ray is very good about that, in part because he was a car owner, so he's been in their shoes, but also because he just happens to be a good human being.

The celebrities ran UMP Modifieds, but this is also a class that runs during our weekly shows, too. They put on some of the best races we see. (Joyce Standridge photo.)

We have a guest suite at the top of the main-stretch grandstand. Occasionally, we have guests like Jimmy Spencer (front) and Dave Blaney (back) who enjoyed the dirt track racing from air-conditioned comfort. Don't worry. They haven't forgotten what it's like to live with sweat in your eyes on a hot summer night. It was just a night off. (Joyce Standridge photo.)

AND WHEN IT GOES WRONG . . .

Still, no matter how hard you try, there are far more opportunities to get it wrong than right. It's a bitch, but it's true. You can spend 60 hours a week getting ready for a race, and then the weather screws you up. The perky weathergirl tells you there's zero percent chance of rain and then giggles when a thunderstorm parks over Pevely. Or you hold off watering Wednesday and Thursday because they're 80 percent sure it's going to rain on Friday. It's that 20 percent that'll get you, for sure. And if it doesn't rain you can count on just enough clouds to scare away part of your crowd while the rest endure dust from the track.

Spring in the Midwest usually means rain by the buckets full. We had a World of Outlaws show one year when we lost a significant part of our parking lot due to the river next-door swelling many times its normal size and turning it into a swimming hole. I thought, "Oh, shit, this is going to be a mess."

Now, a World of Outlaws show brings in a lot of extra people, and it needs to, because the purse is a hell of a lot higher than a regular show. Even the part of the property that wasn't under water was spongy, with lots of puddles and mudholes. Parking was going to be a nightmare. And if people can't find a place to park, they're going to turn around and go home because there aren't a lot of other options.

So, Ann and I got out there and guided people as they came in so we could get everybody in. There were more than a few double-takes, but I think we've established that if something needs doing...

Everybody understands the weather, but there are other things that may not be so obvious. You may be bucking a race down the road that sucks in several of your regular racers. There can be a county fair or country-music show that draws people who would otherwise be race fans that weekend.

It's ulcer territory.

And Ray and I tend to be a little high-strung. He's already had his ulcer, but I'm working on mine and maybe another one for him, thanks to that damned Russ Wallace.

I remember the first night we opened up. We looked like we needed guys in white jackets with butterfly nets ready. I've never seen Ray's eyes that big, not even when I wrecked his race car on the warm-up lap.

"What's wrong, Rayburn?"

"I got the track too wet. *It's gonna be rough! It's gonna be terrible! Wheel packing is gonna take forever!*"

"Don't worry about that," I said, chewing on a bloody cuticle. "We've all driven through big holes before. I'm worried there ain't gonna be no people in the grandstand. *What if nobody comes? And where the hell are the Wallaces?* They're supposed to sign autographs! It's ten minutes to five, they're supposed to start at five, and they're not here yet!"

Well, the Wallaces arrived at five-minutes-to-five, the track was okay, the grandstand was full, and almost everyone had a compliment or two.

So, we found other things to worry about. You can always fall back on what happens when you're not looking, the weather moving in, whether the show gets over at a reasonable hour, if the announcer is entertaining the crowd, and so on. You see, it always looks worse from the inside than it does from the outside.

Thank God. If people on the outside saw what it was really like, they'd bring Maalox instead of money to the gate.

GOING FORWARD

I don't think we will ever meet all the goals we've set for the track, but that's because we set the bar pretty high. We'd like for people to think of I-55 Raceway in the same category with Knoxville, Eldora, Manzanita and the other legendary dirt tracks, but we recognize that we're not there yet. Closer than we were 10 years ago, but still with a lot to achieve.

The thing is, while those tracks have great regular shows, they're famous for their specials. And while we're very happy with the way our special shows have gone, we're most excited about the growth of our weekly racing. I mean, specials are good, but you have only so many of them, so the backbone of the track is the weekly show.

Advertising didn't really matter when Ray was promoting in Farmington, which is down in the Ozark region. He knew that no matter what they did or what kind of show it was, they were going to have a crowd of "X" size. You could advertise all day and night but there were going to be only so many, and they were pretty much there whether it was a special or a weekly show because there was a limited number of things to do in the area.

We've had several charity-benefit races at I-55, including the M&M Night of Stars in 2005, with proceeds going to the Victory Junction Gang Camp, which is one of my favorites. Participants that night included (l-to-r): Bobby Hamilton, Sr., Casey Mears, Dale Earnhardt, Jr. (as flagman), Martin Truex, Jr., "Herman," me, Carl Edwards and Dave Blaney. (Ken Schrader Collection.)

At Pevely, we're much closer to St. Louis, but we're also competing with a lot of other things going on. They publish an entire tabloid of weekend activities in the St. Louis Post-Dispatch every Thursday, and we have to view all that, as well as all the things that aren't advertised in it, as competition for the fan.

So, we have grown, not so much from advertising dollars, but through word-of-mouth. And that's way more important anyway, because you can say just about anything you want in an ad, but you can't put a price tag on a fan telling his or her friends, "Man, I can't go to that concert at the UMB Pavilion. There's a race at I-55 tonight."

Short-track promotion is one of the toughest jobs in America. Especially these days, when you've got to balance the fan's wants with the racer's needs. It's always the same goal, but it isn't always the same route. So you just have to hope the decisions you make end up leaving everybody feeling like their backs have been scratched.

What's It Like Out There, Dude? **15**

I'M NEVER ALONE inside a helmet. After thirty years of driving all kinds of race cars, there are so many people, places and experiences crammed into my memory that I could never assume what I do in a race car is a solo deal. So many people have helped, hindered, shoved, crashed, forgiven, moved, and challenged me that some little bit of all those moments just naturally has to follow me into the race car.

I have confidence that I can drive a race car better than anything else I do, and how well that measures up to anyone else is something I no longer care about.

I honestly hope anybody who wants to race gets the chance to do so, and that they will eventually have that odd combination of contentment to be doing what you want and the never-satisfied hunger that drives you toward a checkered flag.

I still want to win. I want to win every single race I run and have since I was a toddler. I expect I will still feel that way when I'm an old man souping up a wheelchair for the Nursing Home Derby. But if I don't win—if I can't beat the other people on the track—it's okay. Not *wonderful okay*, but acceptable because if I've learned nothing else about myself, I know this much: I *gotta race*.

(Terry Bourcy photo; Ken Schrader Collection.)

I have driven for a lot of great car owners over the years, but now I drive my own dirt late model so I can pick and choose short track events, and I go whenever I can. (Tonya McFall photo; Ken Schrader Collection.)

At the Minnesota State Fair in 1989 they brought in a beautifully restored car and offered me a chance to take it for a spin, complete with the old-style helmet. They didn't have to ask twice. (VR Motorsports Images; Ken Schrader Collection)

When the race starts, I have to give 100 percent concentration to what I'm doing in the car. I can't think about Ann or anybody else until the checkered flag falls—and she understands that. (Ken Schrader Collection.)

I have no idea of the number of times I've been asked what it's like inside a race car. It's a unique experience each and every time I drive, but maybe I can give you some idea of what it's like.

Coming off the fourth turn, I look ahead and see the starter wave the green flag. My foot goes to the floor and the roar of the cars around me penetrates through the helmet and ear plugs wedged in as tight as possible to protect my hearing. Even dulled, the familiar sound jump-starts the adrenalin and a jolt of pure pleasure rockets through my body. Racers will tell you it's like great sex, but that's only because nobody has ever figured out a better comparison. Really, the moment when a race starts is some kind of ecstasy beyond expressing simply in words.

In this brief instant, all things are possible. You still have the chance to win. The odds are probably against you, but you don't think about that as your focus narrows on the coming laps. You might eat the wall. You might do worse than that, but even if you were sure that would happen, you don't want to be anywhere else in the world.

I still have such a great time, on the track and off, mostly because I've accumulated such a great cast of characters in my life and retained nearly all of them. I doubt anybody I know has more fun than I do. I'm at an age where if I haven't grown up by now, it's hopeless.

Now, I'm no fool. I have several businesses and run them reasonably well because I know that there are people whose families literally depend on me for their livelihoods. I take that part very seriously. I benefit from it, too, but my private nightmare is hungry little urchins without milk money because Schrader didn't take his business seriously enough. Bigger urchins without beer money, too. But taking the time to

One of the great things about achieving a certain level of success as a racer is that it's meant we could go all over the country and try driving different kinds of cars. On this occasion, I got to try out Billy Decker's East Coast modified. Talk about fun! (Bill Moore photo; Ken Schrader Collection.)

make sure things get done doesn't mean that having a laugh shouldn't be important, as well. The yoke of responsibility isn't that heavy. And central to it all is the racing.

For the duration of the race I won't think about my family, my business, the past, the future or anything but what's happening on the track. I simply can't afford to. People have some sense of the stress your body experiences in a race car, but unless you've done this, it's hard to imagine the beating your mind takes. In most other sports and games you have brief periods of intense thought or concentration, but unless you are a competition chess player, I can't imagine any recreation that demands so much from your brain.

You have to look forward, and to both sides, and process what you see. At the exact same moment, you have to listen for the

I had to con my sister to chauffeur me to the incredibly fast Winchester Speedway so I could drive Gene Hamilton's very slick-looking midget. That's Rich Vogler on the outside. (Ken Schrader Collection.)

This was my first time at Indianapolis Raceway Park in Howard Linne's midget and clearly I had a few challenges. However, I did get going the right way and always enjoyed racing there. (Jack Gladback photo; Ken Schrader Collection.)

I have enjoyed Silver Crown racing as much as anything I ever did and I drove for great guys like "Boston Louie" Seymour. (Ken Schrader Collection.)

sound of a competitor's engine coming up from behind and process that. If you do hear someone, you have to figure out whether they are far enough alongside that you have to give them room, or if you can move up or down in front of them. Misjudge and you may end up spun out, maybe wrecked, and it doesn't necessarily mean you were at fault. Can you trust the guy behind you? Can you trust the ones alongside?

In the midst of this, you also have to listen to your car, because she's talking to you all the time. Every engine has its own voice and pitch. If you know her well, you know when she's just babbling at you, but still you have to listen for any change. Any little blip can mean she's thinking about tossing a rod through the block. A funny sound that's not just part of her deal can mean the driveshaft is tired. Or the transmission. Or a suspension part. And you have to figure out where and which piece it is, and whether you need to pull in or you can keep going.

You'd better use your sense of smell, too. Tires rubbing on body parts have a distinct odor. So do oil, brake fluid, transmission fluid and rear end grease, and that smell may be your only warning that a catastrophic equipment failure is about to occur.

If that's not enough to fry your brain, you also have to be planning ahead, at least if you think you have a chance to move forward in the field. That guy ahead of you? Knowing him and how he drives is a huge advantage, because you'll have an idea of what he's going to do in specific circumstances. This type of track, maybe he drifts out on the straightaways, or maybe he pinches to the inside in the corners. Whatever his style, if you get to him, you have to hope he continues true to form. You don't mind so much trying to get around him if he's consistent and holds his line, but what if he blocks you because he knows you're faster?

Happens all the time. Take the groove, you think, but give me a fair chance.

When I was a kid, I didn't think about making a living racing. It was more a case of living-to-race than racing-to-live in those days. For a mechanic's kid from working-class Valley Park, talking about dreams of racing full-time would have yielded only laughter, even from people who believed in me. I'm not sure in this new age—where a driver seems to need a sponsor even before he picks up a helmet—that I would be able to repeat the climb. I'd like to think my driving skills would take

me to the top, but I know literally hundreds of short-track drivers whose skill *should have* taken them to Daytona's victory lane. Why it didn't is probably a fascinating story in its own right. What I do know is this: Even if I had never gotten out of Valley Park, I'd be racing every night of the week, in every kind of car I could convince a car owner to bring to the track.

Every race car has her own personality. Some drivers even give individual cars a name. I've gotten out of a race car and called her names…maybe "Sweetheart" or "Darling." Possibly "Junkyard Bait" or "Piece-of-Shit."

A lot of times, what happens during a race isn't really the car's doing. Drivers, other competitors, the track surface, settings and selections for the bolt-ons. All these things contribute considerably to what happens during the race.

But sometimes it just doesn't matter. Some chassis just never respond to all your coaxing and pleading. It's probably some little weld or bend somewhere that doesn't integrate with the rest of the car, but when it happens you're left feeling like the most charita-

ble thing you can do is fire up the cutting torch and send her to race-car heaven.

On this night, however, she purrs. Ever see a sleek young cat stretch and then take off with a self-satisfied launch? Well, that's the way it feels. And when a car responds like that, there's simply nothing else in the world that feels better.

Maybe as good, but never better.

In those moments, your instincts take over and you can actually allow yourself a moment to really feel how wonderful racing can be. You don't even have to be in the lead. Remember Leonardo DeCaprio on the bow of the Titanic yelling into the sky, "I'm King of the World!" That's how you feel when you and your car are completely in sync.

Not that it's as smooth as a ship on the open seas. More like hitting the brakes when they saw the iceberg.

The car is vibrating.

Now, it's always vibrating if the engine is running, because all that horsepower is trying to break free. But once you get underway you pick up all kinds of other shakes, and part of your job is sorting out the normal-okay vibrations from the potentially disastrous ones.

Even when everything is perfect, you know it won't last. Mostly it's tires, because racing tires on any surface wear out at a pace that's light-years ahead of what you get on a passenger car. You can count on a comfortable feeling almost always going away as the laps mount. So you savor it while it lasts.

Throughout the years, a lot of things have changed in my life—certainly the race cars have changed, and the drivers seem to have gotten younger——but what hasn't changed from day one is how it feels to be in a race car. Ninety-nine percent of the time it's incredible. Just ask anyone who's ever driven. Even if they were forced out by injury, or lack of money or age—whatever the reason—that feeling never completely goes

During the time I was with Hendrick Motorsports I ran my own Busch Series team and had a lot of fun with it. (Ken Schrader Collection.)

Just because it was a tiny, 1/10-mile indoor track at the Pontiac Silverdome, it didn't mean you couldn't get on your head. "Smiley" Sitton let me drive his midget again, because, well...shit happens. (Kevin Horcher photo; Ken Schrader Collection)

What's It Like Out There, Dude?   **195**

away. It's the Addictive Personality Factor. You can walk away, but you never forget what it felt like. We're all adrenalin junkies, and as long as we get our fix, very few of us end up doing a Twelve-Step program.

And then there is that one-percent of the time in the car that it's not so beautiful...

The wreck happens so quick there's no time to react. This time I'm not in it, but I've had my share. I've also seen some involving others I wish I hadn't. Nightmare stuff. Most of the time, though, it's just like this one. A guy up ahead starts feeling the pressure coming up on him and he goes into the corner too hard. Or the car shifts. Or the track changes. Or there's something laid down by another car.

In what other sport can a puppy hang out with the big dogs? I was hanging out with some real talent here—from left to right is Bill Faust (his sons are racing now); me; Russ Wallace; Wib Spalding and Harold Workman. I'm not sure I was good enough to be in the group at that point, but I sure thought it was way cool. (Ken Schrader Collection.)

It's been said that I'll drive anything. Well, the truth is that I'm a lot more careful these days about what I get in, but I'm not opposed to trying something new when the opportunity arises. Here, I shared an IMSA sports car ride at the 24 Hours of Daytona in 1986. A teammate wrecked it before we lost any sleep. (Ray's Racing Photos; Ken Schrader Collection.)

There's a hundred different things just lying in wait to screw you up. You can be the best driver on earth and still wreck pretty regularly. Sometimes you're the wrecker, and sometimes you're the wreckee. It's amazing that we continue to race when you consider how hard it is to run straight, fast and true, and how easy it is to go home with your name at the bottom of the pay-off list.

I get a little extra kick of adrenalin as I finesse the steering wheel to avoid the pile-up. Your natural inclination is to yank the wheel when you see stuff going on, but, depending on the track and the conditions, it's usually a whole lot smarter to react with less enthusiasm than to get wild with the steering wheel. Because if the car goes out of control, you'll probably start your own separate pile-up.

I'm amazed at how much I'm still learning about racing. You'd think after all the different types of cars I've driven and the thousands of events I've run, there wouldn't be so much to figure out. But there is.

There's always new gadgets, new set-ups, new ways to cheat, new ways to talk yourself into a ride you'd like to try. Hell, there's even new things to do after the races. As long as you still get a kick out of all that's happening, you can't get old. Racing is a *young-thinking* man's game, not necessarily a *young* man's game. That goes for the gals, too.

There's a mistaken impression that I will drive *anything*. I admit to having driven a few real shitboxes along the way, but I'm pickier these days. I have a few aches and pains from wrecks reminding me that you want to look over the frame, cage and interior pretty closely before you get in one of those things, at any level of the sport.

But the concept that I am *not* a racing snob is absolutely correct. I love a good race, whether it's a street stocker or a Nextel Cup event—

Left: I had a shot at the Indianapolis 500 in May, 1983. Records will show that I ended up having a lot better results when NASCAR came to the Brickyard later. (John Mahoney photo; Ken Schrader Collection.)

Right: July 31, 1988, at Talladega Superspeedway I reached a milestone that probably mirrors a lot of racers' goals when I won my very first Winston Cup race. But you know what? Every win in every type of car feels special, so if you win a street stock race, enjoy it. (Dorsey Patrick photo; Ken Schrader Collection.)

plus everything in between. And I love it best when I'm right in the middle of the mix, running for the lead.

Now, everybody knows even Peter Pan couldn't do this forever. 2006 might be my final year in NASCAR's premier league, but I've got the nice new garage to field Craftsman trucks and ARCA cars for a few years. And when all that goes away, assuming I'm still walking around in approximately the condition I am today, I'll just get in the dirt late model and run every race I can find until I can't anymore. I expect they'll be prying my fingers off the door bars as they haul me to the nursing home.

And you can take that to the bank.

The checkered flag comes out.

I'm disappointed. Not because I didn't win—I know I gave it my best effort. I'm disappointed because the race is over for tonight. If the best years of your life are the years you spend doing what speaks to your heart and soul, then I've been blessed, because you add up all the minutes and hours I've been inside a roll cage and it computes to literally years.

I'm happy inside the car, I'm happy with my life outside my car. And it's been that way for 35 years.

Learn on Your Own Dime 16

A LOT OF PEOPLE have asked how racing has changed in the 35 years I've been driving. I also get asked all the time about how to break into racing and get to the top. It's flattering to think my opinions are wanted, but it's also interesting to watch people's faces shut down when you don't say what they want to hear, or think they're going to hear.

That's not going to stop me from being honest.

I've seen a lot happen over the years that's shaped how I feel about it all. Everybody who lasts long-term in racing arrives at their own conclusions, but I can't think of anybody else who spends quite so much time with vested interests at so many different levels and types of racing as I do. I think buying that many pit passes may be sufficient excuse to offer up my thoughts on the subject.

IF YOU WANT AN EXCUSE, YOU CAN FIND ONE

There's plenty of guys who wanted to race in the Big Time but didn't make it. You can talk to anybody and find a reason.

Had bills to pay.

So does every guy in Nextel Cup, and they had bills every day on the way to where they are.

Had kids to raise.

Kids love to brag about their Dad racing cars, and most of them would rather be at the race track than at piano lessons or soccer practice anyway.

Didn't get the right breaks.

A lot of the "right breaks" are a matter of making something happen rather than sitting around waiting for the phone to ring, or expecting Jack Roush to walk up at the local quarter-mile and hand you a contract.

See, the deal isn't that anybody intended to fail on the way to making it big, but it's easier to make excuses than admit you didn't really try

My first sponsor! I got $1500 to split between the late model and the midget, but it was also the first taste of what a difference sponsorship makes, whether you need $100 or $1,000,000. (Don Figler photo; Ken Schrader Collection.)

hard. Because if you're a race driver, you're supposed to *want* to make it big, and just about everybody would like to imagine how they would do against the best in the land, which means that a lot of guys end up not admitting that they are perfectly content to run on Saturday night.

Well, I'm here to tell you that there's nothing wrong with being a home-boy. I'd like to hear more guys (and gals) say that they're satisfied to stay home and bang fenders with a bunch of other people who are just as happy to stay home. That's admirable—it's certainly no reason to hang your head in shame or live with your head in the clouds. The vast majority of drivers are going to be hobby racers, and God bless 'em all for the thrills and entertainment they bring to fans everywhere.

Don't ever apologize for being a street stock driver—*if* you gave it your all and you're proud of the job you've done. You're every bit as much a race driver as the guys who suit up in Nextel Cup.

BUT MY KID IS THE NEXT JEFF GORDON

I wonder how many millions of dollars Jeff Gordon has cost people. Unintentionally, of course. It was never his idea that so many frustrated racers out there would decide their pension plan would be a son or daughter who makes it to Daytona.

That doesn't stop the craziness.

Well, I said earlier in this book that there's only one Jeff, that his life sometimes sucks because of the intense emotions his career has provoked among the fans, and I don't think another guy with his unique talent will ever come along.

Here's how I think you should go about building a racing career these days, whether you're "the next Jeff Gordon" or not: If you've got a big budget, move down South, get a late model stock car and race as much as you can. After you learn to do that, get an ARCA car and learn that. Then a truck or Busch car, and after mastering that, put together a two- or three-car Nextel Cup team.

I've spent many years now racing with Jeff Gordon, clear back to the open cockpit days when he was too young to shave. I can tell you that there's only one Jeff Gordon. (Mike Adaskaveg photo.)

Don't have the money to do that?

Well, I can't think of very many people who do, so what you do instead is get the laps. You run any piece of shit you can, anywhere you can, because sooner or later you have to learn how to drive.

You can't write a check for that.

There are people who say you need to stay out of bad equipment while you are learning because it's hard to unlearn bad habits.

I totally disagree.

If you run shitboxes and you can do anything at all with them, you learn good habits, because you figure out a lot more than just how to steer a car that's doing everything you want and expect it to do. You learn how to make it do stuff that it *doesn't* want to do. Any idiot can drive a good-handling, well-prepared car. It takes a race driver to make a shitbox get around the track with the good cars, and that separates the race drivers from the wannabes.

Potential drivers (or their parents) also want to know where to get experience.

Doesn't matter.

There's a popular background at various times—a lot of guys right now seem to be coming from a USAC background, but a few years ago it was ASA. But don't look at the kids who seem to come and go—think about the young guys who are doing well these days:

Jimmie Johnson came from off-road and pavement racing;

Tony Stewart came from whatever he could get gas money to do;

Carl Edwards came from more dirt than asphalt;

Jeff Gordon ran everything, mostly dirt when he was real young; and

Kasey Kahne is more dirt than asphalt.

The point is that they all went out and got as many laps as they could, driving everything and anything they could, and got attention because they *demanded* attention by their accomplishments. If there seem to be more dirt-to-pavement drivers coming up and being successful these days, I think it's because a good dirt driver can adapt to

Think that success at the highest level is just a matter of writing a check for the right millions? Or having brilliant mechanical minds? The truth is that everything has to line up and fall into place because even with the best of everything, success can be hard to capture. (Mike Adaskaveg photo.)

Variety is the spice of life, for sure. Learning how to race a stock car beside Russ Wallace, a Johnny Vance sprint car, a NASCAR modified and the Sieveking late model didn't make it more difficult for me to learn how to drive a Winston Cup car. It made it easier! Because the more you master, the more confidence you'll have and the easier it will be to figure out how to make anything work. (Top left: Rocky Rhodes photo; Ken Schrader Collection; top right: Tracy Talley photo, Ken Schrader Collection; bottom: Ken Schrader Collection.)

situations more quickly. Even when you run a single track each week, you deal with so many variables each time on dirt that it makes you learn to adjust your driving as well.

You'd be surprised how much that comes in handy when you get to Daytona.

BUY-A-RIDE AND DEVELOPMENT PROGRAMS

There have always been guys who showed up at NASCAR tracks with checks in hand. It's nothing new, and the checks have been good, too. Cash 'em and you aren't looking for the guy come Monday morning. But I can't think of any buy-a-ride, big success stories.

And I don't mean modest little deals like I did with Elmo back in 1984. A lot of the successful guys brought a little help when they came up, but it was "help," not "buy-a-ride."

If a guy's dream was just to have a cup of coffee at the top level, yeah, there have been plenty of those stories. But if you want a lasting career, thinking that writing a check for a few million dollars is the way to break in, you couldn't be more wrong—or wasteful. It's actually the worst way to try to develop your career because if you don't look good real quick, you won't get the opportunities to stay in a permanent ride.

No matter how many zeroes there are on the check, it won't cancel out a zero behind the wheel.

There's plenty of guys still trying it. We get an unbelievable number of calls and resumes at Schrader Racing, and they're gonna bring money. The check will clear.

But here's the deal—they don't have experience and they don't have enough money to pay for all the shit they're going to tear up trying to get experience.

And the thing of it is, the vast majority of Nextel Cup teams have sponsorship, so they're not looking for money either. I'm sure they wouldn't ignore a $20 million offer, but everybody gets real tired of fixing torn-up cars.

There are development programs, but I'm hearing that some of the top teams are re-thinking that approach. For example, you can take a kid with limited experience, but showing promise, put him in a real good ARCA car, and he probably is going to produce. But, hell, why wouldn't he? He's got the equipment, the pit crew, the perfect situation. With people working on the car who have Cup experience and knowledge, along with the engineers, the new kid on the block has no excuse for not going fast.

But then you take the kid with a year or two of ARCA and put him in a mediocre Busch or Cup ride, and it all goes to hell. Nothing he's done has prepared him for making a shitbox run with the fast guys. So then he starts to feel the stress, because, boy, have times changed in that regard. Twenty-five years ago, you got in Elmo Langley's car or Junie Donlavey's car, and if you showed patience you'd learn how to race with the foxes up front. Now, the kids are in pressure-cookers to produce immediately, or get out. There's plenty more disposable kids where you came from.

I've heard from some good sources that a lot of the monied teams are getting pretty sick of the kids who wreck and wreck and wreck. It's not the money so much as the effort the guys back at the shop have to put into fixing the wadded-up crap, and the sense that some of these kids aren't really learning from their mistakes. They didn't get the chance to make these mistakes on a $10,000 modified back home, so it messes with their heads when they realize the $100,000 cars aren't unlimited.

A MECHANICAL APPROACH

When I was starting out, it was a necessity to work on race cars. Now it's not.

First off, we all had shit that we built from junkyard parts so, basically, you were the only one who knew how you cobbled the car together. You *had* to work on it. But as time went by, technology got into it. Today, you can buy a C.J. Rayburn late model and it's complete. Call C.J., and he will tell you how to set it up. He will also tell you to leave it alone—go have a hot dog or something and don't fiddle with it. Same with a lot of engines these days, so you can get real racey without knowing a lot more than which tires you need.

All the same, I'm an advocate for learning as much as you can anyway. Even though knowing what works at the short-track level is sometimes just the opposite of what works at the Cup level, it's still a huge advantage to understand what you're feeling when you are in a race car. Communicating to your crew is still critical.

We have data from our test sessions, and we have engineers. But they can help us only if we are able to give them feedback. What's

I get asked all the time how to shorten the learning curve. I don't believe you can. But I am just as sure that you can expand your knowledge by picking the brains of the good racers you see. In my case, I had it made because I had my daddy (left), and the guys who got me started like Jerry Sifford (center), and the ones I sought out at the track. That's Gary Bettenhausen on the right. His left arm was useless because of a bad accident, but he wanted to race so bad that he came back from injury and learned how to win with just one arm. Now, that's a race driver. (Left: Ken Schrader Collection; middle: Rocky Rhodes photo; Ken Schrader Collection; right: Ken Schrader Collection.)

changed over the years is that instead of making the changes ourselves, we have to be able to describe what's happening so the crew can interpret and make changes.

Being smart about the cars themselves will never be a disadvantage. Just ask Ryan Newman or Carl Edwards.

TESTING, TESTING, THIS AIN'T THE SAT's

You've probably never heard a race driver tell you he loves to test. A few will say it's not bad, but for the vast majority, it's as close to boring as being in a race car can be. That's still better than flipping burgers, but thank goodness we don't have to do it every week. Of course, I doubt tossing a burger is the direct route to owning the restaurant, where testing race cars often makes the difference between winning and a really long afternoon mid-pack, so it's important.

Here's what a typical test session is like:

You unload. You start with a set-up you think may work, or worked the last time you were at the track.

You climb in the car and go on the track for eight or ten laps at a time while your crew checks the stopwatch.

You come in, the crew de-briefs you, makes a limited number of changes to the car, and you repeat the process.

Again, and again, and again, and again.

Yawn.

Usually you share the expense of renting the track with other teams who have the same manufacturer since the cost can be pretty substantial. The grandstand will be empty, but you need fire and safety crews on hand, as well as some track personnel. If you're lucky, one or more of the other drivers on hand is a pal you can share some laughs with

In July 2005, we took our ARCA car to Gateway International Raceway just outside our hometown of St. Louis for a session. What most people don't know about test sessions is how much time is spent with the car on jacks changing things, and in just talking, figuring out what to try next. (Joyce Standridge photos.)

Even at test sessions, it's not unusual for the press to show up. So, what we have here is a photographer taking a picture of a photographer taking a picture of our crew. Makes sense as sense can be made only in racing. (Joyce Standridge photo.)

while the crews are making changes. Mostly, though, it's a very long day, punctuated with brief bursts of speed to wake you up.

But on Sunday, when you take home a check that you know is larger than it would have been without the test data, you're real glad the crew woke you up and stuffed you back in the cockpit.

I bring up the whole subject of testing because the youngster coming up needs to realize how important it is to be a good test driver. There is absolutely no glamour in it, there won't be a trophy and a check at the end of the day, and if you're lucky the boss won't even think about it, because if he does it's probably a result of your backing the car into the wall.

But test driving is not about mashing the gas. It's about consistency and applying the same repetition each lap, so the engineers can get good measurements and comparisons. You drive as much with your head as your foot.

Which is a good way to drive *all* the time, come to think of it.

Joey Walsh is our dirt late model crew chief, but it's not at all unusual to see him working on the pavement stuff, too. Here he's recording results from the test session. (Joyce Standridge photo.)

The technology rules for the Silver Crown cars had changed little over the decades until 2006, which is one of the reasons they were always so racey. Nobody had a clear advantage in terms of the equipment, so you'd get in them and just drive. Fewer worries about cheater stuff. (Tracy Talley photo; Ken Schrader Collection.)

USING THE RULEBOOK TO GET AHEAD

Another reason to get out-and-about in building a racing career is the exposure to a lot of different rulebooks. In no other sport are there such major differences in equipment or how events are held, even when it's got the same name. Democracy—or maybe lunacy—is at work.

There have been efforts to bring rules more in line, and it's certainly a lot better than it was when I was learning. Back then, every promoter in the country thought he had a better idea than all the rest, and most rulebooks were written to try to keep cars at a given track. I race short tracks mostly in the Midwest and South, so I've seen the improvement that has resulted from organized rules through UMP and the NASCAR Weekly Series. There are groups in other areas of the country making more sense of rules, too, but I'm just not as familiar with them.

Consistent rules are a good thing. And whether it's Saturday night or Sunday afternoon, I think it's valuable to apply NASCAR's thinking on rules when considering changes.

Over the years, there have been a lot of hoops a manufacturer has to jump through to get things approved for NASCAR racing. Turns out it's a good thing because as expensive as this is, it would be so much worse if NASCAR wasn't reluctant to approve new stuff. (Joyce Standridge photo.)

Here's what happens: You come up with a new, trick part. It's going to revolutionize the sport, you think. So, you take it down to Daytona and show it to them.

Their response is that it's got to do three things:

One, it's got to make for a better race. Second, it's got to be cost-effective. And finally, it has to make things safer for the spectators and/or participants.

Well, that's why we don't get a lot of new stuff approved.

If it's an advantage and everybody's got it, then it's no longer an advantage and all it did was drive the cost up. If it makes for side-by-side racing, that's okay, but that's not what most of these things do.

And the safety thing often gets lost in the hysterics that sometimes surround what's done. For example, let's talk restrictor plates.

Restrictor plates are not put on the cars for the drivers.

They're put on the cars for the spectators.

If you missed it, Bobby Allison almost got into the grandstand at Talledega some years ago. Tore down a hundred feet of safety fence, sent projectiles into the stands and hurt a few people, but it might have been racing's luckiest day. If he had gotten through the fence instead of sliding down it, racing—at least at the superspeedway level—wouldn't exist. I don't care if it says on the ticket you bought that the track is absolved of all responsibility for your safety, there are enough sharks trolling the courthouse that a few dozen lawsuits would have been filed before the last ambulance pulled out of the track. It wouldn't have taken but a few fatalities. Massive casualties—it blows the mind to even consider.

So, we're going to be slowed down. And, no matter how we slow down, it's going to be the same problem of cars racing in packs.

We've already got the restrictor plates, and we've got the restrictor-plate engines.

It's four times a year. *Four times.*

Just shut up and run the damned things four times a year, and don't worry about it. You're either in the wreck or you're not. But the alternative is not—and never will be again—to let us go wide-open, because that just isn't going to happen. We absolutely have to keep the race cars out of the fans' laps.

Period.

So let's find something else to fuss about.

BACK TO HOW WE CAN GET STARTED...

I don't see much difference from 35 years ago. Back then, you needed $1,000 and had $100. Now, you need $100,000 and you have $10,000. Obviously, $90,000 versus $900 is a significant dollar figure. But when you've got only ten percent of what you need, you're screwed anyway. That much ain't changed.

A big part of racing is the junk you're left with after you've worn it out or put it through a major wreck. (Ken Schrader Collection.)

This whole thing is still about desire and ability. I know that there are instances of kids with not-as-much desire and ability who seem to get some breaks and showcase their talents a little sooner because of family money or connections. But I still believe that it boils down to the basics.

You don't have to look any farther than the new hero of the sport, Mr. Edwards. He went from running a dirt modified at Moberly, Missouri, to a couple of practice laps in Mike Mittler's truck, to a Silver Crown car, to running good in Mike's truck, to being hired by Jack Roush. It seems like it happened fast, and relatively speaking it did. But, man, he packed a lot of experience into a short time, and ultimately, it was a matter of desire and ability. And—helping Carl hugely—personality, but he couldn't have gotten by solely on that.

There's no way to tell from looking at this photo that the boy in the center is on his way to becoming a superstar in racing. Carl Edwards was just a cute little guy from a middle-class family. But what no photo could contain is how big his desire to succeed is. (Ken Schrader Collection.)

The differences in getting to the race track from the 1970s to the 2000s, but we were just as proud of the rig back in the early days. And the most important thing is that we got to the track. You don't race the haulers. (Top: Ken Schrader Collection; bottom: Joyce Standridge photo.)

It was no advantage to Carl to be related to a Cup driver. I did give him an old school-bus hauler to use, and it says a lot that he didn't think he was too good to use it. He had to get his home-built frames to the track somehow, and they don't pay out at the end of the night based on how pretty the hauler is.

I do think that if you are racing on a budget—and everybody is, it's just a question of how big—you can help your cause in a few ways, like Carl did. Don't worry about fancy trucks and trailers. If what the fast guys are using to tow with intimidates you, the race is already lost. They've got you beat before you unload.

When you're starting out, you are probably hunting sponsors, and for a relatively small amount of money you can keep your stuff looking good. You don't want sponsors to think they'd be ashamed to have their name on your car.

Even when I have a day job (driving in Nextel Cup) to support the night fun (driving my dirt late model), I still have to think about the cost. Tire bills can set back even the best-financed team. (Tonya McFall photo; Ken Schrader Collection.)

If you can run shorter tracks, you don't have to sink a ton of money into your engines. I mean, it can't be breaking all the time, because then you can't finish and show what you can do, but it's a hell of a lot more impressive to see a guy with limited engines managing an eighth place finish than a guy with a $30,000 motor managing an eighth place finish. And the people in the pits know the difference, believe me.

If you know how to build your own car, it's a huge advantage. Good suspension pieces are helpful, but if you can manage to race on tracks that are pretty consistently dry-slick and smooth, you can offset a lot of the benefit of $600 shocks.

The one area that probably makes as much difference as anything is in keeping good, sharp tires on the car. It worked for Carl. It's worked for a lot of guys wanting to work their way up. Even at tracks with tire rules intended to help hold down the cost, it still seems like a deal-buster for many teams.

At every level of the sport, tires seem to be critical to success. Whatever you drive, you'll probably find that you have to buy and haul around plenty. (Joyce Standridge photo.)

TURN OUT THE LIGHTS...

A lot of guys not only don't worry about climbing the ladder to Nextel Cup, they'll never give it a shot because they just don't care. Good for them. But a lot of them are curious about how to make a career last a long time. I'm thinking Don Klein and Red Farmer probably know the answer better than I do, but I can look at them and figure it out: You've just got to want to do it.

And when you stop feeling that way, you don't have to make excuses like you've run out of money or your family wanted you to stop. It's like it is for Rusty Wallace.

Rusty wants to race, but he doesn't want to do some of the other stuff that you have to do if you're going to be Nextel Cup racer. And, there's other things he wants to do that he doesn't have time to do if he's a Nextel Cup driver.

So he retired.

And he doesn't owe any of us an apology for deciding to walk away.

When we were young, Rusty and I thought we would race forever. He's reached the point that he's ready to take a step back, but I'm not. Doesn't make one of us more of a race driver than the other. (Ken Schrader Collection.)

I'm Ready for My Close-up, Mr. DeMille

17

MORE PEOPLE WATCH *Desperate Housewives*, but we've been on the air longer. And, so far, nobody has committed any murders on our show, except maybe to the English language.

Michael Waltrip and I have been doing a television show for ten years now with various other people, and while we seem to be missing out on Emmy awards we're pretty happy with the results. They keep telling us to come back in the spring and there's shows *with* Emmys that don't get that kind of news.

Nobody, however, is more surprised than I am to have ended up a television regular. I know I have a thick Midwestern accent and a voice that's a little higher-pitched than Dave Despain's. I'm not the prettiest boy in the pits either, and damned if I'll do any preparation for the show, so now you understand that it's a bit of mystery why they kept calling me to do *Inside Nextel Cup*.

What I do have working for me is good chemistry with the others, especially Michael, the ability to think on my feet (*or is it on-my-butt, since we're sitting down?*), and a sense of humor that helps to keep the show from taking itself too seriously. For these reasons, and the various talents the other panel members bring to the show, we do relatively well in the ratings.

At least, I think we do okay in the ratings.

I never look at them. When the show's producer says we're "up" I have to take his word for it because I don't verify that. A producer wouldn't lie to you, would he? I mean, he's like a car owner or sanction chief at the track, and we know we can trust them.

Well, anyway, since it demands less of me than high school did—and I got through that—I have continued to do the show through several panelists and producers. You may have seen the finished product on the Speed Channel on Monday nights. Since this book has taken you behind the scenes at the track, we might as well go backstage at the show, too.

NICE OF YOU TO SHOW UP, SCHRADER

We used to tape the show at ten o'clock on Monday morning. I liked that. I wasn't so far into my day that it was an interruption of whatever I needed to be doing at the shop or with other business concerns. When we got a new producer at the beginning of 2005, he decided to move taping back. He wanted 4:00 P.M. I think he might have mulled over a time even later, but it would have squeezed the edit-to-air schedule too much. Ultimately, he decided on 2:00 P.M. as a compromise, and it made sense for everybody—but the panel. The other drivers have things to do, too.

The deal is, the production staff has to go through a lot of tape from the previous day's race and string together highlight reels that we are going to review during the show. If you do the show taping at ten in the morning, the poor folks behind the scenes getting the highlights together have to start their part at some ridiculous hour. Like right after the race concludes and through the night. That's an exaggeration, but it really crimps their style, so the producer moved us to two in the afternoon. He assumed we could still show up sober at that hour.

Inside Nextel Cup tapes at a warehouse on the southeast side of Charlotte. If you envisioned a fancy studio like *Desperate Housewives* has, or even what a fifth-rate comedy on UPN has, you would be wrong. The world of cable is a lot more stripped-down and basic. A lot of television is smoke-and-mirrors anyway, and it doesn't take fancy studios to pull off a cable talk show. A good set and equipment, and who's to know they're boxing stuff for catalog sales at the other end of the building.

When you pull into the lot, you'd never guess that the Speed Channel has a studio there until you pull into the back area and see enough mega-sized satellite dishes to rival NASA. They're pointed in every direction and it's pretty impressive.

The building, on the other hand, looks from the outside like every other in the complex. It's white, it's dull, and it's locked.

Even if you are a big time Nextel Cup driver—like Mikey or Brian Vickers—you have to knock. You don't have a key. It's not that they don't trust us, it's...well, hell, I don't know, but they don't give us keys.

Camera crew double as doormen. And after they let us in, they also have to mike us up, too. But that comes after we change clothes.

Behind the wall at Michael's back is a small area where our neatly pressed shirts and khaki pants are hung in anticipation that we'll actually show up. A few have the Speed logo on them, while others have our sponsors' logos as well as Speed's. It always seems like there are more NAPA shirts than anybody else's, and I don't know if that means they're afraid Mikey's going to get his wrinkled up during the show and need to change, or if they're just testing the rest of us to see if we'll go through the rack to find our own.

There is no changing area. You just get down to the skivvies and put

As I get 'miked up for the show, Dave Despain, Brian Vickers and Michael Waltrip go over notes and prepare. Preparation? Not this cat. (Joyce Standridge photo.)

on the assigned shirt and pants. Yes, there are a few women on the production staff, but they've seen better, so they don't really care.

Much of the floor space is taken up by the set you see when you watch the show. It's really well done, I agree. You'd think we were a major deal when you see it. Step off the set, though, and you're back in the warehouse where the producer is tapping his watch impatiently.

I'm usually on time, but occasionally shop business interferes and I have to scramble to get there. When they finish the interstate loop around Charlotte, it'll be easier, but in the meantime, I'm not getting a ticket for trying to fool the clock.

If I cut it close I can count on catcalls from the rest of the panel, the producer, the camera guys and janitor, if he's there. "Thanks for showing up," is the sarcastic jibe I can repeat on these pages. If there are guests on hand, it usually stops there, but sometimes it sounds like a locker room even if it doesn't look like one. This would bother me only if it was directed solely at me. However, if anybody else is late, they get the razzies, too, so you take it, you change your clothes and you go sit in the chair so you can get an earpiece and a microphone.

Meanwhile, Dave Despain is preparing for the show. Important note: somewhere along the line, the show's owners decided it would be a good idea to have at least one pro on hand. We've had several through the years, and Dave is the designated babysitter right now. He actually checks the Internet, newspapers, television, and for all I know the smoke signals on the horizon, but he always comes prepared. When he first started, the taping took up to two hours for a one-hour show. He wanted to do it right, bless his heart. But we broke him, and we're back to finishing pretty close to our one-hour slot. Despain may despair, but our editors love us for it.

YOU'RE KILLING ME, SCHRADER

They give us clipboards with the segments outlined. They also give us pens, which we use to doodle, write obnoxious notes to each other, and generally play with until the producer snaps at us to behave.

It sounds like we horse around a lot, but really, we understand that this is actually some people's living, so we do care and we do try. We just draw the line at actual preparation, and here's why:

How many shows are there on television these days about racing? How many about NASCAR Nextel Cup? How many do you actually remember not only the title, but anything you heard on them? Yup, a lot of it is forgettable.

They've gone "professional" with a lot of these shows, and while some of them have a real sense of fun to them, they're also interchangeable. I'm never one to argue that putting a lovely lady in front of the camera is a bad idea, but some of those ladies—and gentlemen, as well—wouldn't know a tie rod if it broke off and laid down at their feet. Or who NASCAR's John Darby is and what he means to what we do. (You don't have to, either, but it's our job to know and explain to you when it's appropriate.)

These good-looking kids will come and go, as will their shows, because they are television pros rather than racing pros. What they can do is read a teleprompter like the professionals they are, and offer up a glossy look that appeals to the ever-wanted young male demographic. Mission accomplished—that's what they're supposed to do. For everybody else, which is still a sizable chunk of the racing public, there's Despain's other show, *Wind Tunnel*, and there's us.

What I think viewers get—what I *hope* they get—is a sense of the actual racers' viewpoint. It's also spontaneous, and with that comes an honesty that doesn't feel forced. Sometimes, it's like the viewer is in on a party, sometimes like a brotherhood bitch session, sometimes insight into the way a situation is viewed in the garage, and sometimes—just sometimes—like a really thoughtful observation. We're not doing rocket science on the track, and I think it's a mistake to put too much gravity on what happens.

And just when it seems like we're in danger of going over the edge of taking it all too seriously, something stupid happens. Like the time my cell phone went off.

Twice.

First time was funny, said the producer. The second time, he came roaring through the control-room door during the commercial break and said, "You're killing me, Schrader. You're costing me money."

Not that I think it's actually coming out of his pocket, but I understand. And it wasn't on purpose—I just forgot to turn it off and it was in the jeans on the floor behind the set—but this wasn't church either. *That* would have been bad, this was just disruptive.

At least I wasn't cussing the producer during the break. If something isn't going as well as we'd hoped, the conversations can get kind of heated during breaks. We're nothing if not opinionated, our little group. And Mikey and I have been doing this long enough to have pretty much figured out what works and doesn't. Bring in new people and that dynamic changes. So, while you're listening to the commercial, in the studio the conversation may be a heated little discussion about what we'll talk about in the next segment.

Or not.

Sometimes, we just harass each other about crap that happened at the track yesterday.

CAN WE HAVE YOUR ATTENTION, SCHRADER?

We have plenty of room on the set. Along with our chairs, we each have little telestrators so we can make a point (or just scribble on the screen), but that's it. There's a couple of free-standing signs, and the Speed logo appears on the floor thanks to an overhead light. Lots of room.

Not so generous for the crew. There are four cameras focused on us and they can't just be locked in place. Sometimes adjustments are needed because they have a talking head on one half of the screen while

something else appears on the other half. In studio, the crew has to move the camera to allow the free space for the fill-in. They also occasionally show two, three or all four us in a single shot.

Crammed in between the cameras in the ten-or-so feet of space is a large monitor so we can see the highlights as they roll. (And you thought we were just making things up off the top of our heads!)

When we have a remote from another location, maybe for an interview with somebody else in Nextel Cup racing, often they are shown on our monitor when the hook-up is made. We get into conversations that don't make it to air, but probably ought to. They're not scripted, and they get funny, silly, completely off-center. Getting us back to the professional approach is the producer's job.

"Can we have your attention, Schrader?" comes the disjointed voice from the control room. They're behind a block wall and see only what's on the camera screens.

Well, sure. But your viewers might just want to know that the crew chief stole the winner's trophy from the driver and doesn't plan to give it back.

I'd want to know that.

I also continue to do some television for ARCA. I just do that because I'm a real fan of ARCA and I'm glad I can do something that maybe helps bring them attention.

I know there are people who'd love to trade places and do a television show every week—and I've had a lot of fun over the years doing it—but it doesn't make me who I am. If people want to listen in, and if they enjoy it, then it's really cool. But I'm a racer who happens to occasionally go on television, not the other way around.

I'm sure Alan Bestwick will rest easier knowing that.

(Just kidding, Alan.)

They cleaned us up and pointed a camera. We were a whole lot happier later when we shed the ties—and inhibitions. I still can't tell you some stuff that happened in New York, but trust me, there are no side profiles of any of us on file with the police department. At least, I don't think so. (David Chobat photo; Ken Schrader Collection.)

OKAY, NOW LET'S PARTY

I got on television thanks to racing. I have also been invited several times to the most exclusive party in racing, thanks to having some success in NASCAR—the Cup Series Awards Banquet in New York City. I've gotten on the stage and received some very nice checks, and I've even been shown on television at those deals.

But that's not what I want to talk about. It's the party *after* the party that's worth the trip.

Trust me.

When we went to the NASCAR banquet in New York City it was big for us. In 1985, it was our first time and we didn't know how many, if any, more there would be. Ann and I were especially pleased to be going with Phyllis and Junie Donlavey. (Ken Schrader Collection.)

From time-to-time, we have parties at the shop. What we save on having signs made (I think the can of spray paint to alter the sign cost maybe two bucks) we spend on the kegs and the band. The guests seem to appreciate our priorities. (Ken Schrader Collection.)

The best part of going to the banquet for a long time was seeing the red lights go out on the cameras and then rushing out of the ballroom.

There are many, many stories I can't tell you. I'm pretty sure the statute of limitations hasn't expired yet. But there were a few instances when what we did was just an outrage, rather than hair-raising.

For example, we found out that Dale Earnhardt's suite was large enough to play baseball with members of the New York Yankees—provided we used apples and ice buckets. Apples didn't hold up well, though.

We tried very hard to be sensible one year—really, Mr. France, we did—but Jeff Gordon came down to the room and insisted we go back to the Budweiser suite. So we did. In our pajamas. Most were not in condition to notice, so it really wasn't a big deal.

And the year that teammate Terry Labonte was the champion, we stayed up until 7 A.M. so we could order more food. But only because no champion's room service bill had ever been $25,000, and we knew we could do it.

These days, the affair is pretty stuffy. At most of the post-banquet parties, everybody is there. I mean, *everybody*, which shoots down all the wonderfully juvenile things we used to do. The idea that taking a bunch of yahoos to Manhattan and suddenly they'll be choir boys may have been dreamed up in a board room somewhere, but it used to be shot down in the halls of New York hotels faster than a Harlem sewer rat.

I guess the grown-ups have won. But we dragged our heels magnificently for many years. We did our part to prove every stuck-up New York sportswriter correct that race drivers should be kept down on the farm.

One year on my way to Phoenix I stopped off at the St. Louis Auto Racing Fan Club banquet and look who was their special guest. This was when Bill Elliott was just hitting the radar as a major star, but he has always appreciated all kinds of race cars so it wasn't a surprise to find him trying out this midget. And we agreed, a good party is a good party, no matter where it's held. (Kevin Horcher photo; Ken Schrader Collection.)

Short-track banquets are every bit as much fun and meaningful as the big deals. Here, my life long racing idol and friend, Don Klein, was honored with his family for reaching the milestone of 50 years in racing. I wanna be like Don. (Joyce Standridge photo.)

We behaved so badly NASCAR had to wonder why they didn't drop us off at a Days Inn in New Jersey on the way into town.

It's nice to be invited to those Cup banquets, but really—except for the room-service bill—it's not a lot different at short-track deals. You do what you have to during the banquet, especially thanking the car owner, crew, family and sponsors, but you're working toward the post-banquet stuff. We've had every bit as much fun at some of the short-track events we've attended as we did in New York. About the only difference is that Ann spends a little more on a New York dress, but location (and dress cost) has never kept her from dancing on the table when the band got hot.

I've always said, she cleans up good, but she also knows when to let her hair down.

I'm glad she lets me go along.

At the 1993 NASCAR banquet in New York, Ann tried to push that other guy out of the photo, but she didn't quite make it. (David Chobat photo; Ken Schrader Collection.)

I Ain't Ridin'
Off Into the Sunset

18

I CAN'T THINK OF TOO MANY SPORTS where the participant has control of when he or she walks away. It doesn't always happen in racing, either, but a lot of drivers do pick the time and place.

Some race drivers walk away at the top of their game. Ned Jarrett quit as a defending champion. Freddie Lorenzen was winning regularly when he went back to Chicago. Rusty Wallace was in the Chase for the Championship during his final year.

However, I recall a Nextel Cup driver who lost his ride and then was offered several rides in Busch Grand National and Craftsman Truck but turned them down. See, as far as I'm concerned, he didn't want to be a race driver—he wanted to be a Nextel Cup driver. There's a difference. And he walked away at what he perceived to be the top of his game.

I don't want to walk away.

I don't care about *perceptions*. I want to be a race driver.

If you're going to be a race driver, you gotta be tough. And there's nothing like a modified pile-up to find out just how tough you really are. (Kevin Horcher photo; Ken Schrader Collection.)

I've seen Johnny Benson and Kenny Wallace "go backwards" in terms of classifications and they've never been happier or more content. I've been long-time friends with guys like Danny Lasoski and Billy Moyer, who are as competitive in their 40s as they were when they were fearless kids. But even if they weren't winning, they'd still be racing because it's as important as breathing to them. And I know literally hundreds of guys who never got away from their home tracks, but they're happy in what they do, regardless of where they finish in a race.

I'm going to be one of those guys, as I said earlier, until I come to the fork in the road between the race track and the nursing home. When I forget to turn left, it will be time to retire. But not one minute sooner.

That doesn't make me a better racer than the next guy, but refusing to park the car also doesn't make me any less than the guy who does. I guess people will always argue about when it's the right time to quit racing. I'm just very grateful that I don't have to wait for a cut, or a vote, or anything else. And I'll be just as content—maybe even more so—when I'm rubbing fenders with the guys back at I-55 and Paducah as I've ever been in Nextel Cup.

I have nothing but gratitude to NASCAR and the entire industry, because without them I don't know that I would be able to race as much in my advancing years. And I'll miss the NASCAR brotherhood, probably even more than I realize now. But as much as I like and respect the racers at that level—and they really are as good as the hype—the brotherhood of the short track is equally important to me. I'm not going to get all soppy, but I love these guys, and it's no step backward or down to me to go racing with them. As I've said before, you just change the number of zeroes on the check.

Racing is not the sum-total of my existence, but it's pretty much all I've known. Everything that has happened to me, including personal matters, somehow has been tied to racing. My parents were involved in racing, I met my wife through racing, my children—in spite of having other interests—spend a lot of time with me at the race tracks. All my friends go racing or are racing, or—I'm sorry—they wouldn't last as friends. And sometimes, racing has made my friends' lives even better.

Let me tell you about a special one.

I DIDN'T KNOW YOU WERE GOING TO LIVE SO LONG

I've told you about some of my friends, including The Brain Trust, as well as Bud and Ray, among others. But I can't close this out without telling you a little bit about Steve Bradley.

At first, I knew him just as a race fan. He started coming by the shop and helped a little bit. He wouldn't really *do* much—mostly we just jawed back and forth. But then he started going with us on the road.

On one of these trips, I was driving and pulled over for a brief stop beside the road. Business done, we hopped in and started back down the road.

We got a little ways and I hollered for Steve to hand me a soda.

He didn't answer.

Pissed me off, so I pulled over to see if maybe he really was asleep and not just ignoring me. Got in the back and realized he wasn't there.

I mean—he wasn't in the truck at all!

Steve said it was really funny when he watched the taillights headed down the road—until he couldn't see them anymore. We went 10 miles before we realized he wasn't there so it took a few minutes to get back there. Just long enough for him to start to wonder.

In my defense, it's fair to note that he was so small he could be overlooked. Steve had cystic fibrosis, which had affected his size, but he also had a huge love for racing and an even bigger desire to be treated like everybody else. So, we didn't cut him any slack. He had to take the crap or bail out—and you'll guess which way he went.

I mean, there was a time when he went in the hospital for a tune-up. We called him and told him we were in town.

"Where are you?" he asked.

"Belle-Clair Speedway."

Belle-Clair was his baby. He'd rather be there than anywhere on earth. So, I can't guess it was a huge surprise that a little while later he showed up. Long-sleeved shirt, even though it was July, to cover the IV. He'd checked himself out for the evening. But later, when we dropped him off at the Emergency Room door at 4:30 A.M., he was legally intoxicated by any definition you want to produce.

Should we have treated him with kid-gloves instead? Hell, no,

Steve Bradley wormed his way into our hearts and we sorely miss him still. (Ken Schrader Collection.)

according to Steve. He could always get his meds later on—the important thing was, they were racing at Belle-Clair just once that week.

Another time he decided that he wanted to go to California with us.

"No, Ann and I are going alone," I told him.

"But you told me as long as I was able to go places with you, I could go."

I said, *I didn't know you were going to live this damned long.*

He laughed—but we still didn't take him.

Unfortunately, the disease finally caught up, even though he beat the odds for a long time. He was in his early 30s when he died, which is longer than many C.F. victims survive. I like to think the Budweiser pickled him and the dirt he breathed helped him cough some of that shit out of his lungs. Probably, the truth is that he would have lived even longer if he hadn't hung out with us. But his family believes that the time he spent racing with us gave him quality, if not quantity.

And here's how I really felt about him: Ann and I named our son Sheldon for Sheldon Kinser. But our Sheldon's full name is Sheldon Bradley Schrader.

And now you know where the "Bradley" came from.

TURN YOUR HEAD AND COUGH

Tim Crist is maybe my closest friend in North Carolina. It's kind of a hard call to make because I've got some pretty close pals there, but Tim and I hit it off as soon as we met and we've gotten into a lot of mischief ever since. Even during the off-season, we find things to do.

I never really tried to be an athlete at any other sport, if you discount the ten minutes I played football in high school. But when ESPN had a fishing tournament with pro Jimmy Houston, I tried it out. I didn't win, but I fish better than I play football, so that's something. (Ken Schrader Collection.)

One of the things outside a race car that I really do enjoy is meeting fans and signing autographs. The big deals are hard because you don't get to spend time really talking, but it's better than not meeting at all. (Joyce Standridge photo.)

One winter a few years ago we went to a pro basketball game. Tim knew something was wrong that night when I turned down a beer.

And he was buying.

My leg was bothering me. Tim says I got the twitches, but I just recall having a lot of trouble walking up the steps. And it got worse, until finally I asked to go home before the game was done.

Tim—and later on, Ann—had reason to be concerned. Even though I got up the next morning and went over to the shop to sit in a new race car, I had trouble climbing in and then I could hardly get out. I had to use my arms to pull myself out.

I hate doctors as much as any guy does, but there comes a time you know you're in trouble, and ignoring it won't make it go away.

The doctor diagnosed Guillain-Barré Syndrome. If you are not familiar with it, Guillain-Barré usually begins in the feet or legs and may work its way throughout your body. It can cause altered sensation, numbness, even paralysis. Most people get over it within a few months, but a few don't, and when you are diagnosed you don't know which way you will go.

I had an uncle who ended up paralyzed from the neck down with it, and he got back only about 70 percent usage. Bill Darnell, who owned a midget I drove, also got it and he was greatly affected by it.

Obviously, I beat it, but I have to admit that for a guy who'd never been sick as a kid or more than a little beat-up by race cars, it was a real scary time. You don't know what's going to happen, and you can't do a damned thing about it. The disease runs its course—or it doesn't—and it's maybe worse for your mind than your body while you wait it out.

I was very, very lucky. I was bad enough to be in the hospital for only three days, beginning on the day of the Schrader Racing Christmas party. They didn't stop it—they did drink a toast or ten to the boss—but they wouldn't wait until I got out to have the party. Just because we did-n't know how long that would be. Can you see anything wrong with a Christmas party in February if that's how long it takes? Well, they did.

In fact, it took a couple of months until I got back to where I felt right again, but even at its worst I had only numbness and weakness—never the paralysis. And I never missed a race because of Guillain-Barré.

I bring it up at all only because that's what it will take for me to quit racing altogether—a serious disease or such advanced old age that I put my helmet on backward and don't realize it for five minutes.

I lost part of my thumb when I didn't get out of the way of the truck engine I was working on as it got started a little too quickly. The hospital gave me three options:

They could attach it and sew it to my side to try to get blood flowing through it. There was a chance they could save the tip that way.

I asked to hear the next option.

They could cut a toe off and sew it in place of the missing part of my thumb.

"And the third option?" I asked.

We'll just put some stitches in to close the wound and you can go back to the race track today.

Bingo.

You can't know for sure what life will hand you, but if something bad happens—a heart attack, stroke, cancer or whatever—I'll fight it hard, as much for the right to get back in the race car as for just good sense.

It's the way I am.

Gotta have priorities.

BEFORE I LEAVE NEXTEL CUP. . .

. . .I have a really, really neat deal lined up for 2006: I am driving for the Wood Brothers. By the time you read this, it will be happening, and you may notice a real good smile on my face and a lighter step as I go through the pits. I've driven for the best, and I've enjoyed my time in every car I've been in, even through ups and downs, but this is a real privilege.

If you are not already familiar with them, the Wood Brothers team has been one of the parties responsible for the growth and success of NASCAR racing. Right up there with the Pettys, Bud Moore, Junior Johnson and Mr. Donlavey. Additionally, the Wood Brothers are among the very few who were around in the early days and are still around—and competitive—today.

Originally, it was brothers Glen and Leonard who ran the team, and they became famous for being the first guys to take pit stops real seri-

ous. They recognized that shaving a few seconds off a pit stop meant a quarter or a half a lap on the track in some instances, so theirs were the first pit crews to make the deal look like a ballet.

Some of the greatest drivers in NASCAR history have driven for the Wood Brothers, but probably none was more instrumental in the sport's growth than The Silver Fox, David Pearson. He ranks second all-time in wins, and there aren't very many drivers ever who were tougher, more determined, and more capable. I didn't get to race with him very much—his career was winding down as mine in NASCAR was still in the learning stages—but there's no one I respect more. What he, Glen and Leonard did is the stuff of legends.

These days, the team principals are Glen's children, Eddie, Len and Kim, but really, it's still a family deal that includes extended family members. They respect the history, but it's cool that they also are working really hard to make their own legacy. The shop has been moved from Virginia to North Carolina, and they have aggressively gone after the kind of personnel and equipment it takes to compete with the mega-teams. It's pretty hard to argue with their success, too, as they have been really racey with Ricky Rudd in recent years.

Donnie Richeson: He makes racing fun again, which a lot of people have forgotten how to do. The business has grown so much that it's taken some of it away because of schedules and that, but Kenny puts the priority on it being a good time for everybody around him.

Not long after I started working for him, we decided to go to Toledo to test. He hadn't been there in about 20 years, so when it popped up on the ARCA schedule, he figured we ought to go up there and play for a day so we'd be ready.

Well, afterwards when we left, we stopped at the little restaurant/bar right outside the track. We got a six-pack, and then on the way to the airport we had to stop and get more. It kind of went on like that and by the time we got home, we had to get a driver because nobody was in any shape to drive. I'm not much of a drinker anyway, but you get caught up in the stories and laughter, and next thing you know you need a driver.

We felt like hiring Donnie Richeson was a good fit, and so far that's proven correct. (Joyce Standridge photo.)

They have two Busch cars, two Craftsman truck teams and the Cup car right now. I think they needed somebody a little older who can yell at the kids driving the other stuff and get them pointed in the right direction. Not that I yell much, but I really enjoy being a mentor because I remember what it meant to me to have Don Klein, Wib Spalding, Jerry Sifford, Harold Workman and a lot of other guys take an interest in what I was doing.

When I got the call from Eddie Wood, it was, "Would you sign for a year?"

"Yes."

"There's a good chance it will be longer than a year."

"Well, don't even worry about that. Let's just worry about next year and let the future take care of itself."

I was planning on 2006 in the BAM car as my Schwan...er, swan song. But, there was no contract to be jacked with, so that made it a lot nicer.

We're thrilled that the Wood Brothers have an affiliation with Jack Roush and the Roush/Yates engines, too. We also like that the Wood Brothers team races for a living, not just as a hobby, because that seems to light fires under folks.

We're also happy to be bringing a new sponsor into the sport. I have never had to bring a sponsor to get a ride, and I'm proud that I've maintained a good relationship with every sponsor I've encountered, but it's always special when you get to introduce new ones to the fun and benefit of a racing association.

Mr. Donlavey didn't have a sponsor, but that's when we got started with Schwan's and Red Baron. When I went to Rick Hendrick, sponsors were no problem. He's always had sponsors. When I committed to Petree, Skoal committed to him. I had worked with M&Ms through their Pedigree dog food branch as an associate sponsor on the Hendrick car. And BAM didn't have any sponsors, so we went out and got them one.

Sometimes a sponsor association becomes so famous that many people forget the car owner, car number and even the driver! The Pizza Hut car back in the 1980s was like that. (H.C. Hunter photo; Ken Schrader Collection.)

Now, we've got the Air Force and Motorcraft, along with introducing Little Debbie Snack Cakes. So, for however long I remain in Nextel Cup, these are the people who make it happen, and I thank them very much for making this a fantastic way to wrap up a long career in NASCAR.

THERE'S MORE TO LIFE...

Did I really start to say there's more to life than racing? Well, there is, although it usually has to be scheduled *around* the racing.

I had mentioned earlier that in time our Craftsman Truck and ARCA programs are going to ramp up a little more. That's not changed. It's still in the cards. We'll sneak past our team manager and take the dirt car out as much as possible, too. But occasionally, we do other things, like...

Well, hell, we gave up snow-skiing. Ann is good at it, but I suck. And I don't water-ski. Don't have a boat. Don't want one.

For a while I got pressured into golf tournaments associated with NASCAR events, but I absolutely hated it. So I refuse to do those deals any more.

Okay, there's snow skiing, golf, snorkeling, the infamous annual Float Trip, and bowling. And I'd still rather go racing! (Ken Schrader Collection.)

I Ain't Ridin' Off Into the Sunset

I spend so much time on the road all year racing that I don't care much about traveling. We go to the Bahamas or other places in the sun during the winter to wind down, but I won't be touring the cathedrals of Europe anytime soon.

What does that leave?

Competitive partying. But even that has its odd moments. We started having a float trip around July 4th every year back home on the Ozark Rivers, but the past couple of years people have been showing up literally by the bus load. Friends tell friends what a good time they have, so the friends come along, and then they invite *their* friends, and so on. You get the idea.

So that leaves...racing.

Guess we've come full circle.

I MEAN IT, I AIN'T RIDING OFF INTO THE SUNSET

If it was critical to me to race only at the highest levels, I guess I could say it's 5:00 P.M. in the middle of the winter and it's time to saddle the horses to ride off into the sunset.

But as far as I'm concerned, it's high noon and the horses can stay in the corral.

I've been blessed to race at some of the most famous tracks in the country. Like Indianapolis. Daytona. Talladega. Knoxville. Manzanita.

You see, I liked that places such as Indy paid a hundred grand to start. Yeah, it's got a lot of history, and you have to be impressed with the racers who've run there. It's cool to see your name in the record books alongside the greatest stars in racing history. But the hundred grand pays for a lot of racing parts, and you get to go to a lot of other tracks.

It's a huge kick to run the famous tracks, but y'know it's just as much fun to climb in a late model and run the short tracks you've heard about. (Ken Schrader Collection.)

And there's great history at little bullrings like Macon, too. It's not the same thing...but it is. If a race track, *any* race track, is your home track and you take all your passion for the sport with you when you go there, you're happy just to be able to race there. Then, Macon, Slinger, Manzanita or anywhere, matters just as much and impresses me every bit as much as the big places.

Because what they all have in common—2.5 miles or a quarter-mile, paved or dirt, famous or totally forgotten by time—is that there's a green flag.

And a checkered flag.

And a hell of a good time in between.

THE LAST WORD

My crystal ball is foggy. I try to direct what happens, but you never know. We're planning to stay in North Carolina and race for a while longer, but if it all goes away and I'm bankrupt tomorrow, we'll get by.

My kids were born in North Carolina and have never lived anywhere else, but they've said that if we need to go back to St. Louis, they'll go. Grandma, lots of other relatives and some good friends live there, so it's not as huge a move as you might think. And Dorothy will be going off to college before long, so her life is going to change anyway. Sheldon is just one of those kids who fits in and has fun wherever he is.

My wife is a keeper. I tease her that she got excited about buying our current home in Concord when she found out that the Wal-Mart is only two miles away. The truth is that while she has good taste and has made a very comfortable home for us—and I don't think Wal-Mart had anything to do with it, but she doesn't waste money either—she's still the daughter of a guy who got up every day and punched a time-clock at Anheuser-Busch for more than 30 years. The work ethic is ingrained in Ann, and she's still got her feet on the ground. We've had our ups and downs, like any couple who've been married for a long time, but there's very few women I've met in my life that I would put in the same category as Ann as far as quality of character. Far as I'm concerned, that makes her a trophy wife in the best sense of the word.

Not too long ago we were talking about the day we finally move back to our roots, and Ann said we could just move into the duplex she inherited.

Not enough room, I told her.

Well, we can knock out some walls, she replied.

I realized then that I've come to enjoy the fruits of my labor more than she has. It's a lot more important for Ann to exercise her mind than her credit card. Pretty neat, huh?

For Christmas one year, Ann had the old door from Daddy's shop mounted at our race shop in North Carolina. I think it was probably the best Christmas gift I ever got. (Joyce Standridge photo.)

Ann and the kids have been incredibly supportive of what I do. Obviously, if you are racing 100 times a year, you are not going to be around home a lot. In spite of that, my kids are well-grounded and my wife has taken it in stride. It's the perfect set-up for a racing addict. They are enablers, so I'll blame the way I am on them.

And they'll forgive me for it.

Let me close by saying that I'm not much for television and movies. Haven't got the time. But one of the few good movies about racing is the 1968 Paul Newman flick *Winning.* There's a really good segment in it when Newman's character, Frank Capua, is interviewed after winning the Indianapolis 500.

"Why did you take that extra lap after the checkered flag?" he's asked.

Newman shrugs, and with a goofy little grin he replies, "Because I didn't feel like stopping."

This is the last chapter of this book, but it's nowhere close to the last chapter of my career. Like that fictional character, I don't feel like stopping, so you can just put away your checkered flags.

I didn't write this because I was ready to quit.

I just thought maybe you'd like to catch up.

So, we've got the first 35 years wrapped up, and it's time to start on the next 35. And to get the material for that book, there's just one thing we need to do—*Gotta Race!*

(Joyce Standridge photo.)

35 Years of Racing Records

K EN SCHRADER HAS MAINTAINED RECORDS of nearly every race he ran over the past 35 years. Note that over the years, he never knew that the records would end up in print, so they should be considered to be casual, rather than official records.

Also, in 1984, Ken's briefcase—with all the records in them—was stolen. As a result, the records for 1984 are reconstructed as best as possible, but probably are less reliable than most other years.

At the conclusion of these records is a listing of all the tracks Ken can recall racing, where they are located and the size and type of track.

Legend:

1st F	First of multiple features on same date/same track
2nd F	Second of multiple features on same date/same track
A F	A Feature race on short track
AARA	Allied Auto Racing Association, based in St. Louis area
ACT	American-Canadian Tour
B F	B Feature race on short track
C F	C Feature race on short track
C	Consolation race
CD	Champ Dirt (same as Silver Crown but without USAC sanction)
CT	Craftsman Trucks
D	Dash
F	Feature (short tracks) or Finish (NASCAR races)
GARA	Gateway Auto Racing Association, based in St. Louis area
H	Heat race
IMSA	International Motor Sports Association (sports cars)
IROC	International Race of Champions
LM	Late Model
MARA	Midwest Auto Racing Association, based in Midwest
mph	miles per hour
NASCAR	National Association for Stock Car Auto Racing, based in Daytona
NC	Nextel Cup
NCRA	North Central Racing Association
NW	Northwest Tour
Q	Qualifying position and/or time
S	Semi or consolation race
SC	Silver Crown (Champ Dirt) cars
sec.	seconds
SLARA	St. Louis Auto Racing Association, based in St. Louis area
SW	Southwest Tour
UDTRA	United Dirt Track Racing Association
USAC	United States Auto Club, based in Indianapolis
WC	Winston Cup
WoO	World of Outlaws
WW	Winston West

Date	Track	Type	Car Owner	Race Winner	Finish	Comments
5/2	Lake Hill Speedway	Sportsman	Schrader #100	Jerry Sifford	Q-1st; H-6th; S-2nd; F-7th	Car driven by Bill Schrader
5/8	Lake Hill Speedway	Sportsman	Schrader #100		Q-6th; D-2nd; H-5th; F-1st	Car driven by Jerry Sifford
5/9	Lake Hill Speedway	Sportsman	Schrader #100		Q-5th; H-1st; S-4th; F-14th	Car driven by Bill Schrader
5/15	Lake Hill Speedway	Sportsman	Schrader #100		Q-2nd; D-1st; H-7th; F-2nd	Car driven by Jerry Sifford
5/30	Lake Hill Speedway	Sportsman	Schrader #100	Ken Schrader	Q-9th; D-4th; H-1st; F-1st	Car driven by Ken Schrader for first time
6/6	Lake Hill Speedway	Sportsman	Schrader #100	Ken Schrader	Q-1st; D-6th; H-2nd; F-1st	
6/13	Lake Hill Speedway	Sportsman	Schrader #100	Ken Schrader	Q-1st; D-6th; H-4th; F-1st	
6/20	Lake Hill Speedway	Sportsman	Schrader #100		Q-2nd; D-6th; H-4th; F-18th	
6/27	Lake Hill Speedway	Sportsman	Schrader #100		Q-2nd; D-5th; H-8th; F-6th	
7/5	Lake Hill Speedway	Sportsman	Schrader #100		Q-2nd; D-3rd; H-10th; F-4th	
7/18	Lake Hill Speedway	Sportsman	Schrader #100		Q-2nd; H-1st; F-12th	
7/25	Rolla Speedway	Sportsman	Schrader #100	Ken Schrader	Q-20.51 sec.; H-1st; S-2nd	
8/1	Lake Hill Speedway	Sportsman	Schrader #100		Q-2nd; D-3rd; H-2nd; F-16th	
8/7	Rolla Speedway	Sportsman	Schrader #100		Q-20.44 sec.; F-9th	
8/8	Rolla Speedway	Sportsman	Schrader #100		D-7th; H-1st; F-1st	
8/15	Lake Hill Speedway	Sportsman	Schrader #100	Ken Schrader	Q-23.15 sec.; H-1st; S-4th	
8/21	Lake Hill Speedway	Sportsman	Schrader #100	Ken Schrader	Q-3rd; D-2nd; H-6th; F-1st	First time ever swept a show
8/29	Lake Hill Speedway	Sportsman	Schrader #100	Ken Schrader	Q-1st; D-1st; H-1st; F-1st	
9/5	Lake Hill Speedway	Sportsman	Schrader #100		Q-1st; D-1st; H-1st; F-2nd	
9/12	Lake Hill Speedway	Sportsman	Schrader #100	Ken Schrader	Q-1st; D-5th; H-8th; F-2nd	
9/26	Lake Hill Speedway	Sportsman	Schrader #100	Ken Schrader	Q-18.40 sec.; H-2nd; F-1st	
10/3	Lake Hill Speedway	Sportsman	Schrader #100		D-1st; H-2nd	

Date	Track	Type	Car Owner	Race Winner	Finish	Comments
4/9	Lake Hill Speedway	Late Model	Schrader #100		Q-2nd; D-5th; H-2nd; F-13th	Spun by Russ and broke axle
4/22	Rolla Speedway	Late Model	Schrader #100		Q-21.01 sec.; H-4th	
4/23	Lake Hill Speedway	Late Model	Schrader #100		H-3rd; F-6th	
4/29	Lake Hill Speedway	Late Model	Schrader #100		H-1st; F-8th	Blew left front tire while running 4th
4/30	Lake Hill Speedway	Late Model	Schrader #100		D-2nd; H-2nd; F-12th	Blew right front tire while leading
5/6	Rolla Speedway	Late Model	Schrader #100		Q-22.36 sec.; H-1st; S-4th	
5/7	Lake Hill Speedway	Late Model	Schrader #100		H-6th; F-3rd	
5/13	Rolla Speedway	Late Model	Schrader #100		Q-22.56 sec.; H-1st; S-1st	
5/14	Lake Hill Speedway	Late Model	Schrader #100		D-3rd; H-3rd; F-5th	Lost brakes at end
5/20	Rolla Speedway	Late Model	Schrader #100		Q-23.90 sec.; H-3rd	
5/21	Lake Hill Speedway	Late Model	Schrader #100		H-5th; F-14th	
5/28	Lake Hill Speedway	Late Model	Schrader #100		D-6th; H-3rd	
6/3	Rolla Speedway	Late Model	Schrader #100			Didn't start feature; broke rear cross member
6/4	Lake Hill Speedway	Late Model	Schrader #100		H-6th; F-12th	Wipe out in heat race; broke my racer
6/11	Lake Hill Speedway	Late Model	Schrader #100		H-3rd; F-6th	Blew right front while running 5th
6/18	Lake Hill Speedway	Late Model	Schrader #100		Q-16.28 sec.; H-1st; F-5th	Ran flat out
6/25	Lake Hill Speedway	Late Model	Schrader #100		Q-16.56 sec.; F-7th	Ran flat out 100 laps
7/1	Rolla Speedway	Late Model	Schrader #100		Q-21.53 sec.; S-2nd	

Date	Track	Type	Car Owner	Finish	Comments
7/2	Lake Hill Speedway	Late Model	Schrader #100	Q-2nd; H-4th; F-5th	Spun out in feature
7/9	Lake Hill Speedway	Late Model	Schrader #100	Q-5th; H-3rd; F-3rd	75-lap feature
7/15	Rolla Speedway	Late Model	Schrader #100	Q-23.40 sec.; H-2nd; S-3rd	
7/16	Lake Hill Speedway	Late Model	Schrader #100	Q-5th; H-2nd; F-5th	Wiped out by Jerry in heat; missed handicap
7/22	Rolla Speedway	Late Model	Schrader #100	H-3rd; S-4th	Ran flat out in feature
7/23	Lake Hill Speedway	Late Model	Schrader #100	Q-4th; H-4th; Handi-4th; F-9th	Blew engine running 10th
7/30	Lake Hill Speedway	Late Model	Schrader #100	Q-3rd; H-3rd; F-4th	Broke trailing arm while running 5th
8/6	Rolla Speedway	Late Model	Schrader #100	Q-22.04 sec.; H-2nd; F-2nd	
8/7	Lake Hill Speedway	Late Model	Schrader #100	Q-4th; F-7th	
8/14	Lake Hill Speedway	Late Model	Schrader #100	Q-1st; H-3rd; Handi-3rd; F-4th	100-lap feature
8/19-20	Rolla Speedway	Late Model	Schrader #100	H-2nd; S-1st; F-13th	
8/26	Rolla Speedway	Late Model	Schrader #100	H-1st; S-3rd; F-10th	
8/27	Lake Hill Speedway	Late Model	Schrader #100	Q-5th; H-1st; F-4th	
9/3	Lake Hill Speedway	Late Model	Schrader #100	Q-5th; H-4th; F-4th	
9/9	Rolla Speedway	Late Model	Schrader #100	Q-21.09 sec.; H-2nd; S-3rd	Cooled it in the feature
9/10	Lake Hill Speedway	Late Model	Schrader #100	Q-5th; H-2nd; Handi-4th; F-5th	
9/17	Lake Hill Speedway	Late Model	Schrader #100	Q-9th; H-2nd; F-3rd	

1973

Date	Track	Type	Car Owner	Race Winner	Finish	Comments
3/31-4/1	Springfield (MO) Fairgrounds	Late Model		Dean Roper	Q-29th; H-4th; B F-3rd	Valvoline 100
4/7-8	Rolla Speedway	Late Model		Dick Trickle	Q-13th; H-5th; C-2nd; F-12th	NASCAR 200; was running 8th until pit stop to cool car; wrist pin got loose
4/27	Tri-City Speedway	Late Model	Bob Mueller	Bill Meyers	H-3rd; H-4th; S-3rd	Hit wall easy in heat race
4/28	Rolla Speedway	Late Model	Schrader #100	Larry Phillips	Q-19th	100-lapper; hit wall in 2nd heat; had x-rays at hospital; awful sore; car hurt bad
5/4	Tri-City Speedway	Late Model	Bob Mueller	Wib Spalding	Q-19th; H-4th	Led heat for 7 laps but blew an axle on white flag
5/5	Rolla Speedway	Late Model	Schrader #100	Bob Frueh	Q-7th; H-7th	Car missed all night; found water in gas; blew head gasket; got block and head
6/6	Lake Hill Speedway	Late Model				Rained out; no ride; hot-lapped Marty's car
5/11	Tri-City Speedway	Late Model				Rained out after Handicap; no ride
5/12	Rolla Speedway	Late Model	Schrader #100	Terry Bivens		No ride
5/13	Lake Hill Speedway	Late Model		Harold Workman	Q-10th; H-1st; F-4th	Our 64 Impala
5/18	Tri-City Speedway	Late Model		Louie Jansen		No ride
5/19	Rolla Speedway	Late Model		Terry Bivens		No ride; Pepsi 150
5/20	Lake Hill Speedway	Late Model	Schrader #100	Eddie House	Q-13th (17.05 sec.); H-2nd	Our 64 Impala; lost oil pressure
5/25	Tri-City Speedway	Late Model	Schrader #100	Clyde Lindemann	H-1st; S-1st; F-11th	Our 69 Chevelle
5/26	Lake Hill Speedway	Late Model	Schrader #100		Q-1st (16.15 sec.); H-3rd	Rained out after heats
6/1	Tri-City Speedway	Late Model	Schrader #100	Ron King	Q-12th; H-2nd; S-3rd; F-5th	
6/3	Tri-City Speedway	Late Model	Schrader #100	Wib Spalding	Q-11th; H-3rd; F-5th	
6/8	Tri-City Speedway	Late Model	Schrader #100	John Prior	Q-13th; H-3rd; S-3rd; F-6th	Hit wall in feature
6/10	Lake Hill Speedway	Late Model	Schrader #100	Jerry Sifford	Q-4th; H-4th; F-11th	Our 69 Chevelle; Marty's car in the feature
6/15	Tri-City Speedway	Late Model	Schrader #100	John Prior	Q-10th; H-3rd; F-4th	
6/17	Lake Hill Speedway	Late Model		Paul Lawson	Q-9th; H-4th; F-5th	
6/22	Tri-City Speedway	Late Model		John Prior	Q-2nd; H-2nd; F-12th	Won a Camaro body for free
6/24	Lake Hill Speedway	Late Model		John Prior	Q-6th; Handi-1st	
6/29	Tri-City Speedway	Late Model	Schrader #100	Jerry Sifford	Q-5th; H-1st; Handi-1st	Mid-season championship race; no feature due to Russ's crash

7/1	Lake Hill Speedway	Late Model		Len Gettemeier	Q-2nd; H-2nd; Handi-4th; F-5th	Clyde Lindemann won the postponed mid-season race; Spalding won regular race
7/6	Tri-City Speedway	Late Model		Lindemann; Spalding	Q-5th; H-3rd; Handi-4th; F-4th	Got there late
7/7	Rolla Speedway	Late Model		David Goldsberry	S-2nd; F-7th	New track record; won an extra $100
7/8	Lake Hill Speedway	Late Model		Jerry Sifford	Q-1st (15.37 sec.); H-3rd; F-3rd	
7/13	Tri-City Speedway	Late Model	Schrader #100	Wib Spalding	Q-4th; H-1st; Handi-4th; F-3rd	Mid-season championship
7/15	Lake Hill Speedway	Late Model	Schrader #100	Wib Spalding	Q-1st; H-5th; H-2nd; F-3rd	
7/20	Tri-City Speedway	Late Model	Schrader #100	Ron King	Q-4th; H-2nd; Handi-3rd; F-5th	
7/22	Lake Hill Speedway	Late Model			Q-2nd; H-1st; F-6th	
7/29	Lake Hill Speedway	Late Model			Q-7th; H-2nd; Handi-3rd; F-10th	Overheated running 2nd in feature
8/3	Tri-City Speedway	Late Model		Louie Jansen	Q-7th; H-2nd; Handi-1st; F-14th	Blew engine and hit Rusty in feature
8/5	Lake Hill Speedway	Late Model		Russ Wallace	Q-2nd; H-2nd; Handi-4th; F-6th	Spun out by Russ, leading feature
8/8	Tri-City Speedway	Late Model	Schrader #100	Louie Jansen	Q-7th; H-2nd; F-8th	Worked on Marty's Chevelle all day; took one TT; water in oil; rained out after intermission
8/10	Lake Hill Speedway	Late Model				
8/17	Tri-City Speedway	Late Model	Schrader #100	Wib Spalding	Q-5th; H-2nd; Handi-1st; F-15th	Short on people so all cars paid same
8/22	St. Charles Speedway	Late Model			H-3rd; S-1st; F-5th	200 laps; blew engine running 8th at 140 laps
8/24	Tri-City Speedway	Late Model	Schrader #100	Wib Spalding	Q-11th; H-1st; F-2nd	
8/25	Rolla Speedway	Late Model	Schrader #100	Larry Phillips	Q-8th; H-5th; F-13th	
8/31	Tri-City Speedway	Late Model	Schrader #100	Russ Wallace	Q-19th (32.12 sec.)	Blew new 427 in time trials
9/7	Tri-City Speedway	Late Model	Schrader #100	Wib Spalding	Q-11th; H-2nd; F-8th	Spun in feature
9/9	Lake Hill Speedway	Late Model	Schrader #100	Wib Spalding	Q-3rd; H-1st; F-3rd	
9/14	Tri-City Speedway	Late Model	Schrader #100	Wib Spalding	Q-11th; H-2nd; F-5th	Season championship race
9/21	Tri-City Speedway	Late Model	Schrader #100	Wib Spalding	Q-2nd; H-2nd; Handi-2nd; F-3rd	Season championship race
9/23	St. Charles Speedway	Late Model	Schrader #100	Rusty Wallace	Q-1st; H-2nd; Handi-1st; F-7th	Crashed in feature

1974

Date	Track	Type	Car Owner	Race Winner	Finish	Comments
2/9	New Smyrna Speedway	Late Model	Schrader #100	Bob Senneker	H-8th; F-18th	Put hole in radiator on 80th lap
2/10	New Smyrna Speedway	Late Model	Schrader #100	Jody Ridley	S-2nd	Dropped out of heat race
2/13	New Smyrna Speedway	Late Model	Schrader #100	Jody Ridley		
2/14	New Smyrna Speedway	Late Model	Schrader #100	Pete Hamilton		
2/15	New Smyrna Speedway	Late Model	Schrader #100	Jody Ridley		
4/19	Tri-City Speedway	Late Model	Schrader #100	Lou Thery	H-1st; S-5th; F-6th	Blew engine and totaled car
4/20	Rolla Speedway	Late Model	Schrader #100	Tom Maier	Q-22nd; H-3rd	
4/26	Tri-City Speedway	Late Model	Schrader #100	Wib Spalding	H-1st; S-2nd; F-7th	
4/28	Lake Hill Speedway	Late Model	Schrader #100	Russ Wallace	H-4th; H-4th; D-4th; F-9th	Heat—jumped out of gear and lost oil pressure
	Tri-City Speedway	Late Model	Schrader #100	Bill Scherer		Car vibrated until driveshaft came through the floorboard!
	Lake Hill Speedway	Late Model	Schrader #100	Russ Wallace		Blew up qualifying
5/12	Tri-City Speedway	Late Model	George Egans	Wib Spalding	Q-3rd; H-2nd; D-2nd; F-9th	Overheated all night so took it easy in feature
5/18	Lake Hill Speedway	Late Model		Tom Hannick		Spun bearing in new alum. rod motor in heat race
5/19	Rolla Speedway	Late Model		Larry Phillips	Q-18th	Knocked bearing out after heat
5/24	Lake Hill Speedway	Late Model		Tom Hannick	Q-9th; H-2nd; S-2nd; F-4th	
5/24	Tri-City Speedway	Late Model	Schrader #100	Russ Wallace	Q-6th; H-1st; D-4th; F-6th	
5/26	Lake Hill Speedway	Late Model	Schrader #100	Bob Minor	Q-4th; H-3rd; D-4th; F-5th	
6/2	Lake Hill Speedway	Late Model	Schrader #100	Russ Wallace	F-6th	
6/2	Lake Hill Speedway	SLARA Midget	Bud Hoppe #15	Danny Frye, Jr.		First night ever in midget; just ran the feature

Date	Track	Division	Car	Driver	Results	Notes
6/7	Tri-City Speedway	GARA Late Model	Schrader #100	Len Gettemeier	Q-1st; H-2nd; D-6th	Pulled out of feature; divided $ up evenly
6/9	Lake Hill Speedway	GARA Late Model	Schrader #100	Bill Scherer	Q-9th; H-1st; F-7th	
6/15	Rolla Speedway	Late Model	Schrader #100	Larry Phillips	Q-6th; H-7th; D-6th; S-4th; F-11th	Primary wire came off distributor running 6th in feature
6/14	Lake Hill Speedway	GARA Late Model	Schrader #100	Russ Wallace	Q-12th; H-3rd; S-4th	
6/21	Tri-City Speedway	GARA Late Model	Schrader #100	Wib Spalding	Q-6th; H-4th; F-4th	Dropped valve lining up for heat race
6/23	Rolla Speedway	SLARA Midget	Hoppe #15	Danny Frye, Jr.	H-2nd; D-2nd; F-2nd	Overheated in feature so cooled it
6/28	Lake Hill Speedway	GARA Late Model	Schrader #100	Russ Wallace	Q-6th (15.68 sec.)	Dropped exhaust valve lining up for heat race
6/29	Tri-City Speedway	GARA Late Model	Schrader #100	Russ Wallace	Q-5th; H-3rd; D-1st; F-4th	
6/30	Rolla Speedway	SLARA Midget	Hoppe #15	Bob Wente, Sr.		
6/30	Lake Hill Speedway	GARA Late Model	Schrader #100	Len Gettemeier	Q-7th; H-4th; D-5th; F-11th	New Camaro; threw out driveshaft so drove old Chevelle; running 3rd in feature spun in Rusty's oil; hit wall but not bad.
7/4	Lake Hill Speedway	GARA Late Model	Schrader #100	Bob Minor	Q-3rd; H-4th; D-3rd; F-4th	Transmission locked up in the feature
7/4	Lake Hill Speedway	SLARA Midget	Hoppe #15	Bob Wente, Sr.	H-3rd; F-2nd	Spun running 3rd
7/5	Tri-City Speedway	GARA Late Model	Schrader #100	Leonard Lawson	Q-6th; H-4th; D-2nd; F-11th	
7/6	Capital Speedway	Late Model	Schrader #100	Tom Hannick	H-3rd; F-6th	
7/7	Lake Hill Speedway	SLARA Midget	Hoppe #15	Jon Backlund	Q-2nd; H-4th; D-6th; F-4th	In feature broke the in-and-out box
7/12	Randolph Co. Fairgrounds	Late Model	Schrader #100	Shorty Akers	Q-6th	
7/13	Capital Speedway	Late Model	Schrader #100	Lou Jansen	H-1st; F-2nd	Blew up in feature; broke a rod
7/19	Tri-City Speedway	GARA Late Model	Schrader #100	Arnie Knepper	Q-5th; H-4th; D-1st; F-12th	
7/20	Wayne Co. Fairgrounds	GARA Late Model	George Egans	Russ Wallace	H-3rd; F-6th	
7/21	Lake Hill Speedway	SLARA Midget	Hoppe #15	Wib Spalding	Q-5th; H-4th; D-3rd; F-5th	Mid-season championship
7/27	Tri-City Speedway	GARA Late Model	Schrader #100	Jon Backlund	Q-10th; H-2nd; F-6th	Mid-season championship
7/28	Springfield Speedway	SLARA Midget	Hoppe #15	David Goldsberry	H-6th; D-2nd; F-5th	
8/3	Lake Hill Speedway	GARA Late Model	Schrader #100	Bob Minor	Q-8th; H-3rd; F-13th	Broke transmission lining up for feature
8/4	Rolla Speedway	GARA Late Model	Schrader #100	Danny Frye, Jr.	Q-7th; H-3rd; F-4th	
8/4	Lake Hill Speedway	SLARA Midget	Hoppe #15	Arnie Knepper	Q-5th; H-2nd; D-2nd; F-3rd	
8/10	White Co. Fairgrounds	SLARA Midget	Hoppe #15	Ken Schrader	H-2nd; F-4th	
8/11	Lake Hill Speedway	GARA Late Model	Schrader #100		Q-6th; H-6th; F-4th	
8/14	Tri-City Speedway	Hobby Car	Dennis Satterfield	Bill Scherer	Q-7th; H-2nd; F-1st	1st feature win of season; Dad won mechanic's race
8/16	Tri-City Speedway	GARA Late Model	George Egans	Terry Brumley	H-4th; S-2nd; F-6th	Heat race crash; blew engine in feature
8/18	Rolla Speedway	Late Model	Schrader #100	Bob Minor	Q-5th; H-2nd; F-3rd	Fair race; rained out Saturday so ran on Sunday
	Lake Hill Speedway	Late Model	Schrader #100	Mike Darr	Q-7th; H-2nd; D-2nd; F-12th	Led feature until spun on lap 18 in my own water
	Sedalia (MO) Fairgrounds	Late Model	George Egans		Q-13th	Fair race, was running 10th
	Illinois State Fairgrounds					Blew up qualifying
9/6	Tri-City Speedway	GARA Late Model	Schrader #100	Ken Schrader	Q-3rd; H-1st; D-3rd; F-1st	Also won $25 savings bond; first time Camaro on dirt
9/8	Lake Hill Speedway	GARA Late Model	Schrader #100	Russ Wallace	Q-3rd; H-4th; D-3rd; F-9th	No trouble; just didn't go
9/15	Tri-City Speedway	GARA Late Model	Schrader #100	Ken Schrader	Q-7th; H-1st; D-1st; F-1st	$180 extra plus Firestone tires
9/15	Lake Hill Speedway	SLARA Midget	Hoppe #15	Arnie Knepper	H-1st; F-2nd	
9/15	Tri-City Speedway	GARA Late Model	Schrader #100		Q-4th; H-3rd; D-1st; F-2nd	Burnt piston and nursed it home
9/21	Tri-City Speedway	GARA Late Model	Schrader #100		Q-9th; F-8th	
	Tri-City Speedway	Hobby Car	Bill Broz			
10/19	I-35 Speedway	SLARA Midget	Hoppe #15	Danny Frye, Jr.	H-2nd; F-2nd	On quarter mile; running 2nd and was spun by Red Bailey

1975

Date	Track	Type	Car Owner	Race Winner	Finish	Comments
1/19	Ft. Wayne (IN)	USAC Midget	Hoppe #15	Gary Bettenhausen	Q-5th; H-6th; F-11th	Car quit running on 29th lap; hit the kill button
1/25	Indianapolis Fairgrounds	USAC Midget	Hoppe #15	Dana Carter	Q-24th; H-1st	90 cars
2/7	Auburndale Speedway	Midget	Hoppe #15	Newt White	Q-5th; H-1st; D-2nd	Feature wrecked bad—got knocked out
2/12	New Smyrna Speedway	Late Model	Schrader #100	Pete Hamilton	Q-lousy; H-9th	Dropped out of feature
2/13	New Smyrna Speedway	Late Model	Schrader #100	Pete Hamilton	Q-lousy; H-top 10; D-top 10	Pulled out of feature; no trouble
2/14	New Smyrna Speedway	Late Model	Schrader #100	Jody Ridley	Q-lousy; H-6th	Pulled out of feature; no trouble
2/15	New Smyrna Speedway	Late Model	Schrader #100	Pete Hamilton	Q-lousy; H-5th	Missed show
3/1	Indianapolis Fairgrounds	USAC Midget	Hoppe #15	Ken Nichols	Q-lousy	Also drove Pat Walsh's car
4/6	Lake Hill Speedway	Late Model	Schrader #100	Jerry Sifford	Q-5th; D-4th; S-?; F-9th	
4/13	Lake Hill Speedway	SLARA Midget	Hoppe #95	Newt White	H-4th; F-13th	Also drove Pat Walsh's car
4/13	Lake Hill Speedway	Late Model	Schrader #100	Rusty Wallace	H-3rd; D-6th; F-5th	Also drove Pat's car
4/20	Lake Hill Speedway	GARA Late Model	Schrader #100	Jerry Sifford	H-1st; S-2nd; F-6th	Air cleaner hung up the carb linkage in feature
4/26	Tri-City Speedway	GARA Late Model	Schrader #100	Len Gettemeier	H-1st; S-1st; F-15th	Also drove Pat's car
4/27	Lake Hill Speedway	GARA Late Model	Schrader #100	Jerry Sifford	Q-5th; D-3rd; F-4th	Led 10 laps and bent three intake valves
5/3	Tri-City Speedway	GARA Late Model	Schrader #100	Len Gettemeier	F-4th	Bent two rod bearings in the heat race
5/4	Lake Hill Speedway	GARA Late Model	Schrader #100	Jerry Sifford	H-4th	Car made $10 but I paid $5 to drive it so broke it even
5/9	Lake Hill Speedway	Figure 8	Stanley Rideout	Pat Walsh		Pat drove my Chevelle at Lake Hill and crashed
5/10	Tri-City Speedway	GARA Late Model	Schrader #100	Russ Wallace	H-1st; D-1st; F-2nd	Dropped out running 3rd in heat; feature dropped out leading; battery shorted in both races
5/11	St. Charles Speedway	Late Model	Schrader #100	Jerry Sifford	H-5th; F-5th	Hit wall in heat race; feature spun running 10th
5/16	Lake Hill Speedway	Figure 8	Tim Gore	Pat Walsh		On the half-mile; spun running 4th in heat
5/17	Tri-City Speedway	GARA Late Model	Schrader #100	Russ Wallace	H-6th; D-4th; F-15th	Hit wall in heat and feature
5/26	Sedalia (MO) Fairgrounds	Late Model	Schrader #100	Terry Bivens	H-5th; D-6th; F-2nd	
5/31	Tri-City Speedway	GARA Late Model	Schrader #100	Russ Wallace	H-1st; F-1st	Led until 2 laps to go and broke the rear end
6/7	Tri-City Speedway	GARA Late Model	Schrader #98	Ken Schrader		
6/8	Lake Hill Speedway	SLARA Midget	Hoppe #15		H-1st; F-13th	
6/15	Lake Hill Speedway	Figure 8	Tim Gore	Arnie Knepper	F-1st	Engine trouble
6/21	Springfield Speedway	SLARA Midget	Hoppe #15	Ken Schrader	H-6th; D-6th	Crashed in feature
6/22	Lake Hill Speedway	Figure 8	Tim Gore	Bill Meyers		
6/28	Tri-City Speedway	GARA Late Model	Schrader #100	Ken Schrader	H-2nd; F-1st	
6/29	Lake Hill Speedway	SLARA Midget	Hoppe #15	Arnie Knepper	Q-2nd; H-7th; D-2nd; F-3rd	
7/6	Randolph Co. Fairgrounds	SLARA Midget	Hoppe #15	Larry Patton	Q-15th; H-4th; F-11th	
7/19	Wayne Co. Fairgrounds	USAC Midget	Hoppe #15		Q-5th; H-7th	Paid by qualifying; feature rained out
7/20	Lake Hill Speedway	Figure 8	Tim Gore	Ken Schrader	F-1st	
7/26	Springfield Speedway	SLARA Midget	Hoppe #15	Les Stafford	H-2nd; F-6th	
7/27	Belle-Clair Speedway	SLARA Midget	Hoppe #15	Ken Schrader	H-1st; F-1st	
8/8	Indianapolis Speedrome	USAC Midget	Hoppe #15	Sleepy Tripp	Q-21st; H-3rd; F-9th	
8/9	Tri-City Speedway	USAC Midget	Hoppe #15	Rich Vogler	Q-15th; H-2nd; F-12th	
8/9	Tri-City Speedway	SLARA Midget	Hoppe #15	Arnie Knepper	H-2nd; F-2nd	Johnny Gall got killed
8/10	Lake Hill Speedway	GARA Late Model	Hoppe #15	Russ Wallace	H-1st; S-1st; F-2nd	Pat drove car but Marshall Yost gave me $20 for garage use and hobby car protest
8/15	Springfield Speedway	NAMAR Midget	Wayne Lee #93	West Stafford	S-4th; B F-8th	
8/16	Tri-City Speedway	GARA Late Model	George Egans	Bill Meyers		Blew up in heat race; Pat drove the Camaro

Date	Track	Type	Car Owner	Race Winner	Finish	Comments
8/24	DuQuoin Fairgrounds	USAC Midget		Richard Powell	Q-31st	Missed show; race was called due to dust
8/24	Lake Hill Speedway	SLARA Midget	Hoppe #15	Fred Tiede	H-1st; F-2nd	
9/1	Lake Hill Speedway	GARA Late Model	Schrader #100		S-7th	
	Springfield Speedway	GARA Late Model	Schrader #100	Don Vogler	H-5th; D-1st; F-4th	On the quarter-mile
9/5	Springfield Speedway	USAC Midget	Hoppe #15	Sleepy Tripp	Q-lousy; H-5th; S-2nd; F-9th	
9/6	Tri-City Speedway	SLARA Midget	Hoppe #15	Ken Schrader	H-3rd; F-1st	
9/7	Lake Hill Speedway	SLARA Midget	Hoppe #15	Ken Schrader	H-2nd; F-1st	
9/13	Tri-City Speedway	GARA Late Model	Schrader #100	Bill Meyers	H-2nd; F-12th	Season championship race; running 4th in feature, got hot; ruined the block and head
9/20	Tri-City Speedway	GARA Late Model	Schrader #100	Bill Meyers	Q-5th	First night 427 in car; blew the head gasket
	Springfield (MO) Fairgrounds	Late Model		Larry Phillips	H-6th; S-2nd; F-9th	Changed ratchet at track and then transmission messed up
	Tri-City Speedway	Late Model	Schrader #100	Ed Massie	Q-5th	Broke axle and spun in feature
	Boothill Speedway	IMCA Late Model	Schrader #100		H-6th; S-2nd; F-9th	
	Boothill Speedway	IMCA Late Model	Schrader #100	Freddy Fryer	H-4th; F-11th	

1976

Date	Track	Type	Car Owner	Race Winner	Finish	Comments
4/1	Indianapolis Raceway Park	USAC Midget	Hank Green #67	Sleepy Tripp	Q-19th; H-4th; F-7th	
4/18	Lake Hill Speedway	AARA Late Model	Schrader #100	Kenny Shrum	Q-5th; H-2nd; D-3rd; F-4th	
4/25	Springfield (MO) Fairgrounds	AARA Late Model	Schrader #100	Don Klein	Q-5th (16.81 sec.)	
5/1	Lake Hill Speedway	Late Model	Schrader #100	Larry Phillips	H-3rd; F-18th	
5/2	Belle-Clair Speedway	AARA Mini-Stock	Schrader #100	Jerry Sifford	Q-9th (17.30 sec.)	
5/7	Tri-City Speedway	GARA Late Model	Mike Edwards	Ken Schrader	H-2nd; F-1st	
5/8	Lake Hill Speedway	AARA Late Model	Schrader #100	Don Klein	H-4th; S-3rd; F-15th	
5/9	Belle-Clair Speedway	AARA Mini-Stock	Mike Edwards	Ken Schrader	Q-3rd; H-1st; D-2nd; F-11th	
5/21	Springfield Speedway	SLARA Midget	Hoppe #39	Gene Gennetten	H-1st; F-1st	
5/22	Lake Hill Speedway	AARA Late Model	Schrader #100	Kenny Shrum	Q-8th; H-2nd; F-2nd	
5/23	Lake Hill Speedway	SLARA Midget	Hoppe #39	Ken Schrader	Q-3rd (15.65 sec.)	
5/23	Indianapolis Raceway Park	USAC Midget	Green #67	Bob Wente, Sr.	Q-1st; H-1st; F-1st	
5/29	Sedalia (MO) Fairgrounds	Midget	Green #67	Gene Gennetten	Q-10th; H-5th; S-2nd; F-4th	
5/31	Belle-Clair Speedway	AARA Mini-Stock	Mike Edwards	Scott Stevens	H-4th; F-17th	
6/4	Highland Speedway	SLARA Midget	Hoppe #39	Chuck Taylor	H-2nd; F-2nd	
6/5	Springfield Speedway	USAC Midget	Hoppe #39	Bob Wente, Sr.	Q-4th; H-5th; F-13th	
6/12	Elsberry Speedway	Late Model	Schrader #100	Tevine Pipes	H-6th; S-3rd	
6/18	Tri-City Speedway	GARA Late Model	Schrader #100	Russ Wallace	Q-bad; H-5th; F-2nd	
6/19	St. Charles Speedway	SLARA Midget	Hoppe #39	Duke Derosa	H-1st; S-9th; F-4th	
6/20	Tri-City Speedway	GARA Late Model	Schrader #100	C.C. Corbin	Q-12th; H-4th; F-12th	
6/27	Lake Hill Speedway	AARA Late Model	Schrader #100	Don Klein	H-5th; S-11th; F-5th	
6/27	Riverside Speedway	Midget	Pizza Hut	Thad Dosher	Q-4th	Spun out running 5th
7/4	Randolph Co. Fairgrounds	Midget	Hoppe #39	Steve Cannon	Q-10th; H-4th; F-11th	Dropped out of feature with busted motor mount
7/6	Springfield Speedway	USAC Midget	Schrader #100	Don Klein	Q-2nd; H-2nd; D-3rd	Paid feature according to qualifying due to dust
7/10	Lake Hill Speedway	AARA Late Model	Hoppe #39	Danny Frye, Jr.	Q-3rd; H-1st; D-5th; F-4th	
	Lake Hill Speedway	SLARA Midget	Green #67	Mike Stroud	Q-1st; H-1st; F-2nd	
7/17	Highland Speedway	Midget	Pizza Hut	Roger Branson	H-1st; F-4th	
7/18	St. Charles Speedway	Midget	Pizza Hut		Q-8th	Missed show

Date	Track	Type	Car Owner	Race Winner	Finish	Comments
7/24	Wayne Co. Fairgrounds	Midget	Pizza Hut	Arnie Knepper	Q-4th; H-2nd; D-2nd; F-2nd	
7/25	Belle-Clair Speedway	Midget	Pizza Hut	Gene Gennetten	Q-2nd; H-5th; D-4th; F-5th	
7/31	Springfield Speedway	Midget	Pizza Hut	Arnie Knepper	Q-7th; H-2nd; F-10th	
8/1	Lake Hill Speedway	AARA Late Model	Schrader #67	Kenny Shrum	Q-4th; H-5th; D-2nd	
8/1	Lake Hill Speedway	SLARA Midget	Green #67	Danny Frye, Jr.	H-1st; F-2nd	
8/7	Tri-City Speedway	Midget	Dan Frye, Sr. #79	Jon Backlund	H-3rd; F-12th	
8/8	St. Charles Speedway	Midget	Dan Frye, Sr. #79	Jon Backlund	Q-5th; H-1st; F-5th	
8/15	Lake Hill Speedway	AARA Late Model	Schrader #100	Ken Schrader	Q-3rd; H-5th; D-3rd	
8/15	Lake Hill Speedway	SLARA Midget	Green #67		Q-1st; H-1st; F-1st	
8/15	Lake Hill Speedway	AARA Mini-Stock	Mike Edwards		H-5th; F-5th	
8/18	Indianapolis Raceway Park	USAC Midget	Green #67	Jan Opperman	Q-8th; H-5th; F-4th	
8/20	Belle-Clair Speedway	AARA Mini-Stock	Mike Edwards	Ken Schrader	F-1st	
8/21	Tri-City Speedway	GARA Late Model	Schrader #100	Jerry Sifford	Q-8th; H-1st; F-3rd	Loaded up after heat race because of steering
8/22	Lake Hill Speedway	AARA Late Model	Schrader #100	Kenny Shrum	H-2nd	
8/28	Tri-City Speedway	GARA Late Model	Schrader #100	C.C. Corbin	Q-12th; H-3rd; F-13th	
9/5	St. Charles Speedway	Midget	Dan Frye, Sr. #79	Chuck Taylor	S-11th; F-5th	Crashed in Semi
9/11	Tri-City Speedway	GARA Late Model	Jerry Beinke #32	Russ Wallace		Broke torque tube running 6th in feature
9/18	Tri-City Speedway	GARA Late Model	Beinke #32	Wib Spalding		Fell out of race due to overheating
9/18	Tri-City Speedway	Midget		Bob Bozelli	F-8th	
9/19	Charleston Speedway	Midget	Pizza Hut		Q-10th; H-1st	Feature paid by qualifying due to rain
9/24	Springfield Speedway	Late Model	Beinke #32	Jim Agans	Q-40th; H-8th; B F-6th	
9/26	I-55 Raceway	Late Model	Beinke #32			First night for new track; qualified, then rained out
10/2	Tri-City Speedway	GARA Late Model	Beinke #32	Ken Walton	Q-22nd; S-2nd; F-8th	WIL Gateway Classic
10/17-19	I-70 Speedway	Late Model	Paul Lawson #28	Tom Reffner		Drove relief in the 400-lapper and crashed
11/7	Winchester Speedway	Midget	Green #67	Rich Vogler		Crashed in qualifying

1977

Date	Track	Type	Car Owner	Race Winner	Finish	Comments
3/12	Indianapolis Fairgrounds	USAC Midget	Larry Mullendorf	Sleepy Tripp	Q-38th; C-5th	
4/17	Indianapolis Raceway Park	USAC Midget	Green #100	Gary Bettenhausen	Q-8th (23.80 sec.)	Pulled in both heat and feature; car not handling.
4/23	Tri-City Speedway	Late Model	Schrader #100	Tom Helfrich	H-6th; F-28th	Broke tie rod bolt running 7th; first night new car
4/30	Tri-City Speedway	Late Model	Schrader #100	Ken Schrader	H-4th; F-1st	
5/7	Tri-City Speedway	Late Model	Schrader #100	Wib Spalding	D-2nd; H-2nd; F-15th	
5/15	Lake Hill Speedway	SLARA Midget	Green #67	Ken Schrader	H-1st; F-1st	
5/21	Tri-City Speedway	Late Model	Schrader #100	Jerry Sifford	D-2nd; H-2nd; F-6th	Crashed bad
5/28	Indianapolis Raceway Park	USAC Midget	Green #67	Mel Kenyon	Q-8th (23.86 sec.)	
6/4	Lake Hill Speedway	Late Model	Schrader #100	Kenny Shrum	H-4th; F-7th	Broke rear end in feature
6/5	Lake Hill Speedway	SLARA Midget	Green #67	Ken Schrader	H-2nd; F-1st	Night before the 500 race; broke motor in heat
6/11	Capital Speedway	Late Model	Schrader #100	Shorty Aker	H-4th; F-23rd	
	Tri-City Speedway	Late Model	Schrader #100	Wes Stafford	H-2nd; F-6th	
	Lake Hill Speedway	Late Model	Bill Darnell #14	Bill Holliday	H-1st; F-7th	
	Lake Hill Speedway	Modified	Virgil Range	Don Klein	H-10th; F-6th	Broke ring-and-pinion
6/25	Capital Speedway	Late Model	Schrader #100	Eddie Gray	H-2nd; F-7th	
6/26	Lake Hill Speedway	Modified	Virgil Range	Don Klein	H-3rd; F-3rd	
7/1	Capital Speedway	Late Model	Schrader #100	Ed Kniebel, Jr.	H-1st; F-5th	
7/2	Tri-City Speedway	Late Model	Schrader #100	Kenny Schrum	H-1st; F-7th	Broke axle in heat race
7/9	Tri-City Speedway	Late Model	Schrader #100	Russ Wallace	H-1st; F-7th	
7/16	Tri-City Speedway	Late Model	Schrader #100	Bill Meyers	H-4th; F-4th	

Date	Track	Type	Car Owner	Race Winner	Finish	Comments
7/23	Tri-City Speedway	Late Model	Schrader #100	Kenny Schrum	D-3rd; H-2nd; F-3rd	Crashed on first lap of feature
7/24	Lake Hill Speedway	SLARA Midget	Green #67	Ken Schrader	H-1st; F-1st	
7/30	Tri-City Speedway	Late Model	Schrader #100	Kenny Schrum	D-4th; H-4th; F-18th	Dropped out of heat with broken u-joint
7/31	Belle-Clair Speedway	SLARA Midget	Art Range B-1	Danny Frye, Jr.	Q-9th	Ran both cars; ran out of gas running 6th
8/6	Tri-City Speedway	Late Model	Egans/Jumper	Joe Ross, Sr.	D-6th; H-3rd; F-12th	
8/13	Tri-City Speedway	Late Model	Schrader #100	C.C. Corbin	D-3rd; H-2nd; F-3rd	
8/13	Lake Hill Speedway	SLARA Midget	Range B-1	Gary Hoppe	F-4th	
8/14	Lake Hill Speedway	SLARA Midget	Green #67	Terry Wente	D-1st; H-1st	Dumped it running first
8/20	Tri-City Speedway	Late Model	Schrader #100	Bill Meyers	D-3rd; H-4th; F-18th	Radiator cap loosened up in feature
8/21	State Fair Speedway	Late Model	Schrader #100		Q-15th (26.73 sec.); H-6th	Pulled in semi because wasn't handling
8/26	State Fair Speedway	Late Model	Schrader #100	Jim Whistler	H-1st; F-5th	
8/27	Tri-City Speedway	Late Model	Schrader #100	Bill Meyers	H-4th; F-16th	Radiator clogged up with mud
9/3	Tri-City Speedway	Late Model	Schrader #100	Wib Spalding	H-5th; F-7th	Rain after heats; paid by points
9/8	Farmer City Raceway	SLARA Midget	Range B-1	Duke Derosa	Q-8th; H-5th; S-7th	
9/10	Tri-City Speedway	Late Model	Schrader #100	Wib Spalding	H-3rd; F-23rd	
9/17	Tri-City Speedway	Late Model	Schrader #100	Bill Holliday	D-4th; H-3rd; F-4th	Crashed on 4th lap of feature
9/17	Tri-City Speedway	SLARA Midget	Range B-1	Frye/ Backlund	1st F-2nd	
	Tri-City Speedway	Late Model	Schrader #100	Wib Spalding		
10/1	Ascot Park	USAC Midget	Dan Frye #1	Gary Patterson	Q-18th; H-2nd; F-5th	Missed the show

1978

Date	Track	Type	Car Owner	Race Winner	Finish	Comments
1/15	Allen Co. Expo Center	USAC Midget	Curly Rahn	Rich Vogler	Q-21st; H-1st; S-8th	
2/11	Indy Fairgrounds (indoor)	USAC Midget	Curly Rahn	Cannon/Steiner	Q-9th; H-5th; 1st F-5th; 2nd F-12th	Steve Cannon won 1st F, Tom Steiner 2nd F
2/12	Indy Fairgrounds (indoor)	USAC Midget	Curly Rahn	Rich Vogler	Q-23rd; H-1st	
4/30	Indianapolis Raceway Park	USAC Midget	Howard Linne #98	Johnny Parsons, Jr.	Q-29th; H-5th; S-11th	Spun running 2nd in heat
4/30	Lake Hill Speedway	SLARA Midget	Curly Rahn	Terry Wente	Q-2nd; D-4th; H-3rd	Wire broke on coil lining up for feature
5/10	Tri-City Speedway	Sprint	Dan Frye #51	Shane Carson	H-3rd; F-16th	First night driving a sprint car; pulled in from feature because it wasn't handling
5/14	Lake Hill Speedway	SLARA Midget	Curly Rahn	Jon Backlund	H-4th	Didn't run feature; car wasn't handling
5/19	St. Francois Raceway	Sprint	Frye #51	Hooker Hood	Q-11th; H-3rd; S-7th	
5/20		Sprint	Frye #51	Ron Milton	Q-9th	Car broke lower shaft in heat race
5/26		Sprint	Frye #51			Broke in hot laps; rear end
6/3	Riverside Speedway	Sprint	Frye #51	Terry Gray	F-6th	
6/4	Tri-State Speedway	Sprint	Frye #51		Q-8th (15.71 sec.)	Started 21st; hit wall in heat race
6/10	Tri-City Speedway	Sprint	Frye #51	Ken Schrader	D-2nd; H-2nd; F-1st	
6/11	Tri-State Speedway	Sprint	Frye #51	Cliff Cockrum	Q-15th; H-1st; F-5th	
6/14	Capital Speedway	Sprint	Cook & Marler #4	Chuck Amati	D-5th; H-1st; S-6th	Broke rear end in heat
6/17	Tri-City Speedway	Sprint	Cook & Marler #4	Ken Schrader	H-3rd; F-1st	First night for the new car
6/23		Sprint	Cook & Marler #4		Q-8th; H-3rd; F-6th	
6/24	Tri-City Speedway	Sprint	Cook & Marler #4	Ken Schrader	D-3rd; H-1st; F-1st	
6/25	Tri-State Speedway	Sprint	Cook & Marler #4	Dick Gaines	Q-4th; D-1st; H-4th; F-5th	
7/1	Riverside Speedway	Sprint	Cook & Marler #4	Sammy Swindell	Q-15th	
7/2	Springfield Speedway	Sprint	Cook & Marler #4	Chet Johnson	Q-8th; H-4th; F-4th	Pulled in heat; dropped valve in feature
7/4	Heartland Park	Sprint	Cook & Marler #4	Doug Wolfgang	D-6th; H-2nd; F-8th	Pulled in from dash; gas cap came off
7/7	State Fair Speedway	Sprint	Cook & Marler #4	Jimmy Sills	H-3rd; F-3rd	
7/12	Capital Speedway	Sprint	Cook & Marler #4	Bob Thoman	D-5th; H-2nd; F-10th	
7/14	State Fair Speedway	Sprint	Cook & Marler #4	Rick Ferkel	Q-15th; F-9th	Missouri Nationals

Date	Track	Type	Car Owner	Race Winner	Finish	Comments
7/15	State Fair Speedway	Sprint	Cook & Marler #4	Sammy Swindell	Q-5th; D-8th; F-13th	Missouri Nationals; ran out of fuel running 2nd with 4 laps to go
7/15	St. Charles Speedway	Sprint	Cook & Marler #4	Rick Ferkel	H-3rd; F-9th	
7/18	I-55 Raceway	Sprint	Cook & Marler #4	Gary Scott	D-4th; H-1st; F-3rd	Broke motor in feature
7/21	Richland Co. Fairgrounds	Sprint	Cook & Marler #4	Chuck Amati	Q-3rd; D-2nd; H-3rd; F-2nd	
7/22	Tri-City Speedway	Sprint	Cook & Marler #4	Dean Shirley	D-2nd; H-2nd; F-19th	
7/29	Belle-Clair Speedway	SLARA Midget	Cook & Marler #4	Dean Shirley	H-1st; F-2nd	
7/30	Knoxville Raceways	Sprint	Hoppe #67	Nick Gojmeric	Q-3rd; D-2nd; H-2nd; F-6th	Bent rear axle second lap of feature
8/5	Macon Speedway	Midget	Cook & Marler #4	Bobby Marshall	Q-14th; H-1st; F-20th	Dropped valve in heat
8/8	Knoxville Raceways	Sprint	Cook & Marler #4	Curly Rahn	Q-16th	Knoxville Nationals; crashed running 8th
8/10	Knoxville Raceways	Sprint	Cook & Marler #4	Stan Fox	Q-19th; H-3rd; F-14th	Knoxville Nationals
8/12	Knoxville Raceways	Sprint	Range B-1	Sammy Swindell	B F-8th	Broke right rear hub in feature
8/14	St. Francois Raceway	SLARA Midget	Cook & Marler #4	Bobby Allen	Q-16th; H-1st; F-17th	
8/18	I-55 Raceway	Sprint	Cook & Marler #4	Duke Derosa	Q-1st (14.37 sec.); D-3rd; H-4th; F-3rd	New track record
8/19	State Fair Speedway	Sprint	Cook & Marler #4	Dean Shirley	Q-2nd; D-3rd; F-18th	Flat right rear tire running 5th
8/20	State Fair Speedway	Sprint	Cook & Marler #4	Gene Gennetten	H-4th	Did run feature; broke oil pump in heat
8/26	Tri-City Speedway	Sprint	Cook & Marler #4	Sonny Smyser	D-1st; H-1st; F-2nd	Led first 23 laps; messed up with lapped car
9/1	I-55 Raceway	Sprint	Cook & Marler #4	Dean Shirley	Q-2nd; H-2nd; F-2nd	
9/2	I-70 Speedway	Midget	Gene Hamilton	Ron Milton	Q-18.51 sec.; D-1st	Feature rained out; Gene gave me $100 for new track record
9/4	Springfield Speedway	Sprint	Cook & Marler #4	Ron Milton	Q-2nd; D-4th; H-4th; F-3rd	Sucked intake gaskets in feature and slowed
9/10	Tri-City Speedway	Sprint	Cook & Marler #4	Ken Schrader	D-1st; H-1st; F-5th	$25 bonus for New Track Record
9/24	Springfield Speedway	Sprint	Cook & Marler #4	Bill Rice	Q-11.355 sec.; D-3rd; H-5th; F-1st	Flat tire in feature running 5th
9/30	Capital Speedway	Late Model	Ernie Jumper #33	Ramo Stott	H-2nd; F-18th	Crashed on last lap running 2nd
10/1	State Fair Speedway	Late Model	Jumper #33		H-1st; F-21st	
10/6		Late Model	Jumper #33		Q-32nd; H-9th	NDRA race; qualifying night for Truex 100
10/14	Riverside Speedway	SLARA Midget	Jack Schroeder #20	Tom Steiner	Q-3rd; H-1st; F-16th	Running 4th and busted steering arm off spindle
10/15	Riverside Speedway	SLARA Midget	Schroeder #20	Nick Gojmeric	Q-2nd; D-1st; H-1st; F-2nd	Running 4th on 53rd lap and flipped
11/23	Ascot Park	USAC Midget	Schroeder #20	Rick Goudy	Q-7th; F-17th	

1979

Date	Track	Type	Car Owner	Race Winner	Finish	Comments
1/7	Allen Co. Expo Center (indoor)	USAC Midget	Gene Hamilton #55	Steve Lotshaw	Q-15th; H-1st; F-5th	
1/14	Cincinnati Gardens (indoor)	USAC Midget	Hamilton #55	Bob Wente, Sr.	Q-21st; H-2nd; S-2nd; F-3rd	
1/28	Allen Co. Expo Center (indoor)	USAC Midget	Hamilton #55		Q-16th; H-5th; S-7th	
2/7	East Bay Raceway Park	Sprint	Dan Frye #8		Q-15th; H-5th; S-4th; F-10th	Broke motor in hot laps
2/8	East Bay Raceway Park	Sprint	Frye #8		Q-51st; H-6th	Loaded up after heat because car not working
2/9	East Bay Raceway Park	USAC Midget	Larry Curtis #4	Johnny Anderson	Q-21st; H-2nd; S-10th	
2/25	Cincinnati Gardens (indoor)	USAC Midget	John McDaniels #14	Gary Bettenhausen	Q-7th; H-2nd; F-6th	Qualified right!
3/8	Big H Speedway	WoO Sprint	McDaniels #14	Steve Kinser	A F-10th	
3/11	Big H Speedway	WoO Sprint	Schroeder #20	Steve Kinser	Q-13th; H-5th; S-2nd; F-5th	
3/24	Ascot Park	USAC Midget	Jumper #33	Danny McKnight	Q-19th; H-6th; F-18th	
4/7	State Fair Speedway	NSCA Late Model	Cook & Marler #4	Shane Carson	H-5th; S-4th; F-22nd	Blew up engine in the feature!
4/8	State Fair Speedway	NSCA Sprint	McDaniels #14	Johnny Anderson	H-1st; D-2nd; F-1st	In-and-out box messed up and didn't even start!
4/14	Champaign Motor Speedway	WoO Sprint	McDaniels #14	Ken Schrader	Q-4th; H-1st; F-2nd	Qualified right!
4/21	Tri-City Speedway	Sprint	Jumper #33	Chuck Amati		Poked hole in oil tank in B and ran only 1 lap in A
4/28	Tri-City Speedway	Sprint	McDaniels #14	Bill Meyers		
4/28	Tri-City Speedway	Late Model	Jumper #33		H-3rd	

Date	Track	Division	Car	Driver	Results	Notes
4/29	Tri-State Speedway	Sprint	McDaniels #14	Chuck Amati	Q-6th, H-3rd, F-3rd	
5/5	Tri-City Speedway	Sprint	McDaniels #14	Ken Schrader	H-1st, D-1st, F-1st	
5/6	Tri-State Speedway	Sprint	McDaniels #14	Jim Hirsh	Q-1st, H-3rd, D-4th, F-4th	
5/12	Tri-City Speedway	Late Model	Jumper #33	Mike Wallace	H-2nd, F-11th	Ran out of gas running 3rd
5/13	Tri-State Speedway	WoO Sprint	McDaniels #14	Lee James	Q-1st, F-15th	Crashed in heat; radiator hose broke running 8th
5/20	Tri-City Speedway	Late Model	Jumper #33	Tom Helfrich	H-4th, F-5th	
5/23	Tri-State Speedway	WoO Sprint	McDaniels #14	Steve Kinser	H-3rd, F-5th	
5/26	Indianapolis Raceway Park	USAC Midget	Hamilton #55	Mel Kenyon	Q-14th, F-12th	Broke belt on mag in feature
5/27	Tri-State Speedway	Sprint	McDaniels #14	Chuck Amati	Q-2nd, H-6th	Bent radius rod in feature
6/2	Illiana Speedway	USAC Midget	Hamilton #55 roadster	Bob McClain	Q-5th, H-3rd, F-11th	
6/3	Tri-State Speedway	Sprint	McDaniels #14	Larry Gates	Q-6th, H-4th, F-2nd	
6/13	Tri-City Speedway	Late Model		Larry Phillips	Q-17th, H-7th, F-4th	
6/17	Tri-State Speedway	USAC Midget	Hamilton #55 roadster	Johnny Parsons, Jr.	Q-22nd, H-2nd, F-12th	
6/17	Heartland Park	IMCA Midget	Schroeder #20	Ken Schrader	H-1st, D-1st, Pursuit-2nd, F-1st	Dropped out of feature; lower pulley broke
6/20	St. Charles Speedway	IMCA Midget	Art Range #9	Danny Frye, Jr.	H-5th, Pursuit-2nd, F-3rd	
6/22	Springfield Speedway	USAC Midget	Schroeder #20	Bubby Jones	Q-2nd, H-4th, F-20th	
6/30	DuQuoin Fairgrounds	USAC Midget	Hamilton #55	Sleepy Tripp	Q-1st, H-1st, F-2nd	
6/30	Tri-City Speedway	Late Model	Jumper #33	Kevin Gundaker	H-5th	
7/4	Tri-City Speedway	Late Model	Sandy Anderson #44	Larry Phillips	Q-11th, H-8th, F-13th	
7/7	Springfield Speedway	MARA Midget	Schroeder #20	Dean Shirley	Q-1st, H-1st, D-4th, F-13th	Broke left front radius rod
7/19	Capital Speedway	Late Model	Jumper #33	Tom Frazier	S-2nd, F-5th	Crashed in heat
7/21	Winchester Speedway	USAC Midget	Hamilton #55 roadster	Tripp/Parsons	Q-26th, S-1st, F-13th, F-14th	Sleep Tripp won 1st F; Johnny Parsons won 2nd F
7/29	Belle-Clair Speedway	SLARA Midget	Schroeder #20	Gary Hayes	Q-1st, H-1st, D-3rd, F-last	Lost radius rod bolt
8/3	I-55 Raceway	Sprint	Cook & Marler #4	Gary Scott	Q-2nd, H-1st, D-2nd, F-3rd	
8/4	Tri-City Speedway	Sprint	Cook & Marler #4	Larry Gates	H-2nd, D-1st, F-14th	Running 2nd; broke in-and-out
8/6	Springfield Speedway	Midget	Cook & Marler #4	Chet Johnson	Q-2nd, H-2nd, D-3rd, F-2nd	
8/8	Tri-City Speedway	Late Model	Hamilton #55	Johnny Parsons, Jr.	Q-1st, H-2nd, D-2nd, F-5th	Dropped out of semi
8/8	Tri-City Speedway	Sprint	Jumper #33		H-2nd, D-4th, F-2nd	
8/11	Tri-City Speedway	Late Model	Cook & Marler #4		H-1st, F-2nd	
8/11	Illinois State Fairgrounds	Sprint	Jumper #33	Ken Schrader	Q-3rd, H-1st, D-4th, F-1st	Pulled out of dash
8/17	I-55 Raceway	Late Model	Cook & Marler #4	Ken Schrader	Q-1st, H-2nd, F-1st	
8/18	Tri-City Speedway	Sprint	Cook & Marler #4	Ken Schrader	H-1st, D-1st, F-1st	
8/18	Tri-City Speedway	Late Model	Jumper #33	Joe Ross, Sr.		
8/19	Illinois State Fairgrounds	USAC Late Model	Sievekings	A.J. Foyt		
8/19	Springfield Speedway	Sprint	Cook & Marler #4	Ken Schrader	Q-1st, H-4th, D-4th, F-1st	Crashed in heat and feature
8/21	Belle-Clair Speedway	SLARA Midget	Schroeder #20		Q-7th, H-2nd, D-2nd, F-2nd	Ignition messed up in hot laps; didn't qualify
8/22	WoO Sprint	WoO Sprint	Cook & Marler #4	Sammy Swindell	H-7th; B F-1st; A F-12th	
8/24	Tri-State Speedway	USAC Midget	Hamilton #55	Barry Butterworth	Q-9th, H-3rd, F-9th	
8/25	DuQuoin Fairgrounds	USAC Late Model	Sieveking #68	Rusty Wallace	Q-3rd, F-21st	Feature rained out and paid by qualifying
8/25	Tri-City Speedway	Sprint	Cook & Marler #4	Sonny Smyser	H-2nd, D-1st, F-2nd	
8/29	Tri-City Speedway	IMCA Midget	Schroeder #20	Gary Hayes	H-6th, F-3rd	
8/31	I-55 Raceway	Sprint	Cook & Marler #4	Ron Milton	Q-4th, H-1st, D-3rd, F-2nd	
9/1	Tri-City Speedway	Sprint	Cook & Marler #4	Ken Schrader	H-1st, D-1st, F-1st	
9/1	Tri-City Speedway	Late Model	Jumper #33	Joe Ross, Sr.	H-3rd, D-4th, F-3rd	
9/2	Springfield Speedway	Sprint	Cook & Marler #4	Chet Johnson	Q-1st, H-2nd, D-1st, F-2nd	
9/3	Tri-City Speedway	Late Model	Jumper #33		Q-18th, H-2nd, F-13th	
9/6	Springfield Speedway	MARA Midget	Range #9		Q-5th, H-1st, F-2nd	
9/7	Tri-City Speedway	Sprint	Cook & Marler #4	Larry Gates	Q-2nd, H-3rd, D-4th, F-4th	Illinois Sprint Nationals
9/8	Tri-City Speedway	Sprint	Cook & Marler #4	Larry Gates	Q-5th, H-7th, D-1st, F-3rd Points-3rd	Illinois Sprint Nationals
9/9	Action Track	USAC Midget	Hamilton #55	Johnny Parsons, Jr.	Q-14th, F-23rd	Pulled in with mud in the right front;

Race records for 1979 (continued) and 1980.

Date	Track	Type	Car Owner	Race Winner	Finish	Comments
9/9	Springfield Speedway	Sprint	Cook & Marler #4	Larry Gates	Q-3rd; H-3rd; D-2nd; F-5th	Broke ring-and-pinion
9/14	I-55 Raceway	Sprint	Cook & Marler #4	Larry Gates	Q-5th; H-1st; D-2nd; F-12th	Road Runner 100 Twin 50s; dropped out of second feature with engine trouble
9/15	St. Francois Raceway	Sprint	Cook & Marler #4	Schrader/Thomas	H-3rd; D-2nd; F-1st	Twin 75s; black-flagged in 1st F for smoking; didn't start 2nd feature
9/16	Illiana Speedway	USAC Late Model	Ware/Ruttman		Q-15th	Crashed in heat
9/22	I-55 Raceway	Sprint	Cook & Marler #4	Ken Schrader	Q-2nd; D-4th; F-1st	
9/23	Springfield Speedway	Sprint	Cook & Marler #4	Danny Smith	Q-1st; H-7th; D-3rd; F-4th	Super Weekend
9/29	Springfield Speedway	Sprint	Cook & Marler #4	Danny Smith	Q-4th; H-3rd; F-6th	Dropped out of feature (motor)
9/30	New Bremen Speedway	USAC Midget	Hamilton #55	Tom Bigelow	Q-3rd; H-6th; F-?	Got crashed 1st lap then had right rear flat while leading!
10/6	I-55 Raceway	Sprint	Cook & Marler #4	Randy Standridge	Q-1st; H-1st; D-1st; F-10th	Dropped out of heat; blew two head gaskets in feature
10/13	I-55 Raceway	Sprint	Cook & Marler #4	Tom Corbin	Q-8th	Blew engine 25 laps into feature
10/14	Fairgrounds Speedway	USAC Late Model	Sieveking #75		Q-10th	Dropped out of feature; broke rear end
10/18	Tri-City Speedway	WoO Sprint	Cook & Marler #4	Doug Wolfgang	H-1st; D-4th	Stan Fox and I spun on last lap running 1st and 2nd
10/20	Winchester Speedway	USAC Midget	Hamilton #55 roadster	Steve Lotshaw	Q-1st; H-2nd; F-6th	Didn't make feature; 10th in Busch Bash
10/21	Eldora Speedway	WoO Sprint	Cook & Marler #4		Q-7th; H-6th; S-6th; B F-10th	Qualified for feature tomorrow
10/27	Ascot Park	USAC Midget	Hamilton #55	Tony Simon	Q-26th; H-1st; F-10th	
11/9	Big H Speedway	Midget	Dennis Devea #97	Wente/Backlund	H-2nd	Turkey Night Grand Prix
11/10	Big H Speedway	Midget	Devea #97	Stan Fox	A F-5th	Jimmy Caruthers Memorial; turned over in heat
11/22	Ascot Park	USAC Midget	Hamilton #55	Ron Shuman	Q-15th; F-4th	
11/23	Manzanita Speedway	Midget	Schroeder #20		Q-8th	

1980

Date	Track	Type	Car Owner	Race Winner	Finish	Comments
1/6	Allen Co. Expo Center (indoor)	USAC Midget	Hamilton #55	Terry Wente	Q-33rd	Missed show
1/25	Phoenix International Raceway	Midget	Hamilton #55	Stan Fox	Q-2nd	Copper Classic; broke driveline on 1st lap feature
1/25	Phoenix International Raceway	Late Model	Sieveking #68	Joe Ruttman	Q-23rd; F-11th	
2/6	East Bay Raceway Park	WoO Sprint	Cook & Marler #314	Sammy Swindell	Q-15th; H-6th; F-19th	Steve Stapp went on track during yellow flag and we were disqualified
2/7	East Bay Raceway Park	WoO Sprint	Cook & Marler #314	Doug Wolfgang	Q-53rd; C-1st	Missed show; ran consi
2/8	East Bay Raceway Park	WoO Sprint	Cook & Marler #314	Sammy Swindell	Q-18th; H-3rd; F-10th	
2/9	East Bay Raceway Park	WoO Sprint	Cook & Marler #314	Doug Wolfgang	Q-23rd (157 mph)	Crashed hot lapping for B Main
3/9	Texas World Speedway	USAC Late Model	Sieveking #68	Terry Ryan	Q-12th; H-3rd; F-7th	Running 8th and broke fuel pump
3/14	Devil's Bowl Speedway	WoO Sprint	Cook & Marler #314	Doug Wolfgang	Q-35th; H-3rd	Broke throttle linkage at 30 laps
3/15	Devil's Bowl Speedway	WoO Sprint	Cook & Marler #314	Doug Wolfgang	H-2nd; F-4th	Missed B-Main so went home
3/21	Devil's Bowl Speedway	WoO Sprint	Cook & Marler #314	Ron Shuman	Q-12th	First night for new Stanton car
4/4	State Fair Speedway	NSCA Sprint	Cook & Marler #314	Eddie Leavitt		Broke bird cage in heat; turned over 1st lap of feature
4/11	Tri-City Speedway	WoO Sprint	Cook & Marler #314	Steve Kinser		
4/12-13	Trenton Speedway	USAC Late Model	Sieveking #68	Joe Ruttman	F-11th	Broke tranny in qual; started 20th in F; running 4th at 200 miles and broke coil bracket!
4/18	I-55 Raceway	Sprint	Cook & Marler #314	Terry Gray	H-1st; D-3rd	Leading feature and crashed on 7th lap
4/20	Tri-State Speedway	Sprint	Bill Schmitt #1	Larry Goad	Q-1st; H-7th; F-2nd	Leading till last lap and played lapped car wrong
4/25	I-55 Raceway	Sprint	Cook & Marler #314	Rick Ungar	Q-5th; H-1st; D-1st; F-3rd	

Date	Track	Class	Car	Driver	Results	Notes
4/26	Tri-City Speedway	Late Model	Jumper #33	Mike Wallace	H-4th, F-4th	
4/27	Tri-State Speedway	Sprint	Cook & Marler #314	Dick Gaines	Q-3rd, H-4th, D-3rd, F-8th	Dumped in the feature; finish was rained out
5/2	I-55 Raceway	Sprint	Cook & Marler #314	Ken Schrader	Q-7th, H-1st, D-1st, F-1st	
5/3	Tri-City Speedway	Late Model	Jumper #33	Mike Wallace	H-2nd, D-2nd, F-4th	Blistered right front in feature
5/9	I-55 Raceway	Sprint	Cook & Marler #314	Tom Corbin	Q-2nd, H-3rd, D-3rd, F-2nd	Broke motor qualifying
5/10	St. Francois Raceway	Sprint	Cook & Marler #314	Ken Schrader	Q-2nd, H-1st, D-2nd, F-1st	
5/11	Springfield Speedway	Late Model	Jumper #33	Flea Atkins	Q-1st, H-1st, D-2nd	
5/17	Capital Speedway	USAC Midget	Hamilton #55	Mel Kenyon	H-1st, F-2nd	
5/24	Indianapolis Raceway Park	NSCA Sprint	Cook & Marler #4	John Stevenson	Q-2nd, H-2nd, F-9th	
5/25	Stair Fair Speedway	NSCA Sprint	Cook & Marler #4	John Stevenson	Q-5th, H-6th, F-2nd	
5/26	Capital Speedway	WoO Sprint	Cook & Marler #4	Sammy Swindell	B F-1st, A F-8th	
5/28	I-55 Raceway	Sprint	Cook & Marler #4	Ken Schrader	Q-1st, H-3rd, D-2nd, F-1st	
5/30	St. Francois Raceway	Sprint	Cook & Marler #4	Ricky Hood	Q-2nd, H-2nd	Rained out after heat
5/31	I-55 Raceway	Sprint	Cook & Marler #4	Ken Schrader	H-3rd	Didn't run after heat because of junk in fuel
6/6	Tri-State Raceway	Late Model	Sieveking #68	Baker	Q-1st, D-3rd, F-1st	First night for car (Bopp Chassis)
6/8	I-55 Raceway	Sprint	Cook & Marler #4	Kevin Gundaker	H-1st, D-3rd, F-2nd	Bent valve in heat
6/13	Tri-City Speedway	Late Model	Sieveking #68	Chuck Amati	H-1st, D-6th, F-4th	
6/14	Illinois State Fairgrounds	USAC Late Model	#14/#2	Ramo Stott	Q-10th, F-23rd	
6/15	Kokomo Speedway	Sprint	Sieveking #68	Ricky Hood	Q-15th, H-1st, F-6th	
6/18	Tri-City Speedway	Sprint	Sieveking #68	Rodney Combs	Q-4th (23.87 sec.)	Started last in feature in Steffens #2
6/20	Tri-City Speedway	NDRA Late Model	Jerry Steffens #2	Ron Milton	S-7th	Dropped out hot!
6/21	Tri-City Speedway	NDRA Late Model	Cook & Marler #4	Ron Milton	H-1st	
6/27	I-55 Raceway	Sprint	Cook & Marler #4	Fred Horn	Q-1st (25.00 sec.)	Qual. night; broke water pump with 2 laps to go in heat; tied with Helfrich for 3rd fastest time
6/28	St. Francois Raceway	Late Model	Sieveking #68	Ken Schrader	Q-9th, F-22nd	
7/2	Southern Iowa Speedway	USAC Midget	Hamilton #55 roadster	Ken Schrader	Q-2nd, H-4th, F-1st	
7/4	Illiana Motor Speedway	Sprint	McDaniels #14	Dave Ray	H-1st, D-3rd, F-1st	
7/5	Tri-City Speedway	Midget	Hamilton #55	Tim Green	H-4th, F-16th	Hooked bumpers on lap 25 so pulled in
7/5	Tri-City Speedway	WoO Sprint	McDaniels #14	Ken Schrader	H-1st, D-4th, F-4th	
7/9	Tri-City Speedway	Sprint	Sieveking #68	Rusty Wallace	H-3rd, D-1st, F-1st	
7/11	I-55 Raceway	USAC Late Model	Hamilton #55	Schrader/Kenyon	Q-22nd, H-6th, F-12th	Running 2nd w/4 laps to go and got knocked out
7/13	Winchester Speedway	USAC Midget	Sieveking #68	Kevin Gundaker	Q-8th, 1st F-1st, 2nd F-8th	Oil pressure problems so didn't run feature
7/19	Tri-City Speedway	Late Model	McDaniels #14	Ken Schrader	H-6th, F-3rd	Didn't run heat; oil pressure problems in dash
7/19	Tri-City Speedway	Late Model	Hamilton #55	Ken Schrader	H-1st, D-6th, F-1st	
7/19	Winchester Speedway	USAC Midget	McDaniels #14	Ken Schrader	H-1st, F-1st	
7/20	Interstate 57 Raceway	USAC Midget	McDaniels #14	Ken Schrader	Q-1st, H-3rd, F-1st	First USAC win!
7/23	Tri-State Speedway	Sprint	Hamilton #55	Sleepy Tripp	Q-3rd, D-1st, D-1st, F-1st	
7/28	Colorado National Speedway	USAC Midget	Hamilton #55	Mike Gregg	Q-16th, H-5th, S-8th	
7/30	Colorado National Speedway	USAC Midget	Sieveking #68	Rusty Wallace	Q-31st, H-2nd, F-7th	
8/1	Milwaukee Mile	USAC Midget	Sieveking #68	Kevin Gundaker	Q-21st, F-10th	
8/3	Southern Iowa Speedway	USAC Late Model	Sieveking #68	Tom Hearst	Q-9th, H-3rd, F-4th	
8/6	Tri-City Speedway	USAC Late Model	Sieveking #68	Ken Schrader	B F-1st, A F-5th	
8/7	Tri-State Speedway	NSCA Late Model	Sieveking 368	Ricky Hood	H-3rd, D-6th, F-5th	
8/8	Interstate 57 Raceway	NSCA Late Model	McDaniels #14	Rick Ungar	Q-2nd, H-1st, D-4th, F-2nd	
8/9	Illinois State Fairgrounds	Late Model	McDaniels #14	Terry Ryan	Q-4th, H-1st, F-2nd	
8/10	Tri-City Speedway	Sprint	Sieveking #68	Ken Schrader	F-3rd	Qualifying night; broke trans going out to qualify
8/15	Tri-City Speedway	WoO Sprint	McDaniels #14	Ken Schrader	Q-6th, H-4th, F-1st	Drew 16th starting spot
8/23	DuQuoin Fairgrounds	USAC Late Model	Sieveking #68	Sal Tovella	Q-5th (38.00 sec.); F-5th	No wings

Date	Track	Type	Car Owner	Race Winner	Finish	Comments
8/23	Tri-City Speedway	WoO Sprint	McDaniels #14	Doug Wolfgang	Q-20th; F-16th	Winged show; broke quick-change gears in heat; broke ring-and-pinion in feature
8/24	Tri-State Speedway	Sprint	McDaniels #14	Ricky Hood	Q-2nd; H-5th; D-3rd; F-3rd	Knocked out by Jim O'Conner on first lap
8/27	Charleston Speedway	Late Model	Jumper #33	Dick Taylor	Q-10th (17.05 sec.)	Should have run 2nd but coil shorted out
8/29	Santa Fe Speedway	USAC Midget	Matt Schneider #67	Mel Kenyon	Q-12th; H-4th; F-7th	Broke rear axle in heat & didn't get to run feature
8/30	Indianapolis Raceway Park	USAC Late Model	Sieveking #68	Joe Ruttman	Q-4th (24.43 sec.); F-4th	Super Weekend
8/31	Indianapolis Raceway Park	USAC Midget	Hamilton #55	Mel Kenyon	Q-2nd (23.52 sec.)	Super Weekend
9/7	Milwaukee Mile	USAC Late Model	Sieveking #68	Joe Ruttman	Q-17th (33.68 sec.); F-6th	Wrecked on 86th lap of 100, running 5th
9/12	I-55 Raceway	Sprint	McMillan #25	Tom Corbin		Blew head gasket in heat race
9/14	Action Track	USAC Midget	Hamilton #55	Rich Vogler	Q-19th (24.41 sec.)	Blew engine in feature
9/14	Godfrey Speedway	IMCA Midget	Nick Gojmeric	Danny Frye, Jr.	H-1st; F-2nd	Ran 2nd so Dan could win point championship; we split $
9/19	Capital Speedway	WoO Sprint	McDaniels #14	Steve Kinser	Q-20th; H-4th; B F-1st; A F-8th	
9/20	Tri-City Speedway	Sprint	McDaniels #14	Danny Smith	H-2nd; F-2nd	Ran out of fuel in 1st F; blew engine in 2nd F
9/21	Illinois State Fairgrounds	WoO Sprint	Dallas Driscoll #30	Smith/ Kinser	Q-15th; 1st F-15th; 2nd F-24th	Pulled in; was scaring me so I quit car
9/26	I-55 Raceway	Sprint	McMillan #25	Bobby Davis, Jr.		
9/27	Springfield Speedway	Sprint	McDaniels #14	Frank Hollingsworth	Q-17TH; H-3rd; F-4th	
9/27	Tri-City Speedway	Late Model	Sieveking #68	Larry Phillips	Q-2nd; F-8th	
10/1	Devil's Bowl Speedway	SWIMS Midget	Smiley's #51	Ken Schrader	H-1st; D-1st; F-1st	
10/2	Big H Speedway	SWIMS Midget	Smiley's #51	Johnny Parsons, Jr.	H-1st; F-2nd	
10/3	Big H Speedway	SWIMS Midget	Smiley's #51		H-1st	
10/4	Tri-City Speedway	SWIMS Midget	McDaniels #14	Ken Schrader	F-1st	
10/5	Capital Speedway	WoO Sprint	Sieveking #68	Steve Kinser	H-1st; F-18th	Crashed running 4th
10/10	Capital Speedway	Late Model	Sieveking #68		Q-7th; H-1st	Qualifying night
10/11	Capital Speedway	Late Model	Sieveking #68	Jackson/Nifniger	1st F-5th; 2nd F-4th	
10/12	Illinois State Fairgrounds	USAC Late Model	Jerry Stefner #2	Joe Ruttman	Q-12th; F-14th	
10/18-19	Eldora Speedway	WoO Sprint	Sieveking #68	Steve Kinser	Q-18.015 sec.	Missed show
10/25	Volunteer Speedway	NDRA Late Model	Sieveking #68	Freddy Smith	Q-9th (19.70 sec.); F-16th	Running 6th and put hole in radiator
10/26	Action Track	NDRA Late Model	Sieveking #68	Freddy Smith	Q-6th (15.70 sec.)	Running 3rd and broke flywheel on lap 75
11/3		USAC Silver Crown	Delrose & Holt #14	Gary Bettenhausen	Q-1st (23.31 sec.); F-3rd	Started out in Diz Wilson's car and crashed in hot laps; first Silver Crown race!
11/8-9	Winchester Speedway	AMRA Midget	Hamilton #55	Mack McClellan	Q-3rd (17.34 sec.)	Sammy Sessions Memorial; running 3rd and dropped out (engine)
11/22-23	Phoenix International Raceway	Midget	Hamilton #55	Steve Lotshaw	Q-12th; F-27th	Car missing in qual; broke 4th lap running 4th
11/22-23	Ascot Park	USAC Midget	Hamilton #55	Ron Shuman	Q-19th (21.69 sec.); F-8th	
12/6	Pontiac Silverdome	Midget	Smiley's #51	Gene Gennetten	H-7th; C F-1st; B F-11th	Flipped in heat

1981

Date	Track	Type	Car Owner	Race Winner	Finish	Comments
1/4	Allen Co. Expo Center (indoor)	USAC Midget	Nick Gojmeric #58	Steve Cannon	Q-6th; H-1st; F-5th	
1/25	Allen Co. Expo Center (indoor)	USAC Midget	Gojmeric #58	Bob Wente, Sr.	Q-3rd; H-3rd; F-5th	
1/29-2/1	Phoenix International Raceway	Midget	Hamilton #55 upright	Ken Schrader	Q-2nd; F-1st	
2/8	Daytona International Speedway	ARCA Stock Car	Sieveking #68	Tim Richmond	Q-33rd; F-8th	Blew spark plug on second lap
3/14	Ascot Park	USAC Midget	Hamilton #55	Danny McKnight	Q-18th; H-3rd; F-8th	
3/22	Phoenix International Raceway	Midget	Hamilton #55	Stan Fox	Q-9th (30.90 sec.)	
4/4	State Fair Speedway	NSCA Late Model	Sieveking #68	Tom Hearst	H-2nd; F-3rd	
4/5		Late Model	Sieveking #68	Joe Merryfield	F-10th	Winged late models; started 23rd; running 7th when got tied up with Billy Moyer

Date	Track	Class	Car	Driver	Results	Notes
4/10	Tri-City Speedway	WoO Sprint	McDaniels #14	Steve Kinser	Q-13th; H-1st; F-4th	Was qual. 2nd row and broke motor in heat
4/11	Tri-City Speedway	WoO Sprint	McDaniels #14	Steve Kinser	Q-5th; H-8th; F-2nd	
4/24	Springfield Speedway	WoO Sprint	McDaniels #14	Steve Kinser	Q-12th; H-6th; S-3rd; F-11th	Televised race
4/25	Eldora Speedway	USAC Sprint	Ben Bowen #25	Dave Pepperach	H-2nd; D-1st; F-1st	
4/25	Eldora Speedway	Sprint	McDaniels #14			Broke in hot laps
4/26	Capital Speedway	USAC Silver Crown	Bill Mataki #32	Steve Kinser	H-1st; D-2nd; F-3rd	
5/2	Capital Speedway	USAC Late Model	Sieveking #68	Kevin Gundaker	H-1st; D-1st; F-1st	
5/3	Tri-City Speedway	USAC Late Model	Sieveking #68	Ken Schrader	Q-10th; H-3rd; F-4th	
5/8	Anderson Speedway	USAC Midget	Henseling #54	Jeff Nuckles	Q-1st	Had quick time & disqualified for being too loud!
5/15	Santa Fe Speedway	Midget	Gojmeric #58	Mel Kenyon	H-1st; F-3rd	
5/16	Tri-City Speedway	Sprint	McDaniels #14	Jack Ziegler	H-2nd; F-12th	Ran out of fuel w/3 laps left; running about 6th
5/20	Tri-City Speedway	WoO Sprint	McDaniels #14	Doug Wolfgang		Ran into wall during hot laps
5/22	Indianapolis Fairgrounds	USAC Sprint	Bowen #25	Joe Saldana	Q-3rd; H-1st; D-2nd; F-18th	Night before the 500
5/23	Indianapolis Fairgrounds	USAC Midget	Hamilton #55	Mack McClellan	H-2nd; D-2nd; F-5th	Ran into wall running 2nd
5/26	Winchester Speedway	USAC Late Model	Sieveking #68	Scott Stovall	H-4th	Pulled out of feature
5/26	Winchester Speedway	USAC Midget	Henseling #54	Mel Kenyon	Q-2nd; D-3rd; F-1st	Pulled out of heat
5/29	Springfield Speedway	USAC Midget	Gojmeric #58	Ken Schrader	Q-1st (19.96 sec.); H-4th; F-1st	New track record!
5/30	Illiana Motor Speedway	MARA Midget	Hamilton #55	Ken Schrader	H-1st; D-1st; F-4th	
5/31	Belle-Clair Speedway	SLARA Midget	Gojmeric #58	Ken Schrader	Q-4th; H-2nd; F-5th	
6/5	Lakeside Speedway	USAC Silver Crown	Bowen #25	Smokey Snellbaker	Q-3rd; H-3rd; F-5th	
6/6	Knoxville Raceway	USAC Silver Crown	Blackie Fortune #39	Rich Vogler	Q-7th	
6/10	I-30 Speedway	NDRA Late Model	Sieveking #68	Larry Moore	Q-8th; H-2nd; F-5th	Left gas line loose and caught fire on parade lap of feature
6/11	Warren Speedway	Late Model	Sieveking #68	Don Hester	Q-1st; S-6th	Turned over in heat; drove Hatton midget in semi
6/13	Springfield Speedway	USAC Midget	Gojmeric #58	Rich Vogler	H-3rd; D-3rd; F-10th	First time out for car; dropped out last lap with engine trouble running 3rd
6/14	Illinois State Fairgrounds	USAC Late Model	Sieveking #68	Dean Roper	H-4th; F-5th	Didn't qual. due to right rear torsion arm stripped; started feature 20th
6/14	Godfrey Speedway	USAC Midget	Gojmeric #58	Rich Vogler	Q-1st; H-1st; D-4th; F-3rd	Was getting ready to pass Tripp and something happened to right rear of car
6/19	Macon Speedway	MARA Midget	Gojmeric #58	Sleepy Tripp	Q-2nd; H-1st; F-2nd	
6/20	St. Francois Raceway	Sprint	Ray Marler #38	Ron Milton	Q-2nd; D-2nd	Feature rained out
6/21	Springfield Speedway	Sprint	Marler #38		Q-5th (25.03 sec.)	Qual night; broke motor in heat race
6/26	Tri-City Speedway	NDRA Late Model	Sieveking #68	Pete Parker	S-10th	Pulled out running hot
6/27	Tri-City Speedway	NDRA Late Model	Sieveking #68	Amati/Standridge	Q-2nd; H-8th; D-4th	Mag trouble in make-up feature; hit infield tire in second feature
6/28	Springfield Speedway	Sprint	Marler #38	Doug Wolfgang	Q-12th; H-8th; S-15th; F-9th	Running 2nd dropped out with 7 laps to go
7/3	I-70 Speedway	Sprint	Marler #38	Eddie Leavitt	Q-12th; H-6th; F-7th	
7/5	Williams Grove Speedway	USAC Sprint	Fortune #39	Ken Schrader	Q-1st; H-1st; F-1st	
7/8	Kokomo Speedway	USAC Midget	Gojmeric #58	Lee Osborne	Q-9th; B F-1st; A F-6th	
7/12	St. Francois Raceway	Sprint	Marler #38	Ron Milton	Q-1st (11.60 sec.)	New track record; dropped out of heat; turned over in dash
7/13	Tri-City Speedway	Late Model	Sieveking #68	Kevin Gundaker	Q-6th; F-6th	
7/17	Belle-Clair Speedway	Hobby	Steve Carson #60	Rusty Wallace	Q-2nd; F-5th	
7/18-19	Milwaukee Mile	USAC Late Model	Sieveking #68	Ed Loomis	Q-13th (33.48 sec.); F-18th	
7/19	Angell Park Speedway	BADGER Midget	Wilke Bros. #9	Doug Wolfgang	Q-15th; H-4th; F-7th	
7/24	State Fair Speedway	WoO Sprint	Marler #38	Doug Wolfgang	Q-7th; H-1st; F-18th	Running 4th and steering broke
7/25	State Fair Speedway	WoO Sprint	Marler #38	Doug Wolfgang	H-3rd; F-4th	Broke ring-and-pinion running 2nd
7/26	Tri-City Speedway	WoO Sprint	Marler #38		Q-2nd; H-3rd; F-3rd	
7/26	Belle-Clair Speedway	SLARA Midget	Gojmeric #58		Q-1st (11.45 sec.); H-2nd; D-1st	New track record; feature rained out

Date	Track	Class	Car	Driver	Results	Notes
8/1	Lakeside Speedway		Hamilton #55		Q-8th; H-1st; F-13th	Blew up
8/4	Colorado National Speedway	USAC Midget	Hamilton #55	Dave Strickland, Jr.	Q-14th; H-2nd; F-15th	Broke cam
8/5	Colorado National Speedway	USAC Midget	Hamilton #55	Rich Vogler	Q-13th; H-5th; S-4th; F-5th	Car was illegal and officials told us to run 3rd if we wanted to be paid
8/7	Sycamore Speedway	WOOM Midget	Gojmeric #58	Dennis Devea	H-1st; D-1st; F-3rd	
8/8	St. Francois Raceway	Sprint	Marler #38	Mike Thurman	Q-1st (11.55 sec.); H-1st; D-4th	New track record; turned over in feature
8/10	I-70 Speedway	WoO Sprint	Marler #38	Steve Kinser	Q-7th; H-3rd; F-8th	
8/13	Knoxville Raceway	Sprint	Marler #38	Steve Kinser	Q-13th; H-3rd; F-14th	Qualifying night for non-wing at Nationals
8/14	Knoxville Raceway	Sprint	Marler #38	Gary Scott	Mystery F-7th	
8/15	Illinois State Fairgrounds	USAC Silver Crown	Fortune #39	George Snider	Q-3rd (33.07 sec.); F-16th	Broke engine running 4th at 47 laps
8/15	Knoxville Raceway	Sprint	Marler #38	Steve Kinser	B Dash-3rd; B F-2nd; A F-12th	Knoxville Nationals final
8/16	Illinois State Fairgrounds	USAC Late Model	Sieveking #68	Dean Roper	Q-2nd (35.37 sec.); F-16th	Overheated, water leak
8/16	Springfield Speedway	Sprint	Marler #38	Randy Standridge	Q-2nd; H-4th; D-1st; F-7th	Broke lower shaft while leading
8/18	Kokomo Speedway	WoO Sprint	Johnny Vance #1	Sammy Swindell	Q-17th; H-4th	Running 5th and broke inner tube
8/21	Springfield Speedway	Sprint	Marler #38	Ken Schrader	Q-9th; H-1st; F-1st	Leading feature w/6 laps to go and had flat right rear tire
8/22	Tri-City Speedway	WoO Sprint	Marler #38	Sammy Swindell	Q-6th; H-2nd; F-18th	Crashed running 4th
8/23	Tri-City Speedway	WoO Sprint	Marler #38	Steve Kinser	Q-5th; H-5th; F-15th	
8/29	DuQuoin Fairgrounds	USAC Late Model	Sieveking #68	Ron Milton	H-6th; F-16th	
8/29	St. Francois Raceway	Sprint	Marler #38	Rich Vogler	Q-5th; H-1st; D-1st; F-5th	Running 5th on 80th lap and had right rear go flat
8/30	DuQuoin Fairgrounds	USAC Silver Crown	Fortune #39	Sheldon Kinser	Q-15th; H-6th; F-11th	
9/4	Union County Speedway	USAC Sprint	Bowen #25	Vogler/Gennetten	Q-18th; H-1st; F-4th	New track record; 1st F broke oil cooler lining up
9/5	Union County Speedway	USAC Midget	Gojmeric #58	Cliff Cockrum	Q-1st (15.49 sec.); 2nd F-17th	Started B F last and was running 3rd on 4th lap when the motor went sour
9/6	Tri-State Speedway	Sprint	McDaniels #14			Rented motor from Don Kirn
9/7	Action Track	USAC Sprint	Marler #38	Sheldon Kinser	Q-1st; H-1st; F-4th	
9/9	Paragon Speedway	USAC Sprint	Bowen #25	Ricky Hood	Q-17.01 sec.; H-1st; F-7th	
9/10	Springfield Speedway	Late Model	#0	Roger Long	Q-17th; H-4th; F-12th	
9/11	South Bend Motor Speedway	NAMAR Midget	Bob Seffes #96	Brad Hullings	Q-1st; H-2nd; D-2nd; F-3rd	
9/12	Milwaukee Mile	USAC Late Model	Sieveking #68	Dick Trickle	Q-7th (33.16 sec.); F-5th	
9/13	Action Track	USAC Midget	Hamilton #55	Warren Mockler	Q-12th (25.62 sec.); F-29th	
9/16	Lincoln Park Speedway	USAC Sprint	Vance #1	Sheldon Kinser	Q-terrible; H-2nd; F-8th	
9/18	Devil's Bowl Speedway	Sprint	Marler #38	Goldner/Marshall	H-4th; Qual F-6th	Mark Miner got $400 off top-car repairs DuQuoin
9/19	Devil's Bowl Speedway	Sprint	Marler #38	Ronnie Daniels	A F-3rd	Hut Hundred race; hit wall, bicycled first
9/26	Iowa State Fair Speedway	USAC Late Model	Sieveking #68	Joe Wallace	Q-16th 1st F-2nd; 2nd F-7th	Went over hill qualifying
9/27	Springfield Speedway	Sprint	Marler #38	Ken Schrader	Q-6th; H-7th; F-1st	
10/2	I-70 Speedway	WoO Sprint	Marler #38	Kinser/Swindell	Q-7th (17.44 sec.); H-2nd	
10/3	I-70 Speedway	WoO Sprint	Marler #38	Sammy Swindell	H-1st	
10/10-11	Eldora Speedway	Late Model	Sieveking #68	Joe Wallace	Q-5th; H-1st; F-10th	Overall 5th
10/10-11	Eldora Speedway	Midget	Hamilton #55	Ken Schrader	Q-3rd; F-1st	Super Weekend event
10/10-11	Eldora Speedway	Sprint	Vance #1	Steve Kinser	Q-11th	
10/10-11	Eldora Speedway	Silver Crown	Fortune #39		Q-9th; H-5th; F-6th	
10/17-18	Ascot Park	USAC Midget	Jim Streicher #28	Steve Kinser	Q-18th; H-6th; B F-3rd; A F-11th	
10/24	Ascot Park	Pacific Coast Sprint	Bill Hardy #77	Stan Fox	Q-2nd; H-1st; D-4th; F-3rd	
10/29	Manzanita Speedway	Pacific Coast Sprint	Streicher #28	Tony Simon	Q-20.93 sec.	Broke motor leading with six laps left
10/31	USAC Sprint	USAC Sprint	Hardy #77	Stan Fox	Q-3rd; H-1st; D-1st F-2nd	Broke engine running 4th with 6 laps to go
10/31	Ascot Park	Pacific Coast Sprint	Hardy #77	Sammy Swindell	B F-9th	
11/1	Devil's Bowl Speedway	Sprint	Marler #38	Swindell bros.	Q-21st; H-5th; B F-4th; A F-20th	Crashed first lap of heat
11/6	Devil's Bowl Speedway	NCRA Sprint	Larry Hill #10		H-2nd; F-9th	Broke bird cage bolt 1st lap of A Feature
11/7	Devil's Bowl Speedway	CRA Sprint	Hardy #77			Broke motor in heat race
11/21	Ascot Park	CRA Sprint	Hardy #77	Dean Thompson	Q-27th (20.63 sec.)	Crashed running 5th and had flat right rear; CRA Peabody Classic; hit wall on 2nd lap

Date	Track	Type	Car Owner	Race Winner	Finish	Comments
						qualifying and was out for the night
11/28-29	Phoenix International Raceway	Midget	Hamilton #55	Ken Schrader	Q-3rd (30.40 sec.); F-1st	Race was red-flagged at 16 laps

1982

Date	Track	Type	Car Owner	Race Winner	Finish	Comments
1/3	Allen Co. Expo Center (indoor)	USAC Midget	Gojmeric #58	Dick Pole	Q-1st; H-5th; F-11th	Car kept jumping out of gear
1/17	Allen Co. Expo Center (indoor)	USAC Midget	Gojmeric #58	Allen Brown	Q-2nd; H-5th; D-3rd; F-11th	Hit tire and broke left front radius rod
1/29-31	Phoenix International Raceway	Midget	Hamilton #55	Ken Schrader	Q-1st (28.94 sec.); F-1st	Copper Classic
2/5	Tampa Fairgrounds	Sprint	Marler #38	J. Swindell/Wolfgang	H-3rd; Qual. F-8th	Car bent valve during feature
2/6	Tampa Fairgrounds	Sprint	Marler #38	Doug Wolfgang	F-10th	
2/7	Volusia County Speedway	Midget	Smiley's #51	Gary Koster	Q-1st (20.37 sec.); H-3rd; F-8th	New track record
2/8	Volusia County Speedway	Sprint	Marler #38	Doug Wolfgang	H-4th; B F-3rd; A F-22nd	Dropped out of feature
2/11	East Bay Raceway Park	WoO Sprint	Marler #38	Sammy Swindell	Q-52nd (16.50 sec.)	Missed show
2/12	East Bay Raceway Park	WoO Sprint	Marler #38	Bobby Marshall	Q-15.60 sec.; H-5th; B F-6th	
2/19	East Bay Raceway Park	WoO Sprint	Marler #38	Doug Wolfgang	Q-16.20 sec.; H-7th; B F-8th	
2/20	East Bay Raceway Park	All Star Late Model	Marler #38		Q-13th (17.75 sec.); H-1st	
	East Bay Raceway Park	All Star Late Model	Jim Paulk #8	Kevin Gundaker	1st F-14th; 2nd F-12th	1st F flat RR while running 6th; 2nd F dry sump belt came off while running 6th
3/6	Silverdome	NDRA Late Model	Paulk #8	Jack Boggs	Q-8th; H-2nd; All Star F-9th; F-11th	Running 3rd and lapped car crashed us with 8 to go; 3rd paid $5000
3/11	Devil's Bowl Speedway	Sprint	Marler #38	Sammy Swindell	Q-9th (17.48 sec.)	Crashed 1st lap; heim joint on left rear arm
3/12	Devil's Bowl Speedway	Sprint	Marler #38	Brad Doty	Q-14th (16.16 sec.); H-4th; F-4th	
3/13	Devil's Bowl Speedway	Sprint	Marler #38	Doug Wolfgang	A F-9th	
3/20	Devils' Bowl Speedway	WoO Sprint	Marler #38	Bobby Davis, Jr.	Q-45th; H-5th; C F-2nd; B F-7th	
3/21	State Fair Speedway	WoO Sprint	Marler #38	Sammy Swindell	Q-38th; H-5th; B F-7th	
4/17	Iowa State Fair Speedway	USAC Midget	Hamilton #55	Doug Wolfgang	Q-8TH; h-4TH; f-16TH	Wolfgang won in Nick (Gojmeric's) car; car wasn't running good so I pulled in
4/17	St. Francois Raceway	Sprint	Marler #38	Ken Schrader	Q-13.90 sec.; H-3rd; D-4th; F-1st	
4/18	Tri-State Speedway	All Star Sprint	Fortune #39	Ken Schrader	Q-11th; H-2nd; F-1st	
4/22	Eldora Speedway	USAC Sprint	Fortune #39	Jack Hewitt	Q-14th; H-1st; F-9th	
4/25	Eldora Speedway	USAC Silver Crown	Fortune #39	Danny Smith	Q-13th; H-3rd; F-17th	
4/30	Springfield Speedway	All Star Sprint	Marler #38	Todd Bishop	Q-15th; H-6th; B F-3rd; A F-?	Pulled in during A Feature
5/1	Illinois State Fairgrounds	USAC Silver Crown	Fortune #39	Ken Schrader	F-8th	
5/1	Illinois State Fairgrounds	WoO Sprint	Marler #38	Larry Dixon	Q-3rd (32.95 sec.); Match Race-2nd	
5/1	Springfield Speedway	USAC Midget	Gojmeric #58	Danny Smith	Q-1st; H-5th; S-1st; F-1st	
5/2	Illinois State Fairgrounds	USAC Silver Crown	Fortune #39	Ken Schrader	F-2nd	
5/2	Illinois State Fairgrounds	WoO Sprint	Marler #38	Ricky Hood	H-3rd; F-16th	
5/6	Indianapolis Speedrome	USAC Midget	Rollie Helming #54		H-1st; F-1st	
5/8	Indiana State Fairgrounds	USAC Silver Crown	Fortune #39		H-1st; F-3rd	
5/10	Action Track	USAC Sprint	Fortune #39	Chet Johnson	Q-about 15th; H-1st; F-15th	Hulman Classic; turned over on lap 27, leading
5/14	Paducah International Raceway	USAC Sprint	Fortune #39	Johnny Parson, Jr.	Q-4th; H-2nd; F-3rd	
5/15	Tri-City Speedway	Sprint	Marler #38	Scott Ritchart	H-4th; F-2nd	
5/19	Tri-City Speedway	Sprint	Marler #38	Lee Osborne	H-3rd	Didn't run feature—loaded up
5/19	Tri-City Speedway	Midget	Gojmeric #10	Ken Schrader	H-1st; F-1st	
5/20	Indianapolis Speedrome	USAC Midget	Helming #54		H-3rd; S-4th; B F-2nd	A Feature was rained out
5/22	Tri-City Speedway	Sprint	Fortune #39	Tim Green	H-2nd; F-2nd	
5/23	Tri-State Speedway	Sprint	Fortune #39	Ken Schrader	H-1st; D-4th; F-1st	
5/28	Indiana State Fairgrounds	USAC Sprint	Fortune #39	Ron Shuman	H-4th; F-16th	
5/30	Tri-State Speedway	All Star Sprint	Fortune #39	Steve Kinser	Q-15th; H-2nd; F-7th	Oil pan leak; pulled in 20th lap of 40 laps

Date	Track	Class	Car	Driver	Results	Notes
5/30	Tri-State Speedway	Late Model	Terry Messenger #T5	Kevin Claycomb	Q-10th; H-2nd; F-8th	
6/4	Tri-City Speedway	Sprint	Marler #38	John Stevenson		Blew up in heat race
6/4	Tri-City Speedway	Late Model	Messenger #T5	Bo Smith	H-5th; F-16th	Blew up in feature
6/10	Kokomo Speedway	USAC Midget	Gojmeric #10	Ken Schrader	Q-4th; H-1st; F-1st	
6/12	Tri-City Speedway	Sprint	Marler #38	Tom Corbin	H-4th; F-10th	
6/12	Tri-State Speedway	Late Model	Sieveking #68	Bo Smith	H-5th; F-2nd	
6/13	Tri-State Speedway	Sprint	Fortune #39	Chuck Amati	H-2nd; D-2nd; F-3rd	Ran out of fuel leading
6/16	Tri-City Speedway	Sprint	Fortune #39	Pat McKehan	H-2nd; F-8th	
6/16	Tri-City Speedway	Midget	Gojmeric #10	Ken Schrader	H-1st; F-1st	
6/17	Chandler Motor Speedway	Sprint	Fortune #39	Chuck Amati	Q-1st (16.007 sec.); H-1st; F-2nd	Broke running third
6/19	Tri-City Speedway	Late Model	Sieveking	Bo Smith	H-2nd	Missed show; last chance semi broke power steering hose
6/20	Action Track	USAC Sprint	Fortune #39	Sheldon Kinser	Q-29th (26.50 sec.)	
6/25	Interstate 57 Raceway	Sprint	Marler #38	Cliff Cockrum	Q-9th; H-3rd; F-2nd	
6/26	St. Francois Raceway	Sprint	Marler #38	Rick Pennell	H-1st; F-4th	
6/30	Paragon Speedway	All Star Late Model	Sieveking	Russ Petro	Q-10th (15.94 sec.)	Dropped out of heat race; bent tie rod in feature
7/4	Flemington Speedway	USAC Silver Crown	Fortune #39	Doug Wolfgang	Q-12th (21.12 sec.); F-5th	
7/5	Tri-City Speedway	All Star Sprint	Marler #38	Steve Kinser	Q-5th; H-3rd; F-5th	
7/7	Kokomo Speedway	USAC Midget	Gojmeric #10		Q-14th; H-2nd; F-14th	Crashed in feature
7/10	St. Francois Raceway	Sprint	Marler #38	Ron Milton	Q-2nd to last; H-1st; F-2nd	
7/11	Tri-State Speedway	Late Model	Sieveking	Ken Schrader	H-1st; D-3rd; F-1st	
7/15	Tri-State Speedway	Sprint	Fortune #39	Randy Kinser	H-1st; F-4th	Crashed in dash
7/15	Tri-City Speedway	Midget	Bill Darnell #14	Chucky Koster	H-1st; F-4th	
7/15	Tri-City Speedway	Sprint	Marler #38	Ken Schrader	H-1st; F-1st	
7/16	Macon Speedway	Late Model	Jumper #33	Pete Willoughby	Q-15th; H-last; B F-3rd; A F-19th	
7/17	Springfield Speedway	All Star Sprint	Marler #38	Ron Milton	Q-14th; H-4th; B F-1st; A F-7th	
7/18	Tri-City Speedway	Sprint	Marler #38	Ken Schrader	H-1st; F-1st	
7/18	Tri-City Speedway	Late Model	Sieveking #68	Tom Helfrich	H-1st; F-5th	
7/18	Tri-City Speedway	Midget	Gojmeric #10	Ken Schrader	H-2nd; F-1st	
7/18	Tri-City Speedway	Mini-Stock	Mike Edwards	Ken Schrader	H-1st; F-1st	
7/19	Tri-State Speedway	Sprint	Fortune #39	Rich Vogler	H-3rd; D-3rd; F-3rd	
7/21	Kokomo Speedway	USAC Sprint	Fortune #39	Rich Vogler	Q-3rd; H-1st; F-2nd	
7/23	State Fair Speedway	Sprint	Marler #38	Sammy Swindell	Q-15th; H-2nd; F-5th	
7/24	State Fair Speedway	Sprint	Marler #38	Sammy Swindell	Q-10th; H-3rd; F-9th	
7/25	Tri-City Speedway	Sprint	Marler #38	Ken Schrader	H-1st; D-1st; F-1st	
7/28	Tri-City Speedway	Sprint	Marler #38	Ken Schrader	H-1st; 1st F-5th; 2nd F-1st	Started last in first feature
7/28	Tri-City Speedway	Late Model	Sieveking #68	Tom Corbin		Broke in hot laps
7/30	Santa Fe Speedway	USAC Sprint	Fortune #39	Chuck Gurney	Q-1st (17.505 sec.); h-2nd; f-18TH	Power steering broke running third
7/31	Beaver Dam Raceway	USAC Midget	Gojmeric #10	Ken Schrader	Q-4th; H-1st; F-1st	
7/31	Beaver Dam Raceway	USAC Sprint	Fortune #39	Ken Schrader	Q-10th; H-1st; F-1st	
8/1	I-90 Speedway	USAC Midget	Gojmeric #10	Ken Schrader	Q-8th; H-1st; F-1st	
8/7	Raceland Park	USAC Midget	Gojmeric #10	Mike Gregg	Q-11th; H-2nd; F-3rd	
8/8	Raceland Park	USAC Midget	Gojmeric #10	Stan Fox	Q-15th; H-2nd; F-5th	
8/9	I-70 Speedway	WoO Sprint	Marler #38	Sammy Swindell	Q-25th; H-2nd; F-13th	
8/13	Springfield Speedway	USAC Midget	Gojmeric #10	Rich Vogler	Q-9th; H-3rd; F-2nd	
8/14	Illinois State Fairgrounds	USAC Silver Crown	Fortune #39	Tony Olivero	Q-17th (33.40 sec.); F-8th	
8/15	Illinois State Fairgrounds	USAC Late Model	Darrell Simion #22	Bay Darnell	Q-9th (36.88 sec.); F-19th	
8/18	Macon Speedway	Late Model	Bob Bennett #1	Dick Taylor	H-5th; D-1st; F-7th	Dropped out with overheating
8/21	Raceland Park	USAC Silver Crown	Fortune #39	Doug Wolfgang	Q-3rd (23.11 sec.); F-3rd	
8/22	State Fair Speedway	NSCA Late Model	Sieveking #68	Joe Wallace	Q-2nd (38.04 sec.);	Filled bell-housing full of dirt qualifying and stopped engine

Date	Track	Type	Car Owner	Race Winner	Finish	Comments
8/22	St. Francois Raceway	Sprint	Marler #38	Ron Milton	Q-2nd; H-2nd; D-2nd; F-2nd	
8/29	Belle-Clair Speedway	USAC Midget	Gojmeric #10	Rich Vogler	Q-19th; H-3rd; F-6th	
9/3	Godfrey Speedway	USAC Midget	Gojmeric #10	Rich Vogler	Q-7th; H-5th; B F-1st; A F-5th	
9/4	St. Francois Raceway	Sprint	Marler #38	Ron Milton	Q-5th; H-1st; F-11th	
9/5	Action Track	USAC Sprint	Fortune #39	Larry Rice	Q-10th; H-2nd; F-2nd	
9/5	Tri-State Speedway	Midget	Darnell #14	Ron Mullen	H-5th; F-4th	Did not make A Feature
9/5	Tri-State Speedway	Late Model	Sieveking #68	Tom Helfrich	Q-terrible; H-5th; B F-3rd	Had flat right rear tire; then car wouldn't restart after red flag
9/6	DuQuoin Fairgrounds	USAC Silver Crown	Fortune #39	Gary Bettenhausen	Q-13th (33.28 sec.); F-12th	Had flat right rear tire
9/11	Indiana State Fairgrounds	USAC Silver Crown	Fortune #39	Chuck Gurney	Q-17th (35.20 sec.); F-9th	
9/11	Bloomington Speedway	USAC Sprint	Fortune #39	Rich Vogler	Q-13th; H-1st; F-2nd	
9/12	Action Track	USAC Midget	Hamilton #55	Ron Shuman	Q-10th; (24.23 sec.); F-25th	Shuman won in Nick's car; dropped out of feature
9/19	Capital Speedway	Late Model		Greg Robinson	H-2nd; F-2nd	Lost by six inches!
9/25	I-70 Speedway	Midget	Hamilton #55	Gene Gennetten	H-1st; F-4th	
9/25	I-70 Speedway	Late Model	Sieveking #68	Don Hoffman	H-2nd; F-24th	
9/25	I-70 Speedway	Sprint	Dean Adams #3	Randy Smith	H-4th; F-3rd	
9/28	State Fair Speedway	SWIMS Midget	Hamilton #55	Ron Roberts	H-7th; B F-6th	
10/2-3	Eldora Speedway	USAC Midget	Hamilton #55	Rich Vogler	Q-3rd (18.76 sec.); F-2nd	
10/2-3	Eldora Speedway	USAC Sprint	Fortune #39	Steve Kinser	Q-18th (20.03 sec.); F-18th	
10/2-3	Eldora Speedway	USAC Silver Crown	Fortune ##9	Ron Shuman	Q-8th (19.40 sec.); H-3rd; F-3rd	
10/6	Cowtown Speedway	Midget	Smiley's #51	Ken Schrader	H-1st; D-1st; F-1st	
10/8	Buffalo Park Speedway	Midget	Smiley's #51	Gene Gennetten	Q-1st; D-1st; F-2nd	
10/9		Midget	Smiley's #51	Johnny Parsons, Jr.	B F-1st	
10/10	Heart O' Texas Speedway	Midget	Smiley's #51	Johnny Parsons, Jr.	H-1st; F-13th	
10/16	311 Speedway	USAC Sprint	Fortune #39	Schrader/S. Kinser	Q-10th; H-1st; 1st F-1st; 2nd F-5th	Broke fuel pump in heat race; broke rear end in A
10/17	311 Speedway	USAC Sprint	Fortune #39	Sheldon Kinser	Q-1st (18.50 sec.); H-2nd; F-2nd	Made up a lap
10/21	Manzanita Speedway	Sprint	Fortune 339	Ron Shuman	Q-11th	
10/25	Ascot Park	USAC Midget	Howard Linne #97	Ron Shuman	Q-36th; B F-4th; A F-21st	Flipped in heat race; broke collarbone; winnings include Hard Luck Award; Western World race; Broke axle in Hamilton #55 hot-lapping; motor quit in #97 in feature
12/4	Nazareth Speedway	USAC Silver Crown	Fortune #39/Leyba #6	Keith Kauffman	F-4th	Drew starting position #1; broke oil pump in hot laps; drove #6 and started 30th

1983

Date	Track	Type	Car Owner	Race Winner	Finish	Comments
1/16	Allen Co. Expo Center (indoor)	USAC Midget	Nick Gojmeric	Mike Fedorchek	Q-9th; F-5th	
1/28-30	Phoenix International Raceway	Midget	Linne #98		Q-2nd; F-3rd	Hamilton #55 was snowbound in Texas; Copper Classic
2/5	East Bay Raceway Park	Late Model	Sieveking #68	Gene Genetten	Q-32nd; H-4th	Dropped out running 8th
2/5	East Bay Raceway Park	Late Model	McVay #29	Dunn/Simmons		Crashed B Feature; Jim Dunn and Buck Simmons won features
2/7	East Bay Raceway Park	Late Model	Sieveking #68			
2/9	East Bay Raceway Park	Sprint	Fortune #39	Doug Wolfgang	Q-16th; H-4th; F-10th	
2/11	East Bay Raceway Park	Sprint	Fortune #39	Danny Smith	H-3rd; B F-6th; A F-6th	
2/25-26	Silverdome (indoor)	Midget	Gojmeric #10	Tom Cochran	Q-22nd	
3/5	Illinois State Fairgrounds (indoor)	USAC Midget	Gojmeric #10	Jerry Nuckles	H-2nd; F-3rd	
3/10	Devil's Bowl Speedway	Sprint	Bob Hampshire #63	Jac Haudenschild	H-8th; B F-4th	
3/11	Devil's Bowl Speedway	Sprint	Hampshire #63	Steve Kinser	A F-6th	
3/12	Devil's Bowl Speedway	Sprint	Hampshire #63	Brad Doty		

Date	Track	Class	Car	Driver	Results	Notes
3/17	I-30 Speedway	Sprint	Hampshire #63	Steve Kinser	H-3rd; F-18th	Crashed in feature; broke shoulder
3/26	Nazareth Speedway	USAC Silver Crown	Fortune #39	Gary Bettenhausen	Q-14th (32.60 sec.); F-6th	
4/15	Paragon Speedway	USAC Sprint	Fortune #39	Ken Schrader	Q-3rd; F-3rd; F-1st	Dropped out of feature
4/22	Tri-City Speedway	Midget	Darnell #14	Mike Wallace	H-2nd; F-15th	
4/22	Tri-City Speedway	Late Model	Jumper #33	Arnie Knepper	H-4th; F-3rd	
4/23	Paragon Speedway	All Star Sprint	Fortune #39	Dave Blaney	Q-11th; H-4th; B F-2nd; A F-6th	
4/30	Mottville Speedway	WOOM Midget	Bob Tezak #2	Steve Lotshaw	Q-2nd; H-5th; D-4th; F-15th	Feature broke rear end
5/6	Tri-City Speedway	Midget	Darnell #14	Bob Willig, Jr.	F-4th	Spun in heat race
5/6	Tri-City Speedway	Late Model	Sieveking #68	Ed Dixon	H-1st; F-3rd	
5/8	Action Track	USAC Silver Crown	Fortune #39	Jack Hewitt	Q-2nd; H-1st; F-2nd	Hulman Classic
5/10	Tri-City Speedway	Sprint	McMillan #38	Ken Schrader	H-4th; F-1st	
5/19	Tri-City Speedway	NASCAR Late Model	Sieveking #00	Ken Schrader	Q-1st (23.90 sec.); H-1st; F-1st	Busch Tour
5/20	Santa Fe Speedway	USAC Sprint	Fortune #39	Steve Kinser	Q-1st (17.94 sec.); H-1st; F-3rd	
5/21	Indiana State Fairgrounds	USAC Sprint	Fortune #39	Ken Schrader	H-1st; F-1st	
5/25	Lincoln Park Speedway	USAC Sprint	Fortune #39	Kelly Kinser	Q-8th; H-1st; F-4th	
5/26	Macon Speedway	Late Model	Sieveking	Roger Long	Q-12th; H-3rd; F-9th	Was running 4th and points closed up
5/27	Indiana State Fairgrounds	USAC Silver Crown	Fortune #39	Chuck Gurney	H-5th; F-4th	
5/28	Indianapolis Raceway Park	USAC Midget	Hamilton #55	Ken Schrader	H-1st; F-1st	Night before the 500 race
5/29	Tri-State Speedway	Sprint	Fortune #39	Ken Schrader	Q-5th; H-2nd; F-1st	
5/29	Tri-State Speedway	Late Model	Sieveking #00	Ken Schrader	Q-5th; H-1st; F-1st	
5/30	Springfield Speedway	All Star Sprint	Fortune #39	Randy Kinser	Q-7th; H-4th; F-4th	
6/4	Eldora Speedway	USAC Sprint	Fortune #39	Rich Vogler	Q-2nd; H-3rd; F-5th	
6/4	Eldora Speedway	USAC Sprint	Hamilton #55	Ken Schrader	Q-2nd; H-1st; F-1st	
6/5	Illinois State Fairgrounds	Midget	Hamilton #55	Mel Kenyon	H-1st; F-2nd	
6/8	Charleston Speedway	MARA Midget	Sieveking #00	Bob Pierce	Q-4th; D-6th; F-18th	Busch Tour; dropped out of feature with oil pan
6/10	Hales Corner Speedway	NASCAR Late Model	Gojmeric #10	Kevin Olsen	Q-10th; H-2nd; F-5th	
6/11	Paragon Speedway	USAC Midget	Fortune #39	Danny Smith	Q-15th; H-3rd; F-17th	Dropped out due to overheating
6/12	Tri-State Speedway	All Star Sprint	Sieveking #00	Ken Schrader	Q-4th; H-5th; F-1st	Spence and Greg got $500 each off top
6/15	Macon Speedway	Late Model	Sieveking #00	Roger Long	Q-10th; H-6th; F-3rd	
6/17	Tri-City Speedway	Late Model	Gojmeric #1	Steve Knepper	H-1st; F-20th	
6/18	Tri-City Speedway	Midget	Gojmeric #1	Ken Schrader	Q-6th; H-2nd; F-1st	Dropped out leading last lap
6/19	Action Track	NAMAR Midget	Fortune #39	Ken Schrader	Q-12th; H-2nd; F-2nd	
6/24	Albany-Saratoga Speedway	USAC Sprint	Gojmeric #1	Rich Vogler	H-3rd; F-3rd	
6/25	Fulton Speedway	USAC Midget	Gojmeric #1	Gene Gennetten	H-1st; F-3rd	
6/29		USAC Midget	Gojmeric #1	Nic Fornoro	H-2nd; F-14th	Dropped out running 2nd, with rocker arm
6/30	Macon Speedway	Late Model	Sieveking #00	Sheldon Kinser	Q-5th; H-4th; F-8th	
7/1	Flemington Speedway	USAC Silver Crown	Fortune #39	Jimmy Horton	Q-2nd; F-2nd	
7/3	Nazareth Speedway	USAC Silver Crown	Fortune #39	Ken Jacobs	Q-16th; F-5th	Dropped out of heat race
7/4	Tri-State Speedway	All Star Sprint	Fortune #39	Gary Webb	Q-12th; H-8th; B F-1st; A F-3rd	Busch Tour; overheated; dropped out running 3rd
7/7	Tri-City Speedway	NASCAR Late Model	Sieveking #00	Ken Schrader	Q-4th; F-20th	
7/8	Tri-City Speedway	Sprint	McMillan #38	Ken Jacobs	H-1st; F-1st	
7/10	Pennsboro Speedway	All Star Sprint	Fortune #39	Ken Schrader	Q-10th; H-6th; F-9th	
7/13	I-57 Speedway	Sprint	McMillan #38	Ken Schrader	Q-1st (13.58 sec.); H-1st; F-1st	
7/15	Christian Co. Fairgrounds	MARA Midget	Gojmeric #1	Ken Schrader	H-1st; F-1st	Tried for 6th and went too slow in qualifying; had flat in heat race leading
7/16	Richland Co. Fairgrounds	MARA Midget	Gojmeric #1	Ken Schrader	H-2nd; F-1st	
7/17	Springfield Speedway	Sprint	McMillan #38	Randy Standridge	Q-9th; H-6th; F-4th	
7/20	Kokomo Speedway	USAC Sprint	Fortune #39	Dean Shirley	Q-11th; H-1st; F-5th	
7/21	Macon Speedway	Late Model	Sieveking #00	Gary Webb	Q-24th; H-3rd; B F-2nd; A F-17th	Herald & Review 100; broke tie-rod in feature
7/23	State Fair Speedway	USAC Silver Crown	Fortune #39	Bill Vukovich	Q-9th (23.77 sec.); Challenge-10th	#39 broke in hot laps; ran Larry Hill's car and
7/24	State Fair Speedway	USAC Silver Crown	Fortune #39	Herb Copeland	F-18th	

Date	Track	Class	Car	Driver	Results	Notes
7/27	Paragon Speedway	USAC Sprint	Fortune #39	Jack Hewitt	Q-12th; H-1st; F-3rd	Lost feature by one foot!
7/31	Springfield Speedway	Late Model	Sieveking #00	Jim Harter	Q-7th; H-3rd; F-2nd	
7/31	Springfield Speedway	Sprint	Adams #3	Ken Schrader	Q-3rd; H-4th; D-2nd; F-1st	
8/2	Eldora Speedway	USAC Sprint	Fortune #39	Jack Hewitt	Q-7th; H-2nd; F-14th	Broke rear end in feature
8/3	Eldora Speedway	USAC Sprint	Hampshire #63	Charlie Ford	Q-9th; H-2nd; F-3rd	Nationals
8/4	Eldora Speedway	USAC Sprint	Hampshire #63	Joe Saldana	Q-7th; H-3rd; F-10th	Nationals
8/5	Belleville High Banks	USAC Midget	Hamilton #55	John Johnson	Q-1st (20.34 sec.); H-1st; D-4th; F-4th	Nationals
8/6	Belleville High Banks	USAC Midget	Hamilton #55	Johnny Parsons, Jr.	D-6th; F-3rd	Nationals
8/7	I-70 Speedway	NCRA Champ Dirt	Larry Hill #86	Bob Ewell	H-5th; F-17th	Brake caliper broke
8/7	I-70 Speedway	NCRA Midget	Gojmeric #1	Kevin Doty	H-2nd; F-2nd	
8/8	I-70 Speedway	NCRA Sprint	Adams #3	Doug Wolfgang	Q-8th; H-1st; D-3rd; F-3rd	Kenny Weld Memorial
8/9	Knoxville Raceway	NCRA Champ Dirt	Hill #86	Bob Ewell	H-2nd; F-16th	Fuel pump broke in feature
8/11	Knoxville Raceway	Sprint	C.L. Boyd #65	Bobby Allen	Q-37th; H-10th; B F-18th	2nd night qual for Knoxville Nationals
8/12	Knoxville Raceway	Sprint	C.L. Boyd #65		H-8th	Was running third and engine broke
8/13	State Fair Speedway	Late Model	Sieveking #00	Joe Kosiski	Q-3rd; F-22nd	Dropped out of feature due to stuck valve
8/17	Godfrey Speedway	Sprint	Adams #3	Ken Schrader	Q-3rd; H-1st; D-1st; F-1st	
8/19	Springfield Speedway	USAC Midget	Gojmeric #1	Ken Schrader	Q-7th; H-1st; F-1st	
8/20	Illinois State Fairgrounds	USAC Silver Crown	Fortune #39	Gary Bettenhausen	Q-10th (32.58 sec.); F-3rd	
8/21	Illinois State Fairgrounds	USAC Midget	Hamilton #55	Arnie Knepper	H-2nd; F-4th	
8/21	Illinois State Fairgrounds	USAC Late Model	Simion #22	Dean Roper	F-5th	Broke in hot laps
8/21	LaSalle Co. Fairgrounds	WOOM Midget	Gojmeric #1	Paul Clark		Broke in heat leading; finished 3rd and was docked 2 spots for jumping re-start
8/24	Lincoln Park Speedway	USAC Sprint	Fortune #39	Sheldon Kinser	Q-2nd; H-2nd; F-2nd	
8/26	Godfrey Speedway	USAC Midget	Gojmeric #1	Ken Schrader	Q-15th; H-4th; F-1st	
8/28	Action Track	USAC Sprint	Fortune #39	Jack Hewitt	Q-9th; H-4th; F-2nd	
9/2	Belle-Clair Speedway	AARA Modified	Don Klein #28	Bob Bozelli	Q-14th; H-1st; B F-1st; A F-2nd	Broke in hot laps
9/3	Belle-Clair Speedway	USAC Midget	Gojmeric #1	Ken Schrader	Q-1st (11.70 sec.); H-2nd; D-6th; F-1st	
9/4	DuQuoin Fairgrounds	USAC Late Model	Simion #22	Dean Roper	Q-23rd; H-1st; F-4th	Major crash 1st lap of feature; then major thrash
9/4	Tri-State Speedway	USAC Sprint	Fortune #39	Ricky Hood	Q-4th (23.86 sec.); F-3rd	
9/5	DuQuoin Fairgrounds	USAC Silver Crown	Fortune #39	Gary Bettenhausen	Q-1st (33.88 sec.); F-24th	Hoosier 100; blew up running 2nd in feature
9/10	Indiana State Fairgrounds	USAC Silver Crown	Fortune #39	Chuck Gurney	Q-12th; H-2nd; F-3rd	
9/10	Bloomington Speedway	USAC Sprint	Fortune #39	Larry Martin	Q-15th; F-30th	Hut Hundred; spun and got crashed
9/11	Action Track	USAC Midget	Hamilton #55	Rich Vogler	Q-8th; H-4th; F-4th	
9/11	Jacksonville Raceway	Sprint	Adams #3	Ron Milton	Q-3rd; H-4th; F-4th	
9/15	Paragon Speedway	USAC Sprint	Fortune #39	Kelly Kinser	Q-2nd; H-4th; F-6th	
9/18	Lawrenceburg Speedway	USAC Sprint	Fortune #39	Danny Milburn	Q-3rd; F-6th	
9/24-25	Eldora Speedway	USAC Midget	Hamilton #55	Johnny Parsons, Jr.	Q-2nd; F-3rd	
9/24-25	Eldora Speedway	USAC Sprint	Fortune #39	Jack Hewitt	Q-2nd; F-1st	
9/24-25	Eldora Speedway	USAC Silver Crown	Fortune #39	Ken Schrader	H-1st; F-1st	
10/1	I-55 Raceway	Modified	Sieveking #00	Ken Schrader	A F-1st	
10/2	I-55 Raceway	Modified	Sieveking #00	Rick Bussell	H-4th; 7th	
10/5	Cowtown Speedway	Midget	Smiley's #51	Charlie Swartz	Q-9th (31.36 sec.); F-4th	Modified Nationals
10/9	Illinois State Fairgrounds	Late Model	Sieveking #00	Keith Kauffman	Q-22nd; H-5th; B F-22nd	
10/14	Knoxville Raceway	WoO Sprint	Adams #3	Doug Wolfgang	Q-16th; H-4th; F-17th	Blew engine in feature
10/23	I-70 Speedway	Sprint	Fortune #39	John Mason	Q-about 40th	Blew engine in heat race
10/23	I-70 Speedway	Late Model	Sieveking #00	Jeff Swindell	Q-13th; H-2nd; F-17th	Broke rear end in feature
10/30	Eldora Speedway	All Star Sprint	Fortune #39	Swindell/Shuman	H-2nd; F-18th	Qual night for Winternationals; broke engine running 7th
11/4	Devil's Bowl Speedway	Sprint	Adams #3			Qual night; crashed in feature
11/18	Devil's Bowl Speedway	Late Model	Sieveking #00		H-2nd	

Date	Track	Type	Car Owner	Race Winner	Finish	Comments
11/19	Devil's Bowl Speedway	Late Model	Sieveking #00	Sammy Swindell	A F-17th	Running 8th w/15 laps to go—fuel pump broke
11/20	Devil's Bowl Speedway	NCRA Sprint	Adams #3	Herb Copeland	B F-12th	Motor went sour in B Feature
11/20	Devil's Bowl Speedway	NCRA Champ Dirt	Hill #86	Kevin Olsen	F-6th	Crashed in heat; started 21st in feature
11/25	Ascot Park	Midget	Gojmeric #1	Ray Lawson	Q-32nd; B F-5th; A F-20th	
11/26-27	Phoenix International Raceway				Q-7th; F-6th	

1984

(Ken Schrader's briefcase was stolen during this year, so records were reconstructed as best as could be remembered, but are incomplete.)

Date	Track	Type	Car Owner	Race Winner	Finish	Comments
1/8	Allen Co. Expo Center (indoor)	USAC Midget	Nick Gojmeric	Rich Vogler	Q-23rd (8.56 sec.)	
1/22	Allen Co. Expo Center (indoor)	USAC Midget	Gojmeric	Rich Vogler	Q-5th (7.98 sec.)	
3/10	Illinois State Fairgrounds (indoor)	USAC Midget	Gojmeric	Allen Brown	Q-18th (7.96 sec.)	
5/12	Indiana State Fairgrounds	Sprint	Hyduck #21	Joe Saldana	F-7th	
5/12	Indiana State Fairgrounds	Midget	Wilke Bros. #1	Ken Schrader	H-1st; F-1st	
5/25	Indiana State Fairgrounds	USAC Silver Crown	Pizza Hut	George Snider	H-10th; F-6th	
6/3	Capital Speedway	Late Model	Sieveking	Ken Schrader	H-4th; F-1st	
6/6	Kokomo Speedway	USAC Midget	Hank Green #67	Jerry Knuckles	Q-5th (16.90 sec.); H-1st; F-19th	Vogler and I crashed leading; Hank died
7/1	I-70 Speedway	Late Model	Sieveking	Ken Schrader	H-1st; F-1st	
7/4	East Moline Speedway	Late Model	Sieveking	Roger Dolan	Q-5th; H-1st; D-1st; 1st F-3rd; 2nd F-3rd; 3rd F-3rd	
7/6	Springfield Speedway	USAC Midget	Gojmeric	Rich Vogler	Q-1st (12.96 sec.); H-2nd; D-4th; F-2nd	
7/7	Milwaukee Mile	Midget	Wilke Bros. #1	Dan Boorse	Q-1st (31.72 sec.); F-19th	New track record
7/13	Nashville Speedway	NASCAR WC	Elmo Langley #64	Ken Schrader	Q-27th; F-19th	First Winston Cup race
	Charleston Speedway	MARA Midget	Gojmeric	Kevin Doty	H-1st; F-1st	
	Jacksonville Raceway	MARA Midget	Gojmeric		H-4th	Dropped out of feature
		NDRA Late Model	Sieveking		H-5th	
		NDRA Late Model	Sieveking		F-9th	
	Godfrey Speedway	Sprint	Adams #3	Mike Duvall	Q-8th; H-4th; F-1st	
	East Moline Speedway	Late Model	Sieveking	Ken Schrader	Q-5th; H-1st; D-1st; F-9th	
	81 Speedway	NDRA Late Model	Sieveking	Bob Helm	Q-20th (17.70 sec.)	Qualifying night
	81 Speedway	NDRA Late Model	Sieveking		H-2nd; F-14th	
7/19	I-70 Speedway	NDRA Late Model	Sieveking	Jeff Purvis	Q-26th (21.41 sec.)	Qualifying night
7/20	I-70 Speedway	NDRA Late Model	Sieveking		H-8th	Running 5th and broke dry sump
7/21	State Fair Speedway	USAC Silver Crown	Pizza Hut		Q-21st (22.72 sec.)	
7/22	State Fair Speedway	USAC Silver Crown	Pizza Hut		H-2nd; F-9th	
7/27	Bloomington Speedway	USAC Sprint	McGonial #37	Sheldon Kinser	Q-4th; H-2nd; F-2nd	
7/28	Paragon Speedway	USAC Sprint	McGonial #37	Ken Schrader	Q-2nd; D-3rd; F-1st	
7/29	Belle-Clair Speedway	Midget	Gojmeric	Gene Gennetten	H-4th; F-2nd	100 laps
8/1	Godfrey Speedway	Sprint	Pennell #18	Ken Schrader	Q-1st (11.60 sec.); H-1st; D-4th; F-1st	
8/4	Tri-City Speedway	All Star Sprint	Hyduck #21	Ron Standridge	Q-13th; H-2nd; F-22nd	
8/5	I-70 Speedway	NCRA Champ Dirt	Hill #86		H-7th; S-1st; F-13th	
8/6	I-70 Speedway	Sprint	Adams #3	Sammy Swindell	Q-17th; H-7th	Sucked intake gasket in feature
8/7	Knoxville Raceway	NCRA Champ Dirt	Hill #86	Ron Shuman		Blew up leading semi
8/12	Michigan International Speedway	NASCAR WC	Langley #64	Darrell Waltrip	Q-45.50 sec.; F-33rd	Sat in pits 40 laps w/ignition trouble
8/12	Kokomo Speedway	Sprint	McGonial #37	Randy Kinser	Q-5th; F-4th	Blew up leading heat
8/15	Paragon Speedway	USAC Sprint	McGonial #37	Steve Butler	Q-6th; H-5th; F-4th	Turned over qualifying
8/16	Eldora Speedway	USAC Sprint	McGonial #37	Jack Hewitt	Q-7th; H-1st; F-4th	
8/17	Illinois State Fairgrounds	USAC Silver Crown	Pizza Hut	Chuck Gurney	H-1st; F-19th	
8/17	Springfield Speedway	USAC Midget	Gojmeric	Ken Schrader	Q-5th; H-5th; F-1st	
8/18	Illinois State Fairgrounds	USAC Midget	Gojmeric	Ken Schrader	H-2nd; F-1st	Had flat leading

Date	Track	Type	Car	Race Winner	Finish	Comments
8/18	Illinois State Fairgrounds	USAC Late Model	Simion #38	Ken Schrader	Q-3rd; H-3rd; D-1st; F-1st	
8/18	Springfield Speedway	Sprint	Adams #3	Marvin Carmin	Q-7th; F-5th	
8/24	Milwaukee Mile	USAC Silver Crown	Pizza Hut #55	Mel Kenyon	H-2nd; F-3rd	
8/25	Action Track	USAC Midget	Wilke Bros. #11	Steve Butler	Q-1st; H-1st; F-2nd	
8/26	Springfield Speedway	USAC Midget	McGonial #37	Ricky Hood	Q-5th; H-2nd; F-2nd	
8/31	Tri-City Speedway	Sprint	Gojmeric #37	Ricky Hood	Q-2nd; H-2nd; F-2nd	
9/2	Tri-City Speedway	Midget	Gingerich #37	Tom Bigelow	Q-4th; H-2nd	Broke in feature
9/3	Tri-State Speedway	USAC Sprint	Gingerich #37	Ricky Hood	Q-10th; H-4th; F-2nd	
9/9	DuQuoin Fairgrounds	USAC Silver Crown	Pizza Hut #55	Joe Saldana	Q-5th (32.70 sec.)	Feature crash—big one!
9/9	Springfield Speedway	Sprint	Adams #3	Ken Schrader	Q-4th; F-1st	
9/9	Springfield Speedway	Late Model	Sieveking	Dick Taylor	Q-11th	500 laps
9/15	Indiana State Fairgrounds	USAC Silver Crown	Pizza Hut #55	Steve Chassey	Q-7th (34.46 sec.); F-7th	Started last & won semi; feature—broke rear hub
9/15	Indianapolis Speedrome	USAC Midget	Wilke Bros. #11	Rich Vogler	Q-5th (12.19 sec.); F-3rd	Flat tire in heat race
9/16	Illinois State Fairgrounds	Late Model	Sieveking	Jeff Purvis	S-1st	
9/16	Springfield Speedway	Sprint	Adams #3	Ken Schrader	Q-5th; F-1st	
10/7	Charlotte Motor Speedway	NASCAR WC	Langley #64	Bill Elliott	Q-26th; F-26th	Spent 40 laps in pits w/ignition problems
10/14	North Wilkesboro Speedway	NASCAR WC	Langley #64	Darrell Waltrip	Q-24th; F-17th	Crashed in hot laps
10/19	I-70 Speedway	Late Model	Sieveking	Ken Schrader	H-1st; D-2nd; F-1st	Broke steering arm
10/27	Tri-City Speedway	Sprint	Hyduck #21			Let Mike Sweeney drive in feature; finished 12th
11/4	Atlanta Motor Speedway	NASCAR WC	Langley #64	Dale Earnhardt, Sr.	Q-24th; F-27th	
11/17	Ascot Park	Midget	Agajanian #98	Ron Shuman	Q-30th (20.02 sec.); H-3rd	
11/22	Ascot Park	Midget	Wilke Bros. #11		Q-51st	Car would not run
11/25	Phoenix International Raceway	USAC Midget	Wilke Bros. #11	Rich Vogler	Q-2nd; F-3rd	

1985

Date	Track	Type	Car Owner	Race Winner	Finish	Comments
1/19	Hoosierdome (indoor)	USAC Midget	Wilke Bros. #1	Rich Vogler	H-4th; Team F-2nd, F-3rd	
2/17	Daytona International Speedway	NASCAR WC	Junie Donlavey #90	Bill Elliott	Q-24th; Twin 125-11th, 500-11th	
2/24	Richmond Int'l Raceway	NASCAR WC	Donlavey #90	Dale Earnhardt, Sr.	Q-22nd; F-14th	
3/3	North Carolina Motor Speedway	NASCAR WC	Donlavey #90	Neil Bonnett	Q-16th; F-40th	
3/17	Atlanta Motor Speedway	NASCAR WC	Donlavey #90	Bill Elliott	Q-36th; F-17th	Had flat tire late in race
4/6	Bristol Motor Speedway	NASCAR WC	Donlavey #90	Dale Earnhardt, Sr.	Q-16th; F-10th	
4/14	Darlington Raceway	NASCAR WC	Donlavey #90	Bill Elliott	Q-25th; F-13th	
4/21	North Wilkesboro Speedway	NASCAR WC	Donlavey #90	Neil Bonnett	Q-21st; F-14th	
4/28	Martinsville Speedway	NASCAR WC	Donlavey #90	Harry Gant	Q-22nd; F-16th	
5/5	Talladega Superspeedway	NASCAR WC	Donlavey #90	Bill Elliott	Q-21st (200.70 mph); F-20th	
5/11	I-55 Raceway	AARA Modified	Sieveking	Steve Shive	Q-4th; H-1st; D-6th; F-4th	First night with new modified
5/12	St. Charles Speedway	AARA Modified	Sieveking		Q-3rd; H-1st; D-6th; F-4th	Had flat tire late in race
5/19	Dover International Speedway	NASCAR WC	Donlavey #90	Bill Elliott	Q-18th; F-10th	
5/26	Charlotte Motor Speedway	NASCAR WC	Donlavey #90	Darrell Waltrip	Q-12th; F-38th	
6/2	Riverside International Speedway	NASCAR WC	Donlavey #90	Terry Labonte	Q-24th; F-10th	
6/9	Pocono Raceway	NASCAR WC	Donlavey #90	Bill Elliott	Q-22nd; F-15th	
6/16	Michigan International Speedway	NASCAR WC	Donlavey #90	Bill Elliott	Q-rained out, F-34th	
6/19	St. Charles Speedway	MARA Midget	Schroeder #20	Ken Schrader	H-2nd; D-6th; F-1st	

Date	Track	Type	Car Owner	Race Winner	Finish	Comments
6/22	St. Francois Raceway	Modified	Sieveking #1		H-1st; F-8th	
6/29	I-55 Raceway	AARA Modified	Sieveking #1		S-4th	Broke transmission in feature
7/4	Daytona International Speedway	NASCAR WC	Donlavey #90	Greg Sacks	Q-21st (195.8 mph); F-21st	Lined up by points; broke steering in feature
7/6	I-55 Raceway	AARA Modified	Sieveking #1		Q-3rd; H-5th; D-3rd; F-3rd	Broke engine
7/13	Indianapolis Raceway Park	USAC Silver Crown	Middleton #55		Q-2nd (23.10 sec.); F-2nd	
7/14	St. Charles Speedway	AARA Modified	Sieveking	Ricky Hood	Q-1st (12.53 sec.); H-2nd, -2nd; F-5th	Crashed in first feature
7/20	Flemington Speedway	Modified			H-2nd; F-2nd	
7/20	Flemington Speedway	Modified Sprint			Q-20th; F-15th	
7/21	Pocono Raceway	NASCAR WC	Donlavey #90	Bill Elliott		
7/28	Talladega Superspeedway	NASCAR WC	Donlavey #90	Cale Yarborough	Q-18th (198.34 mph); F-11th	
8/2	Belle-Clair Speedway	AARA Modified	Sieveking #1	Bo Smith	1st F-3rd; 2nd F-9th	Fair race
8/3	I-55 Raceway	AARA Modified	Sieveking #1	Seets	Q-1st (14.49 sec.)	Blew head gasket in heat race
8/11	Michigan International Speedway	NASCAR WC	Donlavey #90	Bill Elliott	Q-24th (161.06 mph); F-20th	Engine broke in feature
8/17	Illinois State Fairgrounds	USAC Silver Crown	Middleton #55	Chuck Gurney	Q-12th	
8/17	Springfield Speedway	USAC Midget	Schroeder #20	Ken Schrader	Q-4th; H-2nd; F-1st	
8/18	Illinois State Fairgrounds	USAC Midget	Schroeder #20	Johnny Parsons, Jr.	H-11th; F-9th	
8/18	St. Charles Speedway	AARA Modified	Sieveking #1	Bo Smith	Q-2nd; H-1st; D-6th; F-12th	Flat tire in feature
8/24	Bristol Motor Speedway	NASCAR WC	Donlavey #90	Dale Earnhardt, Sr.	Q-22nd (17.36 sec.); F-19th	
9/1	Darlington Raceway	NASCAR WC	Donlavey #90	Bill Elliott	Q-32nd; F-14th	Major crash turn three
9/2	DuQuoin Fairgrounds	USAC Silver Crown	Middleton #55	Ricky Hood	Q-13th (32.92 sec.); F-30th	
9/2	Godfrey Speedway	Modified	Sieveking #1		Q-3rd	Crashed in heat race; blew head gasket in feature
9/8	Richmond International Raceway	NASCAR WC	Donlavey #90	Darrell Waltrip	Q-18th (21.17 sec.); F-15th	
9/15	Dover International Speedway	NASCAR WC	Donlavey #90	Harry Gant	Q-25th (26.09 sec.); F-16th	
9/22	Martinsville Speedway	NASCAR WC	Donlavey #90	Dale Earnhardt, Sr.	Q-16th (21.33 sec.); F-26th	
9/29	North Wilkesboro Speedway	NASCAR WC	Donlavey #90	Harry Gant	Q-19th (20.01 sec.); F-15th	
10/6	Charlotte Motor Speedway	NASCAR WC	Donlavey #90	Cale Yarborough	Q-10th; F-25th	
10/20	North Carolina Motor Speedway	NASCAR WC	Donlavey #90	Darrell Waltrip	Q-22nd (26.32 sec.); F-19th	
10/25-26	Peach State Motor Speedway	Late Model	Sieveking	Butch Miller	Q-5th (17.22 sec.); F-14th	
11/3	Atlanta Motor Speedway	NASCAR WC	Donlavey #90	Bill Elliott	Q-26th (33.32 sec.); F-15th	First night with new Shaw car; blew engine
11/17	Riverside International Speedway	USAC Silver Crown	Donlavey #90	Ricky Rudd	F-23rd	

1986

Date	Track	Type	Car Owner	Race Winner	Finish	Comments
1/4	Hoosierdome (indoor)	USAC Midget	Wilke Bros. #11	Nic Fornoro		
2/1-2	Daytona International Speedway	IMSA	Jack Roush #50		F-33rd	Rudd crashed after 9 hours
2/16	Daytona International Speedway	NASCAR WC	Donlavey #90	Geoff Bodine	F-23rd	Daytona 500, blew engine
2/23	Richmond International Raceway	NASCAR WC	Donlavey #90	Kyle Petty	F-21st	
3/2	North Carolina Motor Speedway	NASCAR WC	Donlavey #90	Terry Labonte	Q-16th	Spun on pit road and broke rear end
3/8	Talladega Short Track	Late Model	Sieveking #2		F-21st	Didn't weigh and was disqualified
3/16	Atlanta Motor Speedway	NASCAR WC	Donlavey #90	Morgan Shepherd	H-5th	Blew tire and crashed with 10 laps to go
3/28	Talladega Short Track	Late Model	Sieveking #2		F-13th	Crashed in semi
4/6	Bristol Motor Speedway	NASCAR WC	Donlavey #90	Rusty Wallace	F-10th	Rusty's first win!
4/13	Darlington Raceway	NASCAR WC	Donlavey #90	Dale Earnhardt, Sr.	F-14th	
4/20	North Wilkesboro Speedway	NASCAR WC	Donlavey #90	Dale Earnhardt, Sr.	F-7th	
4/27	Martinsville Speedway	NASCAR WC	Donlavey #90	Ricky Rudd	F-26th	Blew engine running 13th
5/4	Talladega Superspeedway	NASCAR WC	Donlavey #90	Bobby Allison		
5/10	Tri-City Speedway	Late Model	Sieveking #2	Mike Wallace	F-3rd	Crashed in heat race

Date	Track	Type	Car Owner	Race Winner	Finish	Comments
5/11	Springfield Speedway	Late Model	Sieveking #2	Ken Schrader	Q-3rd; H-5th; F-1st	Spun running 6th with 60 laps to go
5/18	Dover International Speedway	NASCAR WC	Donlavey #90	Geoff Bodine	F-10th	Car pushed all day
5/25	Charlotte Motor Speedway	NASCAR WC	Donlavey #90	Dale Earnhardt Sr.	F-23rd	Punched hole in fuel line running 11th
6/1	Riverside International Speedway	NASCAR WC	Donlavey #90	Darrell Waltrip	F-17th	Crash in feature
6/7	Flemington Speedway	Modified	Horton #95		H-3rd	
6/7	Flemington Speedway	Sportsman	#00		H-6th	Dropped valve
6/8	Pocono Raceway	NASCAR WC	Donlavey #90	Tim Richmond	Q-23rd; F-27th	
6/15	Michigan International Speedway	NASCAR WC	Donlavey #90	Bill Elliott	Q-24th; F-20th	
6/21	Tri-City Speedway	Late Model	Sieveking #2	Mike Wallace	H-4th; 1st F-4th; 2nd F-5th	
6/28	Tri-City Speedway	Late Model	Sieveking #2	Mike Wallace	H-1st; F-2nd	
6/29	Tri-State Speedway	Late Model	Sieveking #2	Billy Moyer	Q-15th; H-4th; B F-10th	
7/4	Daytona International Speedway	NASCAR WC	Donlavey #90	Tim Richmond	F-12th	
7/7	Action Track	USAC Late Model	Sieveking #2	Ken Schrader	Q-6th; H-2nd; F-1st	Got there late from Terre Haute; started last
7/7	Tri-City Speedway	Late Model	Sieveking #2	Mike Wallace	F-5th	A Feature rained out
7/10	Macon Speedway	USAC Late Model	Sieveking #2	Ken Schrader	Q-24th; H-5th; B F-4th	
7/13	Indianapolis Raceway Park	USAC Silver Crown	Louis Seymour #29	Tim Richmond	Q-2nd; (22.88 (sec.); F-1st	Blew engine
7/20	Pocono Raceway	NASCAR WC	Donlavey #90	Bobby Hillin, Jr.	F-23rd	No qualifying; points race
7/27	Talladega Superspeedway	NASCAR WC	Donlavey #90	Don Klein	Q-35th (201.4 mph); F-31st	
8/1	Belle-Clair Speedway	AARA Modified	Jumper #33	Rick Beebe	S-8th; F-4th	
8/2	I-70 Speedway	Late Model	Sieveking #2	Rick Standridge	H-5th; F-9th	
8/3	Springfield Speedway	Late Model	Sieveking #2	Tim Richmond	Q-3rd; H-5th; F-9th	
8/10	Watkins Glen International	NASCAR WC	Donlavey #90	Bill Elliott	Q-25th (1:18.40); F-11th	Blew engine
8/17	Michigan International Speedway	NASCAR WC	Donlavey #90	Darrell Waltrip	Q-17th (42.88 sec.); F-11th	Blew engine on 2nd lap
8/23	Bristol Motor Speedway	NASCAR WC	Donlavey #90	Tim Richmond	Q-27th; F-19th	Crashed on 300th lap running 12th
8/31	Darlington Raceway	NASCAR WC	Glen Niebel #20	Jack Hewitt	Q-32nd; F-36th	Running good, broke engine
9/1	DuQuoin Fairgrounds	USAC Silver Crown	Donlavey #90	Tim Richmond	Q-14th (32.40 sec.)	Blew engine
9/7	Richmond International Raceway	NASCAR WC	Donlavey #90	Ricky Rudd	Q-14th; F-25th	
9/14	Dover International Speedway	NASCAR WC	Donlavey #90	Rusty Wallace	Q-17th; F-22nd	
9/21	Martinsville Speedway	NASCAR WC	Donlavey #90	Darrell Waltrip	F-7th	
9/28	North Wilkesboro Speedway	NASCAR WC	Donlavey #90	Dale Earnhardt, Sr.	F-18th	
10/5	Charlotte Motor Speedway	NASCAR WC	Donlavey #90	Kevin Gundaker	F-28th	
10/11	Tri-City Speedway	Late Model	Sieveking #2	Neil Bonnett	H-1st; 1st F-2nd	Ran on ¼-mile; 2nd feature rained out
10/19	North Carolina Motor Speedway	NASCAR WC	Donlavey #90	Billy Moyer	Q-23rd; F-14th	
10/25-26	Tri-City Speedway	Late Model	Sieveking #2	Dale Earnhardt, Sr.	H-3rd; F-9th	
11/2	Atlanta Motor Speedway	NASCAR WC	Donlavey #90	Tim Richmond	F-17th	
11/16	Riverside International Speedway	NASCAR WC	Donlavey #90	Rich Vogler	F-11th	
12/7	Hoosierdome (indoor)	USAC Midget	Seymour #7 & 29		H-2nd; Team 2nd; F-2nd	Drove #7 in Team feature; then #29 because block cracked in #7
12/8	Concord Motorsports Park	Late Model	Sieveking #2	Ernie Irvan	Q-11th; F-11th	Broke quick change gears
12/13	Rosemont Horizon (indoor)	USAC Midget	Seymour #7	Ken Schrader	Q-1st; 1st F-2nd; 2nd F-1st	

1987

Date	Track	Type	Car Owner	Race Winner	Finish	Comments
2/15	Daytona International Speedway	NASCAR WC	Donlavey #90	Bill Elliott	Q-3rd; Twin 125-1st; 500-7th	Daytona 500
3/1	North Carolina Motor Speedway	NASCAR WC	Donlavey #90	Dale Earnhardt, Sr.	Q-3rd; F-10th	
3/8	Richmond International Raceway	NASCAR WC	Donlavey #90	Dale Earnhardt, Sr.	Q-16th; F-13th	
3/15	Atlanta Motor Speedway	NASCAR WC	Donlavey #90	Ricky Rudd	Q-4th; F-29th	
3/29	Darlington Raceway	NASCAR WC	Donlavey #90	Dale Earnhardt, Sr.	Q-1st; R-5th	
4/5	North Wilkesboro Speedway	NASCAR WC	Donlavey #90	Dale Earnhardt, Sr.	Q-13th; F-16th	Blew engine leading

Date	Track	Series	Car	Name	Results	Notes
4/12	Bristol Motor Speedway	NASCAR WC	Donlavey #90	Dale Earnhardt, Sr.	Q-7th; F-17th	Had to start race 26th because missed heat
4/17-18	Concord Motorsports Park	Late Model	Schrader #103	Ernie Irvan	Q-3rd	
4/26	Martinsville Speedway	NASCAR WC	Donlavey #90	Dale Earnhardt, Sr.	Q-20th; F-7th	
5/3	Talladega Superspeedway	NASCAR WC	Donlavey #90	Davey Allison	Q-15th; F-8th	
5/8	Belle-Clair Speedway	AARA Modified	Jumper #33	Ed Dixon	H-5th; S-1st; F-4th	
5/9	Tri-City Speedway			Ken Schrader	F-1st	
5/10	Springfield Speedway	Late Model	Sieveking #103	Ernie Irvan	Q-6th; H-4th; F-4th	
5/16	Concord Motorsports Park	Late Model	Schrader #103	Buddy Baker	H-2nd; F-3rd	
5/17	Charlotte Motor Speedway	NASCAR WC	Donlavey #90	Rodney Combs	Q-4th; F-4th	The Winston
5/22	Lancaster Motor Speedway	6-cylinders	Ira Small			Feature was running 2nd and blew off radiator hose
5/24	Charlotte Motor Speedway	NASCAR WC	Donlavey #90	Kyle Petty	Q-4th; F-29th	
5/31	Dover International Speedway	NASCAR WC	Donlavey #90	Davey Allison	Q-3rd; F-6th	
6/3	St. Charles Speedway	Late Model	Sieveking #103	Billy Moyer	S-3rd; F-5th	Broke seat belt in heat race
6/5	Godfrey Speedway	Late Model	Sieveking #103	Jim Leka	H-5th	Crashed in feature
6/6	Macon Speedway	Late Model	Bob Bennett #99		Q-1st; H-6th; D-4th; 1st F-2nd; 2nd F-2nd	New track record
6/7	Springfield Speedway	Late Model	Sieveking #103		Q-9th; H-1st; F-5th	
6/14	Pocono Raceway	NASCAR WC	Donlavey #90	Tim Richmond	Q-21st; F-17th	
6/21	Riverside International Speedway	NASCAR WC	Donlavey #90	Tim Richmond	Q-19th; F-10th	
6/24	Hales Corners Speedway	Late Model	Sieveking #103	Ray Guss, Jr.	Pursuit: 1st; F-7th	
6/28	Michigan International Speedway	NASCAR WC	Donlavey #90	Dale Earnhardt, Sr.	Q-4th; F-8th	
7/4	Daytona International Speedway	NASCAR WC	Donlavey #90	Bobby Allison	Q-3rd; F-7th	
7/9	Macon Speedway	Late Model	Sieveking #103	Rick Standridge	Q-slow; H-1st; C F-6th	
7/11	Indianapolis Raceway Park	USAC Silver Crown	Seymour #29/Cook #44	Jeff Bloom	Q-4th; F-25th	Herald & Review 100 Broke leading; drove Duke Cook #44 from lap 30 on
7/12	Tri-State Speedway	Late Model	Sieveking #103	Eddie Pace	Q-12th; H-1st; F-6th	
7/19	Pocono Raceway	NASCAR WC	Donlavey #90	Dale Earnhardt, Sr.	Q-21st; F-10th	
7/26	Talladega Superspeedway	NASCAR WC	Donlavey #90	Bill Elliott	Q-26th; F-18th	Race of Champions
8/1	Hialeah Speedway	Late Model		Davey Allison	H-4th; F-8th	Race of Champions
8/2	Auburndale Speedway			Tim Richmond	F-4th	
8/10	Watkins Glen International	NASCAR WC	Donlavey #90	Rusty Wallace	Q-23rd; F-27th	Broke clutch; crashed with Patty Moise
8/16	Michigan International Speedway	NASCAR WC	Donlavey #90	Bill Elliott	Q-4th; F-34th	Broke engine
8/18	Davenport Speedway	Late Model			H-5th	Feature; dropped out
8/22	Bristol Motor Speedway	NASCAR WC	Donlavey #90	Dale Earnhardt, Sr.	Q-3rd; F-27th	Blew tire and hit wall; finished race in Bonnett's car to 10th
8/2]3	Illinois State Fairgrounds	ARCA Stock Car	Jerry Gentile #27	Ron Kelowoski	Q-10th	Blew up
8/23	Springfield Speedway	Late Model	Sieveking #2	Dale Earnhardt, Sr.	Q-10th; H-4th	Crashed in feature
9/6	Darlington Raceway	NASCAR WC	Donlavey #90		Q-18th; F-11th	
9/10	I-70 Speedway	Late Model	Sieveking #2		Q-11th; F-3rd	Crashed running 3rd
9/13	Richmond International Raceway	NASCAR WC	Donlavey #90	Dale Earnhardt, Sr.	Q-18th; F-21st	
9/20	Dover International Speedway	NASCAR WC	Donlavey #90	Ricky Rudd	Q-5th; F-11th	Crashed in feature
9/26	Concord Motorsports Park	Late Model		Ernie Irvan	H-2nd; F-11th	
9/27	Martinsville Speedway	NASCAR WC	Donlavey #90	Darrell Waltrip	Q-11th; F-12th	
10/2	Crossville Raceway	Late Model	#39		H-4th; F-4th	
10/3	Concord Motorsports Park	Late Model		Jack Sprague	F-26th	Big Ten Series; started last; didn't qualify; finished 5th
10/4	North Wilkesboro Speedway	NASCAR WC	Donlavey #90	Terry Labonte	Q-6th; F-15th	
10/11	Charlotte Motor Speedway	NASCAR WC	Donlavey #90	Bill Elliott	Q-10th; F-17th	
10/17	Tri-City Speedway	Late Model	Sieveking #2		F-8th	Crashed but lost 40 laps
10/26	North Carolina Motor Speedway	NASCAR WC	Donlavey #90	Bill Elliott	Q-16th; F-14th	
11/1	Phoenix International Raceway	USAC Silver Crown	Donlavey #90	Ken Schrader	Q-7th; F-1st	

Date	Track	Type	Car Owner	Race Winner	Finish	Comments
11/1	Phoenix International Raceway	Late Model				Blew engine
11/7	Riverside International Speedway	NASCAR WC	Donlavey #90	Ken Schrader	Q-8th; F-30th	
11/8	Riverside International Speedway	NASCAR WC	Donlavey #90	Rusty Wallace	Q-4th; F-1st	Oil on clutch slipping in race
11/22	Atlanta Motor Speedway	NASCAR WC	Donlavey #90	Bill Elliott	Q-38th; F-29th	

1988

Date	Track	Type	Car Owner	Race Winner	Finish	Comments
1/2-3	Volusia County Speedway	Late Model	Sieveking #2	Roy Carruthers	H-1st; F-11th	Crashed heat; pulled out overheating in Feature
1/23	Hoosierdome (indoor)	USAC Midget	Seymour #29	Ken Schrader	H-1st; F-1st	Crashed in team feature
1/24	Nashville Municipal Auditorium	Midget	Seymour #4		F-7th	
2/7	Daytona International Speedway	NASCAR WC	Hendrick #25	Dale Earnhardt, Sr.	Q-31st; F-42nd	Busch Clash
2/13	Daytona International Speedway	NASCAR BGN	Schrader #52	Bobby Allison		Goody's 300: crashed lap 31
2/14	Daytona International Speedway	NASCAR WC	Hendrick #25	Bobby Allison	Q-1st; 125-3rd, 500-6th	
2/21	Richmond International Raceway	NASCAR WC	Arrington #67	Neil Bonnett	F-20th	Qualified 34th in Hendrick #25 and missed show; started Buddy Arrington #67 in 31st
3/5	North Carolina Motor Speedway	NASCAR BGN	Schrader #52	Mark Martin	Q-9th; F-12th	Running 5th ran out fuel with 10 laps to go
3/6	North Carolina Motor Speedway	NASCAR WC	Hendrick #25	Neil Bonnett	Q-5th; F-10th	
3/13	Green Valley Speedway	Southern All Star LM	Sieveking #2	Ed Gibbons	Q-22nd; F-26th	Cut right rear tire 2nd lap of feature
3/20	Atlanta Motor Speedway	NASCAR WC	Hendrick #25	Dale Earnhardt, Sr.	Q-9th; F-10th	
3/26	Darlington Raceway	NASCAR BGN	Schrader #52	Geoff Bodine	Q-15th; F-15th	
3/27	Darlington Raceway	NASCAR WC	Hendrick #25	Lake Speed	Q-1st; F-29th	Blew power steering hose and lost 3 laps
4/10	Bristol Motor Speedway	NASCAR WC	Hendrick #25	Bill Elliott	Q-6th; F-10th	Crashed
4/17	North Wilkesboro Speedway	NASCAR WC	Hendrick #25	Terry Labonte	Q-5th; F-11th	
4/24	Martinsville Speedway	NASCAR WC	Hendrick #25	Dale Earnhardt, Sr.	Q-7th; F-10th	Hit wall by myself and messed car up
5/1	Talladega Superspeedway	NASCAR WC	Hendrick #25	Phil Parsons	Q-6th; F-5th	
5/4	St. Charles Speedway	Late Model	Sieveking #2	Billy Moyer	S-5th; F-7th	Broke fuel pump belt leading heat
5/7	Nazareth Speedway	NASCAR BGN	Schrader #52	Rick Mast	F-33rd	Lined up by points; hole in oil filter and pulled in 14 laps down
5/11	I-55 Raceway	USAC Late Model	Sieveking #2	Willie Kraft	Q-13th; H-1st; F-19th	Overheated in feature
5/14	Indianapolis Raceway Park	NASCAR Modified	Ed Close #6	Mike McLaughlin	Q-1st (21.77 sec.); F-6th	
5/22	Charlotte Motor Speedway	NASCAR WC	Hendrick #25	Sterling Marlin	S-1st; F-7th	Winston Open
5/28	Charlotte Motor Speedway	NASCAR BGN	Schrader #52	Dale Jarrett	Q-15th; F-17th	
5/29	Charlotte Motor Speedway	NASCAR WC	Hendrick #25	Darrell Waltrip	Q-19th; F-6th	
5/30	Macon Speedway	Late Model	Sieveking #2	Rick Standridge	Q-16th; H-1st; S-2nd; F-7th	
6/4	Dover International Speedway	NASCAR BGN	Schrader #52	Bobby Hillin	F-3rd	
6/5	Dover International Speedway	NASCAR WC	Hendrick #25	Bill Elliott	Q-13th; F-21st	Two equalized tires and dropped valve at end
6/12	Riverside International Speedway	NASCAR WC	Hendrick #25	Rusty Wallace	Q-11th; F-20th	Spun twice
6/13-14	Slinger Speedway	Late Model		Butch Miller	Q-23rd (11.78 sec.)	Dropped out due to overheating
6/19	Pocono Raceway	NASCAR WC	Hendrick #25	Geoff Bodine	Q-2nd; F-9th	Ran fast and had a flat
6/19	Hagerstown Speedway	Late Model	Ernie Davis	Gary Schuler	H-1st; F-5th	Spun on 3rd lap
6/22	St. Charles Speedway	Late Model	Sieveking #2	Billy Moyer	H-3rd; F-8th	
6/26	Michigan International Speedway	NASCAR WC	Hendrick #25	Rusty Wallace	Q-11th; F-6th	
7/2	Daytona International Speedway	NASCAR WC	Hendrick #25	Bill Elliott	Q-4th; F-8th	
7/2	Hialeah Speedway	Late Model		Mike Waltrip	Q-2nd; F-2nd	
7/4	Davenport Speedway	USAC Late Model	Sieveking #2	Larry Phillips	Q-5th; H-3rd, F-3rd	
7/9	Indianapolis Raceway Park	USAC Silver Crown	Seymour #29	Bruce Field	Q-7th	Bruce Pathrum show
7/11-12	Slinger Speedway	Late Model	Schrader #2	Butch Miller	Q-15th (11.62 sec.)	Broke leading
7/13	St. Charles Speedway	Late Model	Sieveking #2		F-18th	
7/14	Macon Speedway	Late Model	Sieveking #2		Q-3rd; D-2nd, F-4th	Broke in hot laps; drove Joe Ross, Jr.'s car in F

Date	Track	Type	Car Owner	Race Winner	Finish	Comments
7/15	Kankakee Speedway	Late Model	Sieveking #2	Jim Curry	Q-15th; H-1st; S-1st	Broke ignition coil leading
7/16	Tri-City Speedway	Late Model	Sieveking #2	Tom Helfrich	Q-1st; H-2nd; F-?	Broke in heat race
7/17	Tri-State Speedway	Late Model	Sieveking #2	Jim Curry	S-3rd; F-8th	
7/23	Pocono Raceway	NASCAR WC	Hendrick #25	Bill Elliott	Q-4th; F-2nd	
7/30	Memphis Dirt Track	ROC		Rusty Wallace	F-3rd	
7/31	Talladega Superspeedway	NASCAR WC	Hendrick #25	Ken Schrader	Q-7th; F-1st	First Winston Cup win!
8/4	Lebanon Valley Speedway	Modified	Mark Flury #25	Kenny Brightbill	H-7th; C-3rd; F-6th	
8/5		Modified	Flury #25	Alan Johnson	H-4th	Broke driveline in feature
8/6	Oswego Speedway	NASCAR Modified	Ed Close #6	Mike McLaughlin	Q-10th; H-3rd; F-3rd	Started last; got to 8th and had flat tire
8/7	Cayuga Co. Fair Speedway	NASCAR Modified	Flury #25	Dave Lape	H-7th; C-6th; F-12th	Had flat late in race
8/10	I-35 Speedway	IMCA Modified	Kelly Shyrock #35	Ken Schrader	H-1st; F-1st	Five local drivers versus five Cup drivers
8/12	Black Rock Speedway	Modified	Miller car			Blew up engine with 10 to go
8/14	Watkins Glen International	NASCAR WC	Hendrick #25	Ricky Rudd	Q-8th; F-10th	Crashed running 6th
8/19	Spencer NY	Late Model			H-4th; F-3rd	
8/21	Michigan International Speedway	NASCAR WC	Hendrick #25	Davey Allison	Q-3rd; F-12th	
8/27	Bristol Motor Speedway	NASCAR WC	Hendrick #25	Dale Earnhardt, Sr.	Q-9th; F-21st	
8/28	Peach State Motor Speedway	Late Model	Schrader #2	Dave Mader	Q-11th; F-7th	World Crown 200
9/1	Summerville Speedway	Late Model	Budweiser #1	Dale Earnhardt, Sr.	F-4th	Bruce Pathrum show
9/3	Darlington Raceway	NASCAR BGN	Schrader #52		Q-17th; F-39th	Battery failure
9/4	Darlington Raceway	NASCAR WC	Hendrick #25	Bill Elliott	Q-25th; F-11th	
9/5	Travelers Rest Speedway	Late Model	Hendrick #25	Ken Schrader	F-1st	Bruce Pathrum show
9/11	Richmond International Raceway	NASCAR WC	Hendrick #25	Davey Allison	Q-8th; F-18th	
9/17	Dover International Speedway	NASCAR BGN	Schrader #52	Michael Waltrip	Q-9th; F-28th	Had two flats and lost brakes
9/18	Dover International Speedway	NASCAR WC	Hendrick #25	Bill Elliott	Q-9th; F-35th	Broke engine
9/25	Martinsville Speedway	NASCAR WC	Hendrick #25	Darrell Waltrip	Q-19th; F-4th	Crashed two times; blew right fronts
10/1	Lanier, GA	NASCAR BGN	AACS #2	Rob Moroso	Q-13th; F-10th	Mike Love qualified the car
10/8	Charlotte Motor Speedway	NASCAR WC	Hendrick #52	Rusty Wallace	Q-7th; F-4th	$10,000 for being leader at halfway point
10/9	Charlotte Motor Speedway	NASCAR WC	Hendrick #25	Rusty Wallace	Q-7th; F-7th	
10/16	North Wilkesboro Speedway	NASCAR WC	Hendrick #25	Harry Gant	Q-3rd; F-8th	
10/22	North Carolina Motor Speedway	NASCAR BGN	Schrader #52	Rusty Wallace	Q-15th; F-8th	
10/23	North Carolina Motor Speedway	NASCAR WC	Hendrick #25	Rusty Wallace	Q-21st; F-11th	
10/30	Martinsville Speedway	Modified	Mystic Missle #4	Ray Guss, Jr.	Q-lousy, H-1st	Broke while leading
11/4	Tucson Raceway Park	Late Model	#4	Thirlkettle	H-2nd; F-6th	
11/5	Phoenix International Raceway	Late Model	Schrader #2	Ken Schrader	Q-6th	Brake rotor broke
11/5	Firebird International Raceway				F-1st	
11/6	Phoenix International Raceway	NASCAR WC	Hendrick #25	Alan Kulwicki	F-14th	
11/13	Dixie Speedway	Late Model	Sieveking #2	Billy Moyer	H-4th; F-11th	Bruce Pathrum show
11/20	Atlanta Motor Speedway	NASCAR WC	Hendrick #25	Rusty Wallace	Q-6th; F-6th	
12/11	Concord Motorsports Park		Shorty Baulcom #4		Q-11th; H-2nd; F-7th	

1989

Date	Track	Type	Car Owner	Race Winner	Finish	Comments
1/13	Tulsa Expo Raceway (indoor)	Midget	Kenyon #66			Chili Bowl
1/14	Tulsa Expo Raceway (indoor)	Midget	Kenyon #66			Chili Bowl
1/28	Hoosierdome (indoor)	USAC Midget	Seymour #29			
2/5	Phoenix International Raceway	USAC Silver Crown	Seymour #29			Copper Classic
2/5	Phoenix International Raceway	Late Model	Schrader #52			Copper Classic
2/12	Daytona International Speedway	NASCAR WC	Hendrick #25	Ken Schrader	F-1st	Busch Clash
2/16	Daytona International Speedway	NASCAR WC	Hendrick #25	Ken Schrader	F-1st	Twin 125

Date	Track	Division	Car	Winner	Result	Notes
2/18	Daytona International Speedway	NASCAR BGN	Schrader #52	Darrell Waltrip	F-9th	Spun last lap
2/19	Daytona International Speedway	NASCAR WC	Hendrick #25	Darrell Waltrip	Q-1st; F-2nd	Led most of the day and got beat on fuel mileage
3/4	North Carolina Motor Speedway	NASCAR BGN	Schrader #52			
3/5	North Carolina Motor Speedway	NASCAR WC	Hendrick #25	Rusty Wallace		
3/18	Lanier, GA	USAC Midget	Seymour #29	Mike Fedorchek	Q-3rd; H-2nd; F-3rd	
3/19	Atlanta Motor Speedway	NASCAR WC	Hendrick #25	Darrell Waltrip		
3/26	Richmond International Raceway	NASCAR WC	Hendrick #25	Rusty Wallace		
4/1	Darlington Raceway	NASCAR BGN	Schrader #52			
4/2	Darlington Raceway	NASCAR WC	Hendrick #25	Harry Gant		
4/9	Bristol Motor Speedway	NASCAR WC	Hendrick #25	Rusty Wallace		
4/15	Hickory Speedway	Late Model		Ken Schrader	F-1st	Match race with Rusty and others
4/16	North Wilkesboro Speedway	NASCAR WC	Hendrick #25	Dale Earnhardt, Sr.		
4/22	Pulaski County	Late Model				
4/23	Martinsville Speedway	NASCAR WC	Hendrick #25	Darrell Waltrip		Cut tire running good
4/28	Big Diamond Raceway	Modified	Kohuth modified			
4/30	Nazareth Speedway	NASCAR BGN	Schrader #52			
5/6	Desoto Super Speedway	Late Model	Tom Stimus #1	Ken Schrader	F-1st	
5/7	Talladega Superspeedway	NASCAR WC	Hendrick #25	Davey Allison		
5/13	Indianapolis Raceway Park	NASCAR Modified	Ed Close #6			
5/19	Leesville, SC					Bruce Pathrum show
5/21	Charlotte Motor Speedway	NASCAR WC	Hendrick #25	Rusty Wallace	F-2nd	The Winston
5/27	Charlotte Motor Speedway	NASCAR BGN	Schrader #52			Closed up spark plug on first lap
5/28	Charlotte Motor Speedway	NASCAR WC	Hendrick #25	Darrell Waltrip	F-3rd	Right front tire left loose on last stop
5/29	Macon Speedway	UMP Modified	Schrader-King #52			
6/3	Dover International Speedway	NASCAR BGN	Schrader #52			
6/4	Dover International Speedway	NASCAR WC	Hendrick #25	Dale Earnhardt, Sr.	F-3rd	
6/4	Bridgeport Speedway	DIRT Modified				
6/11	Sears Point Raceway	NASCAR WC	Hendrick #25	Ricky Rudd		Broke rear end gears
6/13	Slinger Speedway	Late Model	Schrader #52			Slinger Nationals
6/14	Tri-City Speedway	Late Model	Schrader-King #52			
6/18	Pocono Raceway	NASCAR WC	Hendrick #25	Terry Labonte		
6/22	Macon Speedway	IMCA Modified				
6/25	Michigan International Speedway	NASCAR WC	Hendrick #25	Bill Elliott		Morgan Shepherd crashed us running good
6/25	Tri-State Speedway	UMP Late Model	Schrader-King #52			Crashed in feature
7/1	Daytona International Speedway	NASCAR WC	Hendrick #25	Davey Allison		
7/1	Oswego Speedway	NASCAR Modified	Close #6	Roger Long		
7/2	Cayuga Co. Fair Speedway	DIRT Modified	Billy Decker #91			
7/3	New York State Fairgrounds	DIRT Modified	Billy Decker #91S			
7/6	Kankakee Speedway	UMP Late Model	Tony Izzo #66			
7/8	Indianapolis Raceway Park	USAC Silver Crown	Seymour #29	Cicconi/Schrader	Q-2nd, 1st F-2nd, 2nd F-1st	Winners were Bob Cicconi and Schrader
7/9	Sanair International Speedway	DIRT Modified	Billy Decker #91	Ken Schrader	H-1st; F-1st	
7/10	Slinger Speedway	Late Model	Schrader #52			Slinger Nationals
7/11	Slinger Speedway	Late Model	Schrader #52			Slinger Nationals
7/12	Viking Speedway	NASCAR Late Model	Schrader-King #52			Busch Dirt Tour
7/13	Macon Speedway	UMP Late Model	Schrader-King #52			
7/21	Albany-Saratoga Speedway	DIRT Modified				
7/22	Flemington Speedway	Late Model	#25 late model	Jimmy Horton	F-1st	
7/23	Pocono Raceway	NASCAR WC	Hendrick #25	Bill Elliott	F-5th	
7/23	Hagerstown Speedway	Late Model				
7/30	Talladega Superspeedway	NASCAR WC	Hendrick #25	Terry Labonte		
8/1	Tri-City Speedway	UMP Late Model	Schrader-King #52			Bruce Pathrum show

Date	Track	Type	Car Owner	Race Winner	Finish	Comments
8/5	Indianapolis Raceway Park	NASCAR BGN	Schrader #52	Geoff Bodine	F-5th	Broke brake line and crashed
8/6	Thompson International Speedway	DIRT Modified	Billy Decker #91			
8/9	Thompson International Speedway	NASCAR North	Schrader #52			
8/10	Lebanon Valley Speedway	DIRT Modified	Billy Decker #91			
8/13	Watkins Glen International	NASCAR WC	Hendrick #25	Rusty Wallace	F-1st	
8/15	Hawkeye Downs Speedway	IMCA Modified		Ken Schrader	F-1st	
8/15	Hawkeye Downs Speedway	IMCA Late Model		Ken Schrader		
8/20	Michigan International Speedway	NASCAR WC	Hendrick #25	Rusty Wallace		
8/20	Tri-State Speedway	UMP Late Model	Schrader-King #52		F-3rd	
8/24	Watertown, NY					
8/26	Bristol Motor Speedway	NASCAR WC	Hendrick #25	Darrell Waltrip	F-13th	Crashed all day long
8/27	Cayuga Speedway	DIRT Modified	Billy Decker #91	Danny Johnson		
9/2	Darlington Raceway	NASCAR BGN	Schrader #52	Dale Earnhardt, Sr.		
9/3	Darlington Raceway	NASCAR WC	Hendrick #25			Brake problems
9/5	Minnesota State Fairgrounds	ASA Late Model	Schrader #52	Rusty Wallace		
9/10	Richmond International Raceway	NASCAR WC	Hendrick #25	Darrell Waltrip		
9/16	Dover International Speedway	NASCAR BGN	Schrader #52			
9/24	Martinsville Speedway	NASCAR WC	Hendrick #25			
10/7	Charlotte Motor Speedway	NASCAR BGN	Schrader #52	Ken Schrader	Q-2nd; F-1st	
10/8	Charlotte Motor Speedway	NASCAR WC	Hendrick #25	Geoff Bodine		
10/15	North Wilkesboro Speedway	NASCAR WC	Hendrick #25			
10/21	North Carolina Motor Speedway	NASCAR BGN	Schrader #52	Mark Martin		
10/22	North Carolina Motor Speedway	NASCAR WC	Hendrick #52			
10/27	Devil's Bowl Speedway	NCRA Late Model	Schrader-King #52	Dick Trickle		
10/28	Devil's Bowl Speedway	NCRA Late Model	Schrader-King #52	Bill Elliott		
11/4	Phoenix International Raceway	NASCAR SW	Schrader #52	Dale Earnhardt, Sr.		ASA car
11/5	Phoenix International Raceway	NASCAR WC	Hendrick #25			
11/19	Atlanta Motor Speedway	NASCAR WC	Hendrick #25			

1990

Date	Track	Type	Car Owner	Race Winner	Finish	Comments
1/11	Tulsa Expo Raceway (indoor)	Midget	Terry Caves #2	John Heydenreich	S-1st; f-5th	Chili Bowl; team car to Steve Kinser
1/13	Tulsa Expo Raceway (indoor)	Midget	Caves #2	John Heydenreich	F-9th	Chili Bowl; started 9th by Thursday race
1/20	Hoosierdome (indoor)	USAC Midget	Seymour #29	Mike Streicher	H-1st; Qual F-1st, F-24th	Broke in feature; was fast
1/27	Mecca Arena (indoor)	USAC Midget	Seymour #29	Bob Meyers	Q-2nd; F-11th	Ran over Swindell trying for 4th
2/4	Phoenix International Raceway	Champ Dirt	Seymour #29	Ken Schrader	Q-1st; F-1st	Copper World Classic
2/5	Phoenix International Raceway	Late Model	Schrader #52	Bob Hanley	F-29th	Ignition wires burned
2/5	Phoenix International Raceway	Super Mod				Qualified 5th but didn't race it
2/11	Daytona International Speedway	NASCAR WC	Hendrick #25	Ken Schrader	F-1st	Bud Shoot-out; started 3rd
2/15	Daytona International Speedway	NASCAR WC	Hendrick #25	Geoff Bodine	F-7th	Twin 125; spun last lap racing for 3rd
2/17	Daytona International Speedway	NASCAR BGN	Schrader #52	Dale Earnhardt, Sr.	Q-20th	Got in #23 car; crash running 10th about 20th lap
2/18	Daytona International Speedway	NASCAR WC	Hendrick #25	Derrick Cope	Q-1st	Had to start back-up car; was super fast; came to 2nd in 25 laps but then broke piston
2/25	Richmond International Raceway	NASCAR WC	Hendrick #25	Mark Martin	Q-13th; F-10th	First Winston Cup short track race finished on lead lap
3/3	North Carolina Motor Speedway	NASCAR BGN	Schrader #52	Dale Earnhardt, Sr.	Q-6th; F-3rd	Ran 6th-8th all day; but then blew up
3/4	North Carolina Motor Speedway	NASCAR WC	Hendrick #25	Kyle Petty	Q-14th; F-4th	Started last in back-up car
3/18	Atlanta Motor Speedway	NASCAR WC	Hendrick #25	Dale Earnhardt,Sr.	H-2nd; F-5th	Started by points
3/24	Desoto Motor Speedway	Late Model	Tom Stimus #1			Cut tire on last lap

Date	Track	Class	Car	Driver	Result	Notes
3/31	Darlington Raceway	NASCAR BGN	Schrader #52	Harry Gant	F-3rd	Was down on motor but handled good
4/1	Darlington Raceway	NASCAR WC	Hendrick #25	Dale Earnhardt, Sr.	Q-6th; F-10th	Was spun by Ernie Irvan
4/8	Bristol Motor Speedway	NASCAR WC	Hendrick #25	Davey Allison	Q-17th; F-6th	Was survival race!
4/14	Pulaski Co., VA	NASCAR Late Model	#47 late model	Clay Highberger	Q-12th (17.10 sec.); F-2nd	Car was loose all day!
4/22	North Wilkesboro Speedway	NASCAR WC	Hendrick #25	Brett Bodine	Q-6th; F-19th	Midget show
4/27	Pulaski Co, VA	ARCA	Seymour #29	Don Shillings	Q-2nd; H-1st; F-2nd	Car was pretty good all day
4/29	Martinsville Speedway	NASCAR WC	Hendrick #25	Geoff Bodine	Q-6th; F-6th	Broke distributor running top 3 all day!
5/6	Talladega Superspeedway	NASCAR WC	Hendrick #25	Dale Earnhardt, Sr.	Q-2nd; F-28th	Broke roller lifter!
5/12	Nazareth Speedway	NASCAR BGN	Schrader #52	Jimmy Hensley	Q-13th; F-31st	Bruce Pathrum show
5/12	Grandview Speedway	Modified	Modified #611	Kyle Petty	F-5th	Winners were Johnny Rumbley and Tink Reedy
5/13	Lonesome Pine Int'l Raceway	NASCAR Late Model	TC Speedway #84	Rumbley/Reedy	Q-4th; 1st F-3rd; 2nd F-4th	4th fastest but penalized 3 seconds
5/20	Charlotte Motor Speedway	NASCAR WC	Hendrick #25	Dale Earnhardt, Sr.	Q-9th; F-2nd	Running good and knocked off left front fender with Robert Pressley
5/26	Charlotte Motor Speedway	NASCAR BGN	Schrader #52	Dale Jarrett	Q-9th	
5/27	Charlotte Motor Speedway	NASCAR WC	Hendrick #25	Rusty Wallace	Q-1st; F-11th	Was running 2nd with 5 to go and lost cylinder
5/28	Macon Speedway	UMP Late Model	Schrader-King #52	Jim Harter	Q-1st; H-4th; D-2nd; F-5th	Was 6th in Bullitt Dash
6/2	Claremont Speedway	Late Model	#25 Pro Stock		F-5th	Started 12th; got to 6th; spun and back to 5th
6/3	Dover International Speedway	NASCAR WC	Hendrick #25	Derrick Cope	Q-10th; F-2nd	
6/6	Kankakee Speedway	UMP Late Model	Schrader-King #2	Bob Pierce	Q-8th; H-3rd; D-6th; F-4th	Had flat w/7 laps to go running 10th
6/10	Sears Point Raceway	NASCAR WC	Hendrick #25	Rusty Wallace	Q-7th (1:40.85); F-18th	Slinger Nationals qualifying night
6/11	Slinger Speedway	ARTGO Late Model	Doug Lane #25		Q-12th	Slinger Nationals; running 3rd in 1st feature and brakes messed up
6/12	Slinger Speedway	ARTGO Late Model	Lane #25	Joe Shear (both)	Q-8th; D-3rd; 1st F-11th; 2nd F-3rd	
6/13	Tri-City Speedway	UMP Late Model	Schrader-King #52 #3	John Gill	H-3rd; F-5th	
6/16	Five Mile Point Speedway	DIRT Modified			Q-5th; F-2nd	
6/17	Pocono Speedway	NASCAR WC	Hendrick #25	Harry Gant	Q-8th (57.27 sec.); F-15th	Made up 2 laps but wasn't fast enough
6/20	Peach State Motor Speedway	All Pro Late Model	Bobby Ray #90	Jody Ridley	Q-17th; F-19th	Was running 6th halfway and got in big crash
6/21	Macon Speedway	IMCA Modified	Dave Dayton #87	Ed Babb	Q-9th; H-1st; F-2nd	
6/24	Michigan International Speedway	NASCAR WC	Hendrick #25	Dale Earnhardt, Sr.	Q-7th	Ran good all day and blew up at the end
6/29	Interstate 79 Speedway	Late Model			H-1st	Feature rained out
6/30	Indianapolis Raceway park	USAC Silver Crown	Seymour #29	George Snider	Q-11th (21.50 sec.); F-2nd	Wrong tires qualifying; was off a little all night
7/1	Tri-State Speedway	UMP Late Model	Schrader-King #52	Kevin Claycomb	Q-17th; H-4th; S-1st; F-9th	
7/2	Lebanon Valley Speedway	DIRT Modified	Dickie Larkin #99	Brett Hearn	H-1st	
7/7	Daytona International Speedway	NASCAR WC	Hendrick #25	Dale Earnhardt, Sr.	Q-6th; F-3rd	Dropped out of feature with brake problems
7/8	Hagerstown Speedway	ARCA Stock Car	Raullo Bros. #6	Ken Schrader	Q-1st; H-1st; F-1st	
7/9	Slinger Speedway	ARTGO Late Model	Doug Lane #17	Ted Musgrave	Q-12th (12.10 sec.)	Fast time was 11.99 sec.; qualifying night
7/10	Slinger Speedway	ARTGO Late Model	Lane #17		Q-14th; D-1st; F-6th	Raced as promoter's option
7/12	Macon Speedway	UMP Late Model	Schrader-King #52	Scott Bloomquist	Q-17th; H-3rd; S-1st; F-4th	Had flat right rear and lost rear brakes; was two laps down
7/13	Lee USA Speedway	Late Model	#64 Pro Stock	Dale Earnhardt, Sr.	H-4th	Was leading w/5 laps to go and got together with 2nd place
7/14	Beech Ridge Motor Speedway	Midget	Seymour #29	Drew Fornoro	H-4th	Was running 3rd and broke rear end
7/15	New Hampshire Int'l Speedway	NASCAR BGN	Schrader #52	Tommy Ellis	Q-37th	Carburetor flooded over; lost 3 laps; pulled in
7/16	St. Francois Raceway	UMP Late Model	Schrader-King #52	Scott Bloomquist	Q-6th; S-3rd; F-8th	Dropped out of heat; started 20th in feature
7/17	St. Charles Speedway	UMP Late Model	Schrader-King #52	Billy Moyer	Q-4th; D-4th; F-3rd	
7/22	Pocono Raceway	NASCAR WC	Hendrick #25	Geoff Bodine	Q-2nd; F-11th	
7/22	Hagerstown Speedway	Late Model	Ernie Davis #25		H-2nd	
7/24	Rockford Speedway	Late Model				Crashed in feature
7/29	Talladega Superspeedway	NASCAR WC	Hendrick #25	Dale Earnhardt, Sr.	Q-26th; F-16th	Match race w/Earnhardt—he won 2 or 3
8/1	Tri-City Speedway	NASCAR Late Model	Schrader-King #52	Ken Schrader	Q-9th; H-1st; F-1st	Busch Tour race on dirt
8/2	Capital Speedway	NASCAR Late Model	Schrader-King #52	Gary Webb	Q-14th; H-3rd; F-17th	Busch Tour; running 5th and broke axle

Date	Track	Type	Car Owner	Race Winner	Finish	Comments
8/3-4	Indianapolis Raceway Park	NASCAR BGN	Schrader #52	Steve Grissom	Q-23rd; B F-7th; A F-27th	Blew head gasket
8/5	Columbus Motor Speedway	NASCAR Late Model				Dropped out with oil leak in rear end
8/10	Black Rock Speedway	Street Stock		Ken Schrader	F-1st	Match race with Ernie Irvan
8/12	Watkins Glen International	NASCAR WC	Hendrick #25	Ricky Rudd	Q-11th; F-9th	Hole in radiator and had to pit unscheduled
8/14	Hawkeye Downs Speedway	Late Model			H-1st	Had flat in feature
8/14	Hawkeye Downs Speedway	IMCA Modified			H-2nd	Broke engine in feature
8/18	Brownstown Speedway	UMP Late Model		Scott Bloomquist		102 cars
8/19	Michigan International Speedway	NASCAR WC	Schrader-King #25	Mark Martin	Q-52nd, H-6th; B F-1st, A F-8th	Qual—bad chassis and motor bad; race—motor blew
8/25	Bristol Motor Speedway	NASCAR WC	Hendrick #25	Ernie Irvan	Q-35th; F-40th	Brake and chassis problems
8/26	Cayuga Speedway	CASCAR			Q-19th; F-12th	Limited late model; started 17th (no qual.); had flat tire in feature
8/31	Summerville Speedway	NASCAR BGN	Schrader #52	Rodney Combs		Bruce Pathrum show; broken ignition
9/1	Darlington Raceway	NASCAR BGN	Schrader #52	Dale Jarrett	Q-9th	Broke water temp gauge and pulled in thinking it was motor problems
9/2	Darlington Raceway	NASCAR WC	Hendrick #25	Dale Earnhardt, Sr.	Q-21s; F-39th	Crashed twice
9/8	Orange County Speedway	Late Model	Bill Meyer #91			Match race with Rick Hendrick!
9/9	Richmond International Raceway	NASCAR BGN	Schrader #52	Dale Earnhardt, Sr.	Q-3rd; F-10th	Crashed off turn 4; scraped right side of car
9/15	Dover International Speedway	NASCAR WC	Hendrick #25	Harry Gant	Q-23rd; F-10th	Led more laps than anyone but crashed hard with Ricky Rudd
9/16	Dover International Speedway	NASCAR WC	Hendrick #25	Bill Elliott	Q-4th; F-27th	
9/23	Martinsville Speedway	NASCAR WC	Hendrick #25	Geoff Bodine	Q-19th; F-5th	
9/30	North Wilkesboro Speedway	NASCAR WC	Hendrick #25	Mark Martin	F-10th	Car was good; best run ever at Wilkesboro
10/6	Charlotte Motor Speedway	NASCAR BGN	Schrader #52	Sterling Marlin	Q-4th; F-35th	Lined up by points so ran qual. race
10/7	Charlotte Motor Speedway	NASCAR WC	Hendrick #25	Davey Allison	F-11th	Ran 2nd half of race and engine laid down
10/13	Orlando Speed World	Big Truck Race				Match race with Harry Gant
10/20	North Carolina Motor Speedway	NASCAR BGN	Schrader #52	Steve Grissom	Q-1st; F-5th	Was too tight all day!
10/21	North Carolina Motor Speedway	NASCAR WC	Hendrick #25	Alan Kulwicki	Q-8th; H-4th; F-7th	Running 4th on last lap and pitting thinking there was one lap to go
10/25	Cajon Speedway	IMCA Modified			Q-14th	
11/2	Tucson Raceway Park	Late Model			Q-2nd; F-2nd	Match races with Earnhardt and M. Waltrip
11/2	Phoenix International Raceway	NASCAR SW		Dick Trickle	F-11th	
11/4	Phoenix International Raceway	NASCAR WC	Hendrick #25	Dale Earnhardt, Sr.	Q-6th; F-2nd	Blew engine
11/18	Atlanta Motor Speedway	NASCAR WC	Hendrick #25	Morgan Shepherd	Q-9th; H-2nd; F-4th	
12/2	Melbourne, Australia	Stock Car	Robin Best #22	Terry Labonte		Drove Thunderbird
12/22	Charlotte Coliseum (indoor)	USAC Midget	Seymour #29	Jim Hettinger		

1991

Date	Track	Type	Car Owner	Race Winner	Finish	Comments
1/5-6	Volusia County Speedway	Late Model	Robert Hanke #74	Ken Schrader	Q-7th (16.62 sec.); F-1st	Tight all day; freed w/5 laps to go & took off
1/11	Tulsa Expo Raceway (indoor)	Midget	Terry Caves #2	Sammy Swindell	H-4th; B F-3rd; A F-18th	Chili Bowl; crash in feature
1/12	Tulsa Expo Raceway (indoor)	Midget	Caves #2	Leland McSpadden	B F-6th	Chili Bowl
1/19	Hoosierdome (indoor)	USAC Midget	Seymour #29	Ted Hines	H-1st; Team F-1st; F-2nd	Raced with Jeff Gordon all day; finally got lead and Hines passed us all w/7 laps to go
2/1-3	Phoenix International Raceway	Late Model	Hanke #74	Junior Hanley	Q-1st; F-3rd	Copper Classic; late model was loose
2/1-3	Phoenix International Raceway	Silver Crown	Seymour #29	Jeff Gordon	Q-2nd	Was off on tires and car started missing
2/10	Daytona International Speedway	NASCAR WC	Hendrick #25	Dale Earnhardt, Sr.	1st 10 lap-3rd, 2nd 10 lap-12th	Busch Clash; crashed in second half
2/14	Daytona International Speedway	NASCAR WC	Hendrick #25	Dale Earnhardt, Sr.	F-12th	Twin 125; started 16th; bad push
2/16	Daytona International Speedway	NASCAR BGN	Schrader #15	Dale Earnhardt, Sr.	Q-4th; F-4th	

Date	Track	Class	Car	Driver	Results	Notes
2/17	Daytona International Speedway	NASCAR WC	Hendrick #25	Ernie Irvan	F-31st	500; hit windshield and tore up front end
2/24	Richmond International Raceway	NASCAR WC	Hendrick #25	Dale Earnhardt, Sr.	Q-5th; F-10th	Too tight to start; then was better
3/3	North Carolina Motor Speedway	NASCAR WC	Hendrick #25	Kyle Petty	Q-2nd; F-2nd	Leading w/11 to go and got yellow we didn't need
3/18	Atlanta Motor Speedway	NASCAR WC	Hendrick #25	Ken Schrader	Q-5th; F-1st	Blew engine running 5th
3/24	Volusia County Speedway	NASCAR BGN	Schrader #15	Kenny Wallace	Q-25th; F-25th	Blew engine in last practice
3/30-31	Hickory Motor Speedway	NASCAR BGN	Schrader #15	Butch Miller	Q-3rd; F-4th	Ran into fence all by myself and lost some laps
4/7	Darlington Raceway	NASCAR WC	Hendrick #25	Ricky Rudd	Q-4th; F-19th	
4/14	Bristol Motor Speedway	NASCAR WC	Hendrick #25	Rusty Wallace	Q-14th; F-29th	Crashed all day!
4/21	North Wilkesboro Speedway	NASCAR WC	Hendrick #25	Darrell Waltrip	Q-9th; F-5th	Was good
4/28	Martinsville Speedway	NASCAR WC	Hendrick #25	Dale Earnhardt, Sr.	Q-3rd; F-23rd	Mark Martin knocked off my front end
5/6	Talladega Superspeedway	NASCAR WC	Hendrick #25	Harry Gant	Q-18th; F-7th	Wasn't bad; just not good enough
5/10	Motordrome 70 Speedway	NASCAR Late Model	Local stock car	Steve Pales	H-5th; F-8th	
5/11	Nazareth Speedway	NASCAR BGN	Schrader #15	Chuck Bown	Q-7th (28.85 sec.); F-31st	Started leaking oil; black-flagged
5/19	Lowe's Motor Speedway	NASCAR WC	Hendrick #25	Davey Allison	F2nd	The Winston
5/26	Lowe's Motor Speedway	NASCAR BGN	Schrader #15	Dale Earnhardt, Sr.	Q-33rd; B F-1st	Broke rocker arm running 5th
5/25	Hickory Motor Speedway	Big Truck		Ernie Irvan	F-2nd	Match race with Ernie & Tracy Leslie
5/26	Lowe's Motor Speedway	NASCAR WC	Hendrick #25	Davey Allison	Q-3rd; F-2nd	Coca-Cola 600
5/27	Macon Speedway	UMP Late Model	Schrader-King #25	Dick Taylor	Q-12th	
6/2	Dover International Speedway	NASCAR WC	Hendrick #25	Ken Schrader	Q-19th; F-1st	Led last 67 laps
6/9	Sears Point Raceway	NASCAR WC	Hendrick #25	Davey Allison	Q-6th; F-5th	Slinger Nationals; crashed 1st lap of 1st feature; had flat running 8th in 2nd
6/10	Slinger Super Speedway	ARTGO Late Model	Doug Lane #25	Morgan; Miller	D-3rd	Broke rocker arm 4 laps to go, running 4th
6/16	Pocono Raceway	NASCAR WC	Hendrick #25	Darrell Waltrip	Q-7th; F-7th	Running good and front lower tray blew off and car wouldn't turn
6/20	Macon Speedway	IMCA Modified	Dave Dayton #87		Q-1st; F-3rd	Crashed car in practice; borrowed Ray DeWitt's car; had to run semi
6/23	Michigan International Speedway	NASCAR WC	Hendrick #25	Davey Allison	Q-8th; F-6th	Busch All-Stars
6/28	Interstate 79 Speedway	ASA Late Model	House car		H-2nd; F-3rd	
6/29	Fairgrounds Speedway		Schrader #52		Q-25th; B F-3rd	
6/29	Tri-City Speedway	NASCAR Late Model	Schrader-King #25	Ken Schrader	Q-4th; H-5th; F-1st	Qualified terrible; crashed in heat
6/30	Fairgrounds Speedway	ASA Late Model	Ray DeWitt	Darrell Waltrip	F-10th	Rained out after 60 laps
6/30	Tri-State Speedway	UMP Late Model	Schrader-King #52	Ken Schrader	Q-14th; H-5th; S-1st; Spec-1st; F-1st	Slinger Nationals; finished rest of 250 lap race on lead lap
7/6	Daytona International Speedway	NASCAR WC	Hendrick #25	Bill Elliott	Q-22nd; F-4th	
7/7		CASCAR			Q-13th; F-13th	
7/8	Slinger Super Speedway	Late Model	Lane #25			Herald & Review 100: rained out after 39 laps; didn't go back to finish
7/9	Slinger Super Speedway	Late Model	Lane #25	Joe Shear	F-7th	Had to go to back after bumped by Larry Phillips
7/10	Slinger Super Speedway	ARTGO Late Model	Lane #25		Q-17th	Qualifying only
7/11	Macon Speedway	UMP Late Model	Schrader-King #25	Kevin Weaver	Q-6th; H-2nd; F-8th	Started 17th by promoter and was up to 10th when blew right front tire
7/12	Lakeside Speedway	ARTGO Late Model	Lane #25	Steve Carlson	Q-15th; H-1st; F-8th	Clutch and brake problems
7/13	Milwaukee Mile	ASA Late Model	Schrader #52			Summernationals
7/13	Lebanon I-44 Speedway	ARTGO Late Model	Lane #25	Tom Harrington	Q-17th	Summernationals
7/14	Milwaukee Mile	ASA Late Model	Schrader #52	Bob Senneker	F-13th	Summernationals; pulled out of feature
7/14	Vermilion County Speedway	UMP Late Model	Schrader-King #25	Scott Bloomquist	Q-10th; H-2nd; F-14th	
7/15	I-55 Raceway	UMP Late Model	Schrader-King #25	Billy Moyer	Q-21st; H-4th; F-7th	
7/16	St. Francois Raceway	UMP Late Model	Schrader-King #25	Kevin Weaver	Q-13th; H-4th; S-1st; F-16th	

Date	Track	Type	Car Owner	Race Winner	Finish	Comments
7/20	Flemington Speedway	NASCAR BGN	Schrader #15	Ricky Craven	Q-4th	Running 2nd on lap 140 and broke rear end
7/21	Pocono Raceway	NASCAR WC	Hendrick #25	Rusty Wallace	Q-2nd; F-23rd	Was super fast and got in crash
7/28	Talladega Superspeedway	NASCAR WC	Hendrick #25	Dale Earnhardt, Sr.	Q-25th; F-40th	Broke camshaft
7/31	Tri-City Speedway	MLRA Late Model	Schrader-King #25	Ken Schrader	F-1st	Broke spur gears in heat; pulled out of feature; (wasn't working)
8/2	Belle-Clair Speedway	AARA Modified	David Jumper	Ed Dixon		
8/4	Heartland Park	ARCA Stock	Schrader #58	Ken Schrader	Q-1st; F-1st	Started 20th
8/10	Seekonk Speedway	Pro Stock	Vinne's #11	Ken Schrader	H-3rd; F-1st	Was leading and broke cam
8/11	Watkins Glen International	NASCAR WC	Hendrick #25	Ernie Irvan	Q-6th; F-30th	Had to hold car in gear for whole feature
8/13	Hawkeye Downs Speedway	IMCA Modified	Bob Harris	Ken Schrader	Q-2nd; h-4th; F-1st	Big truck match race with Ernie Irvan and Tracy Leslie
8/14	Lee County Speedway	IMCA Late Model	Wayne Hennies	Johnny Johnson	H-3rd; F-4th	Hit wall by myself & lost 2 laps; got one back
8/17	Rolling Wheels Speedway	GATR		Ken Schrader	F-1st	
8/18	Michigan International Speedway	NASCAR WC	Hendrick #25	Dale Jarrett	Q-18th; F-10th	
8/21	Kankakee Speedway	UMP Late Model	Schrader-King #25	Kevin Weaver	Q-7th; H-7th; F-7th	
8/24	Bristol Motor Speedway	NASCAR WC	Hendrick #25	Alan Kulwicki	Q-27th; F-3rd	Match race; lost by six inches
8/31	Darlington Raceway	NASCAR BGN	Schrader #15	Dale Earnhardt, Sr.	Q-12th; F-10th	
8/31	New Smyrna Speedway	Super 8		Harry Gant		
9/1	Darlington Raceway	NASCAR WC	Hendrick #25	Harry Gant	Q-9th; F-3rd	
9/7	Richmond International Raceway	NASCAR WC	Hendrick #25	Harry Gant	Q-10th; F-8th	Big crash early involving 16 cars
9/14	Dover International Speedway	NASCAR BGN	Darrell Waltrip #17	Harry Gant	Q-7th; F-5th	Was too tight all day
9/15	Dover International Speedway	NASCAR WC	Hendrick #25	Harry Gant	Q-6th; F-33rd	Match race; won 2 of 3
9/22	Martinsville Speedway	NASCAR WC	Hendrick #25	Harry Gant	Q-9th; F-9th	
9/28	Lanier Speedway	Late Model	Debbie Lunsford	M. Waltrip/Schrader		
9/29	North Wilkesboro Speedway	NASCAR WC	Hendrick #25	Dale Earnhardt, Sr..	Q-10th; F-8th	Match race with Ernie Irvan; Buddy Baker; Dale Jarrett
10/5	Lowe's Motor Speedway	NASCAR BGN	Schrader #15	Harry Gant	F-2nd	Broke engine early running 4th
10/5	Carolina Speedway	Late Model		Irvan/Schrader		Had clutch problems
10/6	Lowe's Motor Speedway	NASCAR WC	Hendrick #25	Geoff Bodine	Q-5th; F-38th	
10/13	New Hampshire Int'l Speedway	NASCAR WC	Hendrick #25	Ricky Craven	Q-23rd; F-4th	
10/19	North Carolina Motor Speedway	NASCAR BGN	Schrader #15	Ernie Irvan	Q-5th; F-14th	Running 2nd and leader had flat w/4 to go
10/20	North Carolina Motor Speedway	NASCAR WC	Hendrick #25	Davey Allison	F-5th	
10/25	Devil's Bowl Speedway	SUPR	Schrader-King #25	Ken Schrader	H-1st; F-1st	Was junk all day!
11/2	Phoenix International Raceway	NASCAR SW	Schrader #3	Ron Hornaday	Q-1st; F-3rd	Major crash; blew right front tire
11/3	Phoenix International Raceway	NASCAR WC	Hendrick #25	Davey Allison	Q-6th; F-17th	
11/17	Atlanta Motor Speedway	NASCAR WC	Hendrick #25	Mark Martin	Q-13th	
11/23-24		Late Model	Schrader-King #24	Mike Head	Q-20th; H-5th; F-6th	

1992

Date	Track	Type	Car Owner	Race Winner	Finish	Comments
1/4	Indoor Arena	Midget	Lou Cicconi #57 TQ	Ken Schrader	Q-13th; H-3rd	Blew engine in feature
1/10	Tulsa Expo Raceway (indoor)	Midget	Wilke Racers #1	Ken Schrader	H-1st; F-1st	Chili Bowl
1/11	Tulsa Expo Raceway (indoor)	Midget	Wilke Racers #1	Sammy Swindell	D-6th; A F-7th	Chili Bowl; spun on first lap with Sammy
1/25	Hoosierdome (indoor)	Midget	Seymour #29 & #4	Russ Gamester	H-4th; F-24th	Crashed running 3rd in team feature; lost wheel in A feature
2/2	Phoenix International Raceway	NASCAR SW	Schrader #25	Toby Butler	Q-2nd (28.56 sec.); F-13th	Copper Classic; car pushed all day; got caught up in a couple of wrecks
2/13	Daytona International Speedway	NASCAR WC	Hendrick #25	Dale Earnhardt, Sr.	Q-35th; F-7th	Twin 125s
2/15	Daytona International Speedway	NASCAR BGN	Schrader #15	Dale Earnhardt, Sr.	Q-11th; F-9th	

Date	Track	Series	Team	Result	Winner	Notes
2/16	Daytona International Speedway	NASCAR WC	Hendrick #25	F-37th	Davey Allison	Started 15th; big wreck back straight
3/1	North Carolina Motor Speedway	NASCAR WC	Hendrick #25	Q-9th (24.97 sec.); F-5th	Bill Elliott	Car was a little tight on entrance all day
3/8	Richmond International Raceway	NASCAR WC	Hendrick #25	Q-13th; F-14th	Bill Elliott	Missed on chassis
3/14	Atlanta Motor Speedway	NASCAR BGN	Schrader #15	Q-9th; F-18th	Jeff Gordon	Handled terrible!
3/14	Atlanta Motor Speedway	NASCAR WC	Hendrick #25	Q-5th; F-41st	Bill Elliott	Broke fan blade and cut tire; crashed
3/29	Darlington Raceway	NASCAR WC	Hendrick #25	Q-15th; F-12th	Bill Elliott	Car missed all day
4/4	Bristol Motor Speedway	NASCAR BGN	Ernie Irvan #4	Q-8th; F-3rd	Harry Gant	
4/5	Bristol Motor Speedway	NASCAR WC	Hendrick #25		Alan Kulwicki	Car was vibrating so I pulled in
4/10	Crossville Raceway	Late Model				Won 2 of 3 match races with M. Waltrip
4/12	North Wilkesboro Speedway	NASCAR WC	Hendrick #25	Q-18th; F-22nd	Davey Allison	Lost one lap w/brake problems in pits; then just didn't handle good
4/17	Batesville Speedway	Late Model	Larry Shaw		Billy Moyer	Cut tire in heat; blew up in feature
4/26	Martinsville Speedway	NASCAR WC	Hendrick #25	Q-18th; F-7th	Mark Martin	Broke rocker arm on lap 350
5/1	Golden Isle Speedway	Late Model				Pathrum show; won 2 of 3 w/Marlin
5/2	Lanier Speedway	Late Model				Earnhardt won 2 of 3 match races
5/3	Talladega Superspeedway	NASCAR WC	Hendrick #25	Q-35th; F-23rd	Davey Allison	Ran terrible all weekend
5/9	Nazareth Speedway	NASCAR BGN	Schrader #15	Q-32nd; F-20th	Todd Bodine	Line up by points & entries; split rear end cooler and lost rear gear; should of run 9th
5/10	Milwaukee Mile	ASA Late Model		34th		ASA started us 21st (wasn't there to qual); Harold Fair spun and I hit him
5/16	Lowe's Motor Speedway	NASCAR WC	Hendrick #25	Q-4th; F-3rd	Davey Allison	The Winston
5/25	Macon Speedway	UMP Late Model	Schrader-King #25	Q-12th; F-8th		Was loose
5/31	Dover International Speedway	NASCAR WC	Hendrick #25	Q-6th; F-23rd	Harry Gant	Was too tight; blew right front tire and spent time in pits fixing car
6/6	Sears Point Raceway	NASCAR SW	Dirk Stevens #3	Q-9th; F-15th	Jon Paques	Lost 2 laps in pits changing rear shocks
6/7	Sears Point Raceway	NASCAR WC	Hendrick #25	Q-13th; F-9th	Ernie Irvan	Was too tight on exit
6/14	Pocono Raceway	NASCAR WC	Hendrick #25	Q-1st; F-4th	Alan Kulwicki	Car pushed off of 2 all day
6/21	Michigan International Speedway	NASCAR WC	Hendrick #25	Q-10th; F-13th	Davey Allison	
6/21	Tri-State Speedway	UMP Late Model	Schrader-King #52	H-3rd; F-5th		
7/4	Daytona International Speedway	NASCAR WC	Hendrick #25	Q-11th; F-6th	Ernie Irvan	
7/22	LaSalle Speedway	UMP Late Model	Schrader-King #52	H-5th; F-8th		Heat—crashed; went brain dead
7/25	Talladega Superspeedway	NASCAR BGN	Schrader #15	Q-18th; F-8th	Ernie Irvan	
7/26	Talladega Superspeedway	NASCAR WC	Hendrick #25	Q-26th; F-9th	Ernie Irvan	
7/29	Beatrice Speedway	IMCA Modified	Bob Harris	H-1st; F-2nd		
7/31	24 Raceway Park	NASCAR Late Model	Schrader-King #52	F-3rd		
8/1	Colorado National Speedway	Late Model	Marshall Cresrown	Q-12th; H-4th; F-3rd		
8/2	Heartland Park	ARCA Stock	Schrader #58	Q-1st; F-29th	Darrell Waltrip	Had brake problems then broke tranny
8/9	Watkins Glen International	NASCAR WC	Hendrick #25	Q-13th; F-21st	Kyle Petty	No brakes all day; was cut short by rain
8/11	Benton County Speedway	IMCA Modified	Bob Harris #25	H-1st		Dropped leading (wiring burnt up)
8/12	Echo Valley Speedway	IMCA Modified	Bob Harris #25	H-1st; F-3rd		Leading & lost left rear wheel; went to back with 13 laps to go
8/13	Dubuque Fairgrounds	IMCA Modified	Harris #25	H-3rd; F-6th		
8/15	Michigan International Speedway	NASCAR BGN	Schrader #15	Q-11th; F-9th	Todd Bodine	
8/16	Michigan International Speedway	NASCAR WC	Hendrick #25	Q-4th; F-11th	Harry Gant	Wrong on fuel mileage
8/23	New Hampshire Int'l Speedway	NASCAR BGN	Schrader #15	Q-32nd; S-2nd; F-5th	Joe Nemechek	
8/29	Bristol Motor Speedway	NASCAR WC	Hendrick #25	Q-6th; F-3rd	Darrell Waltrip	Started 40th; car was too tight to qualify; good to race after a lot of changes
8/30	Cayuga Speedway	ACT	Jerry Gunderman #53	S-3rd; F-2nd	Junior Hanley	Start in back; 2-day show and was only there on Sunday
9/6	Darlington Raceway	NASCAR WC	Hendrick #25	Q-3rd; F-13th	Darrell Waltrip	Rain caught us on a pit stop

Date	Track	Type	Car Owner	Race Winner	Finish	Comments
9/12	Richmond International Raceway	NASCAR WC	Hendrick #25	Rusty Wallace	Q-10th; F-9th	
9/13	I-70 Speedway	NASCAR Late Model	Larry Phillips #75			All-American race; spun out; crash in feature when left front suspension broke
9/20	Dover International Speedway	NASCAR WC	Hendrick #25	Ricky Rudd	Q-9th; F-30th	Car missed all day
9/28	Martinsville Speedway	NASCAR WC	Hendrick #25	Geoff Bodine	Q-28th; F-13th	Should have run 2nd; pit penalty
10/5	North Carolina Motor Speedway	NASCAR WC	Hendrick #25	Geoff Bodine	Q-18th; F-23rd	Car got tight
10/10	Lowe's Motor Speedway	NASCAR BGN	Schrader #15	Jeff Gordon	Q-4th; F-5th	Running 4th & got hot; pulled out
10/11	Lowe's Motor Speedway	NASCAR WC	Hendrick #25	Alan Kulwicki	Q-2nd; F-7th	
10/16-18	Indiana State Fairgrounds	Late Model	Schrader-King #52	Ken Schrader	Q-23rd; H-1st; F-15th	
10/16-18	Indiana State Fairgrounds	Modified	Bob Harris	Mark Martin	Q-1st; F-1st	
10/24	Rockingham Motor Speedway	NASCAR BGN	Schrader #15	Kyle Petty	F-9th	Broke rear drive plate and pulled out
10/25	Rockingham Motor Speedway	NASCAR WC	Hendrick #25	Ken Schrader	F-1st	
10/31	Phoenix International Raceway	NASCAR SW	Schrader #3	Davey Allison	F-6th	
11/1	Phoenix International Raceway	NASCAR WC	Hendrick #25	Bill Elliott	Q-22nd; F-36th	Crashed on lap 94
11/15	Atlanta Motor Speedway	NASCAR WC	Hendrick #25	Gary St. Amant	Q-23rd (17.59 sec.); F-4th	
12/6	Five Flags Speedway	All Pro Late Model	Schrader #3			

1993

Date	Track	Type	Car Owner	Race Winner	Finish	Comments
1/3	Manzanita Speedway	Midget	Jack Yeley	Page Jones	H-4th; F-10th	Ran ½-mile track
1/8	Tulsa Expo Raceway (indoor)	Midget	Wilke #11	Ken Schrader	H-1st; F-1st	Chili Bowl
1/9	Tulsa Expo Raceway (indoor)	Midget	Wilke #11	Dave Blaney	A F-21st	Chili Bowl; running 2nd broke fuel pump belt and dropped out
1/16	Toronto Skydome (indoor)	USAC Midget	Seymour #29	Kenny Irwin, Jr.	Q-6th; H-3rd; F-3rd	Got docked 1 lap in Team Feature
1/30	Hoosierdome (indoor)	USAC Midget	Seymour #29	Kenneth Hickas	H-3rd; Team F-12th; A F-7th	
2/7	Daytona International Speedway	NASCAR WC	Hendrick #25	Dale Earnhardt, Sr.	1st F-10th; 2nd F-2nd	Busch Clash
2/11	Daytona International Speedway	NASCAR WC	Hendrick #25	Jeff Gordon	F-4th	Twin 125
2/13	Daytona International Speedway	NASCAR BGN	Schrader #52	Dale Earnhardt, Sr.	Q-1st; F-2nd	
2/14	Daytona International Speedway	NASCAR WC	Hendrick #25	Dale Jarrett	Q-7th; F-8th	Daytona 500
2/28	North Carolina Motor Speedway	NASCAR WC	Hendrick #25	Rusty Wallace	Q-13th; F-24th	Got tangled up w/lapped car!
3/7	Richmond International Raceway	NASCAR WC	Hendrick #25	Davey Allison	Q-1st; F-20th	Car was shit!
3/20	Atlanta Motor Speedway	NASCAR WC	Hendrick #25	Morgan Shepherd	Q-10th; F-29th	Car ran good and broke rocker cover studs; lost lots of laps
3/21	Texas World Speedway	ARCA Stock Car	Schrader #52	Darrell Waltrip	Q-3rd; F-2nd	J. Hensley qual car; also WW sanction
3/28	Darlington Raceway	NASCAR WC	Hendrick #25	Dale Earnhardt, Sr.	F-4th	Qual rained out; lined up by points
4/4	Bristol Motor Speedway	NASCAR WC	Hendrick #25	Rusty Wallace	Q-7th; F-34th	Hillin spun and we got caught in crash
4/9	State Fair Speedway	IMCA Modified	Bob Harris		H-4th; F-4th	Spun running in 2nd with 3 laps to go
4/10	I-44 Speedway	Late Model	Steve Shive	Rick Wilson	Q-3rd; F-3rd	Bruce Pathrum show
4/11	I-70 Speedway	Late Model	Schrader #52	Mike Eddy	Q-11th; F-3rd	
4/18	North Wilkesboro Speedway	NASCAR WC	Hendrick #25	Rusty Wallace	Q-4th; F-3rd	
4/25	Martinsville Speedway	NASCAR WC	Hendrick #25	Rusty Wallace	Q-13th; F-18th	Running 8th w/8 laps to go and broke rear end!
5/2	Talladega Superspeedway	NASCAR WC	Hendrick #25	Ernie Irvan	Q-8th; F-21st	Running 6th w/20 laps to go and burnt pistons
5/7	Motordrome 70 Speedway	Late Model	Bobby Henry #25	Charlie Cragen	Q-6th; H-2nd; F-5th	
5/9	Milwaukee Mile	ASA Late Model	Schrader #52	Joe Shear	Q-9th; F-11th	Just didn't handle
5/9	Millstream Speedway	UMP Modified	Bob Harris #25	Ken Schrader	F-1st	Started last in feature; also won match race with Jack Hewitt
5/15	Sears Point Raceway	NASCAR SW	Schrader #52	Ron Hornaday, Jr.	Q-3rd; F-3rd	
5/16	Sears Point Raceway	NASCAR WC	Hendrick #25	Geoff Bodine	Q-8th; F-4th	
5/22	Lowe's Motor Speedway	NASCAR WC	Hendrick #25	Martin/Earnhardt	Q-24th for Open; F-2nd; F-4th	The Winston and The Winston Open

Date	Track	Series	Car	Driver	Results	Notes
5/23	Cayuga Speedway	CASCAR	Boomer Borschke	Duke Sawchuk	Q-4th; H-3rd; F-30th	Dropped out of feature
5/29	Lowe's Motor Speedway	NASCAR BGN	Schrader #52	Michael Waltrip	Q-3rd; F-4th	
5/30	Lowe's Motor Speedway	NASCAR WC	Hendrick #25	Dale Earnhardt, Sr.	Q-1st; F-4th	Broke brake line
5/31	Macon Speedway	UMP Late Model	Schrader-King #52	Buffy Clark	Q-2nd; H-3rd; D-5th; F-15th	Blew engine
6/5	Dover International Speedway	NASCAR BGN	Schrader #52	Todd Bodine	Q-5th; F-32nd	
6/6	Dover International Speedway	NASCAR WC	Hendrick #25	Dale Earnhardt, Sr.	Q-12th; F-5th	Dropped out of both features
6/9	Slinger Super Speedway	Late Model	Rick Scalzo #91	Miller/Musgrave	Q-17th; 1st F-20th, 2nd F-14th	
6/13	Pocono Raceway	NASCAR WC	Hendrick #25	Kyle Petty	Q-1st (55.27 sec.); F-2nd	
6/16	Hamilton County Speedway	IMCA Modified	Bob Harris	Bob Harris	H-3rd; F-4th	Spark plug failed & cost top 5 finish
6/17	Lee County Speedway	IMCA Modified	Bob Harris	Bob Harris	H-3rd; F-1st	Got there late and started last
6/20	Michigan International Speedway	NASCAR WC	Hendrick #25	Ken Schrader	Q-4th; F-16th	
6/20	Tri-State Speedway	UMP Late Model	Schrader-King #52	Ricky Rudd	F-6th	Busch Tour; got there in time to start last in heat; started feature 20th
6/23	Tri-City Speedway	NASCAR Late Model	Schrader-King #52	Doug McKennon	H-8th; F-12th	Match race w/Dirk Stevens & local guys
6/24	South Sound Speedway	NASCAR NW	Ron Eaton	Joe Kosiski	F-1st	
6/24	Evergreen Speedway	NASCAR NW	Schrader #25	Ken Schrader	Q-4th; F-1st	
6/27	Evergreen Speedway	NASCAR NW	Schrader #25	Ken Schrader	F-7th	Broke running 2nd w/22 laps left
7/3	Daytona International Speedway	NASCAR WC	Hendrick #25	Rick Carelli	Q-41st; F-3rd	
7/4	Portland International Raceway	NASCAR NW	Schrader #25	Dale Earnhardt, Sr.	F-1st	
7/10	New Hampshire Int'l Raceway	NASCAR BGN	Dick McCabe	Ken Schrader	Q-7th; F-4th	
7/11	New Hampshire Int'l Raceway	NASCAR WC	Hendrick #25	Mike McLaughlin	Q-4th; F-38th	Wrecked two times
7/12	Slinger Super Speedway	Late Model	Hendrick #25	Rusty Wallace	F-17th	Slinger Nationals
7/14	Slinger Super Speedway	Late Model	Schrader #52	Joe Shear	Q-1st; F-6th	Slinger Nationals, broke engine
7/18	Pocono Raceway	NASCAR WC	Hendrick #25	Dale Earnhardt, Sr.	Q-13th; F-33rd	
7/20	Peach State Motor Speedway	All Pro Late Model	Schrader #52	Bill Bigley	Q-6th; F-19th	
7/24	Talladega Superspeedway	NASCAR BGN	Hendrick #25	Dale Earnhardt, Sr.	Q-28th; F-32nd	
7/25	Talladega Superspeedway	NASCAR WC	Schrader-King #52	Dale Earnhardt, Sr.		Broke engine with few laps to go
7/26	Highland Speedway	UMP Late Model	Schrader-King #52	Mark Gansman		
7/30	24 Raceway Park	NASCAR Late Model	Schrader-King #52	Rick Carelli	H-4th; F-3rd	
7/31	Raceland Park	Late Model	Schrader-King #52	Scott Hansen	F-6th	Started last; broke running 6th; lap 50
8/1	Heartland Park	ASA Late Model	Schrader #52	Mark Gansman	F-6th	Running 3rd w/10 laps let and lost brakes
8/1	St. Charles Speedway	UMP Late Model	Schrader-King #52	Ken Schrader	H-4th; F-3rd	
8/2	Salem Speedway	Late Model	Jim Cooper	Mark Martin	H-1st; F-1st	
8/3	Watkins Glen International	NASCAR WC	Hendrick #25	Mark Martin	Q-2nd; F-5th	
8/14	Michigan International Speedway	NASCAR BGN	Schrader #52	Mark Martin	Q-13th; F-8th	
8/15	Michigan International Speedway	NASCAR WC	Hendrick #25	Mark Martin	Q-1st; F-27th	Crashed running 5th w/50 laps to go
8/16	Batesville Speedway	IMCA Modified			H-2nd; D-3rd; F-4th	
8/18	Midway Speedway	IMCA Modified			Q-1st; D-6th; F-7th	
8/20	Anderson Speedway	ASA Late Model	Schrader #52	Scott Hansen	Q-14th; F-19th	Broke right rear shock bracket and hit wall running 7th
8/22	Illinois State Fairgrounds	ARCA Stock Car	Rallaou #33	Bob Keselowski	Q-6th; F-35th	Overheated; dropped out
8/24	LaSalle Speedway	UMP Late Model	Schrader-King #52	Ed Dixon	1st F-8th; 2nd F-7th	
8/25	Hawkeye Downs Speedway	IMCA Modified	Bob Harris		H-2nd; F-10th	
8/28	Bristol Motor Speedway	NASCAR WC	Hendrick #25	Mark Martin	Q-26th; F-24th	Dropped out running 3rd
8/29	Illinois State Fairgrounds	UMP Late Model	Schrader-King #52	John Mason	Q-10th; H-2nd; F-3rd	
9/4	Darlington Raceway	NASCAR BGN	Schrader #52	Mark Martin	F-13th	
9/5	Darlington Raceway	NASCAR WC	Hendrick #25	Mark Martin	Q-1st; F-8th	Big crash early; fixed car & just rode around
9/11	Richmond International Raceway	NASCAR WC	Hendrick #25	Rusty Wallace	Q-12th; F-12th	Pitted wrong (was a good car)
9/15	Madison International Speedway	ASA Late Model	Schrader #52	Scott Hansen	F-4th	Robbie Reiser qual. car. ASA started us 21st; was leading and lost brakes
9/19	Dover International Speedway	NASCAR WC	Hendrick #25	Rusty Wallace	Q-10th; F-2nd	

Date	Track	Type	Car Owner	Race Winner	Finish	Comments
9/26	Martinsville Speedway	NASCAR WC	Hendrick #25	Ernie Irvan	Q-12th; F-13th	
10/3	North Wilkesboro Speedway	NASCAR WC	Hendrick #25	Rusty Wallace	F-10th	
10/9	Lowe's Motor Speedway	NASCAR BGN	Schrader #52	Mark Martin	F-20th	
10/10	Lowe's Motor Speedway	NASCAR WC	Hendrick #25	Ernie Irvan	Q-4th; F-9th	
10/16	Lime Rock Park	NASCAR North	Schrader #52	Ken Schrader	Q-2nd; F-1st	Engine ran hot and dropped out
10/23	North Carolina Motor Speedway	NASCAR BGN	Schrader #52	Mark Martin	F-33rd	
10/24	North Carolina Motor Speedway	NASCAR WC	Hendrick #25	Rusty Wallace	Q-2nd; F-8th	
10/30	Phoenix International Raceway	NASCAR SW	Schrader #52	Scott Hansen	F-2nd	Earnhardt parked us on lap 5; fixed car and just rode around
10/31	Phoenix International Raceway	NASCR WC	Hendrick #25	Mark Martin	F-33rd	Qual in March; didn't feel very good from crash in WC Car on Friday
11/4	Atlanta Motor Speedway	NASCAR BGN	Schrader #52	Ward Burton	Q-3rd; F-11th	Wrecked big time first round; was up to 11th by lap 20 and Spencer spun & collected us
11/6	Las Vegas Park				F-5th	Running 7th and got caught in crash
11/14	Atlanta Motor Speedway	NASCAR WC	Hendrick #25	Rusty Wallace	Q-21st	
12/12	Charlotte County Speedway	Late Model	Mike Garvey		-16th	

1994

Date	Track	Type	Car Owner	Race Winner	Finish	Comments
1/1	Canyon Raceway	IMCA Modified	Jim Doffing #40	Andy Hillenburg	H-1st	Rolled tire off wheel leading!
1/2	Canyon Raceway	IMCA Modified	Doffing #40		F-18th	Chili Bowl; got parked running 7th and then spun later
1/8	Tulsa Expo Raceway (indoor)	Midget	Wilke Racing #11			
1/29	Hoosierdome (indoor)	USAC Midget	Schrader #29			
2/13	Daytona International Speedway	NASCAR WC	Hendrick #25	Jeff Gordon	F-6th	Busch Clash
2/17	Daytona International Speedway	NASCAR WC	Hendrick #25		Q-2nd	Twin 125
2/19	Daytona International Speedway	NASCAR BGN	Schrader #52	Dale Earnhardt, Sr.	F-10th	Blew engine running 2nd w/35 laps to go
2/20	Daytona International Speedway	NASCAR WC	Hendrick #25	Sterling Martin	Q-13th; F-9th	Ran out of gas running 8th on last turn
2/27	North Carolina Motor Speedway	NASCAR WC	Hendrick #25	Rusty Wallace	Q-16th; F-11th	Had one set of tires didn't run good on
3/6	Richmond International Speedway	NASCAR WC	Hendrick #25	Ernie Irvan	Q-24th; F-6th	Tires; one set no good
3/13	Atlanta Motor Speedway	NASCAR WC	Hendrick #25	Ernie Irvan		944 Porsche
3/18	Sebring International Raceway	Sports Car				Chevy; 4th in class; 10th overall
3/19	Sebring International Raceway	IMSA Sports Car			Q-31st; F-4th	
3/27	Darlington Raceway	NASCAR WC	Hendrick #25	Dale Earnhardt, Sr.	Q-6th; F-7th	Stop-and-go penalty for speeding on pit road
4/3	Hickory Motor Speedway	NASCAR BGN	Schrader #52	Ricky Craven	F-13th	Running good & had to pit on green for flat RF
4/10	Bristol Motor Speedway	NASCAR WC	Hendrick #25	Dale Earnhardt, Sr.	Q-22nd; F-2nd	
4/17	North Wilkesboro Speedway	NASCAR WC	Hendrick #25	Terry Labonte	Q-9th; F-9th	Had 3 run-ins with Jimmy Spencer
4/24	Martinsville Speedway	NASCAR WC	Hendrick #25	Rusty Wallace	Q-17th; F-31st	Running 9th at lap 150 & had brake seal go bad
5/1	Talladega Superspeedway	NASCAR WC	Hendrick #25	Dale Earnhardt, Sr.	Q-7th; F-5th	
5/6	Motordrome 70 Speedway	NASCAR Late Model	Cragen	Charlie Cragen	F-7th	
5/7	New Hampshire Int'l Speedway	NASCAR BGN	Schrader #52	Derricke Cope	Q-16th; F-3rd	2nd in match race with Jack Hewitt
5/8	Millstream Speedway	UMP Modified	Bob Harris	Ken Schrader	S-2nd; F-1st	Leading feature and was spun out
5/11	Ukiah Speedway	IMCA Modified			Q-15th; H-2nd	
5/14	Sears Point Raceway	NASCAR SW	Schrader #52	Ken Schrader	Q-2nd; F-1st	
5/15	Sears Point Raceway	NASCAR WC	Hendrick #25	Ernie Irvan	Q-8th; F-9th	
5/21	Lowe's Motor Speedway	NASCAR WC	Hendrick #25	Gordon/G. Bodine	Open-3rd; Winston-3rd	Winston Open and The Winston
5/22	Toledo Speedway	ARCA Stock Car	Schrader #52			Broke engine in hot laps

Date	Track	Type	Car Owner	Race Winner	Finish	Comments
5/28	Lowe's Motor Speedway	NASCAR BGN	Schrader #52		Qual F-3rd	Blew engine
5/29	Lowe's Motor Speedway	NASCAR WC	Hendrick #25	Jeff Gordon	Q-4th	Lost 11 laps working on brakes
5/30	I-55 Raceway	UMP Late Model	Schrader #52		H-5th; F-3rd	Started last in feature because of fuel leak
6/4	Dover International Speedway	NASCAR BGN	Schrader #52	Mike Wallace	Q-33rd	Blew engine running 9th
6/5	Dover International Speedway	NASCAR WC	Hendrick #25	Rusty Wallace	F-3rd	
				(Records missing until August 6)		
8/6	Tri-City Speedway	NASCAR Late Model	Schrader #52	Joe Kosiski	Q-2nd; F-3rd	Busch Tour
8/7	I-70 Speedway	ARCA Stock Car	Schrader #52	Randy Churchill	Q-1st	Tony Roper qualified car; was leading big time and parked car by mistake
8/7	St. Charles Speedway	UMP Late Model	Schrader #52	Ed Dixon	H-4th; F-5th	
8/14	Watkins Glen International	NASCAR WC	Hendrick #25	Mark Martin	Q-2nd; F-4th	Busch Tour
8/15	Iowa State Fair Speedway	NASCAR Late Model	Schrader #52	Bob Hill	Q-17th; H-1st; F-8th	
8/20	Michigan International Speedway	NASCAR BGN	Schrader #52	Bobby Labonte	Q-40th; F-15th	Lost 10th on last lap; ran bad all day
8/21	Michigan International Speedway	NASCAR WC	Hendrick #25	Geoff Bodine	Q-20th; F-11th	
8/23	Sheboygan Co. Fair Park	Modified	Modified #5		Q-2nd; F-4th	
8/24	State Fair Speedway	IMCA Modified	Harris #52		H-1st; F-3rd	Match race with Lasoski finished 1st
8/25	Kingsport Speedway	Hav-a-Tampa LM	Mark Minor	Scott Bloomquist		
8/26	Bristol Motor Speedway	NASCAR BGN	Whitaker #52	Kenny Wallace	F-2nd	
8/27	Bristol Motor Speedway	NASCAR WC	Hendrick #25	Rusty Wallace	Q-33nd F-19th	Toby Butler practiced car
8/28	Milwaukee Mile	ASA Late Model	Schrader #52	Bob Senneker	Q-21st; F-2nd	Led lots of laps and had engine failure
9/4	Darlington Raceway	NASCAR WC	Hendrick #25	Bill Elliott	Q-2nd; F-32nd	
9/5		ASA Late Model	Schrader #52	Mike Eddy		
9/10	Richmond International Raceway	NASCAR WC	Hendrick #25	Terry Labonte	Q-10th; F-9th	Gary Balough practiced car; started in back
9/11	Michigan International Speedway	ASA Late Model	Schrader #52	Bob Senneker	F-4th	Blew engine and hit wall
9/18	Dover International Speedway	NASCAR BGN	Schrader #52	Johnny Benson		
9/23					F-3rd	
9/25	Martinsville Speedway	NASCAR WC	Hendrick #25	Rusty Wallace	Q-14th; F-6th	
10/2	North Carolina Motor Speedway	NASCAR WC	Hendrick #25	Geoff Bodine	Q-27th; F-14th	Hit wall (stupid)
10/8	Lowe's Motor Speedway	NASCAR BGN	Schrader #52			Should have won!
10/9	Lowe's Motor Speedway	NASCAR WC	Hendrick #25	Dale Jarrett	Q-11th; F-4th	
10/16	Mesa Marin Raceway	NASCAR WW	Schrader #52	Ken Schrader	Q-1st; F-1st	
10/23	North Carolina Motor Speedway	NASCAR SW	Schrader #52	Dale Earnhardt, Sr.	Q-24th; F-32nd	
10/29	Phoenix International Raceway	NASCAR WC	Hendrick #25	Rick Carelli		
10/30	Phoenix International Raceway	NASCAR WC	Hendrick #25	Terry Labonte	Q-7th; F-15th	
11/13	Atlanta Motor Speedway	NASCAR WC	Hendrick #25	Mark Martin	Q-38th; F-11th	
11/20	Myrtle Beach Speedway	All Pro Late Model	Schrader #52			
12/11	Tucson Raceway Park	NASCAR CT	Hendrick #24 truck		Q-3rd; F-10th	

1995

Date	Track	Type	Car Owner	Race Winner	Finish	Comments
1/15	Nutter Center (indoor)	Midget	Seymour #29	Michael Lang	H-3rd; S-2nd; F-2nd	Spun leading w/4 laps to go
1/28	Hoosierdome (indoor)	USAC Midget	Seymour #29	Steve Reeves	H-1st; F-11th	
2/8	Phoenix International Raceway	NASCAR CT	Schrader truck	Mike Skinner	Q-2nd; F-3rd	Twin 125; didn't pit for tires
2/16	Daytona International Speedway	NASCAR WC	Hendrick #25	Sterling Marlin	F-5th	Cream-colored car
2/17	Daytona International Speedway	IROC		Dale Earnhardt, Sr.	F-3rd	Dropped valve
2/18	Daytona International Speedway	NASCAR BGN	Schrader #52	Chad Little		
2/19	Daytona International Speedway	NASCAR WC	Hendrick #25	Sterling Marlin	F-9th	Daytona 500: ran 3rd or 4th all day; got right side caved in with 20 laps to go
2/26	North Carolina Motor Speedway	NASCAR WC	Hendrick #25	Jeff Gordon	Q-5th	Crashed with Todd Bodine

3/5	Richmond International Raceway	NASCAR WC	Hendrick #25	Terry Labonte	F-4th	Cut tire & crashed 30 laps to go; running 6th
3/11	Atlanta Motor Speedway	NASCAR BGN	Schrader #52	Johnny Benson	F-2nd	Running 4th w/40 laps to go had flat tire
3/12	Atlanta Motor Speedway	NASCAR WC	Hendrick #25	Jeff Gordon	F-3rd	
3/25	Darlington Raceway	IROC				
3/26	Darlington Raceway	NASCAR WC	Hendrick #25	Sterling Marlin	F-11th	Ricky Craven landed on rear window of car halfway through race
4/2	Bristol Motor Speedway	NASCAR WC	Hendrick #25	Jeff Gordon		Screwed up pit stop! Ran good
4/9	North Wilkesboro Speedway	NASCAR WC	Hendrick #25	Dale Earnhardt, Sr.	F-12th	
4/15	Saugus Speedway	NASCAR CT	Schrader #52	Ken Schrader	Q-3rd; F-1st	
4/23	Martinsville Speedway	NASCAR WC	Hendrick #25	Rusty Wallace	F-6th	Broke engine running in lead pack
4/29	Talladega Superspeedway	IROC		Dale Earnhardt, Sr.	F-7th	Broke gear shift lever & played catch-up all day
4/30	Talladega Superspeedway	NASCAR WC	Hendrick #25	Mark Martin	Q-7th	
5/6	Sears Point Raceway	NASCAR SW	Schrader #52	Ron Hornaday, Jr.	Q-7th; F-9th	
5/7	Sears Point Raceway	NASCAR WC	Hendrick #25	Dale Earnhardt, Sr.		
5/20	Lowe's Motor Speedway	NASCAR WC	Hendrick #25	T. Bodine/Gordon	Open-2nd	Crashed with Jimmy Spencer in The Winston
5/27	Lowe's Motor Speedway	NASCAR BGN	Schrader #52	Chad Little	Qual F-1st; F-5th	
5/28	Lowe's Motor Speedway	NASCAR WC	Hendrick #25	Bobby Labonte	F-11th	Led most of race & blew up leading, 45 laps to go
6/3	Dover International Speedway	NASCAR BGN	Schrader #52	Mike McLaughlin	Q-1st; F-3rd	
6/4	Dover International Speedway	NASCAR WC	Hendrick #25	Kyle Petty		Didn't run good; just survived
6/11	Pocono Raceway	NASCAR WC	Hendrick #25	Terry Labonte		
6/12	Madison International Speedway	Late Model	Gundeman	Reffner/Bickle	Q-5th; Qual H-1st	Miller Nationals
6/13	Madison International Speedway	Late Model	Gundeman		1st F-4th	Miller Nationals; blew up leading 2nd feature
6/15	Macon Speedway	IMCA Modified	Bob Harris		H-5th; B F-1st; A F-4th	Match race
6/16	Limaland Motorsports Park	IMCA Modified			F-2nd	
6/18	Michigan International Speedway	NASCAR WC	Hendrick #25	Bobby Labonte		Had oil leak 2nd lap of race; sat for 25 laps
6/18	Tri-State Speedway	Late Model	Schrader #25		H-3rd; F-13th	Missed on gear big time
6/22	Devil's Bowl Speedway	Late Model	Schrader #52			Pathrum show; Sterling, Michael and Andy Hillenburg
6/24	Brainerd International Raceway	ASA Late Model	Schrader #52	Scott Hansen	Q-1st; Qual H-1st	Ran off course leading with 9 laps to go
6/25	Brainerd International Raceway	ASA Late Model	Schrader #52		F-7th	
7/1	Daytona International Speedway	NASCAR WC	Hendrick #25	Jeff Gordon	Q-26th; F-6th	
7/1	Owosso Speedway	Late Model	Schrader #52	Eric Smith		Only 3 or 4 six-cylinders in the field
7/2	Flat Rock Speedway	ARCA Stock Car		Marv Smith	Q-4th; H-1st; F-7th	Wrecked with Randy Churchill w/8 laps to go and cut right front tire
7/3	I-55 Raceway	UMP Late Model	Jerry Gundeman	Kevin Gundaker	Q-5th; F-2nd	
7/8	New Hampshire Int'l Speedway	NASCAR BGN	Schrader #52	Ricky Craven	F-9th	Blew up in feature
7/9	New Hampshire Int'l Speedway	NASCAR WC	Hendrick #25	Jeff Gordon	Q-10th; F-10th	
7/10	Slinger Super Speedway	Late Model	Schrader #52	Ken Schrader	H-4th; F-5th	Slinger Nationals
7/11	Slinger Super Speedway	Late Model	Schrader #25		Q-9th; H-7th	Slinger Nationals
7/12	Fremont Speedway	Late Model	Jerry Gundeman			Match race and autograph only
7/16	Pocono Raceway	NASCAR WC	Hendrick #25	Dale Jarrett	Q-4th; F-40th	Blew engine
7/18	Knoxville Raceway	NASCAR Late Model	Schrader #25		H-11th; S-1st	All-Star race; dropped out of feature; was up to 8th and had flat tire
7/22	Talladega Superspeedway	NASCAR BGN	Schrader #52			Ran out of gas last lap running 3rd
7/23	Talladega Superspeedway	NASCAR WC	Hendrick #25	Sterling Marlin	Q-4th; F-32nd	Got bumped by #24 and turned over
7/26	Tri-City Speedway	NASCAR Late Model	Schrader #52			
7/29	Michigan International Speedway	IROC				All-Star Race
7/29	Colorado National Speedway	Late Model	Marshall Chesrown	Ken Schrader	F-1st	Got there late; Rick Carelli & I started last row
8/5	Indianapolis Motor Speedway	NASCAR WC	Hendrick #25	Dale Earnhardt, Sr.	Q-10th; F-19th	Running 11th and engine messed up
8/5	Hales Corner Speedway	Late Model	Schrader #52	Ken Schrader	F-1st	Got there in time to start last in feature
8/6	Grundy County Speedway	ARTGO Late Model	Jerry Gundeman			

Date	Track	Type	Car Owner	Race Winner	Finish	Comments
8/13	Watkins Glen International	NASCAR WC	Hendrick #25	Mark Martin	Q-16th; F-36th	Wrecked car in last practice; started last and was up to 20th and engine blew up
8/16	Kalamazoo Speedway	Late Model		Randy Sweet		Led most of race and tires gave up
8/19	Michigan International Speedway	NASCAR BGN	Schrader #52			
8/20	Michigan International Speedway	NASCAR WC	Hendrick #25	Bobby Labonte	Q-36th; F-25th	Car shook itself apart
8/22	Hawkeye Downs Speedway	Late Model			F-10th	
8/26	Bristol Motor Speedway	NASCAR WC	Hendrick #25	Terry Labonte	Q-25th; F-14th	Got up to 6th or 7th & engine broke
8/27	Milwaukee Mile	ASA Late Model	Schrader #52			Got in wreck early
9/3	Darlington Raceway	NASCAR WC	Hendrick #25	Jeff Gordon	Q-38th; F-23rd	
9/4	St. Paul Fairgrounds	ASA Late Model	Schrader #52	Bobby Gill	F-3rd	
9/7	Richmond International Raceway	NASCAR CT	Schrader #52	Terry Labonte	F-5th	
9/9	Richmond International Raceway	NASCAR WC	Hendrick #25	Rusty Wallace	Q-3rd; F-9th	Lined up by points; had brake problems
9/17	Dover International Speedway	NASCAR WC	Hendrick #25	Jeff Gordon	Q-36th; F-12th	Running good & got caught up in crash
9/24	Martinsville Speedway	NASCAR WC	Hendrick #25	Dale Earnhardt, Sr.	Q-15th; F-32nd	Ran like shit
9/25	Martinsville Speedway	NASCAR CT	Schrader #52	Joe Ruttman		
9/30	North Wilkesboro Speedway	NASCAR CT	Schrader #52	Mike Bliss		
10/1	North Wilkesboro Speedway	NASCAR WC	Hendrick #25	Mark Martin	Q-8th; F-8th	
10/7	Lowe's Motor Speedway	NASCAR CT	Schrader #52			
10/8	Lowe's Motor Speedway	NASCAR WC	Hendrick #25	Mark Martin	Q-28th; F-35th	Blew engine
10/13	Mesa Marin Raceway	NASCAR SW	Schrader #52	Todd Bodine	Q-17th; F-3rd	Lined up by rain-out procedure
10/21	North Carolina Motor Speedway	NASCAR BGN	Schrader #52	Ward Burton	F-15th	Got in accident early
10/22	North Carolina Motor Speedway	NASCAR WC	Hendrick #25	Mike Skinner	Q-24th; F-33rd	Burnt up wheel bearing
10/28	Phoenix International Raceway	NASCAR CT	Schrader #52	Ricky Rudd	Q-15th; F-10th	Wrecked about halfway
10/29	Phoenix International Raceway	NASCAR WC	Hendrick #25		Q-18th	
11/5	Homestead-Miami Speedway	NASCAR BGN	Schrader #52			

1996

Date	Track	Type	Car Owner	Race Winner	Finish	Comments
1/20	Hoosierdome (indoor)	USAC Midget	Seymour #29			Had flat tire
2/4	Phoenix International Raceway	NASCAR SW	Schrader			Busch Clash
2/11	Daytona International Speedway	NASCAR WC	Hendrick #25	Dale Jarrett		Twin 125s
2/15	Daytona International Speedway	NASCAR WC	Hendrick #25	Ernie Irvan		Daytona 500
2/18	Daytona International Speedway	NASCAR WC	Hendrick #25	Dale Jarrett		Wheel bearing burned up
2/25	North Carolina Motor Speedway	NASCAR WC	Hendrick #25	Dale Earnhardt, Sr.		
3/3	Richmond International Raceway	NASCAR WC	Hendrick #25	Jeff Gordon		
3/10	Atlanta Motor Speedway	NASCAR WC	Hendrick #25	Dale Earnhardt, Sr.		Blew up engine
3/17	Homestead-Miami Speedway	NASCAR CT	Schrader #52	Dave Rezendes		
3/29	Darlington Raceway	NASCAR WC	Hendrick #25	Jeff Gordon		
3/31	Bristol Motor Speedway	NASCAR WC	Hendrick #25	Jeff Gordon		Throttle stuck in feature
4/6	I-55 Raceway	UMP Late Model	Schrader #52	Randy Korte		
4/14	North Wilkesboro Speedway	NASCAR WC	Hendrick #25	Terry Labonte	F-2nd	
4/21	Martinsville Speedway	NASCAR WC	Hendrick #25	Rusty Wallace	F-3rd	
4/28	Talladega Superspeedway	NASCAR WC	Hendrick #25	Sterling Marlin		Wheel left loose on pit stop & pitted on green
5/5	Sears Point Raceway	NASCAR WC	Hendrick #25	Rusty Wallace		
5/14	Twin Cities Raceway Park	UMP Late Model	Schrader #52			
5/18	Lowe's Motor Speedway	NASCAR WC	Hendrick #25	Michael Waltrip		Winston Open; blew engine
5/26	Lowe's Motor Speedway	NASCAR WC	Hendrick #25	Dale Jarrett		Coca-Cola 600
6/3	Dover International Speedway	NASCAR WC	Hendrick #25	Jeff Gordon		
6/5	Tri-City Speedway	NASCAR Late Model	Schrader #52			Busch All-Star; didn't qualify

Date	Track	Type	Car Owner	Race Winner	Finish	Comments
6/6	Macon Speedway	UMP Modified	Bob Harris			Rained out
6/8	Heartland Park	NASCAR SW	Schrader #52	Mike Cope	Q-1st	Crashed
6/9	Heartland Park	NASCAR CT	Schrader #52			
6/10	Slinger Super Speedway	Late Model	Gundeman #58			Slinger Nationals
6/11	Slinger Super Speedway	Late Model	Gundeman #58			Slinger Nationals
6/16	Pocono Raceway	NASCAR WC	Hendrick #25	Jeff Gordon		
6/23	Michigan International Speedway	NASCAR WC	Hendrick #25	Rusty Wallace		
6/30	Nazareth Speedway	NASCAR CT	Schrader #2			
7/6	Daytona International Speedway	NASCAR WC	Hendrick #25	Sterling Marlin		
7/7	I-55 Raceway	UMP Late Model	Schrader #52			Nationals
7/8		Late Model	Gundeman #58			Nationals
7/9		Late Model	Gundeman #58			
7/14	New Hampshire Int'l Speedway	NASCAR WC	Hendrick #25	Ernie Irvan		
7/21	Pocono Raceway	NASCAR WC	Hendrick #25	Rusty Wallace		
7/23	Macon Speedway	UMP Modified	Bob Harris	Ken Schrader	2nd F-1st	1st Feature-wrecked; 2nd Feature-won
7/28	Talladega Superspeedway	NASCAR WC	Hendrick #25	Jeff Gordon		
7/31	Indiana State Fairgrounds	ARCA Stock Car	Schrader #52		Q-4th	Overheated in feature
8/3	Indianapolis Motor Speedway	NASCAR WC	Hendrick #25	Dale Jarrett		
8/3	Hales Corner Speedway	Late Model	Schrader #52		F-2nd	
8/4	Tri-State Speedway	UMP Late Model	Schrader #52			
8/9	Albany-Saratoga Speedway	UMP Late Model			Q-4th, D-1st, F-4th	Bruce Pathrum show
8/11	Watkins Glen International	NASCAR WC	Hendrick #25	Geoff Bodine		
8/12	Hartford Speedway Park	Late Model	C.J. Rayburn	Billy Moyer		Blew up running 2nd w/about 8 laps to go
8/14	Kalamazoo Speedway	Late Model	Randy Sweet			
8/16		Late Model				Bruce Pathrum show
8/18	Michigan International Speedway	NASCAR WC	Hendrick #25	Dale Jarrett		
8/24	Bristol Motor Speedway	NASCAR WC	Hendrick #25	Rusty Wallace		
9/1	Darlington Raceway	NASCAR WC	Hendrick #25	Jeff Gordon	Q-4th, F-4th	
9/2		ASA Late Model	Schrader #52			
9/7	Richmond International Raceway	NASCAR WC	Hendrick #25	Ernie Irvan		
9/15	Dover International Speedway	NASCAR WC	Hendrick #25	Jeff Gordon		
9/22	Martinsville Speedway	NASCAR WC	Hendrick #25	Jeff Gordon		
9/29	North Wilkesboro Speedway	NASCAR WC	Hendrick #25	Jeff Gordon		Last Winston Cup race at North Wilkesboro
10/6	Lowe's Motor Speedway	NASCAR WC	Hendrick #25	Terry Labonte		
10/20	North Carolina Motor Speedway	NASCAR WC	Hendrick #25	Ricky Rudd		Running 10th w/30 to go and broke rear end
10/27	Phoenix International Raceway	NASCAR WC	Hendrick #25	Bobby Hamilton		
11/2	Las Vegas Motor Speedway	NASCAR WW	Schrader #52	Ken Schrader	Q-1st, F-1st	Winston West
11/3	Las Vegas Motor Speedway	NASCAR CT	Waltrip #17	Jack Sprague	F-7th	
11/10	Atlanta Motor Speedway	NASCAR WC	Hendrick #25	Bobby Labonte		
11/17	Southern National Speedway	ASA Late Model	Schrader #52			

1997

Date	Track	Type	Car Owner	Race Winner	Finish	Comments
2/2	Phoenix International Raceway	NASCAR SW	Schrader #52	Rick Carelli	Q-2nd, F-2nd	
2/13	Daytona International Speedway	NASCAR WC	Andy Petree #33		F-4th	Twin 125
2/16	Daytona International Speedway	NASCAR WC	Petree #33	Jeff Gordon		Daytona 500; Steve Grissom crashed us in middle of race; just limped to finish
2/23	North Carolina Motor Speedway	NASCAR WC	Petree #33	Jeff Gordon	Q-6th, F-18th	Lined up by points; started 8th; lost cylinder
3/2	Richmond International Raceway	NASCAR WC	Petree #33	Rusty Wallace		

Date	Track	Class	Car	Driver	Result	Notes
3/9	Atlanta Motor Speedway	NASCAR WC	Petree #33	Dale Jarrett	Q-35th; F-27th	early in race
3/23	Darlington Raceway	NASCAR WC	Petree #33	Dale Jarrett		Ricky Rudd wrecked us 2/3 way through race and limped around
3/29	I-55 Raceway	UMP Late Model	Schrader #25			
4/6	Texas Motor Speedway	NASCAR WC	Petree #33	Jeff Burton		
4/13	Bristol Motor Speedway	NASCAR WC	Petree #33	Jeff Gordon		
4/20	Martinsville Speedway	NASCAR WC	Petree #33	Jeff Gordon		
5/4	Sears Point Raceway	NASCAR WC	Petree #33	Mark Martin	F-4th	Hit by Ernie Irvan and had flat
5/9	Huntsville Speedway					Pathrum show
5/10	Talladega Superspeedway	NASCAR WC	Petree #33	Mark Martin		
5/10	I-55 Raceway	UMP Late Model	Schrader #25	Randy Korte	Q-3rd; D-4th; F-4th	
5/13	Hawkeye Downs Speedway	IMCA Late Model	Johnny Johnson			
5/14	Anderson Speedway	IMCA Modified				
5/17	Lowe's Motor Speedway	NASCAR WC	Petree #33	Jeff Gordon	H-1st; F-1st	Winston Open
5/25	Lowe's Motor Speedway	NASCAR WC	Petree #33			Running good & had water fitting in cylinder head break
6/1	Dover International Speedway	NASCAR WC	Petree #33	Ricky Rudd	F-6th	
6/8	Pocono Raceway	NASCAR WC	Petree #33	Jeff Gordon		Blew up running good
6/10	Macon Speedway	UMP Modified	Harris #33			
6/11	I-55 Raceway	NASCAR Late Model	Schrader #25		H-5th; S-1st; F-3rd	
6/15	Michigan International Speedway	NASCAR WC	Petree #33	Ernie Irvan		
6/21	California Speedway	NASCAR WW	Petree #3	Ken Schrader	Q-3rd; F-1st	
6/22	California Speedway	NASCAR WC	Petree #33	Jeff Gordon	Q-1st; F-1st	
6/29	Toledo Speedway	ARCA Stock Car	Reolo #39	Ken Schrader		
7/2	I-55 Raceway	UMP Late Model	Schrader #25	Ed Dixon	Q-14th; H-8th	Summernationals; got messed up in heat and didn't run B Feature
7/5	Daytona International Speedway	NASCAR WC	Petree #33	John Andretti	F-15th	
7/13	New Hampshire Int'l Speedway	NASCAR WC	Petree #33	Jeff Burton	Q-1st; F-11th	New Track Record
7/15	Cresco Speedway	UMP Late Model	Schrader #25	Brian Birkhofer	Q-11th; D-7th	Blew up in heat race
7/20	Pocono Raceway	NASCAR WC	Petree #33	Dale Jarrett	Q-7th; F-14th	
7/22	Knoxville Raceway	IMCA Modified	Harris #33	Kelly Schrock	H-1st; F-1st	Broke running 2nd
7/23	Crawford County Speedway	USMS Modified	Harris #33	Ron Jones	H-2nd; F-2nd	
7/25	State Fair Speedway (OK)			Ken Schrader	F-1st	Bruce Pathrum show
7/27	Pikes Peak International Raceway	NASCAR WW	Bill Strausner	Michael Waltrip	Q-1st; F-2nd	Had flat; caught fire; lost 2 laps; made them up and almost won
8/2	Indianapolis Motor Speedway	NASCAR WC	Petree #33	Ricky Rudd	F-11th	Crashed in feature
8/2	Hales Corner Speedway	UMP Late Model	Schrader #52			
8/10	Watkins Glen International	NASCAR WC	Petree #33	Jeff Gordon		
8/17	Michigan International Speedway	NASCAR WC	Petree #33	Mark Martin		
8/23	Bristol Motor Speedway	NASCAR WC	Petree #33	Dale Jarrett	F-6th	
8/31	Darlington Raceway	NASCAR WC	Petree #33	Jeff Gordon	F-6th	
9/4	Richmond International Raceway	NASCAR CT	Schrader #53	Bob Keselowski		
9/6	Richmond International Raceway	NASCAR WC	Petree #33	Dale Jarrett		
9/14	New Hampshire Int'l Speedway	NASCAR WC	Petree #33	Jeff Gordon	Q-1st	Ran terrible
9/21	Dover International Speedway	NASCAR WC	Petree #33	Mark Martin		
9/29	Martinsville Speedway	NASCAR WC	Petree #33	Jeff Burton	F-9th	
10/5	Lowe's Motor Speedway	NASCAR WC	Petree #33	Dale Jarrett	Q-11th; F-15th	
10/12	Talladega Superspeedway	NASCAR WC	Petree #33	Terry Labonte	F-4th	
10/18	Illinois State Fairgrounds	ARCA Stock Car	Jim Coyce #1	Tim Steele	Q-1st; F-2nd	
10/27	North Carolina Motor Speedway	NASCAR WC	Petree #33	Bobby Hamilton		Was terrible all day

Date	Track	Type	Car Owner	Race Winner	Finish	Comments
11/8	Las Vegas Motor Speedway	NASCAR WW	Petree #33	Ken Schrader	Q-4th, F-1st	
11/9	Las Vegas Motor Speedway	NASCAR CT	A.J. Foyt #51	Joe Ruttman	Q-12th, F-18th	
11/16	Atlanta Motor Speedway	NASCAR WC	Petree #33	Bobby Labonte	F-20th	

1998

Date	Track	Type	Car Owner	Race Winner	Finish	Comments
1/11	Tucson Raceway Park	NASCAR WW	Bill Strausser	Butch Gilliland	Q-6th, F-2nd	Got passed w/2 laps to go
2/1	Phoenix International Raceway	NASCAR SW	Schrader #3	Ken Schrader	Q-2nd, F-1st	
2/8	Daytona International Speedway	NASCAR WC	Petree #33	Rusty Wallace	Q-2nd, F-5th	Restarted 3rd but #24 didn't go & got trapped
2/12	Daytona International Speedway	NASCAR WC	Petree #33			Twin 125; hard crash (hit by David Green); broke sternum
2/15	Daytona International Speedway	NASCAR WC	Petree #33	Dale Earnhardt Sr.	F-4th	Daytona 500; started 37th in back-up car
2/22	North Carolina Motor Speedway	NASCAR WC	Petree #33	Jeff Gordon	Q-31st, F-23rd	
3/1	Las Vegas Motor Speedway	NASCAR WC	Petree #33	Mark Martin	Q-37th, F-21st	
3/9	Atlanta Motor Speedway	NASCAR WC	Petree #33	Bobby Labonte	Q-37th, F-17th	
3/22	Darlington Raceway	NASCAR WC	Petree #33	Dale Jarrett	Q-32nd, F-18th	Burned rear end gear qualifying
3/29	Bristol Motor Speedway	NASCAR WC	Petree #33	Jeff Gordon	Q-14th, F-6th	Cut tire and hit wall w/about 30 laps to go
4/5	Texas Motor Speedway	NASCAR WC	Petree #33	Mark Martin		Got spun by Dixon; had to go to rear
4/10	Belle-Clair Speedway	UMP Late Model	Schrader #52	Ken Schrader	H-4th, F-1st	
4/11	I-55 Raceway	UMP Late Model	Schrader #52	Mark Gansman	H-2nd, D-2nd, F-7th	
4/20	Martinsville Speedway	NASCAR WC	Petree #33	Bobby Hamilton	Q-6th, F-10th	
4/26	Talladega Superspeedway	NASCAR WC	Petree #33	Bobby Labonte	Q-4th, F-29th	Got in BIG CRASH!
5/2	California Speedway	NASCAR WW	Petree #15	Ken Schrader	Q-1st, F-1st	
5/3	California Speedway	NASCAR WC	Petree #33	Mark Martin	Q-15th, F-15th	
5/8	Belle-Clair Speedway	UMP Late Model	Schrader #52		H-7th, F-2nd	Match race with Kenny
5/9	I-55 Raceway	UMP Late Model	Schrader #52	Ken Schrader	H-1st, D-1st, F-1st	
5/12	Hawkeye Downs Speedway	UMP Modified	Schrader #52	Kenny Wallace		
5/15	Lowe's Motor Speedway	NASCAR WC	Petree #33			No Bull qualifying race; destroyed car on pit stop
5/16	Lowe's Motor Speedway	NASCAR WC	Petree #33	Jeff Gordon		Winston Open
5/17	Heartland Raceway Park	NASCAR WW	Petree #15			Crashed by Lance Hooper
5/24	Lowe's Motor Speedway	NASCAR WC	Petree #33	Jeff Gordon	Q-14th, F-10th	Broke transmission running 3rd; 10 laps to go
5/31	Dover International Speedway	NASCAR WC	Petree #33	Dale Jarrett	Q-25th, F-15th	
6/5	Richmond International Raceway	NASCAR BGN	Petree #15	Jeff Burton	Q-4th	
6/6	Richmond International Raceway	NASCAR WC	Petree #33	Terry Labonte	Q-7th, F-4th	
6/7	Illinois State Fairgrounds	UMP Modified	Kelly Schrock	Ken Schrader	H-1st, F-1st	
6/7	St. Charles Speedway	UMP Late Model	Schrader #52	Mike Hammerle	H-1st, D-2nd, F-3rd	
6/14	Michigan International Speedway	NASCAR WC	Petree #33	Mark Martin		Got crashed by Earnhardt
6/17	Farmer City Raceway	UMP Modified	Bobby Jacks		H-7th, S-2nd, F-9th	
6/21	Pocono Raceway	NASCAR WC	Petree #33	Jeremy Mayfield	Q-4th, F-43rd	Qual 6th but lead fell out & time disallowed
6/28	Sears Point Raceway	NASCAR WC	Petree #33	Jeff Gordon	Q-27th, F-20th	
7/12	New Hampshire Int'l Speedway	NASCAR WC	Petree #33	Jeff Burton	Q-26th, F-9th	Blew up in dash
7/14	Cresco Speedway	UMP Late Model	Schrader #52	Ken Schrader	F-1st	
7/17	Lawrenceburg Speedway				1st F-4th, 2nd F-8th	Bruce Pathrum show
7/18	Somewhere near Louisville KY				H-2nd	Bruce Pathrum show
7/21	Knoxville Raceway	IMCA Modified	Harris #33			Rained out after heat races
7/22	Crawford County Speedway	USMRS Modified	Harris #33		H-5th, S-2nd	Crashed in feature

Date	Track	Type	Car Owner	Race Winner	Finish	Comments
7/26	Pocono Raceway	NASCAR WC	Petree #33	Jeff Gordon	Q-17th; F-8th	
8/1	Indianapolis Motor Speedway	NASCAR WC	Petree #33	Jeff Gordon	Q-19th; F-10th	
8/1	Hales Corner Speedway	UMP Late Model	Schrader #52	Ken Schrader	Q-7th; H-6th; F-1st	
8/4	Macon Speedway	UMP Modified	Harris #33	Sonny Findling	Q-7th; H-2nd	
8/5	Tri-City Speedway	NASCAR Late Model	Schrader #52		Q-20th; F-7th	Rained out after heat races
8/9	Watkins Glen International	NASCAR WC	Petree #33	Jeff Gordon	Q-16th; F-24th	Had right rear shock go bad
8/15	Michigan International Speedway	NASCAR BGN	Petree #15	Jeff Burton	Q-29th; F-24th	
8/16	Michigan International Speedway	NASCAR WC	Petree #33	Jeff Gordon	Q-10th; F-14th	
8/19	Beaver Dam Raceway	UMP Late Model	Schrader #52	Kevin Weaver	Q-1st; D-3rd; F-3rd	
8/21	Bristol Motor Speedway	NASCAR BGN	Petree #15	Kevin Lepage	Q-32nd; F-6th	
8/22	Bristol Motor Speedway	NASCAR WC	Petree #33	Mark Martin	Q-13th; F-14th	
8/23	Illinois State Fairgrounds	ARCA Stock Car	Ed Rensi #38	Ken Schrader	Q-1st; F-1st	
8/23	St. Charles Speedway	UMP Late Model	Schrader #52	Ken Schrader	H-1st; D-1st; F-1st	
8/30	New Hampshire Int'l Speedway	NASCAR WC	Petree #33	Jeff Gordon	Q-3rd; F-42nd	Crashed by Rusty
9/5	Darlington Raceway	NASCAR BGN	Petree #15			
9/6	Darlington Raceway	NASCAR WC	Petree #33	Jeff Gordon	Q-6th; F-13th	Power steering went out lap 195
9/7	Los Angeles Grand Prix	NASCAR SW	Schrader #52	Steve Portenga		Had ignition problems and pulled in
9/11	Richmond International Raceway	NASCAR BGN	Petree #15	Jeff Burton	Q-2nd; F-4th	Got crashed on 2nd lap
9/12	Richmond International Raceway	NASCAR WC	Petree #33		F-2nd	
9/13	Salem Speedway	ARCA Stock Car	Baird #52	Frank Kimmel		Started by Bill Baird; I got in on first yellow
9/19	Dover International Speedway	NASCAR BGN	Petree #15	Mark Martin	Q-28th; F-39th	Blew engine
9/20	Dover International Speedway	NASCAR WC	Petree #33	Ricky Rudd	Q-18th; F-13th	Spun out by Ernie Irvan on last lap; running 8th
9/27	Martinsville Speedway	NASCAR BGN	Petree #33			Blew engine running 9th
10/3	Lowe's Motor Speedway	NASCAR WC	Petree #15	Mark Martin	Q-15th; F-40th	Blew engine
10/4	Lowe's Motor Speedway	NASCAR BGN	Petree #33	Dale Jarrett	Q-1st; F-24th	Had flat and blew off fender
10/11	Talladega Superspeedway	NASCAR WC	Petree #33	Jeff Gordon	Q-16th; F-9th	Running good for 150 laps and went to shit
10/17	Daytona International Speedway	NASCAR WC	Petree #33	Rusty Wallace	Q-1st; F-22nd	
10/24	Phoenix International Raceway	NASCAR WC	Petree #33	Jeff Gordon		
10/31	North Carolina Motor Speedway	NASCAR BGN	Petree #15			
11/1	North Carolina Motor Speedway	NASCAR WC	Petree #33	Jeff Gordon		
11/7	Atlanta Motor Speedway	NASCAR BGN	Petree #15			
11/8	Atlanta Motor Speedway	NASCAR WC	Petree #33	Jeff Burton		
11/15	Homestead-Miami Speedway	NASCAR BGN	Petree #15			

1999

Date	Track	Type	Car Owner	Race Winner	Finish	Comments
2/7	Daytona International Speedway	NASCAR WC	Petree #33	Mark Martin	F-2nd	Bud Shoot-out
2/11	Daytona International Speedway	NASCAR WC	Petree #33			Twin 125
2/13	Daytona International Speedway	NASCAR BGN	Petree #15			
2/14	Daytona International Speedway	NASCAR WC	Petree #33	Jeff Gordon	Q-1st	Broke rear suspension leading Daytona 500
2/21	North Carolina Motor Speedway	NASCAR WC	Petree #33	Mark Martin		
3/6	Las Vegas Motor Speedway	NASCAR BGN	Petree #15			
3/7	Las Vegas Motor Speedway	NASCAR WC	Petree #33	Jeff Burton		
3/13	Atlanta Motor Speedway	NASCAR BGN	Petree #15			
3/14	Atlanta Motor Speedway	NASCAR WC	Petree #33	Jeff Gordon		
3/21	Darlington Raceway	NASCAR WC	Petree #33	Jeff Burton		
3/27	Texas Motor Speedway	NASCAR BGN	Petree #15			Was crashed by Randy LaJoie
3/28	Texas Motor Speedway	NASCAR WC	Petree #33	Terry Labonte		
4/1	Belle-Clair Speedway	UMP Late Model	Schrader #52		H-3rd; D-4th; F-5th	

Date	Venue	Series/Class	Car	Driver	Result	Notes
4/10	Bristol Motor Speedway	NASCAR BGN	Petree #15			
4/11	Bristol Motor Speedway	NASCAR WC	Petree #33			
4/18	Martinsville Speedway	NASCAR WC	Petree #33			
4/24	Talladega Superspeedway	NASCAR BGN	Petree #15	Rusty Wallace	Q-1st	
4/25	Talladega Superspeedway	NASCAR WC	Petree #33	John Andretti	Q-1st	
5/1	California Speedway	NASCAR BGN	Petree #15			No motor
5/2	California Speedway	NASCAR WC	Petree #33	Dale Earnhardt, Sr.	Q-2nd; F-2nd	
5/7	Belle-Clair Speedway	UMP Late Model	Schrader #52		H-2nd, D-6th, F-7th	
5/8	I-55 Raceway	UMP Late Model	Schrader #52		H-3rd, F-6th	
5/9	Anderson Speedway	ARCA Stock Car	Schrader #99		Q-12th, F-1st	
5/14	Richmond International Raceway	NASCAR BGN	Petree #15	Jeff Gordon		
5/15	Richmond International Raceway	NASCAR WC	Petree #33	Ed Dixon		25-lap qualifying race
5/21	Lowe's Motor Speedway	NASCAR WC	Petree #33	Ed Dixon		
5/22	Lowe's Motor Speedway	NASCAR WC	Petree #33	Ken Schrader		
5/29	Lowe's Motor Speedway	NASCAR WC	Petree #15	Dale Jarrett		
5/30	Lowe's Motor Speedway	NASCAR WC	Petree #33	Terry Labonte		
5/31	Wisconsin International Raceway	NASCAR Late Model	Jeff Victor #52	Jeff Burton		ReMax late models
6/2	Highland Speedway	UMP Late Model	Schrader #52		Q-9th; D-2nd; F-8th	
6/6	Dover International Speedway	NASCAR WC	Petree #33	Bobby Labonte		
6/13	Michigan International Speedway	NASCAR WC	Petree #33	Dale Jarrett		
6/15	Macon Speedway	UMP Modified	John Logue #69		H-5th; F-5th	First car out of feature; bent tie rod
6/16	Farmer City Raceway	UMP Modified	Logue #69		H-2nd; D-6th; F-7th	
6/20	Pocono Raceway	NASCAR WC	Petree #33	Bobby Labonte		Pathrum show
6/25	Watsonville Speedway	Late Model				
6/27	Sears Point Raceway	NASCAR WC	Petree #33	Jeff Gordon	Q-5th; H-4th; F-15th	Flat right rear tire 4 laps to go running 4th
6/30	Action Track	Northern All Stars LM	Schrader #52	Tony Stewart		
7/3	Daytona International Speedway	NASCAR WC	Petree #33	Dale Jarrett		
7/6	Hales Corners Speedway	UMP Late Model	Schrader #52	Billy Moyer	Q-11th; H-4th; S-1st; F-11th	Summernationals race
7/11	New Hampshire Int'l Speedway	NASCAR WC	Petree #33	Jeff Burton		
7/12	Knoxville Raceway	UMP Late Model	Schrader #52	Rick Aukland	H-4th; D-7th; F-13th	
7/12	Knoxville Raceway	UMP Modified	John Logue #69		H-3rd; F-10th	
7/16	State Fair Speedway	UMP Late Model	Schrader #52	Ken Schrader	H-2nd; F-1st	
7/17	I-55 Raceway	UMP Late Model	Schrader #52	Randy Korte	H-6th; F-4th	
7/19	Slinger Super Speedway	Late Model	Victor #52	Schill/Morgan	1st F-14th; 2nd F-14th	Al Schill won 1st; Conrad Morgan 2nd
7/20	Knoxville Raceway	IMCA Modified	Logue #69		H-2nd; S-1st; F-5th	
7/21	Crawford County Speedway	USMLS Modified	Logue #69		H-2nd; F-3rd	
7/25	Pocono Raceway	NASCAR WC	Petree #33	Bobby Labonte		Missed show
7/28	Eldora Speedway	UMP Late Model	Schrader #52		H-6th; S-5th	
7/31	Gateway International Raceway	NASCAR BGN	Petree #15	Dale Jarrett		
8/1	Tri-State Speedway	UMP Late Model	Schrader #52	Scott Hansen	Q-7th; H-4th; F-9th	
8/7	Indianapolis Motor Speedway	NASCAR WC	Petree #33	Jeff Gordon		
8/8	Wisconsin International Raceway	NASCAR Late Model	Victor #52		Q-10th; F-28th	ReMax Series; broke at lap 150 running 4th
8/11	Beaver Dam Raceway	IMCA Modified	Logue #69		H-2nd	
8/15	Watkins Glen International	NASCAR WC	Petree #33			
8/21	Michigan International Speedway	NASCAR BGN	Petree #15	Bobby Labonte		
8/22	Michigan International Speedway	NASCAR WC	Petree #33	Dale Earnhardt, Sr.		
8/28	Bristol Motor Speedway	NASCAR WC	Petree #33	Tracy Leslie		
8/29	Winchester Speedway	ARCA Stock Car	Schrader #52	Jeff Burton	Q-10th; F-19th	Lap 180 (big wreck)
9/5	Darlington Raceway	NASCAR WC	Petree #33			
9/6	Los Angeles Street Race	NASCAR SW	Petree #33			
9/6	Rocky Mountain Raceways	NASCAR WW	Bill Strasser #45		F-8th	Started last, someone else qual. car; blew

Date	Track	Type	Car Owner	Race Winner	Finish	Comments
9/10	Richmond International Raceway	NASCAR BGN	Petree #15			
9/11	Richmond International Raceway	NASCAR WC	Petree #33	Tony Stewart		
9/12	Salem Speedway	ARCA Stock Car	Schrader #99	Ken Schrader	Q-2nd; F-1st	
9/19	New Hampshire Int'l Speedway	NASCAR WC	Petree #33	Joe Nemechek		
9/26	Dover International Speedway	NASCAR WC	Petree #33	Mark Martin		
10/3	Martinsville Speedway	NASCAR WC	Petree #33	Jeff Gordon		
10/9	Lowe's Motor Speedway	NASCAR BGN	Petree #15			Missed show
10/11	Lowe's Motor Speedway	NASCAR WC	Petree #33	Jeff Gordon		
10/17	Talladega Superspeedway	NASCAR WC	Petree #33	Dale Earnhardt, Sr.		
10/23	North Carolina Motor Speedway	NASCAR BGN	Petree #15			Missed show
10/24	North Carolina Motor Speedway	NASCAR WC	Petree #33	Jeff Burton		
10/30	California Speedway	NASCAR WC	Petree #33		Q-11th	
11/6	Phoenix International Raceway	NASCAR BGN	Petree #15	Jeff Gordon		
11/7	Phoenix International Raceway	NASCAR WC	Petree #33	Tony Stewart		
11/21	Atlanta Motor Speedway	NASCAR WC	Petree #33	Bobby Labonte		Crashed in race

2000

Date	Track	Type	Car Owner	Race Winner	Finish	Comments
2/6	Phoenix International Raceway	NASCAR SW	Schrader #99	Rick Carelli	Q-1st; F-16th	New Track Record; terrible loose
2/13	Daytona International Speedway	NASCAR WC	MB2 #36	Dale Jarrett		Got crashed on last lap of Bud Shoot-out
2/17	Daytona International Speedway	NASCAR WC	MB2 #36			Twin 125
2/20	Daytona International Speedway	NASCAR WC	MB2 #36	Dale Jarrett	Q-23rd; F-9th	Daytona 500
2/27	North Carolina Motor Speedway	NASCAR WC	MB2 #36	Bobby Labonte	Q-36th; F-13th	
3/5	Las Vegas Motor Speedway	NASCAR WC	MB2 #36	Jeff Burton	Q-34th; F-16th	
3/12	Atlanta Motor Speedway	NASCAR WC	MB2 #36	Dale Earnhardt, Sr.	Q-42nd; F-23rd	Got in wreck Lap 2
3/19	Darlington Raceway	NASCAR WC	MB2 #36	Ward Burton	Q-36th; F-22nd	
3/26	Bristol Motor Speedway	NASCAR WC	MB2 #36	Rusty Wallace	Q-25th; F-26th	
4/2	Texas Motor Speedway	NASCAR WC	MB2 #36	Dale Earnhardt, Jr.	Q-36th; F-18th	
4/9	Martinsville Speedway	NASCAR WC	MB2 #36	Mark Martin	Q-12th; F-12th	
4/10	Martinsville Speedway	NASCAR CT	Schrader #52			Big wreck
4/16	Talladega Superspeedway	NASCAR WC	MB2 #36	Jeff Gordon	Q-40th; F-36th	Lost laps fixing oil leak
4/22	Las Vegas Motor Speedway	NASCAR WW	Schrader #99		Q-2nd	
4/29	California Speedway	NASCAR WW	Schrader #99	Johnny Benson	Q-1st; F-2nd	
4/30	California Speedway	NASCAR WC	MB2 #36	Jeremy Mayfield	Q-18th; F-24th	
5/6	Richmond International Raceway	NASCAR WC	MB2 #36	Dale Earnhardt, Jr.	Q-34th; F-12th	
5/12	Batesville Speedway	MARS Late Model	Schrader #99	Terry Phillips	H-2nd; F-7th	
5/13	I-55 Raceway	UMP Late Model	Schrader #99	Randy Korte	H-5th; F-3rd	
5/19	Lowe's Motor Speedway	NASCAR WC	MB2 #36	Steve Park	F-13th	No Bull Qualifying Race
5/20	Lowe's Motor Speedway	NASCAR WC	MB2 #36	Matt Kenseth	Q-34th; F-37th	Winston Open; started 20th
5/28	Lowe's Motor Speedway	NASCAR WC	MB2 #36	Tony Stewart	H-1st; F-3rd	Got in one wreck; then wrecked by myself
5/31	Highland Speedway	UMP Late Model	Schrader #99		Q-31s; F-23rd	
6/4	Dover International Speedway	NASCAR WC	MB2 #36	Carl Edwards		
6/6	24 Raceway Park	Modified	John Logue #69	Tony Stewart		Crashed in feature
6/11	Michigan International Speedway	NASCAR WC	MB2 #36	Jeremy Mayfield		
6/19	Pocono Raceway	NASCAR WC	MB2 #36	Jeff Gordon		
6/25	Sears Point Raceway	NASCAR WC	MB2 #36	Jeff Burton		
7/1	Daytona International Speedway	NASCAR WC	MB2 #36	Kurt Busch		
7/8	New Hampshire Int'l Speedway	NASCAR CT	Schrader #52		Q-3rd; F-9th	

Date	Track	Type	Car Owner	Race Winner	Finish	Comments
7/9	New Hampshire Int'l Speedway	NASCAR WC	MB2 #36	Tony Stewart	Q-7th	
7/14	State Fair Speedway	MLRA Late Model	Schrader #52	Terry Phillips	H-1st, F-2nd	
7/15	I-55 Raceway	UMP Late Model	Schrader #52	Ken Schrader	H-1st, F-1st, F-1st	
7/17	Action Track	Northern All Stars LM	Schrader #52	Terry Phillips	H-2nd, F-3rd	
7/19	Crawford County Speedway	Modified	Harris #22	Terry Phillips	H-1st, F-2nd	
7/23	Pocono Raceway	NASCAR WC	MB2 #36	Rusty Wallace	Q-29th; F-19th	Started 20th; no yellows!
7/24	Highland Speedway	UMP Late Model	Schrader	Kevin Weaver	Q-5th, S-4th, F-3rd	Was too tight
7/25	Hawkeye Downs Speedway	IMCA Late Model	Schrader		H-2nd, F-4th	Big wreck lap 2
7/29	Gateway International Raceway	NASCAR BGN	Amick #88	Kevin Harvick	Q-38th; F-43rd	Slinger Nationals; 2 laps down
7/30	Slinger Super Speedway	Late Model	Jeff Victor		Q-22nd (11.88 sec.); F-15th	
8/5	Indianapolis Motor Speedway	NASCAR WC	MB2 #36	Bobby Labonte	F-22nd	Was bad all night
8/5	I-55 Raceway	UMP Late Model	Schrader #99	Ed Dixon	H-6th, F-10th	Got crashed lap 1
8/9	Beaver Dam Raceway	IMCA Modified	Schrock		H-1st, F-2nd	Lost most of time under braking in turn one
8/12	Watkins Glen International	NASCAR WC	MB2 #36	Steve Park	Q-19th; F-18th	
8/20	Michigan International Speedway	NASCAR WC	MB2 #36	Rusty Wallace	Q-12th; F-19th	Ran better; last stop screwed us up
8/26	Bristol Motor Speedway	NASCAR WC	MB2 #36	Rusty Wallace	Q-15th; F-12th	
9/3	Darlington Raceway	NASCAR WC	MB2 #36	Bobby Labonte	Q-8th; F-16th	
9/4	Rocky Mountain Raceway	NASCAR WW	Bill Strausser #10	Bobby Dotter	Q-8th	
9/7	Richmond International Raceway	NASCAR CT	Schrader #52	Rick Carelli	F-7th	Started last; not there for qual on Saturday
9/9	Richmond International Raceway	NASCAR WC	MB2 #36	Jeff Gordon	Q-9th; F-17th	
9/9	Salem Speedway	ARCA Stock Car	Schrader #99	Frank Kimmel	F-34th	
9/10	New Hampshire Int'l Speedway	NASCAR WC	MB2 #36	Jeff Burton	Q-9th; F-10th	
9/17	Dover International Speedway	NASCAR CT	Schrader #52	Kurt Busch	Q-3rd, F-5th	
9/22	Dover International Speedway	NASCAR WC	MB2 #36	Tony Stewart	Q-18th; F-30th	
9/24	Martinsville Speedway	NASCAR WC	MB2 #36	Tony Stewart	Q-39th; F-16th	
10/1	Lowe's Motor Speedway	NASCAR WC	MB2 #36	Bobby Labonte	Q-20th; F-25th	
10/8	Talladega Short Track	Late Model		Dale Earnhardt, Sr.	Q-14th, F-37th	Match race with Red Farmer, car broke
10/14	Talladega Superspeedway	NASCAR WC	MB2 #36	Dale Jarrett	Q-19th; F-18th	Blew up!
10/15	North Carolina Motor Speedway	NASCAR WC	MB2 #36	Kurt Busch	F-17th	
10/22	California Speedway	NASCAR CT	Schrader #52	Garrett Evans	Q-2nd, F-31st	Huge crash on lap 2; car was destroyed
10/28	Phoenix International Raceway	NASCAR SW	Schrader #99	Jeff Burton	F-30th	
11/5	Phoenix International Raceway	NASCAR WC	MB2 #36	Tony Stewart	Q-13th; F-18th	
11/12	Homestead-Miami Speedway	NASCAR WC	MB2 #36			
11/20	Atlanta Motor Speedway	NASCAR WC	MB2 #36	Jerry Nadeau		

2001

Date	Track	Type	Car Owner	Race Winner	Finish	Comments
1/28	Central Arizona Raceway	Late Model	Schrader #99	Steve Drake	H-2nd	Started 7th in heat; blew up in dash; was real fast
2/4	Phoenix International Raceway	NASCAR WW	Schrader	Ken Schrader	Q-3rd, F-1st	
2/4	Phoenix International Raceway	NASCAR SW	Schrader	Ken Schrader	Q-1st, F-1st	Drew pole; was black-flagged then ran out of fuel
2/11	Daytona International Speedway	NASCAR WC	MB2 #36	Tony Stewart	Q-1st; F-16th	Bud Shoot-out
2/15	Daytona International Speedway	NASCAR WC	MB2 #36	Mike Skinner	Q-14th; F-6th	Twin 125
2/18	Daytona International Speedway	NASCAR WC	MB2 #36	Michael Waltrip	Q-28th; F-13th	Big wreck last lap
2/26	North Carolina Motor Speedway	NASCAR WC	MB2 #36	Steve Park	Q-15th; F-22nd	
3/4	Las Vegas Motor Speedway	NASCAR WC	MB2 #36	Jeff Gordon	Q-29th; F-25th	
3/11	Atlanta Motor Speedway	NASCAR WC	MB2 #36	Kevin Harvick	Q-27th; F-8th	
3/18	Darlington Raceway	NASCAR WC	MB2 #36	Dale Jarrett	F-13th	
3/25	Bristol Motor Speedway	NASCAR WC	MB2 #36	Elliott Sadler	Q-10th; F-35th	Wrecked by Little E

Date	Track	Series	Car	Driver	Result	Notes
3/31	Texas Motor Speedway	UDTRA	Schrader #99	Jimmy Mars	F-6th	(Short track race)
4/1	Texas Motor Speedway	NASCAR WC	MB2 #36	Dale Jarrett	Q-13th; F-10th	
4/7	Martinsville Speedway	NASCAR CT	Schrader #52	Scott Riggs	Q-9th; F-29th	
4/8	Martinsville Speedway	NASCAR WC	MB2 #36	Dale Jarrett	Q-32nd; F-25th	Wrecked
4/13	Nashville Superspeedway	ARCA Stock Car	Schrader #99	Ken Schrader	Q-9th; F-1st	Was shit all day; 1 flat; 1 spin
4/14	I-55 Raceway	UMP Late Model	Schrader #99	Kevin Gundaker	H-1st; D-5th; F-4th	
4/15	Monett Speedway	UMP Late Model	Schrader #99	Billy Moyer	H-3rd; S-1st; F-9th	
4/22	Talladega Superspeedway	NASCAR WC	MB2 #36	Bobby Hamilton	Q-36th; F-40th	Was leading and ran out of fuel
4/28	California Speedway	NASCAR WW	MB2 #36		Q-4th; F-6th	We were junk
4/29	California Speedway	NASCAR WC	MB2 #36	Rusty Wallace	F-9th	
5/5	Richmond International Raceway	NASCAR WC	Schrader #52	Tony Stewart	F-17th	Started last; was terrible
5/6	Gateway International Raceway	NASCAR CT	Schrader #52	Ted Musgrave	Q-13th; F-2nd	
5/12	Darlington Raceway	NASCAR CT	Schrader #99	Bobby Hamilton	F-7th	Got there late and started last
5/12	I-55 Raceway	UMP Late Model	Schrader #99	Kevin Gundaker	Q-14th; D-4th; F-7th	
5/15	Farmer City Raceway	UMP Late Model	MB2 #36	Jeff Burton	F-5th	Winston Open
5/19	Lowe's Motor Speedway	NASCAR WC	MB2 #36	Jeff Burton	F-21st	Should of run 5th; pit stop screw up cost us 1 lap
5/27	Lowe's Motor Speedway	NASCAR WC	Schrader #52	Scott Riggs	Q-6th; F-7th	Got tight at end
6/2	Dover International Speedway	NASCAR CT	MB2 #36	Jeff Gordon		Crash on lap 2
6/3	Dover International Speedway	UMP Late Model	Schrader #99	Ed Dixon	F-9th	
6/5	Quincy Raceway	UMP Late Model	Schrader #99	Kevin Gundaker	F-12th	
6/6	I-55 Raceway	UMP Late Model	MB2 #36	Jeff Gordon		
6/10	Michigan International Speedway	NASCAR WC	MB2 #36		Q-33rd; F-14th	Ran in top 10 most all day; didn't pit at end for tires; was still the right decision
6/12	Highland Speedway	UMP Late Model	Schrader #99	Ed Dixon	Q-5th; D-5th; F-3rd	
6/17	Pocono Raceway	NASCAR WC	MB2 #36	Ricky Rudd	Q-3rd; F-9th	
6/24	Sears Point Raceway	NASCAR WC	Schrader #52	Tony Stewart	Q-33rd; F-37th	Broke rear end
6/27	Kankakee Speedway	UMP Late Model	Schrader #52	Bob Pierce	Q-17th; H-3rd; S-1st; F-10th	
6/28	Beaver Dam Raceway	UMP Late Model	Schrader #52	Brian Birkhofer	Q-3rd; H-2nd; F-6th	
6/29	Red Cedar Speedway	WISSOTA	Schrader #52		Q-7th; S-2nd; F-17th	
6/30	Milwaukee Mile	NASCAR CT	Schrader #99	Ted Musgrave	Q-18th; F-8th	Started 20th; one-groove
6/30	I-55 Raceway	UMP Late Model	Schrader #99	Billy Moyer	Q-7th; H-2nd; F-9th	
7/1	DuQuoin Fairgrounds	UMP Late Model	Schrader #99	Billy Moyer	Q-5th; S-3rd; F-5th	
7/7	Daytona International Speedway	NASCAR WC	MB2 #36	Dale Earnhardt, Jr.	F-15th	Broke valve; started leaking & driver hit wall
7/10	Hawkeye Downs Speedway	IMCA Late Model	Schrader #99	Ken Schrader	H-1st; F-1st	Had left rear tire lose air at end
7/15	Chicagoland Speedway	NASCAR WC	MB2 #36	Kevin Harvick	Q-12th	
7/17	Slinger Super Speedway	Late Model	Jeff Victor	Bob Pierce	Q-8th; NASCAR D-1st; F-4th	Ran like shit all day; Slinger Nationals
7/18	Action Track	UMP Late Model	Schrader #99	Jack Sprague	Q-7th; D-3rd; F-7th	
7/21	New Hampshire Int'l Speedway	NASCAR CT	Schrader #52	Dale Jarrett	Q-11th; F-7th	
7/22	New Hampshire Int'l Speedway	NASCAR WC	MB2 #36	Randy Korte	Q-8th; F-22nd	
7/23	Highland Speedway	UMP Late Model	Schrader #52	Rodney Melvin	H-5th; S-2nd; F-12th	
7/25	St. Francois Raceway	UMP Late Model	Schrader #99	Bobby Labonte	H-2nd; D-2nd; F-3rd	
7/29	Pocono Raceway	NASCAR WC	MB2 #36	Jeff Gordon	Q-4th; F-17th	
8/5	Indianapolis Motor Speedway	NASCAR WC	MB2 #36		Q-40th; F-28th	
8/5	Tri-State Speedway	Modified	Dirt Works #17	Ken Schrader	H-1st; F-15th	Led 33 of 40 laps; broke shock
8/8	Beaver Dam Raceway	IMCA Modified	Dirt Works	Jeff Gordon	H-2nd; F-1st	
8/12	Watkins Glen International	NASCAR WC	MB2 #36		F-19th	
8/15	Berlin Raceway	Late Model	Randy Sweet #1	Sterling Marlin	Q-36th; 1st F-5th; 2nd; F-7th	
8/19	Michigan International Speedway	NASCAR WC	MB2 #36	Ken Schrader	Q-38th; F-20th	
8/21	I-30 Raceway	Late Model	Schrader #99	Tony Stewart	H-3rd; F-1st	Left wheel loose; pitted under green; also had flat
8/25	Bristol Motor Speedway	NASCAR WC	MB2 #36	Ward Burton	Q-8th; F-10th	Ran better than that all day
9/2	Darlington Raceway	NASCAR WC	MB2 #36			

Date	Track	Type	Car Owner	Race Winner	Finish	Comments
9/3	DuQuoin Fairgrounds	ARCA Stock Car	Schrader #99	Frank Kimmel	Q-8th; F-4th	
9/6	Richmond International Raceway	NASCAR CT	Schrader #52	Jack Sprague	F-12th	
9/8	Richmond International Raceway	NASCAR WC	MB2 #36	Ricky Rudd	F-23rd	Not there to qualify
9/9	Salem Speedway	ARCA Stock Car	Schrader #99	Frank Kimmel	F-3rd	
9/14	Belle-Clair Speedway	UMP Late Model	Schrader #99		H-3rd; D-5th; F-3rd	I-55 Nationals
9/15	I-55 Raceway	UMP Late Model	Schrader #99	Billy Moyer	H-4th; F-17th	
9/16	Illinois State Fairgrounds	UMP Late Model	Schrader #99	Shannon Babb	Q-1st; H-2nd; F-2nd	
9/23	Dover International Speedway	NASCAR WC	MB2 #36	Dale Earnhardt, Jr.	Q-13th; F-18th	
9/30	Kansas Speedway	NASCAR WC	MB2 #36	Jeff Gordon	Q-28th; F-26th	
10/7	Lowe's Motor Speedway	NASCAR WC	MB2 #36	Sterling Marlin	Q-34th; F-14th	
10/15	Martinsville Speedway	NASCAR WC	MB2 #36	Ricky Craven	Q-20th; F-11th	
10/21	Talladega Superspeedway	NASCAR WC	MB2 #36	Dale Earnhardt, Jr.	Q-36th; F-31st	Had wreck in Saturday Happy Hour; driver lost draft Sunday
10/25	Phoenix International Raceway	NASCAR SW	Schrader #99		Q-2nd; F-3rd	
10/26	Phoenix International Raceway	NASCAR CT	Schrader #52		F-10th	
10/27	Phoenix International Raceway	NASCAR BGN	Schrader #07		Q-10th; F-18th	
10/28	Phoenix International Raceway	NASCAR WC	MB2 #36	Jeff Burton	Q-12th; F-19th	
11/4	North Carolina Motor Speedway	NASCAR WC	MB2 #36	Joe Nemechek	Q-46th; F-42nd	Cut right front; had flat and crashed
11/11	Homestead-Miami Speedway	NASCAR WC	MB2 #36	Bill Elliott	Q-43rd; F-31st	Had two right front flats
11/18	Atlanta Motor Speedway	NASCAR WC	MB2 #36	Bobby Labonte	Q-20th; F-39th	Had brake problems and ran terrible
11/23	New Hampshire Int'l Speedway	NASCAR WC	MB2 #36	Robby Gordon		Started by points; threw off fan belts

2002

Date	Track	Type	Car Owner	Race Winner	Finish	Comments
1/26	Central Arizona Raceway	Late Model	Schrader	Al Purkey	H-7th; B F-3rd	
1/27	Central Arizona Raceway	Late Model	Schrader		F-10th	
2/1-2	Phoenix International Raceway	NASCAR WW	Schrader	Cameron	Q-5th; F-9th	Should have been 3rd or 4th; pit to put fuel cap back on
2/1-2	Phoenix International Raceway	NASCAR SW	Schrader	Ken Schrader	Q-4th; F-1st	
2/10	Daytona International Speedway	NASCAR WC	MB2 #36	Tony Stewart	F-4th	Bud Shoot-out
2/14	Daytona International Speedway	NASCAR WC	MB2 #36	Jeff Gordon	F-3rd	Twin 125
2/17	Daytona International Speedway	NASCAR WC	MB2 #36	Ward Burton	F-26th	Daytona 500; big wreck/ran good
2/24	North Carolina Motor Speedway	NASCAR WC	MB2 #36	Matt Kenseth	Q-2nd; F-35th	Blew engine late in race
3/2	Las Vegas Motor Speedway	NASCAR BGN	Schrader #52	Jeff Burton	Q-29th; F-39th	
3/3	Las Vegas Motor Speedway	NASCAR WC	MB2 #36	Sterling Marlin	Q-29th; F-26th	T. Bodine cut our left rear tire running top 10
3/10	Atlanta Motor Speedway	NASCAR WC	MB2 #36	Tony Stewart	Q-25th; F-24th	
3/15	Darlington Raceway	NASCAR WC	Schrader #52	Ted Musgrave	Q-10th; F-10th	
3/17	Darlington Raceway	NASCAR WC	MB2 #36	Sterling Marlin	Q-8th; F-35th	Big wreck lap 225
3/24	Bristol Motor Speedway	NASCAR WC	MB2 #36	Kurt Busch	Q-18th; F-22nd	
3/29	Joplin 66 Speedway	IMCA Modified	Mike Clark		H-1st	
4/6	Texas Motor Speedway	NASCAR BGN	Schrader #52	Jeff Purvis	Q-26th; F-37th	Blew engine leading
4/8	Texas Motor Speedway	NASCAR WC	MB2 #36	Matt Kenseth	Q-12th; F-34th	Distributor problems
4/13	Martinsville Speedway	NASCAR CT	Schrader #52	Dennis Setzer	Q-16th; F-11th	Missed big on chassis
4/14	Martinsville Speedway	NASCAR WC	MB2 #36	Bobby Labonte	Q-38th; F-24th	2 flats; fire; 40 laps repair
4/21	Talladega Superspeedway	NASCAR WC	MB2 #36	Dale Earnhardt, Jr.	Q-36th; F-24th	Lost draft when ignition switch was cut off by roll-bar padding
4/28	California Speedway	NASCAR WC	MB2 #36	Jimmie Johnson	Q-23rd; F-43rd	Blew up on lap 3; was up to 14th
5/4	Richmond International Raceway	NASCAR WC	MB2 #36	Tony Stewart	F-15th	
5/10	Malden Speedway	MARS Late Model	Schrader #99	Wendell Wallace	H-5th; S-3rd; F-20th	

Date	Track	Series	Car	Driver	Results	Notes
5/14	Farmer City Raceway	UMP Late Model	Schrader #52	Roger Long	Q-15th; H-5th; S-1st; F-10th	
5/15	Paducah International Raceway	UMP Late Model	Schrader #99	Terry English	Q-4th; H-1st; D-2nd; F-4th	
5/18	Lowe's Motor Speedway	NASCAR WC	MB2 #36	Mayfield/Newman	Q-6th; 1st F-2nd; 2nd F-3rd	Engine blew on last lap; pit stop in 1st out 9th
5/19	DuQuoin Fairgrounds	UMP Late Model	Schrader #99	Shannon Babb	Q-2nd; H-5th; F-5th	Contact with small wall in heat
5/20	Dakota State Fair Speedway	UDTRA	Schrader #99	Dale McDowell	Q-21st; 1st F-6th; 2nd F-13th	
5/26	Lowe's Motor Speedway	NASCAR WC	MB2 #36	Mark Martin		
5/31	Dover International Speedway	NASCAR CT	Schrader #52	Ted Musgrave	F-35th	Cut right front tire and hit wall
6/2	Dover International Speedway	NASCAR WC	MB2 #36	Jimmie Johnson		Broke track bar mount 30 laps to go running 20th
6/9	Pocono Raceway	NASCAR WC	MB2 #36	Dale Jarrett	Q-38th; F-16th	Started by points
6/12	I-55 Raceway	UMP Late Model	Schrader #99	Ed Dixon		Missed show
6/16	Michigan International Speedway	NASCAR WC	MB2 #36	Matt Kenseth	Q-18th; H-3rd; F-11th	
6/18	Highland Speedway	UMP Late Model	Schrader #99	Rodney Melvin	Q-18th	Broke rear gear
6/23	Sears Point Raceway	NASCAR WC	MB2 #36	Ricky Rudd	F-1st	Match race with Joe Kosiski
6/26	I-80 Speedway	Late Model	Schrader #36	Ken Schrader	H-1st; F-1st	
6/28	Jacksonville Raceway	UMP Modified	Dirt Works	Ken Schrader		Broke brake caliper bracket off rear end
6/29	Milwaukee Mile	NASCAR CT	Schrader #52	Terry Cook	Q-8th; H-2nd; F-13th	Summernationals
6/29	I-55 Raceway	UMP Late Model	Schrader #99	Shannon Babb	Q-16th; H-4th; F-9th	
6/30	Cayuga Speedway	CASCAR		Matt Kenseth	Q-1st; F-1st	
7/3	South Boston Speedway	ARCA Stock Car	Schrader #99	Ken Schrader	Q-19th; F-25th	Cut oil line and lost two laps
7/6	Daytona International Speedway	NASCAR WC	MB2 #36	Michael Waltrip	Q-5th; H-3rd; F-9th	Summernationals
7/8	Shawano Speedway	UMP Late Model	Schrader #99	Billy Moyer	H-2nd; F-3rd	
7/9	Hawkeye Downs Speedway	IMCA Late Model	Schrader #99			
7/14	Chicagoland Speedway	NASCAR WC	MB2 #36	Kevin Harvick	Q-27th; F-40th	Blew up running 18th; over halfway
7/16	Quincy Raceways	UMP Late Model	Schrader #99	Ed Dixon	H-1st; F-2nd	
7/20	New Hampshire Int'l Speedway	NASCAR CT	Schrader #52	Terry Cook	Q-8th; F-33rd	Brake valve messed up
7/21	New Hampshire Int'l Speedway	NASCAR WC	MB2 #36	Ward Burton	Q-20th; F-24th	
7/23	Slinger Super Speedway	Late Model	Jeff Victor #52	Matt Kenseth	Q-23rd; D-6th; F-24th	
7/24	St. Francois Raceway	Late Model	Schrader #52		F-3rd	
7/24	St. Francois Raceway	Modified	Dirt Works	Scott Webber	F-3rd	Pathrum show
7/27	Ona WV race track			Ken Schrader	F-1st	
7/28	Pocono Raceway	NASCAR WC	MB2 #36	Bill Elliott	Q-25th; F-20th	
7/31	I-55 Raceway	UMP Late Model	Schrader	Ed Dixon	H-1st; D-1st; F-2nd	M & M Night of Stars
8/3	Indianapolis Motor Speedway	IROC		Dale Jarrett	F-3rd	Drove for Lasoski
8/4	Indianapolis Motor Speedway	NASCAR WC	MB2 #36	Bill Elliott	Q-30th; F-14th	
8/6	Action Track	UMP Late Model	Schrader #99	Don O'Neal	Q-3rd; H-2nd; F-7th	
8/7	I-55 Raceway	UMP Modified	Dirt Works		H-2nd; F-4th	
8/11	Watkins Glen International	NASCAR WC	MB2 #36	Tony Stewart	Q-41st; F-28th	
8/13	Wheatland Raceway	MLRA Late Model	Schrader #99		H-3rd	Rained out after heats
8/13	Wheatland Raceway	MLRA Modified	Dirt Works		H-4th	Rained out after heats
8/14	Berlin Raceway	Late Model	Randy Sweet #1	Johnny Benson	Qual F-1st; F-3rd	
8/18	Michigan International Speedway	NASCAR WC	MB2 #36	Dale Jarrett	Q-27th; F-14th	
8/24	Bristol Motor Speedway	NASCAR WC	MB2 #36	Jeff Gordon	Q-40th; F-14th	
9/1	Darlington Raceway	NASCAR WC	MB2 #36	Jeff Gordon	Q-31st; F-26th	
9/2	DuQuoin Fairgrounds	ARCA Stock Car	Schrader #99	Frank Kimmel	Q-4th; F-3rd	
9/5	Richmond International Raceway	NASCAR CT	Schrader #52		Q-14th; F-10th	
9/7	Richmond International Raceway	NASCAR WC	MB2 #36	Matt Kenseth	Q-16th; F-26th	
9/15	New Hampshire Int'l Speedway	NASCAR WC	MB2 #36	Ryan Newman	Q-16th; F-13th	
9/21	Oswego Speedway	Modified	Ted Christopher		Q-2nd; F-21st	
9/22	Dover International Speedway	NASCAR WC	MB2 #36	Jimmie Johnson	Q-27th; F-22nd	Pulled in w/bent wheel/was running 7th
9/28	I-55 Raceway	UMP Late Model	Schrader	Billy Moyer	Q-6th; D-3rd; F-3rd	
9/29	Kansas Speedway	NASCAR WC	MB2 #36	Jeff Gordon	Q-39th; F-28th	Dixon drove GRT car and finished 4th

Date	Track	Type	Car Owner	Race Winner	Finish	Comments
10/4	Talladega Short Track	Southern All Stars LM	Schrader		Q-6th	
10/6	Talladega Superspeedway	NASCAR WC	MB2 #36	Dale Earnhardt, Jr.	Q-31st, F-41st	Was leading and got to car wrestling
10/13	Lowe's Motor Speedway	NASCAR WC	MB2 #36	Jamie McMurray	Q-32nd, F-31st	Engine blew up
10/20	Martinsville Speedway	NASCAR WC	MB2 #36	Kurt Busch	Q-25th, F-26th	
10/27	Atlanta Motor Speedway	NASCAR WC	MB2 #36	Kurt Busch	Q-31st, F-42nd	
11/3	North Carolina Motor Speedway	NASCAR WC	MB2 #36	Johnny Benson	Q-12th, F-22nd	
11/7	Phoenix International Raceway	Late Model	Schrader #99	Paul Menard	Q-2nd, F-22nd	
11/8	Phoenix International Raceway	NASCAR CT	Schrader #52	Kevin Harvick	Q-15th, F-7th	
11/10	Phoenix International Raceway	NASCAR WC	MB2 #36	Matt Kenseth	Q-21st, F-37th	
11/15	Homestead-Miami Speedway	NASCAR CT	Schrader #52	Ron Hornaday, Jr.	Q-17th, F-30th	
11/17	Homestead-Miami Speedway	NASCAR WC	MB2 #36	Kurt Busch	Q-21st, F-27th	
11/23	Lake Cumberland KY track	Late Model	Schrader #99		Q-4th, H-1st, D-2nd, F-4th	Fuel pump (qual); left rear tire loose (race)
11/24	Lake Cumberland KY track	Late Model	Schrader #99		F-2nd	Engine
11/29	Columbus Speedway	Late Model	Schrader #99	Anthony Rushing	F-2nd	Missed weight by 25 lbs; disqualified and 2nd paid $4000; paid for 18th
12/7	River Valley Raceway	Late Model	Schrader #99	David Gentry	Q-1st (14.85 sec.); F-3rd	New Track Record

2003

Date	Track	Type	Car Owner	Race Winner	Finish	Comments
1/19	Manzanita Speedway	Late Model	Schrader #99	Pat Doar	Q-6th	Broke tie rod in Semi
1/21	Manzanita Speedway	Late Model	Schrader #99	Bill Frye	H-2nd, F-18th	Spun out running 6th; no damage; pulled in
1/23	Central Arizona Raceway	Late Model	Schrader #99	Pat Doar	H-1st, F-5th	
1/25	Central Arizona Raceway	Late Model	Schrader #99		H-1st	
1/26	Central Arizona Raceway	Modified				Pulled in; running good but caught in crash
2/1-2	Phoenix International Raceway	NASCAR WW	Schrader	Jeff Taylor	Q-2nd, F-1st	
2/1-2	Phoenix International Raceway	NASCAR SW	Schrader	Ken Schrader	Q-1st, F-8th	
2/13	East Bay Raceway Park	STARS Late Model	Schrader #99	Bryan Germone	Q-17th, H-4th, S-2nd, F-25th	Feature pulled in
2/4	East Bay Raceway Park	X-treme Late Model	Schrader #99	Steve Francis	Q-35th, H-6th, S-4th, F-21st	Was promoter's option
2/5	East Bay Raceway Park	STARS Late Model	Schrader #99	Rick Eckert	Q-27th, H-2nd, F-11th	Renegade STARS
2/8	Daytona International Speedway	NASCAR WC	BAM #49	Chub Frank	Drew 11th, F-6th	Bud Shoot-out
2/3	Daytona International Speedway	NASCAR WC	BAM #49	Dale Earnhardt, Jr.	F-15th	Twin 125
2/16	Daytona International Speedway	NASCAR WC	BAM #49	Michael Waltrip	Start-28th, F-42nd	Daytona 500; got wrecked by Ward Burton
2/23	North Carolina Motor Speedway	NASCAR WC	BAM #49	Michael Waltrip	Q-35th, F-24th	Got caught in pits by yellow
3/2	Las Vegas Motor Speedway	NASCAR WC	BAM #49	Dale Jarrett	Q-28th, F-28th	
3/9	Atlanta Motor Speedway	NASCAR WC	BAM #49	Matt Kenseth	Q-42nd, F-38th	Blew engine
3/16	Darlington Raceway	NASCAR WC	BAM #49	Bobby Labonte	Q-15th, F-17th	Pitted and got caught by yellow
3/23	Bristol Motor Speedway	NASCAR WC	BAM #49	Ricky Craven	Q-3rd, F-37th	Blew right front running 7th
3/30	Texas Motor Speedway	NASCAR WC	BAM #49	Kurt Busch	Q-42nd, F-24th	
4/6	Talladega Superspeedway	NASCAR WC	BAM #49	Ryan Newman	Q-41st, F-33rd	Lap 4 big accident; had to fix car
4/12	Martinsville Speedway	NASCAR CT	Schrader #52	Dale Earnhardt, Jr.	Q-9th, F-14th	
4/13	Martinsville Speedway	NASCAR WC	BAM #49	Dennis Setzer	Q-4th, F-10th	
4/16		SUPR	Schrader #99	Jeff Gordon	B F-2nd; A F-10th	
4/17	Macon Speedway	USMTS Modified	Dirt Works #99	Scott Slay	H-3rd, F-9th	
4/18	Paducah International Raceway	UMP Late Model	Schrader #99	Justin Boney	Q-5th, H-3rd, F-9th	
4/19	I-55 Raceway	UMP Late Model	Schrader #99	Terry English	Q-1st, D-1st, F-1st	
4/25	Cajon Speedway			Kenny Wallace	F-2nd	Pathrum show
4/26	California Speedway	NASCAR WW	Schrader #99	Steve Portenga	Q-3rd, F-2nd	
4/27	California Speedway	NASCAR WC	BAM #49	Kurt Busch	Q-41st, F-30th	
5/3	Richmond International Raceway	NASCAR WC	BAM #49	Joe Nemechek	F-24th	

Date	Track	Class	Team	Driver	Result	Notes
5/4	Toledo Speedway	ARCA Stock Car	Schrader #99	Frank Kimmel	Q-1st; F-28th	Led first 105 laps & had engine problems
5/9	Memphis Short Track	MARS Late Model	Schrader #99	Jeff Taylor	H-1st; F-4th	
5/11	Tri-State Speedway	UMP Late Model	Schrader #99	Kevin Claycomb	H-1st; F-6th	
5/13	Farmer City Raceway	UMP Late Model	Schrader #99	Roger Long	Q-22nd; S-3rd; F-9th	
5/13	Farmer City Raceway	UMP Modified	Dirt Works #99		H-4th; S-1st; F-10th	
5/14	Paducah International Raceway	UMP Late Model	Schrader #99	Terry English	Q-4th; H-3rd; F-5th	
5/14	Paducah International Raceway	UMP Modified	Dirt Works #99	Jim Schersek	H-2nd; F-3rd	
5/16	Lowe's Motor Speedway	NASCAR CT	Schrader #52	Ted Musgrave	Q-21st; F-11th	Winston Open
5/17	Lowe's Motor Speedway	NASCAR WC	BAM #49	Jimmie Johnson	F-13th	600-mile race
5/25	Lowe's Motor Speedway	NASCAR WC	BAM #49	Jimmie Johnson	Q-30th; F-28th	Lined up by points
5/30	Dover International Speedway	NASCAR CT	Schrader #52	Jason Leffler	F-6th	
6/1	Dover International Speedway	NASCAR WC	BAM #49	Ryan Newman	Q-25th; F-26th	Lost brakes; big crash
6/8	Pocono Raceway	NASCAR WC	BAM #49	Tony Stewart	Q-bad; F-43rd	
6/10	Quincy Raceway	IMCA Modified	Dirt Works #99	Henry Orlonjay	H-1st; S-6th	
6/15	Michigan International Speedway	NASCAR WC	BAM #49	Kurt Busch	Q-28th; F-42nd	Got wrecked lap 2
6/17	Highland Speedway	UMP Late Model	Schrader #99		F-2nd	
6/22	Sears Point Raceway	NASCAR WC	BAM #49	Robby Gordon	Q-42nd; F-33rd	
6/24	Hales Corner Speedway	UMP Late Model	Schrader #99	Billy Moyer	Q-28th; H-8th; F-18th	Summernationals; wrecked in B
6/27	Jacksonville Raceway	UMP Modified	Dirt Works #99		H-6th; F-2nd; F-8th	
6/28	Milwaukee Mile	NASCAR CT	Schrader #52			
6/28	I-55 Raceway	UMP Late Model				
7/5	Daytona International Speedway	NASCAR WC	BAM #49	Justin Allgaier	Q-7th; F-41st	Blew engine
7/8	Hawkeye Downs Speedway	IMCA Late Model	Schrader #99	Greg Biffle	H-1st; F-1st	
7/11	Red Cedar Speedway	WISSOTA	Schrader #99	Ken Schrader	H-3rd; F-3rd	
7/13	Chicagoland Speedway	NASCAR WC	BAM #49	Ryan Newman	Q-43rd; F-28th	Set field by points; had brake problems
7/20	New Hampshire Int'l Speedway	NASCAR WC	BAM #49	Jimmie Johnson	F-36th	Crashed on 2nd lap by slow car
7/23	Lake Erie Speedway		Hoover Racing	Glen Gault, Jr.		
7/27	Pocono Raceway	NASCAR WC	BAM #49	Ryan Newman	Q-34th; F-26th	
7/29	Action Track	UMP Late Model	Schrader #99	Don O'Neal	H-3rd; F-7th	
7/30	I-55 Raceway	UMP Late Model	Schrader #99	Justin Allgaier		
8/1	Indianapolis Raceway Park	NASCAR CT	Schrader #52	Carl Edwards	Q-3rd; D-3rd; F-2nd	M & M Night of Stars
8/2	Indianapolis Motor Speedway	NASCAR WC	BAM #49	Kevin Harvick	Q-13th; F-7th	
8/6	Independence Motor Speedway	Late Model	Schrader #99			Missed show
8/9	I-55 Raceway	UMP Late Model	Schrader #99			
8/10	Watkins Glen International	NASCAR WC	BAM #59	Robby Gordon	Q-39th	
8/12	Joplin 66 Speedway	Modified	Dirt Works #99		H-1st; F-3rd	
8/13	Napa Race Park	Modified	Dirt Works #99		H-2nd; D-3rd; F-6th	
8/14	Farley Speedway	Late Model	Schrader #99			Missed show
8/17	Michigan International Speedway	NASCAR WC	BAM #49	Ryan Newman	Q-30th; F-8th	
8/20	Bristol Motor Speedway	NASCAR CT	Schrader #52	Travis Kvapil	Q-14th; F-13th	Started last due to engine change
8/23	Bristol Motor Speedway	NASCAR WC	BAM #49	Kurt Busch	Q-26th; F-12th	Flat running 6th with 50 laps to go
8/31	Darlington Raceway	NASCAR WC	BAM #49	Terry Labonte	Q-38th; F-38th	Crashed twice; hood blew up
9/1	DuQuoin Fairgrounds	ARCA Stock Car	Schrader #99	Tony Stewart	Q-4th; F-2nd	
9/3	Sheboygan Co. Fair Park	Modified	Schrader #52		H-7th	Car was shitbox
9/4	Richmond International Raceway	NASCAR CT	Schrader #52	Tony Stewart	Q-25th; F-33rd	Qual rained out; lined up by points; alternator quit during race
9/6	Richmond International Raceway	NASCAR WC	BAM #49	Ryan Newman	Q-27th; F-25th	
9/7	Columbus Speedway			Bill Cunningham	Q-19th; F-7th	
9/7	Tri-City Speedway			Jimmy Spencer	H-2nd; F-5th	
9/13	New Hampshire Int'l Speedway	NASCAR CT	Schrader #52		Q-5th; F-11th	
9/14	New Hampshire Int'l Speedway	NASCAR WC	BAM #49	Jimmie Johnson	Q-20th; F-37th	Car was bad and then engine blew up

Date	Track	Type	Car Owner	Race Winner	Finish	Comments
9/21	Dover International Speedway	NASCAR WC	BAM #49	Matt Kenseth	Q-23rd; S-2nd; F-9th	Lined up by points
9/26	Talladega Short Track	Southern All Stars LM	Schrader #99			
9/28	Talladega Superspeedway	NASCAR WC	BAM #49	Michael Waltrip	Q-7th; F-21st	
10/5	Kansas Speedway	NASCAR WC	BAM #49	Ryan Newman	Q-43rd; F-28th	Missed show
10/11	Lowe's Motor Speedway	NASCAR WC	BAM #49	Tony Stewart	Q-7th; F-8th	
10/18	Martinsville Speedway	NASCAR CT	Schrader #52	Jon Wood	Q-1st; F-1st	
10/18		ARCA Stock Car	Schrader #99	Ken Schrader	Q-18th; F-22nd	
10/19	Martinsville Speedway	NASCAR WC	BAM #49	Jeff Gordon	Q-12th	Flat running 7th w/15 laps to go
10/25	Dixie Speedway					Track supplied car; broke in feature
10/27	Atlanta Motor Speedway	NASCAR WC	BAM #49	Jeff Gordon	Q-40th; F-26th	Running 8th w/15 laps to go; wrecked by Newman
10/30	Phoenix International Raceway	NASCAR SW	Schrader #99	Eddie McKean	Q-12th; F-11th	
10/31	Phoenix International Raceway	NASCAR CT	Schrader #52	Kevin Harvick	Q-4th; F-17th	
11/2	Phoenix International Raceway	NASCAR WC	BAM #49	Dale Earnhardt, Jr.	Q-34th; F-27th	
11/9	North Carolina Motor Speedway	NASCAR WC	BAM #49	Bill Elliott	F-32nd	Blew engine
11/14	Homestead-Miami Speedway	NASCAR CT	Schrader #52	Bobby Hamilton		Missed show
11/16	Homestead-Miami Speedway	NASCAR WC	BAM #49	Bobby Labonte		
11/21	Kentucky Lake Speedway	Late Model	Schrader #52	Steve Francis	Q-8th; H-2nd; F-6th	
11/22	Kentucky Lake Speedway	Late Model	Schrader #99	Scott Bloomquist	S-2nd; F-16th	
11/28	Columbus Speedway	Late Model	Schrader #99		Q-2nd; D-1st	
11/29	Columbus Speedway	Late Model	Schrader #99	Mike Boland	F-2nd	
12/6	I-20 Speedway	Late Model	Schrader #99	Jack Pennington	Q-17th; F-7th	

2004

Date	Track	Type	Car Owner	Race Winner	Finish	Comments
1/8	Tulsa Expo Raceway (indoor)	Midget	Jerry Russell #20K		H-4th; B F-9th	Chili Bowl
1/13	New Smyrna Speedway	Late Model	Schrader #99	Steve Francis	H-4th; B F-4th	Kyle Petty Benefit; crash in feature
1/7	Central Arizona Raceway	Late Model	Schrader #99	Terry Phillips	H-3rd; S-4th; B F-11th; A F-16th	Missed A F; needed to be in top 3 of B F
1/18	Manzanita Speedway	Late Model	Schrader #99	John Andusa		
1/20	Central Arizona Raceway	Late Model	Schrader #99			Rained out
1/23	Central Arizona Raceway	Late Model	Schrader #99			
1/25	Phoenix International Raceway	NASCAR SW	Schrader #99	Eddie McKean	Q-3rd; F-7th	
1/25	Phoenix International Raceway	NASCAR WW	Schrader #99	Ken Schrader	F-1st	
2/3	Volusia Speedway Park	WoO Late Model	Schrader #99	Steve Francis	Q-5th; H-4th; F-12th	First World of Outlaws late model race ever
2/4	Volusia Speedway Park	WoO Late Model	Schrader #99	Bart Hartman	Q-13th; H-4th; F18th	
2/7	Daytona International Speedway	NASCAR NC	BAM #49	Dale Jarrett	Q-14th; F-13th	First Nextel Cup race; random draw for Shoot-out
2/8	Volusia Speedway Park	WoO Late Model	Schrader #99	Scott Bloomquist	Q-1st; H-1st; F-15th	
2/12	Daytona International Speedway	NASCAR NC	BAM #49	Elliott Sadler	F-18th	Twin 125; started 22nd
2/15	Daytona International Speedway	NASCAR NC	BAM #49	Dale Earnhardt, Jr.	F-40th	Started 37th in Daytona 500; Rusty caused wreck
2/22	North Carolina Motor Speedway	NASCAR NC	BAM #49	Matt Kenseth	Q-18th; F-27th	Had flat & hit wall; then got hit by Jimmie Johnson when I was coming in pits
2/27	Pike County Speedway	Late Model	Schrader #99	Kenny Merchant	H-1st; F-3rd	
2/28	Pike County Speedway	Late Model	Schrader #99	David Ashley	H-2nd; F-4th	
3/7	Las Vegas Motor Speedway	NASCAR NC	BAM #49	Matt Kenseth	Q-31st; F-32nd	
3/13	Atlanta Motor Speedway	NASCAR CT	Schrader #52	Bobby Hamilton	Q-10th; F-10th	
3/14	Atlanta Motor Speedway	NASCAR NC	BAM #49	Dale Earnhardt, Jr.	Q-24th; F-24th	
3/21	Darlington Raceway	NASCAR NC	BAM #49	Jimmie Johnson	Q-16th; F-22nd	
3/28	Bristol Motor Speedway	NASCAR NC	BAM #49	Kurt Busch	Q-19th; F-6th	
4/4	Texas Motor Speedway	NASCAR NC	BAM #49	Eliott Sadler	F-19th	
4/4	Nashville Superspeedway	ARCA Stock Car	Schrader #99		Q-8th; F-5th	

Date	Track	Series	Car	Driver	Results	Notes
4/17	Martinsville Speedway	NASCAR CT	Schrader #52	Rick Crawford	Q-24th; F-36th	Punched hole in radiator
4/18	Martinsville Speedway	NASCAR NC	BAM #49	Rusty Wallace	Q-26th; F-40th	Crashed by Nemechek on lap 118
4/23	Talladega Short Track	Late Model	Schrader #99	Jerry Goodwin	Q-1st; F-2nd	
4/25	Talladega Superspeedway	NASCAR NC	BAM #49	Jeff Gordon	Q-39th; F-23rd	
5/1	California Speedway	NASCAR WW	Schrader #99	Ken Schrader	Q-8th; F-1st	
5/2	California Speedway	NASCAR NC	BAM #49	Jeff Gordon	Q-32nd; F-20th	Passing points
5/7	Lakeside Speedway	TORA	Schrader #99	Kyle Berk	Q-1st; F-2nd	
5/8	Batesville Speedway	IMCA Modified	Dirt Works	Scott Bloomquist	F-19th	
5/15	Richmond International Raceway	NASCAR NC	BAM #49	Dale Earnhardt, Jr.		
5/16	Toledo Speedway	ARCA Stock Car	Schrader #52	Ken Schrader	H-1st; F-1st	
5/19	Paducah International Raceway	Late Model	Schrader #99	Terry English	Q-2nd; H-3rd; F-2nd	
5/19	Paducah International Raceway	Modified			H-3rd; F-6th	
5/21	Lowe's Motor Speedway	NASCAR CT	Schrader #52	Dennis Setzer	Open-9th; 1st F-9th; 2nd F-13th	All-Star race; was voted in to race by fans
5/22	Lowe's Motor Speedway	NASCAR NC	BAM #49			
5/28	Lowe's Short Track	Southern All Star LM	Schrader #99	Mike Balzano	H-3rd; F-3rd	
5/29	Lowe's Short Track	Southern All Star LM	Schrader #99	Jimmie Johnson	H-1st; F-9th	Pathrum show
5/30	Lowe's Motor Speedway	NASCAR NC	BAM #49	Chad Chaffin	Q-41st; F-31st	
6/4	Dover International Speedway	NASCAR CT	Schrader #52	Mark Martin	Q-16th; F-5th	Broke panhard mount on truck mount
6/5	Waterford Speedbowl					
6/6	Dover International Speedway	NASCAR NC	BAM #49	Scott Riggs	1st F-1st; 2nd F-3rd	
6/6	Highland Speedway	UMP Late Model	Schrader #99	Jimmie Johnson	Q-15th; F-34th	
6/8	Hawkeye Downs Speedway	IMCA Late Model	Schrader #99	Ed Dixon	Q-7th; H-1st; F-5th	BIG CRASH in heat race
6/12	Pocono Raceway	ARCA Stock Car	Schrader #52	Ryan Newman	Q-32nd; F-2nd	Lined up according to points
6/13	Pocono Raceway	NASCAR NC	BAM #49	Jeff Gordon	Q-18th; F-25th	Brake bleeder came loose
6/15	Quincy Raceway	UMP Late Model	Schrader #99	Madden	H-5th; F-3rd	Started 14th
6/18	Raceway 7	Late Model	Schrader #99	Jeff Gordon	Q-28th; F-39th	Crashed in heat and in feature
6/20	Michigan International Speedway	NASCAR NC	BAM #49	Matt Taylor	Q-18th; F-23rd	Engine blew up
6/27	Sears Point Raceway	NASCAR NC	BAM #49	Tony Stewart	Q-12th; F-8th	
6/29	Laurens County Speedway	Late Model	Schrader #99	Ed Dixon	Q-29th; F-35th	
7/3	Daytona International Speedway	NASCAR NC	BAM #49	Ken Schrader	Q-7th; F-5th	Mayfield cost us 6 spots with 10 to go
7/6	Highland Speedway	UMP Late Model	Schrader #99	Ken Schrader	H-2nd; D-7th	
7/9	Red Cedar Speedway	WISSOTA	Schrader #99	Ryan Hemphill	H-2nd; D-4th; F-2nd	
7/10	I-55 Raceway	UMP Late Model	Schrader #99	Matt Taylor	Q-40th; F-27th	Got caught in wreck
7/11	Chicagoland Speedway	NASCAR NC	BAM #49	Ken Schrader	H-7th; 1st F-3rd; 2nd F-11th	Got sent to back in heat
7/11	Vermilion County Speedway	Modified	Jeff Leka	Kurt Busch	H-6th; F-4th	
7/13	St. Francois Raceway	UMP Late Model	Schrader #99	Bill Elliott	H-3rd; F-1st	Blew engine
7/13	St. Francois Raceway	UMP Modified	Dirt Works	Jimmie Johnson	Q-2nd; D-1st; F-1st	
7/14	Clarksville Speedway	UMP Late Model	Schrader #99	Ken Schrader	Q-5th; D-2nd; F-2nd	
7/14	Clarksville Speedway	UMP Modified	Dirt Works	Jeff Aikey	Q-2nd; F-23rd	
7/16	Gateway International Raceway	ARCA Stock Car	Schrader #99	Chad Chaffin	H-1st; D-4th	
7/17	I-55 Raceway	UMP Late Model	Schrader #99	Jeff Gordon	H-2nd; F-1st	
7/21	Red Hill Speedway	UMP Modified	Brian Shaw #1	Denny Eckrich	Q-17th; F-37th	
7/25	New Hampshire Int'l Speedway	NASCAR NC	BAM #49		1st F-2nd; 2nd F-2nd	
7/31	Lorain County Speedway	UMP Late Model	Schrader #99		Q-40th; F21st	Blew engine
8/1	Pocono Raceway	NASCAR NC	BAM #49		Q-2nd; H-6th; D-5th; F-1st	Big wreck in feature; running 3rd
8/3	Farmer City Raceway	UMP Late Model	Schrader #99		H-1st; F-2nd	Engine blew up
8/4	Independence Motor Speedway	UMP Late Model	Schrader #99		Q-12th; F-34th	Pathrum show
8/6	Indianapolis Raceway Park	NASCAR CT	Schrader #52		Q-31st; F-18th	Got wrecked by Musgrave
8/6	Indianapolis Motor Speedway	NASCAR NC	BAM #49		H-1st; F-7th	
8/9	Fiesta City Speedway	Late Model	Schrader #99		H-5th; F-14th	
8/10	Deer Creek Speedway	WDRL Late Model	Schrader #99			

Date	Track	Type	Car Owner	Race Winner	Finish	Comments
8/15	Watkins Glen International	NASCAR NC	BAM #49	Tony Stewart	F-25th	Match race in small-engine sprint cars with K. Petty; T. Stewart; D. Blaney
8/18	Adrian Speedway	Modified	Dirt Works	Ken Schrader	H-4th; F-13th	Qualifying rained out
8/21	Sharon Speedway	Sprint		Ken Schrader	F-1st	No power steering
8/22	Michigan International Speedway	NASCAR NC	BAM #49	Greg Biffle	F-28th	Wasn't there to qual; started last promoter's opt.
8/25	Bristol Motor Speedway	NASCAR CT	Schrader #52	Carl Edwards	Q-1st; F-10th	Big wreck front straight; was down 80 laps
8/26	Volunteer Speedway	Late Model	Schrader #99	Randell Chupp	S-5th; F-14th	Blew engine and big crash
8/28	Bristol Motor Speedway	NASCAR NC	BAM #49	Dale Earnhardt, Jr.	Q-26th; F-32nd	Had flat running 3rd with 10 laps to go
9/5	California Speedway	NASCAR NC	BAM #49	Eliott Sadler		Crashed by Sprague
9/6	DuQuoin Fairgrounds	ARCA Stock Car		Frank Kimmel	Q-1st; F-8th	
9/9	Richmond International Raceway	NASCAR CT	Schrader #52			
9/11	Richmond International Raceway	NASCAR NC	BAM #49	Jeremy Mayfield		Sunoco Super Series; crashed in feature
9/12	Columbus Motor Speedway	Late Model	Schrader #99	Ken Schrader	Q-17th; F-37th	Started by points due to rain
9/14	Lee County Speedway	Late Model	Schrader #99	Ken Schrader	H-6th; 1st F-1st; 2nd F-1st	
9/18	New Hampshire Int'l Speedway	NASCAR CT	Schrader #52	Travis Kvapil	Q-18th; F-12th	Broke track bar bracket at end of race
9/19	New Hampshire Int'l Speedway	NASCAR NC	BAM #49	Kurt Busch	F-16th	
9/22	New Egypt Speedway	House car		Frank Cozze	Q-29th; B F-9th; A F-17th	Broke driveshaft
9/22	Dover International Speedway	NASCAR NC	BAM #49	Ryan Newman	F-25th	
10/1	Talladega Short Track	Late Model	Schrader #99	Ray Cook	Q-33rd; 1st F-2nd; 2nd F-8th	Paid feature by qualifying—got too late
10/2	Talladega Short Track	Southern All Stars LM	Schrader #99	Earl Pearson Jr.	Q-25th; 1st F-2nd; 2nd F-24th	Lined up by draw
10/3	Talladega Superspeedway	NASCAR NC	BAM #49	Dale Earnhardt, Jr.	Q-37th; F-20th	Lined up by points; had fuel pump problems running 4th
10/6	Adrian Speedway	MLRA Late Model	Schrader #99	Jeff Turner	H-2nd; F-7th	
10/8	Lakeside Speedway	MLRA Late Model	Schrader #99		H-6th	Running 10th and got wrecked
10/10	Kansas Speedway	NASCAR NC	BAM #49	Joe Nemechek	Q-32nd; F-27th	
10/13	Lowe's Short Track	Late Model	Schrader #99	Chris Madden	F-6th	
10/16	Lowe's Motor Speedway	NASCAR NC	BAM #49	Jimmie Johnson	Q-30th; F-21st	Big pit stop problems
10/23	Martinsville Speedway	NASCAR CT	Schrader #52	Jamie McMurray	Q-34th; F-17th	
10/24	Martinsville Speedway	NASCAR NC	BAM #49	Jimmie Johnson	Q-20th; F-31st	
10/31	Atlanta Motor Speedway	NASCAR NC	BAM #49	Jimmie Johnson	Q-37th; F-23rd	Lined up by points; dead battery
11/4	Phoenix International Raceway	NASCAR SW	Schrader #99	Eddie McKean	Q-4th; F-3rd	Crashed in feature (driver screwed up)
11/5	Phoenix International Raceway	NASCAR CT	Schrader #52	David Starr	Q-2nd; F-12th	
11/7	Phoenix International Raceway	NASCAR NC	BAM #49	Dale Earnhardt, Jr.	Q-18th; F-20th	Broke driveshaft in feature
11/13	Darlington Raceway	NASCAR CT	Schrader #52	Kasey Kahne	Q-20th; F-10th	
11/14	Darlington Raceway	NASCAR NC	BAM #49	Jimmie Johnson	Q-33rd; F-30th	
11/20	Homestead-Miami Speedway	NASCAR CT	Schrader #52	Kasey Kahne	Q-21st; F-33rd	
11/21	Homestead-Miami Speedway	NASCAR NC	BAM #49	Greg Biffle	Q-44th; F-25th	
11/26	Columbus Speedway	Late Model	Schrader #99	Anthony Rushing	Q-2nd; F-23rd	Feature DNF; had trouble leading on lap 31!
11/27	Columbus Speedway	Late Model	Schrader #99	Clint Smith	Q-2nd; F-2nd	
12/4	Cleveland Speedway	Late Model	Schrader #99		Q-3rd	

2005

Date	Track	Type	Car Owner	Race Winner	Finish	Comments
1/8	Talladega Short Track	Late Model	Schrader #99		Q-3rd in group; F-4th	Was leading heat and had problem with yellow flag on last lap
1/15	Central Arizona Raceway	Late Model	Schrader #99	Don O'Neal	H-2nd; F-7th	
1/16	Central Arizona Raceway	Late Model	Schrader #99	Billy Moyer	H-7th; S-5th; F-17th	
1/18	Central Arizona Raceway	Late Model	Schrader #99	Terry Phillips	H-2nd; F-11th	

Date	Track	Division	Car	Driver	Results	Notes
1/20	Central Arizona Raceway	Late Model	Schrader #99	Ken Schrader	H-1st; F-1st	Big wreck—upside down
1/21	Central Arizona Raceway	Late Model	Schrader #99	Steve Francis	H-1st, F-20th	Had flat right front running 5th
1/22	Central Arizona Raceway	Late Model	Schrader #99	Steve Francis	H-1st, F-18th	Lost cylinder
1/29-30	Phoenix International Raceway	NASCAR WW	Schrader	David Gillian	Q-3rd; F-31st	
1/29-30	Phoenix International Raceway	NASCAR SW	Schrader	Burney Lamar	Q-19th; F-2nd	
2/7	East Bay Raceway Park	NARA Late Model	Schrader #99	Don O'Neal	Q-39th; H-4th; S-3rd	Big wreck in heat race
2/8	East Bay Raceway Park	NARA Late Model	Schrader #99	Tim McCreadie	Q-about 73rd of 115 cars	
2/9	East Bay Raceway Park	NARA Late Model	Schrader #99	Terry English	Q-about 70th; H-6th; B F-3rd	
2/12	Daytona International Speedway	NASCAR NC	BAM #49	Jimmie Johnson	Q-5th; F-16th	Flat tire in heat; loaded up
2/14	Volusia Speedway Park	UMP Late Model	Schrader #99	Rick Eckert	Q-27th; H-2nd; F-12th	Daytona 150 qualifying race
2/15	Volusia Speedway Park	UMP Late Model	Schrader #99		Q-about 48th	Blew engine; Daytona 500
2/17	Daytona International Speedway	NASCAR NC	BAM #49			Was decent all day
2/20	Daytona International Speedway	NASCAR NC	BAM #49	Jeff Gordon	Q-38th; F-14th	Dirt track; 5th in passing points (61 cars); spun first lap and knocked off nose
2/27	California Speedway	NASCAR NC	BAM #49	Greg Biffle	H-2nd; F-22nd	
3/4	Texas Motor Speedway	SUPR	Schrader #99			
3/5	Texas Motor Speedway	SUPR	Schrader #99	Kelly Boen	Q-4th; F-6th	Dirt track; 4th in passing points (54 cars)
3/13	Las Vegas Motor Speedway	NASCAR NC	BAM #49	Jimmie Johnson	Q-14th; F-34th	Changed engines & started in back; 2 wrecks
3/20	Atlanta Motor Speedway	NASCAR NC	BAM #49	Carl Edwards	Q-28th; F-26th	
4/3	Bristol Motor Speedway	NASCAR NC	BAM #49	Kevin Harvick	Q-30th; F-23rd	Big wreck back straight
4/9	Martinsville Speedway	NASCAR CT	Schrader #52	Bobby Labonte	Q-16th; F-14th	
4/10	Martinsville Speedway	NASCAR NC	BAM #49	Jeff Gordon	Q-11th; F-24th	
4/16	Texas Motor Speedway	SUPR	Schrader #99		H-7th; S-5th	Started last; wrecked 2nd lap of qualifying
4/17	Phoenix International Raceway	NASCAR NC	BAM #49	Greg Biffle	Q-30th; F-23rd	Dirt track
4/23	Texas Motor Speedway	NASCAR NC	BAM #49	Kurt Busch	Q-30th; F-38th	Got in two wrecks
4/24	Salem Speedway	ARCA Stock Car	Schrader #99	Chad Blount		Josh Richardson qual 11th; got there after Phoenix; had engine problems in feature
4/24	Tri-City Speedway	UMP Late Model	Schrader #99	Michael Kloos	H-6th; S-1st; F-13th	Match races
4/29	Talladega Short Track	Late Model	Schrader #99	Chris Madden	Q-2nd; D-1st; F-3rd	
5/1	Talladega Superspeedway	NASCAR NC	BAM #49	Jeff Gordon	Q-42nd; F-8th	Lined up by points; big crash w/Dave Blaney
5/7	Darlington Raceway	NASCAR NC	BAM #49	Greg Biffle	Q-28th; F-18th	Victory Junction Gang night
5/14	Richmond International Raceway	NASCAR NC	BAM #49	Kasey Kahne	Q-40th; F-30th	Was tight all day
5/15	I-80 Speedway	NASCAR Late Model	Schrader #99		H-5th; F-11th	
5/17	Mt. Vernon Raceway	UMP Late Model	Schrader #99	Rodney Melvin	Q-8th; H-1st; D-2nd; F-2nd	
5/18	Paducah International Raceway	NASCAR CT	Schrader #52	Rodney Melvin	Q-3d; H-1st; F-4th	
5/20	Lowe's Motor Speedway	NASCAR NC	BAM #49	Kyle Busch	F-36th	Blew engine
5/21	Lowe's Motor Speedway	ARCA Stock Car	Schrader #99	Brian Vickers	Q-6th; F-9th	
5/22	Toledo Speedway	Dixie Thunder	Schrader #99	Ken Schrader	Q-27th; F-1st	
5/25	Lowe's Dirt Track	Southern All Star LM	Schrader #99	Dennis Franklin	H-3rd; F-3rd	
5/27	Lowe's Dirt Track	NASCAR NC	BAM #49	Jimmy Owens	F-8th	
5/29	Lowe's Motor Speedway	NASCAR CT	Schrader #52	Jimmie Johnson	F-9th	
6/4	Dover International Speedway	NASCAR NC	BAM #49		F-14th	
6/5	Dover International Speedway	Late Model	Schrader #99	Greg Biffle	Q-26th	
6/8	Eldora Speedway	NASCAR NC	Schrader #99	Kenny Wallace	Q-5th; H-3rd; F-4th	
6/12	Pocono Raceway	NASCAR NC	BAM #49	Carl Edwards	Q-19th; F-20th	
6/15	I-55 Raceway	UMP Late Model	Schrader #99	Brian Shirley	Q-8th; D-1st; F-7th	
6/18	Michigan International Speedway	NASCAR CT	Toyota #17	Greg Biffle	Q-38th; F-28th	
6/19	Michigan International Speedway	NASCAR NC	Schrader #99	Rodney Melvin	Q-10th; H-1st; F-6th	
6/21	Highland Speedway	UMP Late Model	Schrader #99	Ron Bartels	Q-11th; H-4th; F-6th	
6/25	Antioch Speedway	Late Model	John Soares #99			
6/26	Sears Point Raceway	NASCAR NC	BAM #49	Tony Stewart	Q-19th; F-35th	Blew engine

Date	Track	Series	Car	Driver	Results	Notes
7/2	Daytona International Speedway	NASCAR NC	BAM #49	Tony Stewart	Q-40th; F-10th	Got there late and started last (23rd)
7/5	Poplar Bluff Speedway	Late Model	Schrader #99		H-3rd; D-3rd; F-3rd	
7/7	Quincy Raceway	UMP Late Model	Schrader #99		H-6th; F-3rd	
7/8	Red Cedar Speedway	WISSOTA	Schrader #99		H-6th; F-9th	
7/10	Chicagoland Speedway	NASCAR NC	BAM #49	Dale Earnhardt, Jr.	F-26th	
7/10	Vermilion County Speedway	UMP Modified	Wallace #23	Arby Burton	F-8th	
7/13	Stafford Motor Speedway	Silver Crown	Seymour #29	Ken Schrader	F-1st	Match race with Sammy Swindell; Bentley Warren; Carl Edwards & Dave Blaney
7/14	Fonda Speedway	IMCA Modified		Ken Schrader	H-3rd; F-2nd	
7/16	Wiscasset Raceway				H-1st; F-1st	
7/16	New Hampshire Int'l Speedway	NASCAR NC	BAM #49	Tony Stewart	Q-41st; F-26th	Running 20th & got punted by Jason Leffler
7/20	Thunder Road	ACT	Phil Scott #1	Joey Laguerre	H-5th; S-1st; F-9th	Pathrum show; Kenseth; Martin and Kahne
7/23	Jennerstown Speedway					
7/24	Pocono Raceway	NASCAR NC	BAM #49	Kurt Busch	Q-12th; F-31st	Engine sucked
7/27	Clarksville Speedway	UMP Late Model	Schrader		F-4th	
7/29	Gateway International Raceway	ARCA Stock Car	Schrader	Joey Miller	Q-1st; F-3rd	
7/30	I-55 Raceway	UMP Late Model	Schrader #99	Randy Korte	H-1st	
7/31	Tri-City Speedway	UMP Late Model	Schrader #99		Q-13th; H-4th; F-12th	Crash in dash
8/3	I-55 Raceway	UMP Late Model	Schrader #99		H-4th; F-10th	
8/5	Indianapolis Raceway Park	NASCAR CT	Schrader #52	Dennis Setzer	F-35th	M & M Night of Stars
8/7	Indianapolis Motor Speedway	NASCAR NC	BAM #49	Tony Stewart	Q-11th; F-22nd	Started by points (rain); power steering in race
8/9	Dakota State Fair Speedway	WISSOTA	Schrader #99		H-1st	Blew engine running 2nd; w/2 laps to go
8/10	Echo Valley Speedway	WDRL Late Model	Schrader #99		S-4th; F-11th	Flat tire in heat
8/12	Elkins Speedway	Late Model			H-4th; F-9th	
8/14	Watkins Glen International	NASCAR NC	BAM #49	Tony Stewart	Q-28th; F-32nd	Out of fuel on last lap
8/18	Portsmouth Raceway Park	Late Model	Schrader #99	Ken Schrader	Q-1st D-5th; F-1st	
8/19	Michigan International Speedway	ARCA Stock Car	Schrader #99	Steve Wallace	Q-8th; F-3rd	
8/21	Michigan International Speedway	NASCAR NC	BAM #49	Jeremy Mayfield	F-25th	
8/24	Bristol Motor Speedway	NASCAR CT	Schrader #52	Mike Skinner	Q-7th; F-11th	
8/27	Bristol Motor Speedway	NASCAR NC	BAM #49	Matt Kenseth	Q-7th; F-11th	
9/4	California Speedway	NASCAR NC	BAM #49		Q-31st; F-29th	
9/5	DuQuoin Fairgrounds	ARCA Stock	Schrader #99	Kyle Busch	Q-5th; F-34th	Threw belts off
9/8	Richmond International Speedway	NASCAR CT	Schrader #52	Frank Kimmel	Q-26th; F-15th	
9/10	Richmond International Speedway	NASCAR NC	BAM #49	Mike Skinner	Q-42nd; F-19th	
9/13	Lee County Speedway	Late Model	Schrader #99	Kurt Busch	H-1st; F-2nd	
9/17	New Hampshire Int'l Speedway	NASCAR CT	Schrader #52	Rick Crawford	Q-20th; F-18th	
9/18	New Hampshire Int'l Speedway	NASCAR NC	BAM #49	Ryan Newman	Q-40th; F-40th	Blew two tires
9/25	Dover International Speedway	NASCAR NC	BAM #49	Jimmie Johnson	Q-42nd; F-28th	
9/27	North Alabama Speedway	Late Model	Jeff Taylor #5		Q-5th	
9/29	Batesville Speedway	Modified	Schrader #99	Shane Clanton	H-2nd; F-11th	
9/30	Talladega Short Track	Late Model	Schrader #99	Jimmy Owens	Q-5th; F-2nd	Broke driveshaft; running 2nd
10/1	Talladega Superspeedway	Southern All Star LM			Q-10th; F-7th	
10/2	Talladega Superspeedway	NASCAR NC	BAM #49	Dale Jarrett	F-26th	Blew tire 5 laps to go and wrecked
10/6	Lakeside Speedway	TORA	Schrader #99	Kyle Berck	H-4th; F-8th	50 cars
10/7	Lakeside Speedway	MLRA Late Model	Schrader #99	Denny Eckrich	H-5th; S-1st; F-9th	71 cars
10/8	Lakeside Speedway	MDRL	Schrader #99	Kyle Berck	H-2nd; F-21st	High passing points car; pulled in feature
10/9	Kansas Speedway	NASCAR NC	BAM #49	Mark Martin	Q-24th; F-17th	
10/12	Lowe's Dirt Track	Late Model	Schrader		H-5th or 6th	Ran good
10/15	Lowe's Motor Speedway	NASCAR NC	BAM #49	Jimmie Johnson	Q-40th; F-34th	
10/22	Martinsville Speedway	NASCAR CT	Schrader #52	Ricky Craven	Q-28th; F-11th	
10/23	Martinsville Speedway	NASCAR NC	BAM #49	Jeff Gordon	F-13th	Blew engine

Date	Track	Series	Car	Driver	Result	Notes
10/30	Atlanta Motor Speedway	NASCAR NC	BAM #49	Carl Edwards	F-34th	
11/6	Texas Motor Speedway	NASCAR NC	BAM #49	Carl Edwards	F-29th	
11/10	Phoenix International Raceway	NASCAR SW	Schrader #99	Ken Schrader	Q-1st; F-1st	
11/11	Phoenix International Raceway	NASCAR CT	Schrader #52	Todd Bodine	Q-36th; F-24th	
11/13	Phoenix International Raceway	NASCAR NC	BAM #49	Kyle Busch	Q-33rd; F-30th	
11/20	Homestead-Miami Speedway	NASCAR NC	BAM #49	Greg Biffle	Q-34th; F-22nd	
11/25	Columbus Speedway	Late Model	Schrader #99	David Breazle	H-3rd; F-10th	
11/26	Columbus Speedway	Late Model	Schrader #99	Michael England	H-2nd; F-11th	
12/2	East Bay Raceway Park	Crate Racing USA	Schrader #99		Q-5th D-1st	Screwed up on get-go qualifying lap
12/3	East BayRaceway Park	Crate Racing USA	Schrader #99	Jimmy Owens	F-5th	Pulled in feature; bent tie-rod

Ken Schrader—Tracks Raced

(Track info in bold indicates tracks at which Ken won races)

Track	Track	Size/Type
311 Speedway	**Madison NC**	**4/10-mi dirt oval**
Action Track	**Terre Haute IN**	**1/2-mi dirt oval**
Adrian Speedway	Adrian MO	1/3-mi dirt oval
Albany-Saratoga Speedway	Malta NY	4/10-mi dirt oval
Allen Co. Mem. Expo Center	Ft. Wayne IN	1/10-mi paved (indoors)
Anderson Speedway	**Anderson IN**	**1/2-mi paved oval**
Angell Park Speedway	Sun Prairie WI	1/3-mi dirt oval
Antioch Speedway	Antioch CA	1/4-mi dirt oval
Ascot Park	Gardena CA	1/2-mi dirt oval
Atlanta Motor Speedway	**Hampton GA**	**1.54-mi paved oval**
Atomic Motor Speedway	Oak Ridge TN	1/3-mi dirt oval
Auburndale Speedway	Winter Haven FL	1/4-mi paved oval
Batesville Speedway	Batesville AR	3/8-mi dirt oval
Beatrice Speedway	Beatrice NE	3/8-mi dirt oval
Beaver Dam Raceway	**Beaver Dam WI**	**1/3-mi dirt oval**
Beech Ridge Motor Spdwy	West Scarborough ME	1/3-mi paved oval
Belle-Clair Speedway	**Belleville IL**	**1/5-mi dirt oval**
Belleville High Banks	Belleville KS	1/2-mi dirt oval
Benton County Speedway	Vinton IA	1/4-mi dirt oval
Berlin Raceway	Marne MI	4/10-mile paved oval
Big Diamond Raceway	Minersville PA	3/8-mi dirt oval
Big H Speedway	**Houston TX**	**1/4-mi dirt oval**
Black Rock Speedway	Dundee NY	5/8-mi dirt oval
Bloomington Speedway	Bloomington IN	1/4-mi dirt oval
Brainerd Int'l Raceway	Brainerd MN	3-mi road course
Bridgeport Speedway	Bridgeport NJ	5/8-mi dirt oval
Bristol Motor Speedway	Bristol TN	1/2-mi paved oval
Brownstown Speedway	Brownstown IN	1/4-mi dirt oval
Buffalo Park Speedway	Carrollton TX	1/4-mi dirt oval
Cajon Speedway	El Cajon CA	3/8-mi paved oval
California Speedway	**Fontana CA**	**2-mi paved oval**
Can-Am Motorsports Park	LaFargeville NY	1/4-mi dirt oval
Canyon Raceway	Peoria AZ	3/8-mi dirt oval
Capital Speedway	**Jefferson City MO**	**3/8-mi dirt oval**
Carolina Motorsports Park	Kershaw SC	2.3-mi road course
Carolina Speedway	Gastonia NC	4/10-mi dirt oval
Cayuga County Fair Spdwy	Weedsport NY	3/8-mi dirt oval
Cedar Lake Speedway	New Richmond WI	3/8-mi dirt oval
Central Arizona Raceway	**Casa Grande AZ**	**3/8-mi dirt oval**
Champaign Motor Speedway	Champaign IL	1/4-mi dirt oval
Chandler Motor Speedway	Chandler IN	3/8-mi dirt oval
Charleston Speedway	**Charleston IL**	**3/8-mi dirt oval**
Charlotte Coliseum	Charlotte NC	1/10-mi paved (indoor)
Charlotte County Speedway	Punta Gorda FL	3/8-mi paved oval
Chicagoland Speedway	Joliet IL	1.5-mi paved oval
Christian County Fairgrounds	Taylorville IL	dirt oval
Cincinnati Gardens	Cincinnati OH	1/10-mi paved (indoors)
Claremont Speedway	Claremont NH	1/3-mi paved oval
Clarksville Speedway	**Clarksville TN**	**1/4-mi dirt oval**
Cleveland Speedway	Cleveland TN	3/8-mi dirt oval
Colorado National Speedway	Erie CO	1/2-mi dirt oval
Colorado National Speedway	**Erie CO**	**3/8-mi paved oval**
Columbus Motor Speedway	Columbus OH	1/3-mi paved oval
Columbus Speedway	Columbus MS	3/10-mi dirt oval
Concord Motorsports Park	Concord NC	1/2-mi dirt oval
Concord Motorsports Park	Concord NC	1/2-mi paved oval
Cowtown Speedway	Ft. Worth TX	1/4-mi dirt oval
Crawford County Speedway	Denison IA	1/2-mi dirt oval
Cresco Speedway	Cresco IA	4/10-mi dirt oval
Crossville Raceway USA	Crossville TN	3/8-mi dirt oval
Dakota State Fair Speedway	Huron SD	3/8-mi dirt oval
Darlington Speedway	Darlington SC	1+-mi paved oval
Davenport Speedway	Davenport IA	1/2-mi dirt oval
Daytona International Speedway	**Daytona FL**	**2.5-mi paved oval**
Daytona International Speedway	Daytona FL	3.56-mi paved road course
Deer Creek Speedway	Spring Valley MN	3/8-mi dirt oval
Desoto Super Speedway	**Bradenton FL**	**3/8-mi paved oval**
Devil's Bowl Speedway	**Mesquite TX**	**1/2-mi dirt oval**
Dixie Speedway	Woodstock GA	3/8-mi dirt oval
Dover Int'l Speedway	**Dover DE**	**1-mi paved oval**
Dubuque Fairgrounds Speedway	Dubuque IA	3/8-mi dirt oval
DuQuoin State Fairgrounds	DuQuoin IL	1-mi dirt oval
East Bay Raceway Park	Gibsonton FL	1/3-mi dirt oval
East Moline Speedway	East Moline IL	1/4-mi dirt oval
Echo Valley Speedway	West Union IA	4/10-mi dirt oval
Eighty-one (81) Speedway	Wichita KS	3/8-mi dirt oval
Eldora Speedway	**Rossburg OH**	**1/2-mi dirt oval**
Elkins Speedway	Elkins WV	3/8-mi dirt oval
Evergreen Speedway	**Monroe WA**	**5/8-mi paved oval**
Fairgrounds Speedway	Nashville TN	5/8-mi dirt oval
Fairgrounds Speedway	Nashville TN	5/8-mi paved oval
Fairgrounds Speedway	Springfield MO	
Farley Speedway	Farley IA	1/2-mi dirt oval

Track	Track	Size/Type
Macon Speedway	**Macon IL**	**1/5-mi dirt oval**
Madison Int'l Speedway	Oregon WI	1/2-mi paved oval
Malden Speedway	Malden MO	3/8-mi dirt oval
Manzanita Speedway	Phoenix AZ	1/2-mi dirt oval
Manzanita Speedway	Phoenix AZ	1/3-mi dirt oval
Martinsville Speedway	Martinsville VA	1/2-mi paved oval
Mecca Arena	Milwaukee WI	1/10-mi paved (indoors)
Memphis Dirt Track	Memphis TN	1/2-mi dirt oval
Memphis Motorsports Park	Memphis TN	1/4-mi dirt oval
Memphis Motorsports Park	Memphis TN	1/2-mi dirt oval
Mesa Marin Raceway	**Bakersfield CA**	**1/2-mi paved oval**
Metrolina Speedway	Charlotte NC	1/2-mi dirt oval
Michigan Int'l Speedway	Brooklyn MI	2-mi paved oval
Midway Speedway	Crooksville OH	3/8-mi dirt oval
Millstream Speedway	**Findlay OH**	**1/2-mi dirt oval**
Milwaukee Mile	West Allis WI	1-mi paved oval
Monett Speedway	Monett MO	3/8-mi dirt oval
Moroso Motorsports Park	Palm Beach Gardens FL	2.25-mi road course
Motordome 70 Speedway	Smithton PA	1/2-mi paved oval
Mottville Speedway	Mottville MI	1/4-mi paved oval
Mountain Motor Racing Comp.	Whitesburg KY	3/8-mi dirt oval
Mt. Vernon Raceway	Mt. Vernon IL	1/4-mi dirt oval
Mutter Center	Dayton OH	1/10-mile paved (indoors)
Myrtle Beach Speedway	Myrtle Beach SC	1/2-mi paved oval
Name unrecalled	Binghamton NY	
Name unrecalled	Branson MO	dirt oval
Name unrecalled	Chula Vista CA	
Name unrecalled	Elsberry MO	
Name unrecalled	Fort Smith AR	
Name unrecalled	Jackson TN	
Name unrecalled	Lake Cumberland KY	
Name unrecalled	Leesville SC	
Name unrecalled	**Marshall MO**	
Name unrecalled	Mt. Pleasant MI	
Name unrecalled	Niagara Falls NY	1/10-mi paved (indoors)
Name unrecalled	Ona WV	
Name unrecalled	Watertown NY	
Name unrecalled	Wichita Falls TX	
Napa Race Park	Benton MO	3/8-mi dirt oval
Nashville Munic.Auditorium	Nashville TN	1/10-mi paved (indoors)
Nashville Superspeedway	**Lebanon TN**	**1-1/3 mi paved oval**
Nazareth Speedway	Nazareth PA	1-mi dirt oval
Nazareth Speedway	Nazareth PA	1-mi paved oval
New Bremen Speedway	New Bremen OH	
New Egypt Speedway	New Egypt NJ	1/2-mi dirt oval
New Hampshire Int'l Spdwy	Loudon NH	1-mi paved oval
New Smyrna Speedway	New Smyrna FL	1/2-mi paved oval
New York State Fairgrounds	Syracuse NY	1-mi dirt oval

Track	Track	Size/Type
North Alabama Speedway	Tuscumbia AL	3/8-mi dirt oval
North Carolina Motor Spdwy	Rockingham NC	paved oval
North Wilkesboro Speedway	North Wilkesboro NC	paved oval
Norway Speedway	Norway MI	1/3-mi paved oval
Oglethorpe Speedway Park	Savannah GA	1/2-mi dirt oval
Orange County Speedway	Rougemont NC	3/8-mi paved oval
Orlando Speed World	Orlando FL	1/3-mi paved oval
Oswego Speedway	Oswego NY	5/8-mi paved oval
Owosso Speedway	Ovid MI	3/8-mi paved oval
Paducah International Raceway	Paducah KY	3/8-mi dirt oval
Paragon Speedway	**Paragon IN**	**3/8-mi dirt oval**
Peach State Motor Speedway	Jefferson GA	1/2-mi dirt oval
Pennsboro Speedway	Pennsboro WV	1/2-mi dirt oval
Phoenix International Raceway	**Avondale AZ**	**1-mi paved oval**
Pike County Speedway	Magnolia MS	3/8-mi dirt oval
Pikes Peak International Raceway	Fountain CO	1-mile paved oval
Pocono Raceway	Long Pond PA	2.5-mi paved oval
Poplar Bluff Speedway	Poplar Bluff MO	3/8-mi dirt oval
Portland International Raceway	**Portland OR**	**1/2-mi paved oval**
Portsmouth Raceway Park	**Portsmouth OH**	**3/8-mi dirt oval**
Quincy Raceways	Quincy IL	1/2-mi dirt oval
Raceland Park	Denver CO	7/16-mi dirt oval
Raceway 7	Conneaut OH	1/2-mi dirt oval
Randolph County Fairgrounds	Sparta IL	5/8-mi dirt oval
Ransomville Speedway	Ransomville NY	3/8-mi dirt oval
Red Cedar Speedway	Menomonie WI	3/8-mi dirt oval
Red Hill Speedway	**Sumner IL**	**3/8-mi dirt oval**
Richland County Fairgrounds	Olney IL	dirt oval
Richmond International Raceway	Richmond VA	3/4-mi paved oval
River Valley Raceway	Arkadelphia AL	3/8-mi dirt oval
Riverside Int'l Motor Speedway	**Riverside CA**	**Road course**
Riverside Speedway	Kansas City MO	1/4-mi dirt oval
Riverside Speedway	West Memphis AR	2.54-mi road course
Road Atlanta	Braselton GA	1/4-mi paved oval
Rockford Speedway	Loves Park IL	1/4-mi paved oval
Rocky Mountain National Speedway	Commerce City CO	3/8-mi dirt oval
Rocky Mountain Raceways	Salt Lake City UT	3/8-mi paved oval
Rolla Speedway	Rolla MO	1/2-mi paved oval
Rolling Wheels Speedway	Elbridge NY	5/8-mi dirt oval
Rome Speedway	Rome GA	1/2-mi dirt oval
Rosemont Horizon	Chicago IL	1/10-mi paved (indoor)
Salem Speedway	**Salem IN**	**1/2-mi paved oval**

Track	Track	Size/Type
Twin Cities Raceway Park	North Vernon IN	3/8-mi dirt oval
Ukiah Speedway	Ukiah CA	mi paved oval
Union County Speedway	Liberty IN	3/8-mi dirt oval
US 30 Speedway	**Columbus NE**	**1/3-mi dirt oval**
Vermilion County Speedway	Danville IL	3/8-mi dirt oval
Viking Speedway	Alexandria MN	1/2-mi dirt oval
Volunteer Speedway	Bulls Gap TN	4/10-mi dirt oval
Volusia Raceway Park	Barberville FL	1/2-mi dirt oval
Volusia Raceway Park	**Barberville FL**	**1/2-mi paved oval**
Warren Speedway	Warren AR	1/4-mi dirt oval
Waterford Speedbowl	Waterford CT	3/8-mi paved oval
Watkins Glen International	Watkins Glen NY	2.45-mi road course
Watsonville Speedway	Watsonville CA	1/4-mi dirt oval
Wayne County Fairgrounds	Fairfield IL	1/2-mi dirt oval
Wheatland Raceway	Wheatland MO	3/8-mi dirt oval
White County Fairgrounds	Carmi IL	1/2-mi dirt oval
Williams Grove Speedway	Mechanicsburg PA	1/2-mi dirt oval
Winchester Speedway	**Winchester IN**	**1/2-mi paved oval**
Wiscasset Raceway	**Wiscasset ME**	**1/3-mi paved oval**
Wisconsin Int'l Raceway	Kaukauna WI	1/2-mi paved oval

CANADA

Track	Track	Size/Type
Cayuga Speedway	Nelles Corner ON	5/8-mi paved oval
Sanair International Speedway	St-Pie QC	4/5-mi paved oval
Toronto Sky Dome	Toronto ON	1/10-mi paved (indoors)
Name unrecalled	London ON	

AUSTRALIA

Track	Track	Size/Type
	Melbourne	

Track	Track	Size/Type
Santa Fe Speedway	Hinsdale IL	1/4-mi dirt oval
Santa Fe Speedway	Hinsdale IL	1/2-mi dirt oval
Saugus Speedway	**Saugus CA**	**1/3-mi paved oval**
Sears Point Raceway	**Sonoma CA**	**2.52-mi road course**
Sebring Int'l Raceway	Sebring FL	3.7-mi road course
Sedalia's State Fair Spdwy	Sedalia MO	1-mi dirt oval
Sedalia's State Fair Spdwy	**Sedalia MO**	**1/2-mi dirt oval**
Seekonk Speedway	**Seekonk MA**	**1/3-mi paved oval**
Sharon Speedway	**Hartford OH**	**3/8-mi dirt oval**
Shawno Speedway	Shawno WI	1/2-mi dirt oval
Sheboygan Co. Fair Park	Plymouth WI	1/3-mi dirt oval
Silverdome	Pontiac MI	1/10-mi paved (indoors)
Slinger Super Speedway	**Slinger WI**	**1/2-mi paved oval**
South Bend Motor Speedway	South Bend IN	1/4-mi paved oval
South Boston Speedway	**South Boston VA**	**4/10-mi paved oval**
South Sound Speedway	Tenino WA	3/8-mi paved oval
Southern Iowa Speedway	Oskaloosa IA	1/2-mi dirt oval
Southern National Speedway	Kenly NC	4/10-mi paved oval
Spencer Speedway	Williamson NY	1/2-mi paved oval
Springfield Speedway	**Springfield IL**	**1/4-mi dirt oval**
St. Charles Speedway	**St. Charles MO**	**1/4-mi dirt oval**
St. Francois C'nty Raceway	**Farmington MO**	**1/3-mi dirt oval**
Stafford Motor Speedway	**Stafford Springs CT**	**1/2-mi paved oval**
State Fair Speedway	Oklahoma City OK	3/8-mi dirt oval
State Fairgrounds	St. Paul MN	1/2-mi dirt oval
State Fairgrounds	Shreveport LA	1/2-mi paved oval
State Fairgrounds	Springfield MO	1/2-mi dirt oval
Summerville Speedway	Summerville SC	4/10-mi paved oval
Sycamore Speedway	Sycamore IL	1/4-mi dirt oval
Talladega Short Track	Talladega AL	1/3-mi dirt oval
Talladega Superspeedway	**Talladega AL**	**2.66-mi paved oval**
Tampa State Fairgrounds	Tampa FL	1/2-mi dirt oval
Texas Motor Speedway	Ft. Worth TX	1.5-mi paved oval
Texas Motor Speedway	Ft. Worth TX	4/10-mi dirt oval
Thompson Int'l Spdwy	Thompson CT	5/8-mi paved oval
Thunder Road	Barre VT	1/4-mi paved oval
Toledo Speedway	**Toledo OH**	**1/2-mi paved oval**
Travelers Rest Speedway	Travelers Rest SC	4/10-mi dirt oval
Trenton Speedway	Trenton NJ	1.5-mi paved oval
Tri-City Speedway (PA)	Franklin PA	1/2-mi dirt oval
Tri-City Speedway	**Granite City IL**	**1/4-mi dirt oval**
Tri-City Speedway	**Granite City IL**	**1/2-mi dirt oval**
Tri-State Speedway (OK)	Pocola OK	3/8-mi dirt oval
Tri-State Speedway	**Haubstadt IN**	**1/4-mi dirt oval**
Tucson Raceway Park	Tucson AZ	3/8-mi dirt oval
Tucson Raceway Park	Tucson AZ	3/8-mi paved oval
Tulsa Expo Raceway	**Tulsa OK**	**1/4-mi dirt (indoor)**
Twenty-four (24) Raceway Pk	Moberly MO	4/10-mi dirt oval

Index